Norman Entomg
Quechee, VT.
1992

NEW ENGLAND
IN THE ENGLISH NATION
1689-1713

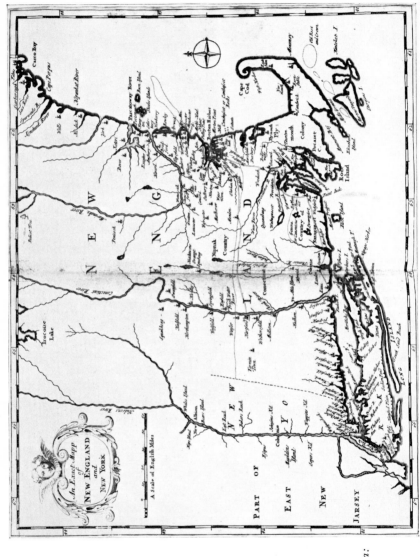

From Cotton Mather,
*Magnalia Christi Americana:
or, the Ecclesiastical
History of New-England*
(London, 1702)

New England
in the English Nation
1689-1713

by

PHILIP S. HAFFENDEN

CLARENDON PRESS · OXFORD
1974

Oxford University Press, Ely House, London W.1

GLASGOW   NEW YORK   TORONTO   MELBOURNE   WELLINGTON
CAPE TOWN   IBADAN   NAIROBI   DAR ES SALAAM   LUSAKA   ADDIS ABABA
DELHI   BOMBAY   CALCUTTA   MADRAS   KARACHI   LAHORE   DACCA
KUALA LUMPUR   SINGAPORE   HONG KONG   TOKYO

ISBN   0   19   821124   4

© *Oxford University Press 1974*

Printed in Great Britain by Butler and Tanner Ltd, Frome and London

To
Professor Gerald S. Graham

Preface

IN this volume I have drawn heavily upon the work of others. The indebtedness to the thought and research of Professor G. M. Waller, Susan Reed, and the late Perry Miller is particularly great. But much is also owed to the inspiration of *The Glorious Revolution in America*, a pioneering study produced by Professors Michael G. Hall, Lawrence H. Leder, and Michael G. Kammen; to Professor Carl Bridenbaugh for his profound insights into society and religion and to Professor Bernard Bailyn who has skilfully charted so many aspects of colonial America.

The research upon which this book was founded was made possible by a fellowship at the John Carter Brown Library at Providence, Rhode Island, in 1967. The unique collection of printed works which this library possesses and its fine collection of maps were supplemented by the resources of the Rhode Island Historical Society, the Providence Athenaeum, and the John Hay Library of Brown University. It is difficult to express adequately my sense of gratitude to the staff of the John Carter Brown Library and to the Librarian, Mr. Thomas R. Adams. Combining high standards of scholarship and service with human warmth and vivacity they created an atmosphere which remains in my mind as the ideal for academic pursuits.

I am most grateful to patient colleagues for aiding the completion of this work: to Mr. F. C. Mather and Professor J. S. Bromley who have read part of the manuscript and offered valued criticism; to Mr. Brynmor Pugh for his advice and guidance in exploring the medieval background to the concept of nation. I owe a particular debt to Dr. Trevor Reese of the Institute of Commonwealth Studies, London, who to further this project gave generously his encouragement and his time.

All dates are in Old Style, unless otherwise indicated. January 1 has been taken as the beginning of the new year, although in citing from documents current usage has been adopted, e.g. 1 January 1699/1700, and original spellings and punctuation retained.

Southampton,
December 1971   P.S.H.

Contents

Map of New England	*frontispiece*
Abbreviations	viii
Introduction	ix
I. Revolution and Settlement in the colonies, 1689–1692: the commitment to Protestantism and representative government, and the role of Massachusetts Bay	1
II. New England and the English: 'A Nation within a Nation'	38
III. The Nine Years War and Massachusetts Bay, 1689–1697	72
IV. The Supports of the Massachusetts Tradition and the Sources of Provincial Wealth	120
V. The Face and Purpose of the Adversaries: a survey of the fields of battle and the debatable ground	162
VI. Massachusetts Bay in the War of the Spanish Succession	204
VII. Against Port Royal and Quebec: Anglo-Massachusetts co-operation and the aftermath of failure, 1707–1713	243
Bibliography	291
Index	311

Abbreviations

ADM	Admiralty papers, British Public Record Office.
AHR	*American Historical Review.*
B. M	British Museum.
C.S.P.C.	*Calendar of State Papers, Colonial series.*
Cal. Treas. Books	*Calendar of Treasury Books.*
Cal. Treas. Papers	*Calendar of Treasury Papers.*
CO	Lords of Trade and Board of Trade papers for the colonies, British Public Record Office.
Conn. Hist. Soc. Coll.	*Connecticut Historical Society Collections.*
D.A.B.	*Dictionary of American Biography.*
Essex I.H.C.	*Essex Institute Historical Collections.*
H.M.C.	*Historical Manuscripts Commission Publications.*
Mass. Archives	Massachusetts Archives.
Mass. Col. Soc. Publ.	*Massachusetts Colonial Society Publications.*
Mass. Hist. Soc. Coll.	*Massachusetts Historical Society Collections.*
Mass. Hist. Soc. Proc.	*Massachusetts Historical Society Proceedings.*
Mass. Hist. Soc. Publ.	*Massachusetts Historical Society Publications.*
N.H. Provincial Papers	*New Hampshire Provincial Papers.*
New York Col. Docs.	*New York Colonial Documents.*
New York State Hist. Soc. Coll.	*New York State Historical Society Collections.*
New York State Hist. Assoc. Proc.	*New York State Historical Association Proceedings.*
Penn. Col. Rec.	*Pennsylvania Colonial Records.*
Prot. Episc. Hist. Soc. Colls.	*Protestant Episcopal Historical Society Collections.*
Royal Hist. Soc. Trans.	*Royal Historical Society Transactions.*
W & MQ	*William and Mary Quarterly.*

Introduction

THE failure of the first British empire to endure as a political entity may be ascribed to the deficiencies of its statesmen. But if the communities of which it was composed were unable at a critical stage—or stages—to produce leaders whose vision transcended parochial horizons this may imply that the contemporary images of empire as a source for speculation were inadequate or fatally restricted.

In the seventeenth century Sir Josiah Child, when devising a blue-print for national growth, had observed that profit and power ought jointly to be considered. But whereas the tenets of mercantilism, as applied before 1776, yielded an unrivalled wealth, sustaining protracted conflict with France, and providing the English colonists by 1763 with the highest standard of living in the world, the systematic or imaginative use of power for political ends remained merely the dream of a few men—administrators mainly, during the early years of the eighteenth century; later, more eminent Anglo-American politicians such as the elder Pitt, Benjamin Franklin, and James Otis. This company included individuals of outstanding ability and high intelligence but also men whose balance of intellect is questionable and others whose narrowness of mind is incontrovertible.

Inability to solve or even to recognize, for much of the time, the problem of rationalizing the political relationships of English communities fringing the Atlantic—the sole means of preserving power—left the way open for the growth of divergent interpretations of what these relationships really were. It led ultimately to imperial bifurcation and the loss to Britain of the more promising sources of strength—that is, the most populous and enterprising mainland colonies which by their attainments and aspirations represented the best of European achievement.

As successor states of the first British empire the united colonies, subsequently renamed the United States of America, had laid—within little more than a decade after their separation from England, though not without protracted suffering, alarm, and misgivings—the foundation of a political system which substantially solved the problem imperfectly posed by Child. However, the remnant of old empire, which now burgeoned into new growth, drew conscious instruction not from the achievement of the former colonists, which to contemporaries long remained questionable, but from its own failure to retain their loyalty. Representative institutions were recognized as the birthright of Englishmen but, apart from an uninspired and halting movement for imperial federation preceding World War I, they were gloomily acknowledged as an insuperable barrier to political integration. In Britain the success of the American union was facilely attributed to its operation within a continuous landmass which made possible close and abiding relationships denied to communities separated by salt water, such as the former Atlantic empire had been.

The American experience after 1776 might seem to argue, however, that the failure of the first empire lay not in the dynamic process associated with the institution of representative government but rather in the readiness of English and Scottish leaders to accept as politically efficient the baldly materialistic canons of mercantilism. The consequences of this blindness were largely hidden for three-quarters of a century between 1689 and 1763, half the life of the old empire, by the omnipresent French menace which acted as a substitute for an imperial constitution and imposed a unity that to many observers, as indeed to later American patriots, seemed a fixed and sufficient reality. The stage was set for this prolonged and nervous drama (mistakenly conceived by later generations as a golden age) by the Glorious Revolution of 1688 and its derivative disturbances in North America and the West Indies. These events offered to England's overseas possessions a shared experience unique in its political annals. No preceding occasion had created such unity or revealed so clearly a frame of mind common to both sides of the Atlantic. The nearest comparison, if comparison it may properly be called—the restoration of Charles II—was observed with scant enthusiasm in New England even if cordially acknowledged elsewhere. But in 1689, apart from the Irish of the Leeward Islands, there was scarcely a true Jacobite to be found in the western hemisphere.

Almost as if by instinct the English had closed ranks, contending only in their claims of loyalty to the new Protestant sovereign, and had resolutely prepared to confront a traditional foe in the struggle the outcome of which was by no means certain. In 1689 there was to be perceived in the colonies something of the spirit which sustained Britain in 1940: the nation, though not isolated from support in Europe, had experienced purification. For months to come, the English nation was united by sentiment in a bond more meaningful than the narrowly calculated profit and loss of the old colonial system. The successful accession of William, joyfully anticipated in many provinces with incautious regard for legalities and the maintenance of public order, and widely accompanied by a lucid affirmation of religious and political principles, ensured the rejection of absolutism and popery and made inevitable the survival of assembly government as a central feature of colonial politics.

Henceforth there was an in-built resistance to French practices and procedures, however successful they might appear to be in the administration of the rival empire, and a distrust of centralization not merely by reason of the inevitable encroachment upon local power it would bring but because of its association with Bourbon and Stuart despotism. The intellectual climate in the colonies was now averse to the orderly but ambitious plans pursued under the Stuarts and still favoured by those of their administrators who had retained important office. If it had been otherwise, time of war was not the occasion to define in close legal terms a relationship between the colonies and the mother country emotionally enacted at the time of James's abdication. Moreover there was little in the English past to argue its necessity. King William, distinguishing accurately between what was practicable and what was not, aimed to retain the wide support granted to him for dispossessing James. His colonial policy, one of caution and compromise—the consequence of a mind centred on the curtailment of French power in Europe—though firmly committed to the principle of religious toleration, pursued no striking innovations in the political structure of the empire.

Of all the mainland colonies none welcomed the Protestant succession more fervently than Massachusetts, or New England, as she was commonly called. In the eyes of her Churches it brought deliverance from an Egyptian bondage, for property-owners a security which the land registration and taxes of a previous reign had seemed to deny, and to the mercantile classes hope, if not assurance, of a sympathetic remodelling of the navigation laws. Massachusetts was more than a mere province: her historical experience was arguably unique. Alone of all the overseas plantations of Europe she had avoided at the outset the customary feebleness and the humiliating poverty of spirit. The outstanding calibre of the first political and spiritual leaders, their assurance, and sense of purpose provided a natural focal point for the reverence of later generations. Settlement was swiftly followed by a significant period of isolation, the product of England's embroilment in civil war, and by a quasi-independence which persisted in some measure until the revocation of the first charter in 1684. A sense of tradition, initially communicated through the weekly sermons, the best of which were printed and circulated throughout the churches, pervaded the whole community.

By the last quarter of the seventeenth century Massachusetts possessed a historical past which encouraged the unconscious arrogation of many of the attributes of nationhood. It would be wrong to suggest that she was viewed by her settlers as on a par with the states of Europe, but the descriptive terms of her own theocracy defined her as an Israel separated from them, as from her colonial and Indian neighbours, by the attention with which God favoured a chosen people. The position of England in this relationship was anomalous and at times obscure. Her function was never unimportant but was assumed or implied rather than defined. If in the beginning the Bay colony was the City upon a Hill, the beacon lit by the first settlers, then England formed the uplands of the Protestant plain which it sought to inspire. So the earliest churches had reasoned until disenchantment with the progress of the Puritan Revolution after the mid-1640s had all but ended their equivocation and encouraged an 'inwardness' which dominated for several decades the colony's sense of mission and absorbed much of its intellectual activity.

Now the success of Stuart policy, culminating in the despotic rule of Sir Edmund Andros (1686–9), had humiliated the theocrats, alienated the commercial classes, and rendered impossible the continuance of this frame of mind. The exhausting sacrifices of New England during King Philip's War (1675–6), an economic recession, and the threat under James II of settlement by Irish papists added to the grave uncertainties about the Puritan future of Massachusetts. The substitution of William for James as king of England, and the sequence of events which followed it in Boston and the surrounding countryside gave to New Englanders a sense of having returned to the mainstream of the English nation by their own volition. But with the rapid onset of major conflict, and awareness of the ambitious projects of conquest conceived by Count Frontenac, governor of New France, the sense of crisis deepened. Although powerful elements within the colony contended for a return of the charter of 1629 and its attendant privileges, there was a growing recognition before 1691 that no turning back of the clock was possible. Provincial policy, it was understood, must henceforth be approved by the mother country, if not subordinated to her needs, not merely out of respect for the length of her arm but as a step towards sharing her more abundant material resources.

In the influential annual election sermons, when the purposes of the community were searchingly reviewed before the newly-gathered Assembly, repeated references echoing the duty unto Caesar took on a meaning which reached beyond the palpably limited powers of the General Court. Against a background of profound insecurity in which the barbarities of war waged by the Indian allies of France threatened to drive in the frontiers, provincial leaders aspired to a special relationship with old England. This never achieved precise political form and was, at most, pathetically insubstantial, but it created within the English nation a new lodgement for the concept of pre-eminence which had formed an essential part of the definition of Massachusetts ever since John Winthrop's sermon on the *Arbella* inaugurated the federal covenant. This provided small material comfort but, until the ill-fated Canada expedition of 1711 shattered the prospects of mutual respect and understanding, it helped to bolster the hopes of New Englanders that the province would not be lightly abandoned to papists and heathens.

CHAPTER I

Revolution and Settlement in the colonies, 1689-1692: the commitment to Protestantism and representative government, and the role of Massachusetts Bay

THE Glorious Revolution was for the colonial empire, as for England, a memorable occasion and a historical watershed. In one sense it marked the end of an important phase of growth and the beginning of another. By the close of the 1680s, as the third generation of settlers reached towards manhood, the initial problems of adjustment to the American wilderness had been left behind by the established communities. Frontier regions remained, but even here the accumulated wisdom and the achievements of a century of planting supported a spirit of optimism. The future for Carolina was still unclear, it is true, but Pennsylvania, the most recent venture, was away to a promising start, Philadelphia having begun the precipitous rise which in less than a century would create the second city of the British empire. Population estimates, prepared for the Lords of Trade by assiduous colonial governors, offered considerable assurances for widespread increase, yet for some observers this was seriously outweighed by the hostile presence of the eastern Indians, who had threatened to destroy New England in King Philip's War (1675-6), and by the graver, if uncertain, menace of the French empire. But the accession of William III and the restraints imposed on the royal prerogative helped to redress the balance by re-uniting the English nation in support of constitutional monarchy.[1] In this sense 1689 marked the beginning of a period of consensus: for henceforth the political precepts upheld in England were subscribed to by the overwhelming majority of colonists. Fundamentally the empire was now committed to the principle of representative government and

[1] For commentary on the deeper uncertainties which remained, see J. H. Plumb, *The Growth of Political Stability in England, 1675-1725* (London, 1967), p. 1.

to the Protestant religion.[1] Because of this New England, a region hitherto seriously at odds with the English policy-makers, could set aside her anti-monarchical sentiments and in broad terms identify her interests with those of the mother country. In a further sense, although one hidden from contemporaries, the abdication of James II marked the end of the concerted drive for centralization. Had the schemes of James come to fruition they would have created a governmental structure similar to that of New France: uniformity and administrative coherence would have been achieved at a price. Instead the Revolution assured that the traditional units of government would remain substantially intact, and that plans for their modification would be advanced only with great caution.[2] Persistent diversity, however, was no more than tolerated. It was not seen by Englishmen as an expression of unity, as was the case during the first part of the twentieth century.

Throughout the seventeenth and the eighteenth century most of the colonial empire was acutely sensitive to major disturbance in Britain. Each flutter of the imperial heart produced a provincial twitch. But in part these agitations were the consequence of contrived manipulation by assemblymen, northern merchants, local patriots, or just plain demagogues. In particular the astute politicians of Massachusetts had maintained a form of independence until 1684 by careful observation of the conflicts, tensions, and divisions of English political life. Intelligence from home was used for defensive purposes, especially to safeguard the charter of 1629. Other communities were less skilful but few neglected altogether opportunities thrust before them. Yet provincial politicians were no more free to operate in a political vacuum than were those in England. Local rivalries and personal animosities created a climate, with its own seasons, which was sometimes more and sometimes less amenable to the pursuit of essential

[1] J. R. Pole, *The Seventeenth Century. The Sources of Legislative Power* (Charlottesville, Va., 1969), pp. 5–6.

[2] Three forms of colonial government survived down to the American Revolution. Royal provinces such as Virginia, New York, New Hampshire, and Massachusetts, had their governor appointed by the king. In proprietary colonies, granted by charter to individual subjects, the governor was nominated by the proprietors, subject to royal approval. On the mainland in the 1690s these were the most numerous and included Pennsylvania, East and West New Jersey, Maryland, and the Carolinas. The corporate colonies of Connecticut and Rhode Island, which were quasi-independent, elected their own governors.

provincial interests. In regarding colonial politics as a monolithic conspiracy aimed at frustrating or deflecting imperial policy English administrators were seriously at fault. Colonists who exaggerated the degree of freedom and depth of design of the policy-makers in Britain similarly erred.

In examining the effects of the Glorious Revolution on the empire it is important, first of all, to determine to what extent events in England were the direct cause of, and to what extent they were the excuse for, political turmoil which shook much of the colonial world. Not all colonies suffered upheaval. Boston, and subsequently Massachusetts, rose against Edward Randolph and the governor, Sir Edmund Andros. In New York the legal government was overthrown by a faction led by Jacob Leisler. Maryland rebelled against the proprietor, Lord Baltimore. In South Carolina, for reasons almost exclusively local, there was a successful rising against Seth Sothell, a hated governor. But Virginia avoided serious trouble, Connecticut calmly adjusted to it, and the Jerseys escaped it altogether. In the West Indies the change from Stuart to Orange, from peace to war, from Catholic to Protestant monarch, was achieved with relative ease. Thus it was not entirely true that when Whitehall took fever every imperial limb was similarly agitated.

The most striking consequence of the abdication of James and the accession of William was that it provided the transatlantic empire with a unifying external threat, namely the aggrandizement of France. This dangerous force had been variously viewed in earlier decades. James II took careful steps to confine the bounds of French power in North America. Indeed the Dominion of New England, which had collapsed when news of the abdication was received, had been designed, in some measure, to counter the threat of New France. Yet James, like his brother Charles, was open to the charge of equivocation. No one could be certain that Catholicism was not ultimately more important than imperial dominion. For the northern colonies in particular, the contrasting simplicity of purpose of William of Orange, in seeking to counter the domination of Louis XIV and his religious aspirations, offered an important bridge to the schisms which divided England for so long. No wonder Mather called it 'the Happy Revolution'. Thus most colonies perceived the need to put their house in order as a preliminary to confronting the hereditary foe and his feared design of proselytization or extirpation. The accession of William provided the empire with a clear military purpose: the defence of Protestantism. In so doing it achieved what the economic aspects of the old colonial system could never hope to achieve: it revived the importance of membership of the English nation.[1] Patriotism, whether geared to provincial interest or to the wider community of Englishmen, moved individuals to drastic action. Men acclaimed the Revolution England had wrought and rejoiced at being enabled to repeat in the colonies her political example. In New England men were further motivated by the need to safeguard embedded traditions.

For William, however, it was essential to shore up imperial walls and undesirable that time be expended in debating the means to be employed.[2] Thus all provincial initiative in support of the Protestant accession gained some form of acknowledgement from England, if only temporary, and raised hopes of permanent concessions. The encouragement to Roman Catholicism, which under James II accompanied the ill-formed plans for a new administrative order, was pathetically feeble but sufficed to alarm Protestants over a wide area. In Jamaica, under the Duke of Albemarle, the expectations of Roman Catholics were for a brief while raised high. Governor Albemarle, instructed to protect and favour all papists, had been aided in his task by Dr. Churchill, appointed chief pastor

---

[1] 'That a colony so considerable as *New-England* should be discouraged is not for the Honour and interest of the *English Nation*; in as much as the People there are generally Sober, Industrious, Well-Disciplined and apt for Martial Affairs; so that he that is Sovereign of *New-England* may by means thereof (*when he pleaseth*) be Emperour of *America*.' 'A Narrative of the Miseries of New England by reason of an Arbitrary Government Erected there,' attributed to Increase Mather and printed in W. H. Whitmore (ed.), *The Andros Tracts* (3 vols., The Prince Society, Boston, Mass., 1868–74), ii. 1–14.

[2] See Increase Mather, 'Brief Account of the Agents, 1691', in *Narratives of the Insurrections, 1675–90*, ed. C. M. Andrews (New York, 1915). 'Help against France', Mather had been advised, was more important 'than [regaining] the [original] Charter'; see also Revd. Gershom Bulkeley, 'The People's Right to Election', in *Conn. Hist. Soc. Coll.* (Hartford, Conn., 1860), i. 71. 'It is a time wherein there is a strong engagement to root out the Protestant Religion. *Europe* is upon this account in flames, the Ax is laid to our own Root, if it be so, it is a time wherein we had need to *strengthen the things that are weake*, to join heart and hand together against the French and Pagan-Force and Cruelty, and to unite heaven and Earth . . . for the preservation of ourselves and posterity . . . surely there is no time to fall to Faction and parties and to promote private interests.'

for the island. In time the Bishop of Panama would sanguineously claim that all the English there had been converted, but in fact the number seems to have been very small. In Barbados, alarm was caused through the energetic activity of Sir Thomas Montgomery, and Mr. Willoughby Chamberlayne. The former was a native of Barbados, a young man of considerable estate and reputation who had been in touch with the leading Catholic dignitaries of the Privy Council in England, including Father Petre and Lord Sunderland. News of his zeal is alleged to have reached as far north as Virginia, for he may have held hopes of enlisting Catholic help from the mainland to deliver the island over to the French of Martinique. Chamberlayne, like Montgomery, was a recent convert to Rome, and in direct correspondence with the governors, priests, and Jesuits of the neighbouring French islands. Mass was held in his house and arrangements made for Father de Forest to come over from Martinique to advance the conversion of the young. But by the time of the flight of James few had changed their faith through the activities of either Montgomery or Chamberlayne.

On the mainland, Roman Catholic strength was centred in Maryland, which had been originally founded as a refuge for Catholics and remained under the proprietorship of the Calvert family. Elsewhere, especially in Virginia and New York, the small increase in the number of Catholics, some of whom became office-holders, gave reason to fear that more widespread schemes for conversion were developing behind the scenes. In each of the three areas there was concern over the allied threat to political liberties, though in Virginia the effect of this on public order was less serious. Here, more skilfully than in contemporary England, Assembly powers had been significantly restricted. The legislative session at the beginning of James's reign was a stormy one, the burgesses vigorously resisting an attempt to deprive them of control over taxation. In August, as a mark of his displeasure, the king ordered the governor to dissolve the Assembly. James was angry that his veto power should have been questioned,[1] though in fact the prerogative had gained by denying the legislature the right to

---

[1] The burgesses protested against the king's claim to annul acts of Assembly. They petitioned the king to give up the right of repealing law by proclamation. T. J. Wertembaker, *Virginia under the Stuarts* (New York, 1959), pp. 242–3; *Journals of the House of Burgesses of Virginia, 1659/60–93*, ed. H. R. McIlwaine (Richmond, Va., 1914), pp. 304–5, 309, 313, 316–7, 325–6, 329.

elect its own clerk and by the measures taken against individual burgesses. Arthur Allen and John Smith, influential members of the House, had suffered loss of civil and military employment; Charles Scarburgh had forfeited membership; while later, in 1688, William Anderson—a fourth—was detained seven months in the common gaol without trial and denied benefit of Habeas Corpus.

In face of such measures, designed to terrorize and to cow, Virginians, with fluctuating hopes, waited for events in England to bring them some relief. Initial restiveness against the accession of a Catholic monarch reached a peak at the time of Monmouth's rebellion when fears were expressed that the colony might espouse the duke's cause.[1] Thereafter the advancement of the king's co-religionists was received with superficial equanimity, even approbation; but beneath the surface fear and resentment steadily grew. Under direction from England, the governor, Lord Howard of Effingham, himself a Roman Catholic, dispensed with the oaths of allegiance and supremacy and admitted papists to the Council. When James issued the edict suspending laws against Nonconformists the news was celebrated by the firing of guns and the beating of drums, the burgesses expressed their official approval, and a Roman Catholic was duly elected member for Stafford County. All counties seem to have responded with voluntary and unaffected enthusiasm to the governor's command to celebrate the birth of the Prince of Wales.[2] Outlay in liquor alone for the single county of Rappahannock was 10,000 pounds of tobacco—a very considerable sum. This, however, may not indicate respect for the Stuarts so much as delight at an excuse for a drinking orgy. Some accession to Roman Catholic strength now took place. By 1689 it was believed, probably wrongly, that the entire Council as well as a proportion of the county justices had been converted.[3] Among the people at large, Mass was celebrated by the priest Raymond in the houses of several leading citizens—Captain Robert Jordan, Mr. Henry Ruddick, Mr. Charles Egerton. The papist marriage

[1] CO5/1357, 79, 80, 95–6; Wertembaker, op. cit., p. 242.

[2] P. A. Bruce, *Institutional History of Virginia in the Seventeenth Century* (New York, 1910), ii. 284; D. Boorstin, *The Americans: The Colonial Experience* (New York, 1964), p. 137.

[3] Suspicion was directed in particular against Isaac Allerton and John Armistead, but both were subsequently confirmed as councillors by William III. *C.S.P.C.*, 1689–92, no. 99.

ceremony was openly performed. But though Stafford County bordering on Maryland was nervously watched by the rest of the province, and anxieties were expressed at the proposed planting of the Catholics, there is no indication of any spectacular growth of the Catholic community.[1]

For Maryland, the disturbed state of provincial affairs preceded the accession of James II. In some respects the situation was not unlike that in Virginia, for here also the relative powers of governor and Assembly were in dispute. But in general the background was more complex. Long-standing opposition to the proprietary grant stemmed from an economic root. Freemen without voting rights paid equal taxes with the rich, so it was claimed, while depression in the 1680s brought resentment among the planters and merchants against Lord Baltimore's economic policy. Religion also accentuated divisions. The ratio of Protestants to Catholics was overwhelmingly against the latter who constituted a mere 1,500 out of a population of about 25,000. But in 1681 the proprietor, long under suspicion of unduly favouring his co-religionists, had been charged with partiality before the Privy Council. Here, the Crown was not directly involved and the vague project which saw the vacation of the proprietary charter as a step to the consolidating of the tobacco colonies under one royal governor did not contribute, as far as is known, to the revolution in Maryland in 1689.[2]

To the north, in this year, with the exception of Pennsylvania, lay the vast Dominion of New England, stretching from the Delaware to the remote St. Croix. Originally embracing the New England settlements under the government of Sir Edmund Andros, located in Boston, it had been hastily extended in 1688, after only two years existence, to include New York and the Jerseys. Within this structure the most important features of representative government had ceased to exist. There is no doubt that the Assemblies throughout the English colonies had served in the past, and would continue to serve, as something more than a means of securing the rights and privileges of Englishmen. As instruments to advance the ambition and influence of provincials, their abolition

---

[1] Such as there were represented a novel element in the composition of Virginia. In 1681 Governor Culpeper had reported that the province lacked a single papist.

[2] *Quo warranto* proceedings against the charter were initiated in 1686, but never completed.

had lessened the opportunities, in crude numerical terms, of many who sought a significant role in colonial affairs.

This was true for New York, where the re-location of the main centre of government 200 miles eastward visibly worsened the position of an *arriviste* class which by its vigour had greatly accelerated economic growth under English rule. The pattern of background disturbance—preceding revolution—was again complex, extending over several decades at least to the time of the first seizure from the Dutch. The bewildering effects of transition from Dutch to English rule, twice experienced, had accompanied the economic decline of the 1670s and had been followed by further political change from proprietary to royal province when James ascended the throne. Some Catholics had subsequently been admitted to office. But the fears of those denied influence were heightened by the knowledge that men indifferent to religion were prepared to compromise for the sake of acquiring or retaining power. Many of the leading merchants, as well as Lieutenant-Governor Nicholson, were suspected of readiness to sacrifice English Protestantism for the sake of private gain. In the background there lurked Thomas Dongan (a Roman Catholic Irishman and former governor of the province before its transfer to the control of Sir Edmund Andros) now residing at Hempstead in East New Jersey. No governor had moved with more resolution than Dongan to block the aggressive schemes of New France and its Indian allies, even while England and France were nominally at peace. Even so he was viewed with apprehension as a potential rallying-point for Catholic strength and, after the abdication of James, was suspected of conspiring with the French for the sake of the Stuart monarchy and the welfare of his religion. The populace of New York, exposed by geographical factors to invasion from the north, and agitated by high taxes, grew convinced that a plot was afoot against its liberties. These calculations and assessments were not wholly wanting in foundation or logic, but clearly they were advanced by men whose interests in part at least, were narrow and selfish.[1]

The seat of the revolutionary disturbances in North America was Boston; its most important source of support the surrounding

---

[1] Leder, pt. II in *The Glorious Revolution in America*, ed. M. G. Hall, L. H. Leder, and M. G. Kammen (Chapel Hill, N.C., 1964), p. 85.

countryside; the main instrument was the colony of Massachusetts Bay, by reason of its established ideals and the utilization of its traditional structure of communication. The role of Massachusetts is accordingly distinguished from that of any other colony in that here was initiated a sequence of events the repercussions of which were felt directly throughout the enlarged Dominion of New England, and which indirectly helped to sustain the anti-proprietary government in Maryland. In 1684, caught at last in the web of English legal procedures, Massachusetts had suffered the annulment of the charter of 1629 after nearly three-quarters of a century of quasi-independent status.[1] This purposeful society, led by a cautious and skilful theocracy adept at obscuring its true intentions and at contending for rights without acknowledging responsibilities, possessed some of the important attributes of nationhood. The restraint and sophistication of its leaders under the stress of Stuart vacation of the throne more closely compares with the direction of events in Scotland or even England than in Maryland or New York. Discontented elements under the theocracy—primarily a rising mercantile class—may have viewed the establishment of firm English rule with favour; a larger body of the people doubtless regarded the change with a curiosity not hostile. However this does not alter the fact that Stuart policy had here ushered in a more abrupt break with the past than in any other colony either in the West Indies or on the mainland.

Loss of representative institutions, including the subversion of town government, the overthrow of an educational system, and uncertainty of land title, combined with the threat to the churches of New England to alienate all sections of the community as effectively as would the Stamp Act of 1765. With few impediments to his will, and aided by the hated Edward Randolph, who as surveyor-general of the colonies and a member of the Council sought to apply the letter of the law to the navigation system, Sir Edmund Andros imposed a despotic control the ultimate purpose of which could not be clearly divined. But the remark of the former president of the Council, Joseph Dudley, to the Revd. John Wise

---

[1] For details of the attack on the charter governments of New England see P. S. Haffenden, 'The Crown and the Colonial Charters, 1675-88', *W &MQ*, 3rd ser. xv (1958), 297-311, 452-66; V. F. Barnes, *The Dominion of New England* (New Haven, Conn., 1960), pp. 21, 28-9; H. L. Osgood, *The American Colonies in the Seventeenth Century* (Gloucester, Mass., 1957), iii. 331-3, 378-97.

of Ipswich that they had no more privileges left them than not to be sold for slaves offered little hope for the future. Whether this was to be seen as a prelude to Anglican domination or a return to Rome, it implied a fearful prospect portending the permanent shift of control from the theocrats or visible saints, and perversion of the ultimate spiritual end of society. However, the fact that no Catholic had obtained office east of the Hudson River, and the readiness of James in the latter half of his reign to advance religious toleration, as a means to escape the consequences of his earlier actions, persuaded many New Englanders that the governor not the king was the focal point of evil.[1] Because of this, Increase Mather in London sought assurance from James that the colony's true interests would be safeguarded. But not all ills stemmed from England's policy. Indeed even those that did evidenced God's displeasure with Massachusetts and were seen by her minister as the consequence of lapse from grace by her people. Mather was influenced in his interpretation of their fate by his study of the Old Testament prophets and their reflections on the vicissitudes of the Jewish kingdoms. The depth of God's wrath had earlier been indicated by the harrowing experience of King Philip's War which had left behind it exhaustion and uncertainty. Accordingly the task of New England, as customarily defined, was to seek God's purpose for His chosen people and to pursue it unerringly; to ascertain the significance of His external instruments, whether they be nations, rulers, or officials, and determine whether it was His will they should be resisted, overthrown, or supported. Repentance was essential but since it was recognized as God's wish that Massachusetts should prosper, the problem of selecting the right path was less difficult than it might otherwise have seemed. A godly way was an orderly way and for this reason violent change was not readily justifiable, nor indeed sought.[2]

The advantages of negotiating with James II for political safeguards were lessened when news reached Boston in December 1688 that an invasion of England from Holland was to be antici-

---

[1] Many New Englanders were suspicious of the intention behind the Declaration of Indulgence. See Danforth to Mather, 8 Nov. 1687, cited in C. M. Andrews, *Colonial Self-Government, 1652–1689* (New York, 1904), p. 304; cf. Barnes, *Dominion*, p. 127.

[2] See below, ch. ii, pp. 49–50.

pated.[1] Shortly afterwards, under instructions from England, Governor Andros announced that William of Orange had landed there, and calling for unity ordered the people to be on guard against surprise by a foreign power. The position of James was known to be insecure and rumours of the movements of William added to the tensions which beset the colony. But throughout the winter more certain news was lacking and not until March did Massachusetts have knowledge of the flight of James.[2] Then opposition to the character of the government which had motivated the representations to the king in 1688 was heightened by the fear that Andros would turn the colony over to the French. With the advantages of hindsight the constructions of the New Englanders may easily be ridiculed.[3] There was, however, ample reason to mistrust the political judgement and intent of the Stuart king and to fear that the loyalty of administrators in New England would compound his errors. Even so, the immediate actions of Andros did not justify suspicion that he designed precipitate action harmful to Massachusetts.

During the winter the governor had been at the frontier with

[1] *Mass. Hist. Soc. Coll.*, 5th ser. viii. 486; 6th ser. iii. 495. The king's letter to Governor Andros warning him to prepare for landing or invasion (16 Oct. 1688) was sent by a vessel which reached Boston at the beginning of January. By the same convoy Mather and other New England agents warned their friends to 'prepare for an interesting change'. G. Chalmers, *Political Annals of the Present United Colonies . . . to the Peace of 1763 . . .* (London, 1780), i. 469, ii. 20, 33–4; J. H. Palfrey, *A Compendious History of New England* (Boston, Mass., and New York, 1873), iii. 571n.

[2] E. Channing, *History of the United States* (New York, 1926–7), ii. 198–9. The 'Address of the Nonconformist Ministers' to William was printed at Boston before the end of the month and John Nelson, military head of the movement, wrote to a friend on 25 Mar. that James, having been defeated, had fled. William of Orange issued a circular letter to the colonies on 12 Jan. directing all colonial officials to remain in their places, but Increase Mather, acting as agent for Massachusetts, saw to it that no copy was sent to Boston. *New York Hist. Soc. Coll.* (1868), p. 36; *C.S.P.C.*, 1689–92, no. 8. See also *Narratives of the Insurrections*, p. 277. In 'New England's Faction Discovered, 1690', by C.D., it was claimed that the revolt was intended for January 1688 and that 'those concerned in the late Revolution were then to have acted the like parts, at which time no account of the Prince of Orange's intention of coming into England [was] known in that land.' C. M. Andrews believed there was no certain evidence of a conspiracy formed at this early date. Ibid., p. 257n.

[3] J. R. Brodhead, *History of the State of New York* (New York, 1871), ii. 550, alleged that it was well understood in France that Andros would declare for the Dutch prince should he become sovereign.

his regular soldiers in anticipation of attack by the French and
Indians. He was thus absent from Boston until the end of March
and accordingly out of touch with public feeling. Yet he did nothing
to placate the colonists' fears, nor did he indicate the limits of his
loyalty to James. Whether to have done so would have prevented
an uprising it is difficult to say. Nothing short of a sweeping reversal
of previous policies could have allayed the general detestation he
had aroused. He might, it is true, have attempted a more devious
game and sought to win support from sections of the community
alienated by the land-registration policy, but such a course without
official sanction from England was incompatible with his nature
as the obedient administrator. As it was, since his ulterior motives
were distrusted, every move he made was suspect. In circumstances
such as these the absurd rumours were circulated that he had
furnished the Indians with arms and ammunition in several
localities and encouraged them to attack the English Settlements.[1]
In fact, his purpose was to maintain order: no more than this.
His resources for this task were pitifully small. In the absence from
Boston of his two regular companies he depended on the cannon
and men of the fifth-rate frigate *Rose*. But the capacity of the *Rose*
to offer aid was restricted by the grievances of the crew which
before April had led to a number of minor mutinies.

The insurrectionists were presented with a quasi-legal justification by learning of the 'Declaration' which William issued upon
undertaking the invasion of England. By this, all magistrates
whom James had unjustly turned out were forthwith to resume
their employment though it was questionable whether it was ever
intended to apply to the colonies. The news was carried from
Nevis by one John Winslow, son of a Boston merchant.[2] Winslow
was duly sentenced to imprisonment by Justice Foxcroft for
bringing a traitorous and treasonable libel into the country, but
by this time the damage had been done. It has been suggested
that the uprising had been planned days or weeks before,[3] but
there is no decisive evidence to uphold such a claim. Moreover,
there is much to support the view that the colony's leaders, while

---

[1] 'The Revolution in New England Justified', *Andros Tracts*, i. 101ff.

[2] Palfrey, op. cit. iii. 574. T. Hutchinson, *History of the Colony and Province
of Massachusetts Bay*, ed. L. S. Mayo (Cambridge, Mass., 1936), i. 317, says
that the news was brought from Virginia.

[3] Osgood, op. cit. iii. 419.

wishing William well in his undertaking, refrained from committing themselves for the soundest possible reasons until the outcome
of events in England was plainly visible.[1] William's success would
be their success but should he fail they would be no worse off than
before. Some concessions had already been forthcoming from
James, and if the invasion from Holland proved abortive James
might conceivably continue to seek the support of the dissenters.
Removal of Andros might well result from this. However, it
would seem that their hand was forced.

Fear of desertion by the common soldier from the war against the
eastern Indians, and alarm at the behaviour of the country people,
especially those to the northwards, induced the more sensible
gentlemen at Boston to assume control when disturbances did
occur, in order to avoid the onset of bloody revolution.[2] According
to Samuel Mather, New England's objectives were achieved once
the criminals (namely the former government) were reserved for
the justice of the English Parliament: they were to be committed
as enemies of the Prince of Orange, and of New England's English
liberties. It was essential that the people be prevented from
eroding authority beyond this point. Such limitation of aims was
a rational move: social change had no scriptural sanction, and a
complete break with Britain, as experiences under the Restoration
had taught, was neither practicable nor desirable.

It is highly unlikely that the theocracy planned to use an ill-
controlled mob as its instrument; contemporary sermons ring
with abhorrence of political disorder. But whatever the source
there now occurred a popular uprising. Both North-Enders and

---

[1] Andrews, *Narratives of the Insurrections*, p. 317; Hall, pt. I in *Glorious
Revolution*, ed. Hall, Leder, and Kammen, pp. 38–40; and see *Andros Tracts*,
iii. 145, 191–202. Belief in a conspiracy is supported by material in Brodhead,
History of the State of New York, ii. 537. It is here suggested that Mather, in
cornering William Jephson, secretary to William III and cousin of Lord Wharton
to prevent the confirmation of all office-holders who were non-papists, prepared
the ground for the overthrow of Andros.

[2] This is confirmed in 'An Account of the Late Revolutions in New-England'
by A.B., *Andros Tracts*, ii. 191–202; M. G. Hall, *Edward Randolph and the
American Colonies, 1676–1703* (Chapel Hill, N.C., 1960), p. 50. This tract, by
an unknown author or authors, suggests a consultation among the more eminent
men about the middle of April. 'They considered the *Directions* given in the
Prince's Declarations (of which at last we had stolen a sight) and the *Examples*
which the whole kingdom of *England* (as far as we could learn) had set before
us.'

South-Enders sprang to arms.[1] In face of disorders Andros and
Randolph hastened to the new fort at Fort Hill for safety. But
from the beginning the government was unable to counter popular
determination with comparable resolution. Even the regular
soldiers lacked spirit in opposing the Bostonians, and after the
capture of Captain George by a gang headed by Robert Small,
ship's carpenter of the *Rose*, all but a few supporters of Andros
were soon taken. Finally the governor himself, along with Randolph, was apprehended attempting to escape from the fort to
the questionable security of the frigate *Rose*.[2] Shortly afterwards
the 'Castle' on Castle Island was induced to surrender and the
frigate, with ship- as well as battery-guns now trained upon her,
hauled down her colours. That afternoon of 18 April the country
people whom the leaders of the province had affected to fear—
some thousands of horse and foot so it was reported—came
armed into the town 'in a great heat and rage', according to Samuel
Prince. They were pacified only by Randolph being bound in
chains and cords. The attempt by Governor Andros to escape
dressed as a woman failed.

The leaders were eager, according to their later admission, to
follow the examples which the whole kingdom of England had
set before them. Their success was evident.[3] Not a man's life had
been lost. There was neither bloodshed nor rapine. As in England,
members of the Church of England assisted the overthrow of
despotism. A revolution had been made; it was secured two days
later when a Council for the Safety of the People and the Con-
servation of the Peace was set up. There was no immediate danger
of it being reversed: there was some possibility, however, that
its impedance might not be permanent, that the revolution might
lead to a restoration. The designs of the 'moderates'—many of

---

[1] The armed men were under the command of John Nelson and John Foster,
both of whom have been classed as among the moderates of the day. For comment
on Nelson see *Mass. Hist. Soc. Proc.* (1863–4), p. 370. According to the account
of Nathaniel Byfield the eruption was spontaneous. North-Enders reported
South-Enders were in arms and vice versa.

[2] Byfield says the fort was insufficiently fortified. Andros probably neglected
this to spend money on frontier defences. For further details see ch. iii, p. 78,
n. 6.

[3] Andrews, *Narratives of the Insurrections*, p. 277; *Andros Tracts*, i. 75–9,
ii. 194; R. N. Toppan and A. T. S. Goodrick, *Edward Randolph; Including His
Letters and Official Papers* (The Prince Society, Boston, Mass., 1898–1909),
v. 57, vi. 271–8; *C.S.P.C.*, 1689–92, nos. 152, 196, 261.

them Bostonians—to maintain a close dependence on England, in accord with political and economic realities, was opposed by men from the towns of the colony who urged a return to former autonomy, and agitated for the right to participate in determining the future form of government. As a concession two conventions were held in May at which representatives attended, but the contention that the mode of settlement rested with 'the People' was successfully resisted.[1] Yet it says much for New England discipline and respect for the law that though indecision and doubt persisted as to the legal position of the government now in possession, extravagant action was avoided. 'Every man gave himself the Laws of good Neighbourhood.' It was questioned whether government by the committee should continue until word came from England or whether the overthrow of a government, regarded as illegal, had ushered in the return of the former government by charter. These things agitated New England, but the unidentified 'A.B.' was right in saying that King William and Queen Mary had been proclaimed 'with such a Joy, Splendour, Appearance and Unanimity as had never before been seen in these Territories'. Monarchy had at last assumed an acceptable form.[2] Though there were many difficulties ahead in shaping and defining the new form of government, and though New Englanders would not exert their will in these matters with the same ease and with the same success achieved in revolution, nevertheless a New England more closely bound to the mother country than ever before had now emerged.

The first news of the invasion of England reached New York in February 1689.[3] Nicholson sent word to Andros but tried to keep his own province in the dark. Information, however, reached the public from Maryland, yet, as in Massachusetts, reaction in a physical sense was delayed. It was not until 26 April that disturbances began: a direct consequence of the great 'suprizall' at Boston. With the *de jure* government of the dominion overthrown

---

[1] R. C. Simmons, 'Massachusetts: Godliness, Property and the Franchise in Puritan Massachusetts', *Journal of American History*, iv (1968), 502.

[2] Perry Miller, *New England Mind from Colony to Province* (Cambridge, Mass., 1953), pp. 158–9; and below, ch. ii, pp. 40–2. See p. 13, n. 2 above for reference to 'A.B.'

[3] Leder, pt. II in *Glorious Revolution*, ed. Hall, Leder, and Kammen, pp. 99, 102.

the problem for New York was primarily one of maintaining order. The administrative machinery available was the lieutenant-governor and his council of four, the mayor and aldermen of the city and the chief officers of the trained bands. It was an unquestioned assumption that a lead would be provided by the lieutenant-governor. Joint meetings between these officials continued for about six weeks until early June. Although the government was at a loss to raise money for fortifications the city was kept reasonably calm. But outside there was greater reason for disquiet. Soon after the beginning of May information about the disturbed state of the counties of Westchester, Queens, and Suffolk began to come in. The militia of Queens, in arrears with its pay, expelled its officers and elected substitutes, while from the towns of Southampton, Easthampton, and Huntington came demands that the fort should be placed in the hands of men whom the county could elect and trust.[1] By 15 May most of the militia of the three counties was drawn up at Jamaica, about fourteen miles from New York, in order to threaten the city.

Tension continued throughout May but a minor difference at the end of the month between a subordinate officer of the militia and a regular was injudiciously magnified by Nicholson as a mutiny and as a bid by the militia to take over control of the city.[2] His own fears and incautious utterances, including a wild threat to burn the city, facilitated a quarrel with some of the leading figures such as Cuyler and De Peyster. There was now substance to popular suspicion seeking a specific outlet for its fears that his intentions were harmful to the best interests of the province.[3] Moreover under James II, Nicholson had compromised his Protestantism for the sake of good standing in England. In the crisis Nicholson's worst adversary was to be his own indecision, at a time when bold action might have restored a situation by no

---

[1] Ibid., pp. 102–3, 106; E. B. O'Callaghan and Berthold Fernow (edd.), *New York Col. Docs.* (15 vols., Albany, N.Y., 1856–87), iii. 592–3.

[2] Leder, pt. II in *Glorious Revolution*, ed. Hall, Leder, and Kammen, p. 108. Nicholson alleged that the militia refused to obey him or their colonels.

[3] The safety of the province was rumoured to be threatened at a number of specific points. Irish and other papists, hunted out of Boston, were believed to be on the way. The regular soldiers within the city were said to be Roman Catholics, and there was widespread talk of a plot to massacre the inhabitants of Staten Island before burning New York. *C.S.P.C.*, 1689–92, no. 458.

means out of hand. As it was he deferred to the Board of councillors, which had hitherto proved a valuable aid in preventing widespread disorder.

In one respect Nicholson's problem was comparable to that of the 'sensible people of New England' in that, empowered by the fall of his superior, Governor Andros, he was required to assume control of a movement technically revolutionary in character. So far, backing from the more sober elements had facilitated the retention of order. The task of rendering it secure looked relatively simple. But though New Yorkers may have been largely loyal to his administration or, at the worst, indifferent, Nicholson faced an active minority, for which we might read 'the populace', which included leaders of capacity and social influence.[1] These contested vigorously with a government which, unlike that in Boston, felt unsure of its right to rule. The aversion to bloodshed in the colonial revolutions of 1689 was near-universal, and from fear of it the Board advised that Fort James be given over to the militia.

The governmental situation still remained fluid. No clear leader had yet emerged from the bid to assume military power.[2] Nicholson had blundered in deferring to the Council, but his action was not decisive. His second major error was to quit the colony. Jacob Leisler—a wealthy militia-captain of German birth, and Dutch descent—had already begun to come to the fore the day following the take-over of the fort. On 1 June, he proclaimed that the lieutenant-governor and all the Council were rogues, papists, and traitors, and creatures of the late King James for whom they intended to secure the province.[3] But two days later official news was received of the proclamation of William and Mary in England, and the continuance of all Protestants in office. The easy course for Nicholson was now to proclaim William and Mary. In so doing

[1] Leder, pt. II in *Glorious Revolution*, ed. Hall, Leder, and Kammen, p. 85. New York's first historian, William Smith, claimed there was a 'general dis-affection to the government' prevailing among the people, partly as a consequence of Catholic settlement in New York and the establishment of a Latin school under the care of a suspected Jesuit. 'The whole body of the people trembled for the protestant cause.' *The History of the Province of New York from the first discovery to 1732* (London, 1776), pp. 80–1.

[2] G. H. Guttridge, *The Colonial Policy of William III in America and the West Indies* (Cambridge, 1922), p. 2.

[3] Minutes of the Council 4 June, Document relating to the administration of Jacob Leisler, *New York Hist. Soc. Coll.* (1868), pp. 269–70.

he would have cleared himself of suspicion and cut the ground from under Leisler's feet.[1] Instead, again leaning heavily on Council advice, he preferred to sail for England.

Thus after 6 June, government was practically thrust in the hands of Leisler and the militia-captains who, forming a Committee of Safety, proclaimed the new monarchs, and denounced as papists all who would not give their support. Leisler having used the mayor and aldermen to assist him in the proclamation subsequently suspended them.[2] Shortly after a letter from William arrived with instructions for Nicholson, and in his absence addressed to such as for the time being 'do take care for the preservation of their Majesties peace and Administering the Laws'. This sufficed to provide Leisler with temporary authority. The committee was dismissed: some of the councillors fled to Albany. A convention was now resolved upon, and invitations issued to the counties and towns to choose delegates. The northern area of the province, Suffolk, and part of Queens refused to participate. Delegates of the remaining parts of the colony met on 26 June. From their hands Leisler received powers to repel foreign enemies and suppress internal disorders.

Albany stayed aloof and on 1 August the officials and commonalty there formed a convention to secure interest of Their Majesties until further orders from England. An attempt by Leisler in October to take over Albany failed though it produced dissension among his opponents. But in January 1690 Albany again refused to recognize him. The following spring he called an assembly which met on 24 April but was dissolved a few days later. During all this period the home government had never shown the slightest tendency to recognize him: the reason he remained unchallenged in power so long is explained by the exigencies of domestic and European affairs. The behaviour of Boston had made possible this revolution, and Boston's example had facilitated the task of the

---

[1] Leisler's own cause was perhaps irrevocably damaged by the failure of his envoy, Joost Stoll, to arrive in England before Nicholson and his companion, an episcopal clergyman named Ennis. William Smith, the historian, sympathetic to Leisler but not uncritical of him, observed that the disturbances were falsely ascribed to aversion to the Church of England rather than zeal for the Prince of Orange, causing Leisler and his party to miss the rewards and notices which his activity for the Revolution justly deserved. Smith, op. cit., p. 83.

[2] E. B. O'Callaghan, *The Documentary History of the State of New York* (Albany, N.Y., 1849), ii. 56.

discontented and fearful.[1] But once again the accidental instruction
of the mother country had acted as a powerful force in providing
the revolutionaries with a justification. Thus the inhabitants of
Suffolk County sought to 'secure our English nation's liberties
and properties from Popery and slavery and from the intended
invasion of foreign French design'. Suffolk justified its action in
terms of self-preservation 'being without any to depend on for
the present'.

In Maryland the controversy between the proprietary and the
Lower House of Assembly was joined in 1688 as the reign of James
II drew to a close. The Lower House opposed the proprietary's
plan to stop the export of bulk tobacco from the Chesapeake Bay
area.[2] In November, a petition listed seven grievances, among
which were complaints of militia-officers relieving inhabitants of
their stores of meat and provision by violence, the exacting of
sterling money for the support of the proprietor instead of mer-
chantable tobacco, as was provided for by the act of 1671, and the
exaction of unlawful fees.[3] Even so, at the beginning of 1689 the
deputies of Baltimore were impressed more by the peace and quiet
of the province than by fears of domestic disturbance, although
rumours of stirring events in England were reported by the Council
as perplexing the colony.[4] Baltimore was instructed by the Privy
Council in February to have William and Mary proclaimed in
his proprietary and the new oath of allegiance administered there.

For various reasons it was not until the following September
that news reached Maryland through official channels.[5] Accordingly, uncertainty as to the intention of the proprietor encouraged

[1] Smith claims that intelligence from England of designs there in favour of
the Prince of Orange blew up the coals of discontent and elevated the hopes of
the disaffected: op. cit., p. 81. But he believed that no man dared to spring into
action until after the rupture in Boston. Andrews (*Colonial Self-Government
1652–1689*, New York, 1904, p. 325) similarly argued that there would have
been no grounds for, or fears of, a revolt had it not been for the example of
New England. But cf. E. S. Lovejoy, 'Equality and Empire: The New York
Charter of Liberties, 1683', *W & MQ*, 3rd ser. xxi (1964), 493–515.

[2] W. H. Browne *et al.* (edd.), *Archives of Maryland* (Baltimore, Md.,
1883–), xiii. 198–9; Kammen, pt. III in *Glorious Revolution*, ed. Hall, Leder,
and Kammen, pp. 158–9.

[3] Ibid., p. 160.

[4] Osgood, op. cit. iii. 488.

[5] The messenger having died at Plymouth, Baltimore's instructions never
reached America: Kammen, pt. III in *Glorious Revolution*, ed. Hall, Leder,
and Kammen, p. 167.

confusion and rumours. By March there were whispers of a conspiracy involving the Indians and Catholics, as there were in
New York and Massachusetts. Certain Catholic members of the
Council, including Henry Darnall and Edward Pye, were believed
to be preparing for a general attack on the Protestants in co-operation with the several thousand Indians alleged to be massed on
the border. The source of information was ludicrously unsound.
But the rumours were inflated from several quarters (including
Virginia). Impartial investigation labelled them false, nevertheless
they persisted, encouraged by the belief that orders for the proclamation of William and Mary, carried out in Virginia, had been
suppressed by the proprietary. Under these circumstances the
Protestants became more and more impatient. In fact, the Council,
without formal instructions, was damned by irresolution and
feared to take the decisive step in acknowledging the new monarchy.

By the middle of June, Maryland alone of all the provinces
remained in allegiance to James Stuart. But as in New York weeks
of disquiet passed before rebellion broke. When it did it was
because the decision of the rebels triumphed over the vacillation
of the provincial government. Information brought to the Council
in mid-July, that John Coode, a braggart and swashbuckling
clergyman, planter and militia-captain of St. Mary's County,
was raising men in the Potomac settlements, led to a summoning
of the Council.[1] Meanwhile, Coode was joined by men from
Charles County and moved to take the State House at St. Mary's.
The attempt by a Council member, Colonel Digges, to defend
the capital broke down, his men refusing to fight against superior
numbers. It is noteworthy that the Protestant Association under
Coode's guidance included not only earlier grievances and the
machinations and growing influence of the Roman Catholics in
its written justification but also the application of the 'nulifying
and suspending power' which gave the revolution elements in
common with that in England.

---

[1] It has been suggested that he was put forward by the others as a figurehead.
After Coode, the most prominent leaders were Henry Jowles of Charles County,
Nehemiah Blakiston, collector of the royal customs on the Potomac, and Kenelm
Cheseldyne, Speaker of the late Assembly. Bernard C. Steiner, 'The Protestant
Revolution in Maryland', American Historical Association, *Annual Report for
1897* (Washington, D.C., 1898), pp. 289–302.

The efforts of the remainder of the Council to organize resistance under President William Joseph failed.[1] Supported by an indifferent militia and faced with a larger and more determined enemy armed with cannon, the government forces capitulated. Again there was a bloodless colonial revolution with the suspected adversaries unseated but not harmed. Joseph was promised a safe conduct out of the province. Henceforth papists were to be excluded from office, but other officials were unaffected. The subsequent revolutionary procedure is interesting and less of a 'tragick comedy of rebellion' as Peter Sayer called it.[2] A convention was arranged for the end of August with four delegates from each county. Perhaps only a fraction of the people participated in the elections, but all save one county was represented at this gathering which lasted a fortnight. A committee of secrecy quickly reporting on charges of conspiracy with the northern Indians led the House to inform its neighbours as far north as New England of the complicity of Baltimore's deputies in plotting against the Protestants. But by 4 September the House had made provisions for a steering committee and temporary financial expedients. It then dispersed to wait instructions from England.[3] The deputy-governors Darnall and Sewall remained at large using their utmost endeavours to stir up the people and causing alarm to the militia. In due course Darnall fled for New England; two other deputies were apprehended; three more fled to Virginia. The peaceful revolutionaries remained in power until 1691. In April of 1690 a second convention met and drew up arrangements for a provisional government to consist of Coode and a committee of twenty (two from each county). Cordial relations with the revolutionaries in New York had been established for some time, and the comforting fiction was circulated to them that the great men of Maryland, New York, and New England had been a cabal against the Protestant interest.

Other provinces escaped rebellion. It is not easy to understand

---

[1] He was a man who believed completely in the divine right of kings. His 'high prerogative' ideas could not be acceptable to many provincials. Power, he thought, descended from God to the king, to the proprietor, and thence to the Assembly. Ibid, p. 285.

[2] Peter Sayer to Lord Baltimore, 31 Dec. 1689, *Archives of Maryland*, viii. 158–60; Kammen, pt. III in *Glorious Revolution*, ed. Hall, Leder, and Kammen p. 175.

[3] Ibid., p. 185.

why in every case. The problems confronting Connecticut and Rhode Island were relatively simple. The New England revolution was made in Massachusetts, at Boston. This removed for the two westerly colonies their central government, which was arguably their *de jure* government. To preserve law and order they were obliged to adopt some expedient: it was not possible, even if desirable, to do nothing. The easiest and most profitable course was to resume their old form of government which, it could be convincingly argued, had been overthrown by the arbitrary actions of James II. In Connecticut this was canvassed immediately news of the deposition of Andros was known. Few were opposed, although Gershom Bulkeley of Wethersfield desired the dominion administration to continue, and persuaded his townsmen to boycott the Hartford convention, to which most towns sent delegates.

Here, with little debate of alternatives, it was decided that those in place and power when Sir Edmund Andros took the government should regain office. The General Court was constituted: Governor Treat and Deputy-Governor Bishop resumed their function, as did the magistrates elected two years earlier. All present military officers were confirmed. The Court's first measure was to order the enforcement of all legislation enacted according to the charter 'before the late interruption'. No future alterations were to be made save according to the charter. Shortly after, on 13 June, with news of the accession of William and Mary, the Court was once more convened and the new monarchs proclaimed. Connecticut had almost unshakeable confidence in the authority of its chartered foundations, although with cautious prudence it prayed for ratification and confirmation from England.[1] The colony had shown resolution and near unanimity. But the situation demanded decisive action: the eastern Indians were on the warpath and news had come in from New York that several pickaroons threatened the seaboard area. This was not the time to create a government permanent or temporary, which brought division. As Treat wrote to his agent 'The true and real ground of the procedure of the colonists in assuming the government was, "SALUS POPULI EST SUPREMA LEX".' In fact, the people had been little consulted, their participation carefully limited. Governor Treat and his council, the latter slightly broadened, were presented

---

[1] Palfrey, op. cit. ii. 385–6.

to the freemen of the colony for approval. The government could not be modified by the alteration of one name: it must be rejected or accepted *in toto*.[1]

In Rhode Island, the successor government was less easily established, although there was no disorder, for the people themselves were unanimous that charter government should be resumed. On May Day, the customary election date, inhabitants and freemen elected in Newport the officers whom Andros had displaced. But for nine months there was no chief magistrate. Walter Clarke, the former governor, being uncertain as to his authority, refused to serve. Accordingly the Assembly elected an alternative, but he, too, prudently declined office.[2] Finally Henry Bull, an octogenarian Quaker, agreed to become governor. Meanwhile on 24 April, the government of Plymouth colony had been quietly resumed by Governor Hinkley.

The Jerseys suffered even less disturbance than Connecticut and Rhode Island. Under the Dominion of New England for only a short time, they were little troubled by the Viceregal administration. Andros had seized the government of East Jersey on 11 August 1688, and West Jersey a week later. But although great modifications were experienced in the judicial system, office-holders in general were not removed. After the capture of Andros and his aides in April 1689, East and West Jersey were without a central government for more than three years, but the machinery of provincial government continued to function, and petty courts, town government, and other local agencies followed the procedures employed before they had been taken over by the Dominion of New England. This happened despite the number of New Englanders in the province, the proximity of New York, and the proportion of Scots who might be suspected of sympathizing with James Stuart. But in fact the Jerseys avoided enlarged fears of conspiracy or Indian attack. Two factors may well go a long way to explain this. Of importance was the distance of the provinces from the main Indian frontier, as was also the limited extent of the period it had spent under the control of New England. But if recent experience here differed from that of Massachusetts, the history was not unlike Maryland's. No province in 1689 had

---

[1] Richard S. Dunn, *Puritans and Yankees. The Winthrop Dynasty of New England, 1630–1717* (Princeton, N.J., 1962), pp. 288–9.
[2] Palfrey, op. cit. ii. 168.

seen more troubled decades than East Jersey, while disgust with
the proprietors equalled that felt against the Calverts. On the
other hand, the proprietors, though associated with the Stuarts,
were not Roman Catholics, and the Scots inhabiting the Jerseys
might be suspected of Jacobitism but not Catholicism. The
grounds for fearing popular support for James were weak since
the Scots were lowlanders and covenanters who had suffered
persecution from the Stuarts.[1] Moreover, unlike Maryland and
New York, there was no active and able élite aggrieved by its
exclusion from political influence. The proprietors of the Jerseys
had stayed at home.

The proprietor of Pennsylvania, William Penn, was also in
England at the time of the Revolution and under a cloud of
suspicion because of his friendship with the Stuarts.[2] This, and
Quaker tolerance, led the revolutionary government of New York
and the rightful government of Virginia to fear that Pennsylvania
would become a centre of Jacobite resistance, drawing in the
French and Indians with fatal consequences for most other
colonies.[3] Evidence of support for James after news of his abdication is scanty. Yet the province continued to be a source of anxiety
for its neighbours. Although Penn had early information of
William's landing, for various accidental reasons it was not until
November that he was proclaimed.[4] In the eyes of the lieutenant-
governor of Virginia Pennsylvania rated as one of the 'loose

[1] William A. Whitehead (ed.), *Archives of the State of New Jersey*, 1st ser.
(Newark, N.J., 1880), ii. 288, 544, iii. 14; *New York Col. Docs.* ii. 656, 701,
747. But some Jacobitism was revealed in the early months of the Revolution—
sufficient to give Leisler cause for alarm. He first blamed the Quakers whom
he accused of encouraging if not outdoing the Roman Catholics in supporting
James II. But only two Jacobites were named: Richard Townley, a former
New Yorker and member of the Council, and Secretary James Emott, clerk of
the Council. These were alleged to have drunk the health of King James and
openly to have declared—as late as 1690—that James had never vacated the
throne of England. Leisler informed the Bishop of Salisbury that the raging
spirit of malice was a great obstruction to his administration. But perhaps because the charge derived from Leisler, neither Towner, Emott, nor the unnamed
planters were ever proceeded against.

[2] Penn probably wished James to be restored but would seem to have taken
no active steps against William and Mary. James wrote to him for help but Penn
claimed never to have corresponded with him after he left England. C. P. Keith,
Chronicles of Pennsylvania, 1688–1748 (Philadelphia, Pa., 1917), i. 246. See also
W. Hepworth Dixon, *History of William Penn: Founder of Pennsylvania* (New
York, 1902)—where James's request for assistance is printed in full.

[3] *C.S.P.C.*, 1689–92, nos. 490, 1302.   [4] See Guttridge, op. cit., p. 37.

governments' of North America of which he intended to be very watchful.[1]

Virginia did not escape disturbance. But Virginia was neither in the dominion, nor under proprietary government, nor possessed of any sizeable Catholic minority, as we have seen. She was, however, vulnerable to Indian attack and subject to a Catholic governor who had faithfully carried out the orders of James II. Such enthusiasm as there was for the king, still conceivably maintained when the birth of the Prince of Wales was celebrated, rapidly faded. In 1688, Colonel Charles Scarborough, High Sheriff of Accomack County, and churchwarden of his parish, had the temerity to complain openly to the governor that James was wearing out the Church of England by replacing vacancies with men of other persuasions.[2] For this he was deprived of his magistracy and summoned before the General Court, although apparently not otherwise punished. Edmund Bowman, a wealthy merchant, was charged with a similar offence, and James Collins was imprisoned for criticizing the king's conduct. Henry Pike of Northampton County precipitately toasted the Prince of Orange as king in March and suffered arrest for it; but by the time news of the proclamation was received by the Council under Nathanial Bacon's presidency, severe punishment was meted out to whoever dared to drink to the health of James.[3]

Virginia's more serious threat, or so many professed to believe, stemmed from her exposure to the machinations of the Catholic minority of Maryland.[4] Imported from her sister colony was the fabrication that the papists conspired with 10,000 Senecas and

---

[1] *C.S.P.C.*, 1689–92, no. 1583.   [2] Bruce, op. cit. i. 268.

[3] William was proclaimed on 27 Apr. at 11 a.m. before the courthouse door in the county of James city. By 23 May every other county had followed suit. Henrico County Deeds, 1688–97 (transcript), pp. 48–9. John Broome was arraigned for styling William 'Rouge, Villain, Rebell and Traytor', and for comparing him disadvantageously to Oliver Cromwell. He charged that Parliament now sitting in England was no parliament but a company of bad men got together by the power of the sword. Roger Loveless of Rappahannock County was ordered twenty lashes with all the force the constable could lay on for wishing the death of William. *Virginia Calendar of State Papers, 1652–1781*, ed. W. Palmer (Richmond, Va., 1875), p. 23; Bruce, op. cit. i. 268, ii. 286.

[4] The Virginian administration blamed the 'inconsiderate and over hasty intelligence' of Marylanders as being partly the cause 'of our Inhabitants being violently carried into ruinous imaginacōns': Steiner, loc. cit., p. 296; *Executive Journals of the Council of Virginia*, ed. H. R. McIlwaine (Richmond, Va., 1925), i. 92.

9,000 Nanticoke Indians to cut down all Protestants.[1] Their fears inflamed by John Waugh, a minister of Stafford County, who preached of the danger of a Catholic dynasty, Potomac and Rappahannock Counties flew at arms.[2] Aided by Buer Harrison and John West, Waugh had inspired the formation within Stafford County of armed bands. In neighbouring Rappahannock, William Heather, Timothy Davis, George Lambert, and William Gannock led an array armed with swords and muskets which proclaimed that all government had dissolved. Locally no Catholic had moved to justify such alarm, with the possible exception of Captain George Mason, a magistrate, militia-commander, and member of an influential family who was removed from office on the suspicion of encouraging riotous behaviour.[3]

The real menace to order came from the Protestants, some of whom had proclaimed an interregnum and sought to create anarchy for their own profit. The purpose of these bands, so the Council alleged, was to rob, plunder, and pillage loyal subjects and to stir up rebellion in both Maryland and Virginia. Fortunately the executive, stronger and more resolute than any other on the mainland, was adequate to the emergency. The absence of Lord Howard of Effingham in England removed a serious source of embarrassment for those prepared to endorse the cause of William. Had he been present an inevitable focal point for popular fears would have existed. As it was, under the guidance of Nicholas Spencer, a province moving towards rebellion was skilfully calmed and restored to civil order. The leaders of the tumult were taken into custody by the Sheriff of Stafford County, and put upon the ketch *Deptford* for safety.[4] The Virginian government

---

[1] *C.S.P.C.*, 1689–92, no. 56.

[2] Richard Hildreth, *The History of the United States of America* (New York, 1877), ii. 90.

[3] He was made sheriff in 1699. Bruce, op. cit. i. 601.

[4] Ibid. i. 270. They were to be removed to Nominy, there to be examined by Nicholas Spencer and two other Council members. If found guilty they were to be kept in close custody, removed from Stafford County and transported to Northampton across Chesapeake Bay. Waugh probably regained his liberty, for on 23 Oct. he was again charged with stirring up the people of Stafford by his sermons, having failed to answer the summons of the General Court. By 12 Dec. he was suing for debt in Stafford County Court, and Captain George Mason, relieved of his command of the militia earlier in the year for his part in the disturbances, was acting security for him. *Executive Journals of the Council of Virginia*, i. 104–5, 522; Stafford County Court Orders, 1664–8, 1689–92, p. 11.

succeeded where that of Maryland failed in tracing the Indian informant who had brought the so-called Catholic 'plot' to light. Unfortunately he was murdered before he could be questioned.[1] Though only a relatively small part of Virginia was directly affected by the disturbances—that abutting troubled Maryland—fear of the French and Indians terrified the people of the more remote regions during the early months following the abdication of James when loyalties were uncertain and security threatened from several quarters.[2]

In Virginia, revolution was avoided by a determined executive able to keep its head. Similarly in the Leeward Islands Sir Nathaniel Johnson, a skilled governor of impeccable integrity, prevented a dangerous situation from becoming uncontrollable. Johnson, an avowed supporter of James II, was confronted with French power in Guadeloupe and Martinique and embarrassed by Irish Catholics within his administration in the shape of 'white servants' on the islands of St. Kitts and Montserrat. An ideal situation for fears of conspiracy to arise—not involving the native Indians, for the Caribbs had by now been exterminated, but directed against the Frenchmen and Roman Catholics. Johnson was not a Catholic: during the late indulgences of King James, as he stated in his defence, he had avoided the error of many devout Protestants who had attended Mass out of curiosity. Nor had he ever kept company with any Roman Catholic priests, save on three or four public occasions. Had he so wished, and been prepared to change his religion, he could have obtained lucrative employment in England. But this too he rejected. Upon receiving orders to proclaim William he did so but immediately penned his resignation. His purpose was to avoid serving as an unwitting instrument of the French by causing division within his own administration. He sought nothing further than the welfare of England and her colonies, and the safeguard of her interests against foreign enemies. To this end he was prepared to remain in office and defend the Leewards faithfully until his successor arrived.

Antigua took him at his word, being content to return to his leadership temporarily. Nevis, however, was less calm. An innocent

[1] *C.S.P.C.*, 1689–92, nos. 91–2.
[2] See William Byrd Letter Book, Virginia Historical Society Library, MSS5: 2B 9965/1, p. 461.

exchange of letters with the Count de Blenac over an administrative matter, subsequently used by Blenac to offer proposals of a more significant co-operation, had met no response from Johnson. The people of Nevis suspected otherwise. Fearing a French invasion the island population, swollen by a large number of refugees, passed through what Sir Alan Burns has called 'an outbreak of nerves'. The experience is not well-documented but would seem to bear close comparison with that of Maryland and New York. It was prevented in part from paralleling the more serious developments of those colonies by the stability of Antigua and the rapid installation of Johnson's successor, Colonel Christopher Codrington. Johnson commissioned him lieutenant-governor on 25 July, and sailed immediately for retirement to South Carolina. The Leewards had been generally fortunate to have escaped so lightly. Serious disorder had arisen a month earlier when the Irish in St. Christophers had repudiated the English government.[1] Having declared themselves for King James, they burned and killed forcing the Protestants to retire to the fort for safety. The Irish then withdrew to the French part of the island.

Barbados, where the Protestants had the situation well in hand, offered to send help to the Leewards. Possibly Montgomery aimed to deliver the island to the French of Martinique. But Governor Stede, for the sake of security, had shown good sense and indeed great courage in having Montgomery as well as Chamberlayne committed. He had also forbidden the saying of Mass, and rendered Catholics incapable of public employment. This was before William's accession was known. In May, proclamation of the new sovereign took place 'in the most splendid and glorious manner Barbados could afford'.[2] It was a Protestant occasion though dramatically qualified by the absence of the clergy, one only of whom attended the celebrations. The absentees were non-jurors who by scruple of conscience felt bound by their oath of allegiance to James II. But the schism was short. After a few Sundays without service or sermon they yielded their support to the revolutionary settlement. Stede boastfully attributed this to his powers of persuasion. 'As they were rather doubting than stubborn they soon complied.'

---

[1] *C.S.P.C.*, 1689–92, no. 312.
[2] Ibid., 1689–92, no. 155.

Elsewhere the transition from James to William was smooth. The Duke of Albemarle had died in Jamaica on 16 October 1688. But Albemarle was recognizably the least satisfactory of all Stuart governors, and James while still king had cancelled all his proceedings, a step which William gladly affirmed. When news of Albemarle's death was received Hender Molesworth, then in England, was appointed governor; while in Jamaica, government having devolved automatically on Sir Francis Watson, president of the Council, martial law was sensibly proclaimed. As far as men of means were concerned—those who had lost influence under Albemarle—the causes of grievance were over. Conceivably the planters were so many Vicars of Bray who cared not who was king so long as they flourished.[1] Jamaicans in general would seem to have had confidence in the ability of their government to counter the religious menace inspired by French power, to sustain law and order, and protect property, even though no Assembly was to be called until the new governor arrived. By 1692 the Jews, regarded as a 'great and growing evil', had replaced the Catholics as a major concern of the colony.

South Carolina remained in a disturbed state but this was unrelated to the main political events in England. There had occurred in 1688 an insurrection against the unpopular rule of Governor Seth Sothel, and Virginia continued to be concerned lest the lack of stable government should encourage disorder among its own poor and unruly elements. The proprietors of the Carolinas avoided compromise. Lord Craven, a dedicated and intelligent member of the Lords of Trade, as Colonel of the Coldstream Guards, had remained loyal to James until the eleventh hour, offering to defend Whitehall even as the Dutch battalions were moving down upon St. James's Park. But unlike Maryland, there was no mishap here in recognizing the change of sovereign. William was expeditiously proclaimed on the order of the proprietor and the province scarcely distracted from its domestic turmoil.[2]

Thus we may consider the effect on the western empire as a whole. There was no bloodshed. Save for John Pain in Maryland, none died either for the defence of James or for the sake of William

[1] Agnes M. Whitson, *The Constitutional Development of Jamaica, 1660–1729* (Manchester, 1929), p. 80.
[2] Nicholson to Lords of Trade, 10 June 1691, *C.S.P.C.*, 1689–92, no. 1583.

and Mary. A few were threatened—Randolph, and subsequently the deputy-governors in Maryland; but it is doubtful if even Randolph was ever in danger of losing his life. As was said in Maryland 'they hurt not the least hair of the Papists' head or wronged them one farthing of their Estates, notwithstanding the continual provocations of them.'[1] The uncertainty of government in England produced severe strain and encouraged the dangerous belief that government in the colonies had dissolved. But as has been seen this did not inevitably lead to disorder. All the West Indian governments and South Carolina escaped in spite of local incendiary material which could have produced conflagration. Virginia was saved by firm leadership and community awareness of the dangers of anarchy. Only north of the Potomac did the disturbed state of England provoke violent political change. And even here direct revolutionary activity was limited to three centres: St. Mary's, New York, and Boston. What happened elsewhere was a peaceful endorsement of these actions through the re-assumption of power.

The colonial disturbances of 1689 presented the newly established government of William III with intricate problems of adjustment and settlement. The war with Louis XIV which shortly followed rendered their solution more difficult and obliged the mother country to seek compromises which were not desired administratively. The pressing need was to facilitate the employment of imperial manpower and resources in such a way that a critical war could be sustained on a broken front extending over several thousand miles. Whatever William might have wished from a military standpoint it was impracticable in time of war to restore the Stuart structure of centralization once it had broken down, or to pursue the ambitious schemes for the empire of which it had formed a part. But for Whitehall the attractions of a move in this direction were never wholly lost. From time to time down to 1713 and beyond, revived plans and some incipient substance would cast a shadow across the provincial politics of North America. As it was, an empire—loosely-jointed but locally vigorous—had affirmed its faith in the Protestant religion, in English liberties in general, and in representative government in particular. The

[1] Kammen, pt. III in *Glorious Revolution*, ed. Hall, Leder, and Kammen, p. 186.

political task of William's government was thus restricted: to restore or sustain executive power in the colonies while respecting the principles of 1689. Mercantilist objectives, inherited from the Stuarts, remained unchanged. But it was now more difficult than it otherwise might have been to ensure that adequate local defences were maintained and when the situation demanded, that effective co-operation was achieved with the metropolitan forces. Meanwhile difficult decisions had to be taken about the seizure of power in Maryland, New York, and New England; defence considerations demanded that steps should be taken to counter the defects of the proprietary system of government and the pacific influence of the Quakers.

For Maryland, the result of the Revolution was the substitution of a royal governor and a strengthened legislature in place of the proprietary control of the Calvert family. The plantations committee, advised by the Attorney-General on the strength of Lord Baltimore's charter rights, were concerned only for the king's interest. Their interim proposal gave support to Coode's government yet permitted the proprietor or his agents to collect the customary revenue.[1] In 1691, claiming that the province had fallen into disorder and confusion, the Crown directly assumed the government and the following spring Lionel Copley arrived as the new royal governor. In a short while the convention was called together for the last time, dissolved, and replaced by a regular assembly. Thus William's government had accepted the Maryland revolution and had used the semblance of order it imposed as a stopgap, while devising a compromise which recognized the facts of the revolution without wholly denying proprietary rights.

In distinction from its policy towards Maryland and New England, the home government never showed any inclination to recognize Leisler's government in New York, the power of which in any case did not extend to Albany. Here appointees of the former administration firmly committed to William, remained in office. From 1 August a convention met regularly under the mayor's presidency, and debated the imminent threat from New France. But defence costs proved far beyond the capacity of so small an

---

[1] *C.S.P.C.*, 1689-92, nos. 708, 752.

outpost. The promise of men from Connecticut was not of itself
sufficient assurance of survival, while Leisler refused help without
prior recognition of his government. His attempt in October to
reduce Albany by force misfired but the shock of the Schenectady
raid of February 1690 and the counsel of New England prepared
the frontier region for submission to the control of the seaboard.
Meanwhile in England, Henry Sloughter was appointed governor
of New York on 25 September 1689. He was later described as
'utterly destitute of every qualification for government, licentious
in his morals, avaricious and poor'. Although a commission was
prepared by mid-November, for various reasons he was not ready
to sail until the following autumn, reaching New York in March
1691. Neither Leisler nor the interests he stood for were represented on the new council, though his enemies—Phillipse, Van
Cortlandt, and Bayard—had all been nominated. Because of
Sloughter's shortcomings, had Leisler behaved discreetly he must
have lived to regain some of the influence now lost. Instead by
refusing to surrender the fort and hand over power to the king's
representative, he ensured that New York would be cursed with
domestic turbulence for many years to come. The leaders of the
social class which his regime had replaced now turned on him in
fury, and the governor, becoming the willing tool of the faction,
resolved to make Leisler pay with his life for his presumption.
Perhaps the most important event in Leisler's career was the
speech he made from the scaffold, for the influence of his aspirations was extended by his death.

Elsewhere, apart from New England, the main effect of the
colonial disturbances was to introduce new governors and to
revise political groupings. The most important change related to
Pennsylvania. In May 1689, the Lords of Trade had recommended
a strengthening of the interest of the Crown in this as well as in
the other proprietary provinces of Carolina and Maryland. The
matter was deemed worthy of the consideration of Parliament.
Lacking the means or will for defence Pennsylvania could offer
easy access to the enemy if a major attack developed. So Virginia
feared. New York, heavily burdened with the expenses of the
Albany frontier, desired to bring its Quaker neighbours here and
in the Jerseys under direct control for the purpose of revenue, a
proposal reported on by the Lords of Trade in 1691 after close
scrutiny. A compromise was effected bearing some comparison

with the contemporary accommodation of New England and Maryland. Benjamin Fletcher, Sloughter's successor, would take over the government of Pennsylvania and half the militia of New Jersey. He was empowered to nominate a lieutenant-governor and a Council not exceeding twelve persons, members of which he was also enabled to suspend. As a concession to the proprietorship, Quakers holding public office were permitted to sign a declaration of fidelity instead of taking the oath. William Penn regarded the premises upon which this decision was taken as false. He denied that the French could make their way into Pennsylvania, and contended strenuously for his rights as an Englishman to the country and government of Pennsylvania which, he argued, were inseparably his property.[1] As has been indicated, for the Jerseys the changes initially were less far-reaching. But in 1692, after an endeavour to put the provinces in a better state of order had failed, a writ of *scire facias* was issued against the proprietors of East and West Jersey impeaching their charters.[2]

For Virginia, Nicholson was created lieutenant-governor in 1691 and Sir Edmund Andros governor in 1692 superseding Lord Howard of Effingham.[3] Thus, two of the key figures in the important administrative experiment of James II were employed under William in the senior colonial dominion of the Crown. This was a clear, and a justified, endorsement of their value as servants. But for Virginia there were few changes in the style of government, and Carolina similarly continued as before under proprietary governors. Likewise in the West Indies, there were no far-reaching governmental changes at the commencement of King William's reign. In Jamaica, William O'Brien, Earl of Inchiquin, an Irish soldier who had fought on the Boyne, was appointed governor on 11 September;[4] Christopher Codrington was confirmed governor

---

[1] Ibid., 1689–92, nos. 2267–8.

[2] John E. Pomfret, *The Province of East New Jersey, 1609–1702* (Princeton, N.J., 1962), pp. 276–7.

[3] Lord Howard of Effingham had been proposed, with a Mr. Savage to be his lieutenant-governor. Later, in July, Lord Lumley was suggested as an alternative to Savage. *C.S.P.C.*, 1689–92, nos. 109, 224.

[4] Ibid., 1689–92, no. 413. At one time he had been captain-general of the king's forces in Africa and Vice-Admiral of the Royal Citadel at Tangier. Frank Cundall, *The Governors of Jamaica in the Seventeenth Century* (London, 1936), p. 124.

of the Leeward Islands on the same day and on 5 July, James Kendall was named for Barbados, arriving the following year.[1]

Thus very few men were brought into colonial administration as a result of the abdication of James II. Andros was not returned to New England—that would have been mere folly. His services, as those of Nicholson, were employed elsewhere though it could not be said that either men suffered real demotion. Johnson was not retained in the Leewards because of his wish to retire. Where possible the revolutionaries who had risen in the name of William III and Protestantism were upheld, either as a temporary expedient, as in the case of Massachusetts and Maryland, or as the permanent government, in the case of Connecticut and Rhode Island. Only Leisler and Milborne were repudiated and then not until the royal administration was ready to assume power. There had been some changes in government with a view to strengthening royal power. This occurred notably in Pennsylvania, the Jerseys, and Massachusetts. More drastic changes were considered but rejected largely because of the exigencies of war. Generally speaking William would have wished to be the heir of James in every respect of his colonial policy save repudiation of representative assemblies, but in clinging to the latter and in choosing to fight the French he effectively disinherited the empire from much of the pre-revolutionary past. For most colonial Englishmen this was a relief. To the people of Massachusetts it was a significant act of God. Yet in giving support to the Protestant Succession and in accepting war as its consequence there was an affirmation of principle and a realignment of resources which for Massachusetts gave rise to hopes that would not be fulfilled.

Of all the colonies Massachusetts was the most sophisticated politically, the most enterprising economically, and the most

---

[1] There had been earlier proposals. Lord Colchester and Colonel Molesworth for Jamaica; for the Leewards, Sir H. Belasyse and Lt.-Col. Gypson. But on 16 May (following the proposal of 4 May) Sir James Lesley was given for the Leewards with Col. Hill for St. Christophers; Col. Blakiston for Montserrat; Captain Fowkes or Lt.-Col. Hamilton for Antigua. On 3 July the list of 16 May was confirmed. Inchiquin was not mentioned until September. But none of those proposed as governor for the Leeward Islands was accepted. On 7 Sept. the Lords of Trade advised that they had prepared a commission for Nicholas Sankey, but the king, on hearing that Johnson had surrendered the government to Codrington, confirmed the latter's appointment. *C.S.P.C.*, 1689–92, nos. 109, 127, 224, and 411.

articulate. Through her representatives in London during the closing months of the reign of King James she had sought advantage from the king's express need of an alliance with the dissenters. Now, in an effort to safeguard those ancient liberties which charter government had traditionally sustained, she contended ambitiously with the government of William III. William had, early on, raised hopes by denouncing the assault of his predecessor upon both English and colonial charters. In so doing he lessened the room for manoeuvre open to the English government. Increase Mather, still in London and alert to opportunities to advance his region's interest, first sought from the new king explicit assurance that the charter existence of colonial Massachusetts had been terminated by a series of formal illegalities in 1684. He succeeded only in preventing Secretary Jephson from sending a circular letter confirming all governors, a significant achievement which effectively destroyed any faint hope of restoring the government of Sir Edmund Andros.[1] William subsequently felt his way more cautiously. Shortly after the coronation a new Privy Council for Trade and Plantations was appointed (16 February) before which Mather, Sir William Phips, and Sawyer were called. The committee was not at all convinced by the contentions of the Massachusetts agents and viewed with respect the process of *scire facias* by which the charter of 1629 had been vacated. It was agreed, however, that a provisional government to replace the administration of Andros should be approved.

News of this decision reached Massachusetts on 1 December 1690, serving to diminish advantageously the political uncertainties still faced by those responsible for demolishing the Dominion of New England.[2] Details of royal plans had yet to be worked out and two more years passed before they were put into effect. During this time the Lords of Trade advanced a strong argument for recreating at least part of the dominion as a counter to the threat of French invasion. In reviewing the settlements from the St. Croix to the Delaware they recommended the imposition of such a government as would enable the people to oppose the French defensively and offensively. On the frontiers of the north and north-east, where the brunt of French and Indian incursions were borne, the settlers themselves held a

---

[1] See above, p. 11, n. 3.   [2] Dunn, op. cit., p. 261.

similar perspective. Criticism of the reversion to political frag-
mentation went hand in hand with the call for a viable union
regulated from England. Edward Randolph, who had arrived in
England in the spring of 1690 accompanied by Sir Edmund Andros
and Joseph Dudley, quickly regained influence. He enlarged upon
native criticism of the provisional governments in New England
and added his own views about governmental disorder and infringe-
ment of the navigational laws. Neither the condemnation of
Andros nor the restoration of charter government was desirable;
nor, especially in time of war, could the former independency of
New England be allowed to revive. Slowly the government edged
towards compromise.

Mather's hopes of using Parliament to legalize a restoration
faded before the latter's dissolution by William in February 1690.
Then, on 22 April 1691, Lord Sydney was instructed to inquire
whether the agents of New England would accept a charter from
the king which left to Their Majesties the power of commissioning
the governor and Council but permitted the legislature to meet
once a year, or more frequently, should the governor think fit.[1]
William had rejected election of the executive but was prepared
to accept nomination by the agents as a means to securing an
appointment acceptable to Massachusetts. Moreover, the General
Court could veto the governor's control of the militia in use
abroad, while the elective Council or Upper House, enlarged from
eighteen to twenty-eight members, would escape the interference
of an appointed royal chamber.[2] These privileges, it was contended, were as large as those enjoyed by any corporation within
the royal dominions. However, the power of Massachusetts was
to be trimmed in one important respect. The degree of toleration
accorded under the dominion government to those outside New
England Churches was to be advanced through the creation of a
property franchise of forty shillings freehold giving the vote to
almost all adult males irrespective of religion.

The issue of boundaries was likewise a sensitive one. Should
Massachusetts include Maine and Plymouth? The former had
long been associated with her: the latter had been part of the
Dominion of New England. The Massachusetts agents, working
for the most extensive territory amenable to control from Boston,

[1] Barnes, op. cit., pp. 259–60.   [2] Osgood, op. cit. iii. 441–2.

urged also the annexation of Nova Scotia. These wishes were cordially acknowledged but New Hampshire was granted independent provincial status and both Connecticut and Rhode Island continued as separate governments.

Mather, who misconstrued the nature of his influence in London, appeared to believe that as agent of a powerful colony he could accept or reject the royal proposals as he saw fit. For his presumption he was sharply reminded that he was not the plenipotentiary from a foreign state. In certain respects this was an ill-considered rebuke—evidence of England's equivocation in her behaviour towards Massachusetts—for he had been treated all along as something more than the mere representative of an overseas corporation. The partnership of old and New England had existed, albeit briefly, as a political reality. For her virtue in endorsing the English Revolution Massachusetts had many of her former privileges and some of her territorial pretensions confirmed. But in endorsing so much of a defiant past which James and the Lords of Trade had sought to counter and repudiate, William implicitly sanctioned the continuance of an *imperium in imperio*. Was it so egregious a blunder on the part of Massachusetts to assume this was now transformed into a type of partnership in an empire whose political form, so ill-defined in theory, approximated more nearly to a confederation in practice? The revolutionary experiences were novel and important because they had been shared with the whole English nation. Because the ends were similar the disturbances in the plantations of North America and the West Indies, like the political upheaval in the British Isles, could be roundly approved by the people of Massachusetts. The nation had moved as one and was seen to be sound in pretty well every part. Yet the views of other colonists were important only in so far as they accorded with those of Massachusetts and were amenable to influence from Boston. Inevitably the main focus of attention, henceforth, was on England for reasons which were emotional as well as political.

In due course it will be considered how far Massachusetts was equipped for the role of partnership, which internal factors upheld or weakened her pretensions, and to what extent they were modified by the stresses and catastrophe of war.

CHAPTER II

New England and the English: 'A Nation within a Nation'

MASSACHUSETTS was not the only purposive English settlement in the New World but by 1691 after the absorption of Plymouth colony she stood forth unexcelled in vitality and potential resources and in clarity of intent. This is not to say that sharp conflicts of opinion within the province were absent concerning the value of the new charter as a political foundation and the nature and role of the theocratic superstructure. Under scrutiny the homogeneity of Massachusetts appears highly complex if not questionable, but to the contemporary external observer the patterns of behaviour established in the earliest years of settlement, and pursued with little substantial variation thereafter down to the overthrow of the Andros regime, left little doubt that here was a self-assured, aggressive, and well-defined political entity. Although it is true that the problems faced by New Englanders had altered radically as their circumstances had altered, it was not apparent to concerned outsiders that this society had experienced any real change of heart. English administrators looked for humility but failed to perceive it.

Massachusetts, or New England, as she was frequently called—to the disgust of those who saw the assumption of a regional name as a significant conceit—was both depressed and inspired by the past. No earlier colony in history could claim among its founders a comparable galaxy of talented and educated men. Nor could the purity of their religious aims be seriously disputed. An independent and persevering spirit facilitated the growth of prosperity and ensured that political opportunities were firmly grasped and exploited. The consequence was a form of autonomy under which there had taken place in the half-century before 1684 a set of experiences particularly amenable to representation in clear and simple form. Upon such foundations and through the continuing genius of her people Massachusetts confronted the mother country with qualities which to a considerable degree offset the very great

inferiority in numbers and material resources.[1] Community vigour
is undeniable but does not wholly explain why the leaders of the
Bay colony after 1689 frequently spoke as if old and New England
were on roughly equal terms as the pre-eminent members of a
trans-oceanic polity.[2] In their eyes religious factors, including
spiritual vitality, redressed if not outweighed the material imbalance. Not surprisingly they aspired to a special relationship
which gave to this concept some form of acknowledgement.
Moreover, because of it they were predisposed to perceive in
English enactments which were favourable to the colony hidden
meanings beyond those intended—a further conceit which did not
pass unnoticed in the mother country.

In the past, friction between Massachusetts and England had
been a persistent feature of the relationship, significantly lessened,
if not suspended, only by the distant cordialities of the Puritan
interregnum. At times it had risen to dangerous intensities, as in
the 1630s when Massachusetts had prepared to defend her
chartered liberties by use of force if necessary. During the
Restoration serious charges of religious persecution and evasion of
the navigation laws gave rise to a prolonged and basically hostile
confrontation which endured for a quarter of a century. As a
sequel to this, the collapse of the Andros regime appeared as a
skilful yet devious exploitation of England's distraction and the
delays of transatlantic communication. With these aids Puritan
resolution had once again been successfully asserted at the expense
of imperial welfare.

New Englanders, of course, had reason enough to fear and
detest the Stuarts who, as instruments of Catholicism, had
threatened to destroy the colony's purpose and replace it by
antithetical concepts and principles. Save for questionable
protection against England's enemies, implicit encouragement for
the shipbuilding industry, and regulated opportunities for trade

---

[1] The population of England and Wales was estimated in 1688 as 5,318,100:
David Ogg, *England in the Reigns of James II and William III* (Oxford, 1955),
p. 30. That of Massachusetts and Maine was approximately 70,000. Another
36,000 were to be found in the rest of New England—6,000 in Rhode Island,
6,000 in New Hampshire, and 24,000 in Connecticut. J. T. Adams, *Revolutionary New England, 1691–1776* (Boston, Mass., 1923), p. 30.

[2] See especially S. E. Morison, *Intellectual Life of Colonial New England*
(New York, 1956).

with the West Indies, the dynasty afforded little that was not attainable by other means. Apart from the belated offer of toleration made by James II to Increase Mather, and the promise of protection for Harvard College against the designs of Edward Randolph, no part of the Old Colonial system had been visibly tailored to suit New England. The Stuarts had coerced and even threatened to dragoon. Only at the eleventh hour did they endeavour to woo or placate. This began a brief and novel chapter in Anglo-Massachusetts relations but it sprang palpably from the dire predicament of James and was thus of doubtful worth. In any case it was abruptly terminated by his abdication. Nothing had happened to disprove the belief brought to New England by the founding fathers and confirmed by later experiences that the Stuarts were essentially bad kings.

After 1689 there was no major reform of English institutions which would augment the similarities of old and New England. The Anglican Church and the House of Lords remained as distinguishing differences between the two societies. But modifications in the constitution restricted the exercise of the prerogative within the realm and prepared the way for the rule of virtuous monarchs. Thus was provided a powerful new bond drawing the two countries closer together.

The charge has frequently been levelled at New England that her theology was anti-monarchical in intent. To New Englanders, however, there was nothing inherently wrong in the institution of monarchy, as countless sermons reveal.[1] God had sent to the Israelites, his chosen people and the exemplar of New England, good kings as well as bad.[2] Now, having shared a revolution with England and having facilitated its success, or so it was argued, they found it possible to describe the English monarchy in terms which were favourable, and at times even sycophantic. In contrast to his English predecessors, William of Orange was not merely a Protestant but a Dutch Calvinist of the strictest orthodoxy who ruled

---

[1] This is not to deny the contention—made by J. R. Pole, *The Seventeenth Century. The Sources of Legislative Power*, p. 69—that they were 'natural' republicans.

[2] Revd. John Norton, *An Essay Tending to Promote Reformation* (Boston, Mass., May, 1708), p. 21. 'A good King and Queen is a great blessing, and God's love . . . . Kings have a great influence upon the People. Like King, like People. So it was with the children of Israel; so it hath been with other Nations.'

justly in fear of God. To contemporary New Englanders the change of climate was dramatic—'a morning without clouds unto the Protestant World'. Henceforth a tribute to the king and his consort Queen Mary, a woman of comparable Protestant virtue, especially when viewed against the preceding 'Romish Delilah',[1] forms an essential part of sermons delivered to mark occasions of political consequence. Thus Cotton Mather in 1689 observed with fulsome tribute:

We now see upon the British Throne, a KING whose unparalleled zeal for the Church of the Lord Jesus Christ at the Lowest Ebb, hath made Him the Phoenix of this Age; a KING in whom Courage and Prudence make a Temper which is to be no where seen but in the greatest Heroes; a KING that scornfully rejected a Sovereignty over his own Country, when he might have had it; a KING that rises to say, That he cannot have so unworthy a concept of God, or so base Thoughts of Mankind as to believe that any one person should be designed by the Almighty King, to trample and oppress a society placed under him; a KING that so abhors all persecution, that when he accepted the Crown of Scotland he explained a clause in the Coronation Oath, with this Proviso, I will not be obliged to be a Persecutor; a KING with whom we see a QUEEN whose virtues had long since Enthroned her in the Hearts of the whole English Nation.[2]

The feeling of relief at the Protestant accession was manifestly very great and verbal expressions of gratitude are to be anticipated. It would be absurd to expect any developed sense of reciprocal obligation towards the monarchy springing from this source alone, though in 1690 Increase Mather did describe a 'great service to be done for their Majesties... by securing their interest in this large Territory, and Consequently in all America'. However, unless we are to represent Mather as first and foremost an Anglo-American, and only secondarily a supporter of the theocracy, we must take this statement for what it appears to be: namely an exposition of New England's interest which can be expediently represented as that of old England's simply because the interests of the two were now in certain important respects identical. Indeed Mather in the same sentence speaks of the need to make a 'brisk Salley forth upon the French territories, which must be a

[1] Mary of Modena.
[2] Revd. Cotton Mather, *The Wonderful Works of God—a Thanksgiving Sermon* (Boston, Mass., Dec. 1689), pp. 36–7.

Perpetual obstacle to the Thriving of these plantations'. It was, of course, mere casuistry to argue, as he did on so many occasions, that 'the cause of the Revolution was also the service of their Majesties.' It *was* so in the sense that this was also the service of New England. The sentiment 'We are undone if we do not venture all' directly related to the opportunity presented to New England to pursue its interests without fear of serious check from England. This was indicated in the election sermon of 1693 when Increase Mather urged New Englanders to pray for their king and queen: 'as long as they reign, New England is secure.' Conceivably a virtuous expenditure of effort might reap the reward of positive English support if the English could be effectively instructed as to their own interests.

Such beliefs were underpinned by developed notions of the responsibilities of the monarchy expounded from the pulpit. In 1691 an anonymous pamphleteer had written: 'I would fain know of our Publicans, how many Cities and Countries have ever revolted and turned Commonwealth for being too well used.'[1] The onus was on the monarchy to sustain its merit. Though fulsome praise of William and Mary continued throughout their reign, upheld and encouraged by the possibility of assassination and fear of a Jacobite plot, New England ministers persisted in expressing and developing their ideal towards which all rulers were expected to aspire. However, William, by his excellence, sustained the hopes raised at the time of his accession. His nobility of character and personal restraint encouraged ministers to speak of his rule as evidence of God's pleasure with New England: in such rulers, 'Righteousness and Religion ... will be as a Torch on an Hill, whose Light and Influence will be vastly extensive: everyone will be advantaged to see their good works, and to Glorifie God for and in them .... They will be a good Copy'.[2]

William, characterized as a blameless man who fought the battles of the Lord,[3] was, at times, represented as the ideal itself, to be set apart from every other king who had ever ruled New England,

---

[1] *The Humble Address of the Publicans of New England* (London 1691), p. 14.

[2] Revd. Samuel Willard, *Character of a Good Ruler, as it was Recommended in a Sermon* (Boston, Mass., 1694), p. 14.

[3] Joshua Scottow, *A Narrative of the Planting of Massachusetts Colony. Anno 1628* (Boston, Mass., 1694), p. 61; Increase Mather, *The Great Blessing of Primitive Counsellours* (Boston, Mass., 1693), p. 21.

especially in that he had been independently chosen as monarch by New Englanders in preference to James. His importance was not to be questioned. Upon his shoulders rested the fate of Europe, and the preservation of the Church of God. No one person, it was contended, had held such an exalted role for a thousand years.[1] By the end of the Nine Years War he was hailed as a great king, of such stature as no other nation could boast. Not only had he safeguarded property and land, neither of which had been safe under Andros, but by parliamentary legislation he had advanced the privileges of the English nation 'richly worth all the millions of Money that have been spent since the Revolution', having previously saved three kingdoms from the chains of popery and slavery.[2] Through God's will he had also 'put an Hook in the Nostrils of a Leviathan (Louis XIV) and made him disgorge at the Peace of Ryswick cities and countries which contain as much in Bigness as all the Kingdom of England'.[3] Such achievements gained the esteem of New England, and after his death he remained particularly revered, 'like holy Hezekiah', out of respect for the moral elevation and regulation he had brought to the hierarchy of the Church and for the high standards he had demanded from the men he advanced.[4]

After the accession of Anne, Anglican and High Church by persuasion, praise of the monarchy became more formalized, but William's successor was repeatedly extolled for maintaining the high moral values he had established and for her many edicts against vice and immorality.[5] Thus to a degree it was possible to acknowledge her publicly as in tune with New England's purpose, for the theocrats were persuaded of her irreconcilable enmity towards 'everything that had a tendency to draw down the Wrath of an Almighty and Sin Hating God on the Kingdoms and Plantations over whom she sways her Imperial scepter'. She not only

---

[1] *Primitive Counsellours*, p. 21.

[2] Revd. Nicholas Noyes, *New England's Duty and Interest to be an Habitation of Justice and a Mountain of Holiness Containing Doctrine, Caution, and Comfort* (Boston, Mass., May 1698), p. 79.

[3] Revd. Cotton Mather, *A Pillar of Gratitude* (Boston, Mass., May 1700), p. 34.

[4] See Revd. Benjamin Colman, pastor of Boston Church, *The Piety and Duty of Rulers: To Comfort and Encourage the Ministry of Christ* (Boston, Mass., 1708), p. 4.

[5] Miller, *New England Mind*, pp. 163–4.

favoured religion but engaged to defend and promote the interest of it.[1]

So much suggests respect for individual monarchs voiced through the mouths of the leading ministers of the province. But those who officially represented the institution of monarchy on the American continent were frequently assessed by colonials as being inferior in character to local leaders and sometimes in abilities also.[2] The esteem in which the monarchy was held would not be enhanced by a royal governor acting in any way which was unseemly or ill-advised, especially when his pretensions were beyond his resources. Thus Governor Dudley's choleric encounter with two stubborn New England carters was a confrontation in miniature in which the monarchy, by proxy, was worsted and held up to ridicule by native virtue.[3] The attempt of Governor Andros to escape his captors in female dress added nothing to the lustre of the institution. One may suppose that the physical distance of the English throne from its American subjects did something to counter this and helped to preserve some of the main attributes of majesty, yet these too were vulnerable and easily offset by such gossip—inevitably enlarged upon—as filtered across the Atlantic. The peccadilloes of William were insufficient to diminish his stature in the eyes of the average New Englander, though aggrieved settlers close to the New York border might be inclined to curse him as another damned Dutchman. The dangers he faced,

---

[1] John Rogers, *A Sermon Preached at the Election* (Boston, Mass., May 1706), pp. 34–5. Benjamin Colman, in praise of the royal proclamation for 'Preventing and Punishing Vice, Profanities and Immorality', compared Anne to William. 'No Earthly Prince can go by a more perfect Rule than this by which God governs', *Piety and Duty*, pp. 4, 16, 20, and 30. See also Norton, *Essay*, p. 21, who urged that the royal proclamations should be followed by reforming societies, as in old England.

[2] This was not true of Massachusetts whose governors before 1713, with two notable exceptions, were New England-born. One of those who were not was Sir Edmund Andros. The Earl of Bellomont, who was the other, created a good impression and was highly praised by New Englanders. Neighbouring governors were far less impressive and it is unlikely that Massachusetts went uninformed of the scandal of Lord Cornbury's administration in New York, which Lewis Morris likened to that of Gessius Florus in Judaea. See Charles Worthen Spencer, 'The Cornbury Legend', *New York State Hist. Assoc. Proc.* xiii (1914), 309–10, 319; L. H. Leder, *Robert Livingston, 1654–1728 and the Politics of Colonial New York* (Chapel Hill, N.C., 1961), p. 200.

[3] Vernon L. Parrington, *Main Currents in American Thought* (New York, 1954), i. 127.

particularly the attempt on his life leading to an association for his
defence, and the taking of an oath to protect him by members of
the legislature, invested him with a certain hallowed role so that he
came to be seen, and was so represented in New England sermons,
as the symbol of Protestantism.[1] His birthday celebrations in
Boston were well attended thenceforth, not only by royal officials
but by others of the community.[2] On his death Samuel Sewall
observed to Governor Dudley: 'The cloaths your Excellency sees
us wear, are a true Indication of our inward Grief for the Departure
of King William'.[3]

Anne similarly gained something from the Jacobite attempt
against her. She possessed clear personal qualities: her generosity,
even in questionable causes, was undeniable. But she was a woman,
not a warrior, and rumours of her coarse addiction to drink
reaching the ports of a New England which officially regarded
intemperance as a cardinal sin could not have endeared her to the
Congregational ministers, even if to the layman it made her
appear decidedly human. Yet, while something of the personal
loyalty which New Englanders gave to the image of William
departed when Anne came to the throne, this was still an acceptable
monarchy in contradistinction from the Universal Monarchy of
Louis XIV and its Stuart imitators.

Perhaps it is unwise to attach too much importance to the celebration of royal birthdays but such occasions were reminders to
New Englanders that they lived under monarchy, even if for many
its main justification was an excuse for excessive drinking. Samuel
Sewall rarely failed to record this annual event, though the manner
of its observation generally provokes his disapproval. Sewall was
no enthusiastic monarchist: the virtues of this institution sprang
from personal sources alone. He is better defined as a fairminded
New Englander of a serious religous nature, who as a diarist felt
compelled to comment on an event which because of its important
role in colonial life he was unable to ignore. When he spoke to
Governor Dudley against having illuminations, especially in the
Town House, on the occasion of the queen's birthday, his wish was
to honour both God and the queen but to avoid profanation of the

---

[1] Samuel Sewall, *Diary, Mass. Hist. Soc. Coll.* 5th ser. v–viii (Boston, Mass.,
1878–82), i, 433. For details of the plot see Ogg, *James II and William III*,
pp. 426–7.

[2] Sewall, *Diary*, i. 462.   [3] Ibid. ii. 58.

Sabbath. But Governor Dudley would not be moved. It would be hard to forbid, he argued, considering how good the queen was, and what military successes God had given her. The last, a telling point, could not be denied save on very narrow grounds. Accordingly on 6 February between eight and nine in the evening bells began to ring in celebration.

Sewall regarded the coronation celebration which fell on Sunday, 23 April, with even greater sourness. He dourly notes in his diary:

Lord's Day: April 23, 1704.

There is great firing at the Town, Ships, Castle, upon account of its being the Coronation-day, which gives offence to many; see the Lords Day profan'd. Down the Sabbath, Up St. George.

This was not republicanism but an attitude of mind which expected the monarchy to conform to local values and practices. On the queen's birthday the following year, out of respect for his views, he was not called to the Council chamber to drink her health. Instead he went to hear Willard's catechizing lecture.[1] But he continued to regret explicitly the excesses associated with tributes to the monarchy. Surprisingly in 1710 he agreed to join the Council in treating the governor to wine and dine, presumably at the *Green Dragon*. 'Cost us 5s apiece', he observed without relish. Business was mixed with pleasure for afterwards the company returned to the council chamber where they burned £6,000 of decayed bills. 'When the Candles began to be lighted I grew weary and uneasy and even slipped away without drinking.'[2]

To many New Englanders, not given to profundities, the distinction between the good of William's rule and the evil that preceded it needed no instruction. Even so the nature of monarchy in particular and rulers in general was constantly elaborated from the pulpit, so that the community as a whole was conscious that it should be governed according to clearly defined practices and standards. Divine Law, formulated by God the sovereign as lawgiver, and collectively constituting a 'constitution, sacred and inviolable', was the foundation for all earthly political activity.[3]

---

[1] Sewall, *Diary*, ii. 101, 123.

[2] Ibid. ii. 273. In 1714 he refused an invitation at John Netmaker's to drink the queen's health in the tavern at South End, describing the company as disorderly: 6 Feb. 1713/14, Sewall, *Diary*, ii. 419–24.

[3] Alice Baldwin, *The New England Clergy and the American Revolution* (Durham, N.C., 1928), pp. 13–14.

The power of God was absolute, but by reason of His natural perfection it was not used in an arbitrary and unjust manner. The end of His government and laws was the good of mankind. Civil government, ordained by God, should therefore possess purpose in accord with Him.[1] So the clergy taught. This then was the starting-point to which the inviolable rights and liberties of the people were attached. Though God might specify His desires more precisely at times, as He had done for the Jews in the past, the form of government was generally less important than the ends it pursued.

The divine status of rulers was no less elevated than the earthly status. They were God's vicegerents and were sometimes honoured with the title of gods.[2] But they were no more than delegates: they laboured to conform to God's pattern and imitate His government, and were expected to study and understand the laws of God, both natural and revealed.[3] But since God had voluntarily limited His power, their power too was prescribed, and rulers who abused their people or who erred in their understanding aroused God's resentment and forfeited His sanction.[4] This applied not to kings alone but to parliaments, governors, and colonial assemblies: all political entities were likewise obliged to regulate their political behaviour. It was not the purpose of rulers to be oppressive and arbitrary even if their power had been acquired by conquest.

Thus rulers whose standards fell, or who failed to attain the avowed objective, transgressed twofold. They sinned against the people and they sinned against God. Samuel Willard spelled out these main precepts and their ramifications in the 1694 election-day sermon which was explicitly entitled 'Character of a Good Ruler'. The character of a 'Good Ruler' was recommended in the

---

[1] Ibid., p. 16.

[2] Psalm 82:6.

[3] Baldwin, op. cit., p. 33; Revd. Joseph Belcher, pastor of Dedham Church, *The Singular Happiness of Such Heads or Rulers as are able to chuse out their People's Way and will also endeavour their People's Comfort* (Boston, Mass., May 1701). 'Though there is not a Body of Civil Law drawn up in the Scripture to which every Polity is to confined; yet there are sufficient general directions and Rules to be gathered from thence . . .' *Character of a Good Ruler*, p. 26.

[4] *Singular Happiness*, p. 36; Revd. Solomon Stoddard, pastor of Northampton, *The Way for a People to Live Long in the Land that God hath given them* (Boston, Mass, May 1703), p. 11.

word of God but was also usefully exemplified in those who deserved that epithet in that it instructed others how to demean themselves in their authority and showed what qualities to look for in selecting lesser officials and public servants.[1] 'He must be just, ought not to assert his Power illimitedly and arbitrarily but in conformity to the law of God and the Right of Nature for God's Honour.'

It was of the highest consequence, contended Willard, that civil rulers should be just men and such as ruled in the fear of God. They must be informed men, for ignorance was the foundation for error: 'without knowledge the mind cannot be good.' They must be of good character: 'one whom neither flattery nor bribery may be able to remove out of the way', hating ambition and covetousness,[2] and preferring the public benefit above all private and separate interests whatever. 'Everyman in his place owes himself to the good of the whole, and if he does not so devote himself he is unjust.'

Further, it was essential that the ruler should be one who would take care to promote religion as well as honesty, and to do his utmost to ensure that the true religion might be countenanced and established. The demand for competence was extensive and the burden of responsibility heavy, for happiness was never easily achieved nor misery easily avoided.

When men can enjoy their Liberties and Rights without molestation or oppression; when they can live without fear of being born down by their more potent Neighbours; when they are secured against Violence, and may be Righted against them that offer them any injury, without fraud; and they are encouraged to serve God in their own way, with freedom and without being imposed upon contrary to the Gospel precepts, now they are an happy People.[3]

No one held power save 'Durante bene placito'. Officials were stewards who held office under trust. Civil government was not seated in particular persons or families by natural right and God might call public servants to a reckoning at any time.[4] The tenure of thrones operated within such a framework. As Willard observed, 'God sets up and he pulls down dynasties'. The only way for

---

[1] *Character of a Good Ruler*, p. 5.
[2] Ibid., p. 10.
[3] Ibid., p. 16.
[4] Ibid., p. 20.

rulers to build up their own Houses was to emulate the best kings of Israel.[1]

At the annual election of the General Court, and on other formal occasions, these precepts of conduct were often pointedly and precisely directed at local rulers for the purpose of advising and instructing those new to the responsibilities of office. But royal officials and dignitaries in England who influenced the nation's destiny in general, as well as that of the colonies in particular, were also aimed at. At a time when a ruler of express piety and purpose sat on the throne of England they served as a commentary on the past and a chart for the future, indicating the restrictions under which kings must operate and the limitations of England's power over the colonial peoples. However, they should not be narrowly seen as a reaction to the imposition of external control.

To the ministers, control and restraint in various forms were essential aspects of politics. The people, like their rulers, had responsibilities. Faction must be avoided: 'levellism' and 'murmurings' were sins. The doctrine of submission to rulers carried to extravagant heights was dangerous. But it was equally dangerous to the state to depress obedience to a mere nullity. One would expose a people to oppression and sullen tyranny, the other to confusion and lawless anarchy. Ebenezer Pemberton argued in 1710:

Doubtless God has not left a State without a Regular remedy to Save itself, when the Fundamental Constitution of a People is overturned; their Laws and Liberties, Religion and Properties are openly Invaded and ready to be made a Publick Sacrifice.

However, it was not reasonable to suppose, concluded Pemberton, that a God of Order had ever invested any men of a private station, 'who can with a Nodd inflame and raise the Multitude with a Lawless Power, on pretence of Public Mismanagements, to Embroyl the State, Overturn the Foundations of Government'.

Revolution or even civil disturbance was not lightly to be entered upon or encouraged. They could best be avoided if rulers fulfilled their role as guardians and in emulation of 'the Lord Paramount of Heaven and Earth' governed not by unaccountable will but by stable measures. Even so there was an absolute necessity of superiority and power in some and 'Inferiority and Submission as to

---

[1] Ibid., pp. 18–19.

others'. 'Nothing was more unequal than equality', Pemberton believed. 'Levellism' was 'an open defiance to God, his Wisdom and Will, as well as the Reason of Mankind'.[1]

Many other ministers stressed the importance of obedience and gave voice to fears of licentious behaviour. Such notions of mutual responsibility were directly related to the relationship of the General Court and the people of Massachusetts, but their applicability to the relationship with England is obvious and inescapable. Civil government existed in the world for the common good of mankind. Bad government was better than none at all, 'for who is there', said Belcher in 1701, 'but will grant that Tyranny (except it grow to a great extremity indeed) is better than Anarchy—without this the world would be, *ipso facto*, in a state of war and fall into endless disorders.' Multitudes without fear of God and without law were vile.[2]

For those who were heads or rulers, to be able to choose out 'the People's way' was a matter of considerable moment. Incapacity in this direction could be ruinous and fatal for the community as a whole. But rulers must be given a chance to pursue their designs. Solomon Stoddard in 1703 vigorously attacked unconstructive criticism of government.[3] The children of Israel, he warned, had often fallen into this sin and smarted for it. Criticism of necessary burdens or of failure to achieve immediate success was unhelpful and to be avoided. But, contended Stoddard, 'they murmur also when in their complaints they talk rudely and rebelliously: these murmurings are the froth of the discontented spirit; murmurers are like the raging sea, that cast forth mire and dirt.' 'Murmuring' was undesirable, because it weakened the hands of rulers, was a preparation for sedition, and a degree of rebellion. It was also a sin, or the reflection of sin, since 'murmurers' were those who as 'complainers walking after their own lusts', pretended to be great sufferers. Men that murmured against their rulers revealed an unruly and ungoverned spirit.

Thus a duty of the people was to assist their rulers to maintain order for they could not do so without popular co-operation. Rulers

---

[1] Pemberton was singled out by Alice Baldwin for his readiness to place a large share of responsibility for domestic turbulence squarely on the shoulders of the ruler. *New England Clergy*, pp. 37, 174.

[2] *Singular Happiness*, p. 31.

[3] *Way for a People, passim.*

were few in comparison and without assistance the ends of government could never be achieved. The renewal of war with France
gave especial point to his contentions. With biblical sanction
Stoddard stressed the importance of political obedience: 'Submit
yourself to every ordinance of man for the Lord's sake. Whether it
be to the King as Supream, or unto Governors, as those that are
set by him. Obey them that have to rule over you and submit
yourselves.' But he also argued strongly for a clear understanding
of mutual obligations:

Let Rulers and Ruled doe their duty one to another, and that will keep
them from all sorts of heinous transgression against the first or second
Table of the Law: if Rulers be remiss in their work, that opens a door
to a world of wickedness, iniquity will break in like a flood upon a
People; as when there was no King in Israel every man did what was
right in his own eyes; or if the People be headstrong and will not submit
to Government; they will quickly cast off the Government of God and
take a licentious liberty; but so long as government is duly managed by
Rulers and submitted to by the People the substance of the Covenant
will be kept.[1]

In the main, however, ministers on political occasions gave more
weight to the obligations of power than to the duties of submission.
The greater the office bestowed by God, the greater the service
expected. 'The End of God in furnishing people with intellectual
abilities and cloathing them with Authority' said Joseph Easterbrook, 'was to promote the weal and benefit of others.' It was
commonly averred that people were not made for rulers, but rulers
were set up for the sake and good of the people.[2]

The charter of 1691, as a foundation for government, was
complementary to the natural regulations which it was believed
should govern the conduct of rulers. From the start Elisha Cooke
and his followers were disinclined to accept it in place of the former
instrument of government. But the established clergy, in fear that
this wildness of opposition would disturb the disorderly-natured,
who had been curbed from disturbance only with difficulty in
1689, did not support them in this. In defending the new provincial
charter of 1691 Increase Mather stressed how it secured liberty
and property 'the fairest flower of the state' and more valuable still

<hr>

[1] Ibid., pp. 4, 6, 19.
[2] Revd. Joseph Easterbrook, *Abraham the Passenger, his Privilege and Duty
described.* (Boston, Mass., May 1705), p. 13.

N E—C

'the enjoyment of the Blessed Gospel in its purity and Freedom'.[1]
'Although there is a restraint of your power in some things that
were granted in the former Charter,' he admitted, 'yet there are
more Ample Privileges in other things that may be a Perpetual
Advantage to the Colony.' Nor was a murmuring spirit the right
way to obtain more, he warned. In the main the clergy viewed the
new charter in the manner of Samuel Willard.

A good Charter is Doubtless preferable to a bad one; it is a great Privilege to be secured from being hurt by any but ourselves; but let Charter
Privileges be never so Excellent, Good Rulers only make us Happy
under them.[2]

Charters were a helpful but contingent aid to the pursuit of the
ends of government. Many of the rights of Englishmen which the
people of Massachusetts valued were comprehended by the 1691
charter in that a governor in Council could no longer make laws
or impose taxes, as had Andros, without the consent of a representative assembly. Further, no governor could cause any subject,
or his children, or servants, to be sent out of the province.[3]

The charter was also viewed as an important indication of New
England's excellence in earthly things. Whatever rights or privileges
were acquired, through this or any other instrument, were soon
regarded as evidence of the high esteem in which the province was
held. This state of mind, encouraged by the Mathers, served to
enhance the achievement and to ensure the maintenance of what
had been secured in the negotiations between 1689 and 1691.
Increase pointed to 'peculiar Charter Privileges', granted to the
people of Massachusetts, 'which no other English Plantation in
the world has'.[4] No other colonists, not even the king's subjects
in England, were enabled to nominate a governor's Council.
Cotton Mather sustained this argument:

It was a fruit of the Royal Justice, as well as Goodness in His Majesty, to
Endow New England with a Charter of Liberties above the rest of the
Plantations. . . . We have a Royal Charter which Effectually Secures unto
us all Christian Liberties and all English Liberties. . . . We have a Royal

---

[1] '[The vacation of the Charters] denied the Common Rights which all
English men justly reckon themselves born unto . . . . We were but slaves.'
The Wonderful Works, p. 42.
[2] *Character of a Good Ruler*, pp. 21–4, and see Miller, *New England*, pp. 167,
177, and 465.
[3] *Primitive Counsellours*, p. 21.
[4] Ibid., p. 21.

Charter, so sheltering us, That no Counsellors, nor Judges, nor Justices, can hereafter be Arbitrarily imposed upon us. Yea we have some Advantages not only above any other Nation but above any part of our own Nation.[1]

For a variety of reasons New Englanders cherished a pre-eminence which manifested itself in diverse ways. They claimed to have risked all for the sake of Protestantism:

Even before... the Prince of Orange was King of England, and that at a time when they knew no more than that his Highness was landed in England, with a design to endeavour the delivering the Kingdom and the Churches of God from Popery, Slavery and Arbitrary Power, which as they lookt upon as an Heroick and Glorious Undertaking; so they also accounted it their Duty to embark themselves in the same Cause; though they knew not what the Issue of so mighty a Work would be.[2]

They were, so they believed, distinguished for their loyalty to William. The Mathers several times claimed as much. In instructing Lord Bellomont as to the pleasures of his gubernatorial office, lest a full appreciation had escaped him before departure from England, Increase spoke of the fervour of New England's attachment to the throne. A decade earlier, possibly for narrow political advantage, Cotton had twice made this point in sermons subsequently printed.[3] First he had claimed New Englanders to be the most loyal people throughout the empire, and then four months later had shown how easily this point might be demonstrated.[4]

It would be wrong to dwell upon the precise political objectives of the Mathers and to ignore the fact that they here expressed a widespread need: the desire of the peole of New England to identify themselves by reference to a wider community as a means to demonstrate their excellence, perhaps also to help ease their

---

[1] *Pillar of Gratitude*, pp. 38–9. See also Revd. Cotton Mather, *The Short History of New England. A Recapitulation of Wonderful Passages Which have Occurr'd First in the Protections and then in the Afflictions of New England* (Boston, Mass., 1694), p. 18. 'Not our former hedge [he is here referring to the charter of 1629] but another . . . . There is in these things yet an Hedge about us in respect whereof we are known above all the Families of the Earth . . . a hedge which cannot, without the concurrence of our own Hands, be plucked up.'

[2] *A Brief Relation of the State of New-England* (London, 1689), p. 161.

[3] Revd. Increase Mather, *The Surest Way to the Greatest Honour* (Boston, Mass., May 1699), p. 33, estimated there were not 100 Jacobites in the whole province. He may have meant 'non-resisters' rather than subjects loyal to James Stuart.

[4] *Wonderful Works*; Cotton Mather, *The Serviceable Man* (Boston, Mass., Mar. 1690).

self-doubts and brutal criticism.[1] Thus, although many of New England's governors during this period were natives of the region and scarcely needed to be informed of its special importance, this fact was nevertheless repeated endlessly. In 1703 Solomon Stoddard contended that, though the maintainance was limited, a governor might live more happily in Massachusetts than in any other of the English plantations because of the advantages of good society and spiritual opportunities.[2] Inevitably the latter consideration predominated in the thought of the ministers. Increase Mather made it clear to the Earl of Bellomont that in coming to New England he was the recipient of a great honour.

It may be thought to be beneath the Character of so illustrious a Person to accept of the Government of so mean a People; but *My Lord* considering that they are the Lords people give me leave to say to you, that the God of Heaven has put honour upon you in committing so many of His Jewels to your charge.

Increase proudly recalled for his countrymen and for the benefit of the Earl how an honourable person in England, interceding with King William on behalf of his New England subjects, had argued that proportionate to the number of people there were more good men in New England than in any other place in the world.[3]

William, it was noted with satisfaction, had agreed that they were indeed a good people—a power of judgement which manifestly enhanced his value as a monarch. But favourable external valuation was less common than prejudiced and uninformed comment or the witty sneers of a Ned Ward. Hence the interest and satisfaction with which it was received. Sometimes the source of praise is a surprising one—as for example the printed work of Sir Josiah Child which, in labelling New England 'the most prejudicial Plantation to this Kingdom', described the inhabitants as 'a people whose Frugality, Industry, and Temperance, and the happiness of whose laws and institutions, promise to them long life with a wonderful increase of People, Riches and Power'. Massachusetts he termed a 'most industrious colony'.[4] Such things pleased and had their utility even when mixed with unhelpful observations on the relationship of old and New England. Hence

---

[1] In courage New Englanders were compared with the people of Northern Ireland and Londonderry—'those brave souls': *A Brief Relation*, p. 161.

[2] *Way for a People*, p. 16.   [3] *Surest Way*, p. 36.

[4] Sir Josiah Child, *A New Discourse of Trade* (London, 1694), pp. 229, 233.

'The Address of the Publicans of New England' (1691) argued that
in relation to the record of this people their political privileges were
inconsiderable. Here in potent and developed form was the notion
of separateness and disposition different from and above the other
colonies. 'These New England colonies were the Envy of the
Tyranny and the Glory of England.' There the people were:
Civilly good, far above all the other Collonies that ever were, for there
could be nothing seen but Religion, Industry, and Sobriety; their
Women employed in one ingenuous thing or other, and far from the
common temptations to Pride, Pomp and Lust: their Young Men
industrious, everyone improving himself in his way and preserved from
Idleness and Debauchery, their Old Men sitting honourably at the
Gates, thinking well and speaking right. . . . Where their Young were
loved, and the old honoured, and where few or no Complaining for
want were heard in the Streets. . . .

This record contrasted with that of most other English plantations
which, it was alleged, were inhabited by a people who 'commonly
cannot, or may not have any Principles of Honour, Honesty,
Industry'.[1] Such lavish and wide-ranging praise, though it may
have been locally composed, was naturally cherished. But external
valuation, which underpinned for the New Englander his own
difficult concept of the place of New England in the world, welcome though it may have been, particularly if emanating from an
exalted source, was nevertheless inferior to divine judgement which
could be accurately assessed only by the tortuous thought of the
ministers. As Cotton Mather observed 'We are more vile than
every other Nation, if we dont own ourselves as vile as any
Nation. . . .'[2]

To the New England mind the endeavours to christianize the
Indians were of considerable importance, the 'vindication of New
England' which should also be the emulation of the world: 'for
shame let not poor little New England be the only Protestant
country that shall do any notable thing for the propagation of the
Faith, into those Dark corners of which are full of cruel Habitations.' The celebrated John Eliot who had had such success in
spreading the gospel among the Indians of New England was

---

[1] The achievement in education was beyond dispute. 'New England hath
upon the best account which can be mentioned outdone all America—"pro
more academiarum in Anglia"': *A Brief Relation*, p. 161; *Humble Address of
the Publicans*, pp. 20–1.
[2] *Pillar of Gratitude*, pp. 7–8.

representated as the archetypal New Englander in whom all the
New English principles and practices were to be found. Mather
told Lord Wharton 'in one Eliot you see what a people 'tis that you
have counted worthy of your Notice.'[1] Achievement and display
had clearly acquired an important defensive purpose, for in reminding his countrymen in 1714 how in the midst of the most
troubled period of the late war they had expressed their charity to
their friends in the Caribbean islands by sending them bounty,
Cotton Mather warned 'Let not ignorant strangers abuse New
England, until they outdo that Poor Country in the Things that
every one must confess to be Laudable.'[2] Yet the accuracy of some
external criticism was acknowledged, as was the bad reputation that
New Englanders had gained as promise-breakers.[3]

New Englanders were a people in covenant with God and 'under
a Comfortable Relation to him'. They were also a people which had
'proportionably more of God among them than any part of mankind beside'.[4] Samuel Cheever said in 1712 'it is most certain that
we are by Profession the Lord's People.'[5] The nature of origins
was an important feature upon which the distinction of Massachusetts rested. New England differed from all other plantations, it
was argued, in that they were built upon a worldly interest,
whereas New England was founded upon an interest purely
religious 'not so much in respect of the Faith of the Gospel . . .
as of the Order of it'.[6] But this was a means indicative of an end,
for here was a people of whom the God of Heaven had said 'This
people have I formed for myself.'[7] Because of the covenant,
ministers could speak without embarrassment of 'the God of New-

---

[1] Revd. Cotton Mather, *Early Piety: Exemplified in the Life and Death of
Mr Nathaniel Mather* (London, 1689), frontispiece; p. 133.
[2] Cotton Mather, *Duodecennium Luctuosum. The History of a Long War
with Indian Salvages and their Directors and Abettors from the Year 1702 To the
Year 1714* (Boston, Mass., 1714), p. 24. Samuel Sewall observed of this event
that 'a country so ready to serve Her Majesty, and to help their fellow Subjects,
ought to have a room in the Thoughts of all good Men in the *English* Nation.'
'A Memorial of the Present Deplorable State of New England', *Mass. Hist.
Soc. Coll.* 5th ser. vi. 42.
[3] *Duodecennium Luctuosum*, p. 10.
[4] Revd. Cotton Mather, *The Present State of New-England* (Boston, Mass.,
Mar. 1690), p. 35.
[5] Revd. Samuel Cheever, *God's Sovereign Government among the Nations*
(Boston, Mass., May 1712), p. 38.
[6] *Surest Way*, p. 40.
[7] *Pillar of Gratitude*, p. 3.

England (our Father's God and Ours)' who was capable of especial kindness and favour to Massachusetts.[1] Yet if references were frequently made to England and the plantations as a means of indicating the excellence of New England, so was the comparison frequently drawn between New England and Ancient Israel. 'Behold', it was said 'you may see an Israel in America.'
'Tis the prerogative of New England above all the Countries of the World, That it is a Plantation for the Christian and Protestant Religion. You may now see a land filled with Churches, which by Solemn and Awful Covenants are dedicated unto the Son of God.[2]
The closeness of the comparison, sense of common identity even, is nowhere better illustrated than in a sermon in which Cotton Mather, speaking at length about the roots and views of a people, finally said: 'My hearers all this while know not whether I am giving an Account of Old Israel or of New England so Surprising has been the parallel.'[3] New Englanders, without self-consciousness, employed the term 'Our English Israel', or 'Our New English Israel'.[4] Thus New Englanders belonged to two worlds— spiritual and material—in both of which they held distinction.[5]

Internal unity was essential for the preservation of these privileges and of the covenant, particularly when an external menace of savage severity threatened the community. Loose-livers were charged as being the cause of the province's ills: 'This people of God is now in such Distress and Danger as it never saw before; and I ask not your leave to tell you, that you are the Authors of it all. Tis you that bring whole Armyes of Indians and Gallic Blood Hounds in upon us.'[6]
As has been observed, the danger of anarchy was strongly denounced by the ministers, but traditionally education and the family were invoked as instruments of order.[7] Heads of families

---

[1] *A Sermon Preached at the Election*, p. 42.   [2] *Serviceable Man*, p. 27.
[3] *Pillar of Gratitude*, p. 5.   [4] *Early Piety*, p. 22.
[5] In 1694 Joshua Scottow defined New England's purpose as 'the Enlargement of Christ's Kingdom and His Majesty of England's Dominions'. *A Narrative of the Planting of Massachusetts Colony. Anno 1628*, p. 10.
[6] *Present State*, p. 28.
[7] 'God hath given this Part of these Ends of the Earth to his son for a Possession. . . . I need not mind you of Schools of Learning to encourage and uphold them. . . . If learning should utterly fail here, this Land would be reduced to Primitive Darkness.' *Essay Tending to Promote Reformation*, p. 25; and see Bernard Bailyn, *Education in the Forming of American Society: Needs and Opportunities for Study* (Chapel Hill, N.C., 1960), pp. 15-18, 75-8.

vested by God with power over those under their charge, were, it was argued, in some respects appointed kings and prophets in their own houses for the good government and education of those under their care. Families were 'the master out of which Church and Commonwealth were formed', for good government, at this level, facilitated the work of public rulers. Without it the burden of rulers was intolerable, their efforts unlikely to bear fruit.[1]

Concern for the instruction of youth, the foundation of every well-ordered commonwealth, led some ministers in the first decade of the eighteenth century—notably Ebenezer Pemberton—to raise alarm at the number of parents unfit to be entrusted with the care of their own children. This was all the more serious because public means of education for the rising generation were 'under sensible damps'. He urged that the instruction of youth, according to the places likely to be held in the state, be regarded as a birthright and a public good.[2] The following election sermon, six months later, contained like sentiments, and indeed the decay or languishment of education and family unity was a serious element of the jeremiad.

The gloom of the sermons extended to the traditional political framework which no longer offered security:

When 'twas Judged that some of the Provinces in Israel were breaking off from the Rest and setting up for themselves, and intending no more to bear the name of the united colonies, what said the man of God unto them in Numb. 32.23. 'Behold, ye have sinned against the Lord, and be sure your sin will find you out.'[3]

In the face of an uncertain future, internal unity was an urgent essential. When the war was but a few months old Cotton Mather, speaking of times of great distress and danger for the people of God, called for voice and action to sustain the effort 'let the venture look never so big and black'. He pointedly attacked the private spirit, a 'detestable neutrality in the multitudes of men, that let the People of God sink or swim; . . . they would not care tho' the Houses of their Neighbours were Burnt, if their own Apples might be Roasted at the Flame.'[4] Even if the form of the jeremiad was traditional it would be absurd to assume that men were so accustomed to the cataloguing of woes that they were unaffected by

---

[1] Revd. Ebenezer Pemberton *Sermon Preached in the Audience of the General Assembly at Boston* (Boston, Mass., Nov 1705), p. 21.

[2] Pemberton, ibid., p. 21; Rogers, *A Sermon Preached at the Election*, p. 44.

[3] *Present State*, p. 24.   [4] Ibid., pp. 21, 23.

the allusions, both implicit and explicit, to present perils. Since they were an educated, indeed a sophisticated people, wide horizons and extensive perils were made visible to them. They were constantly reminded of the Protestant past, 'the dark time of the Romish Apostasy', two hundred years ago when 'the unsearchable Judgements of God, gave up all Europe unto the Chains of Darkness which Popery, that is but a Disguised and Ravished Paganism, laid upon it'. This was followed by the Reformation when 'Antichrist lost half of his Empire'.[1]

Against this background, references to 'Our Nation', meaning 'the English Nation', express an emotive element in New England thought which is significant. There was a desire not merely to honour the Protestant past of England but also to be associated with her contemporary achievements.[2] Unreserved tributes to that part of the English nation which dwelt across the Atlantic are not frequent and many are a means of demonstrating the superior virtues of the New English. But Cotton Mather was explicit when he justified the name 'New England' by commenting that England had nowhere in America a daughter that so much resembled her. 'It is no little Blessing that we are part of the English Nation. Our Dependance on, and Relation to, that brave Nation, that man deserves not the Name of an Englishman, who despises it.'[3] He also contrasted the skill and fortitude of the English in preserving their liberties with the failure of all the other nations of northern Europe. In a tendentious piece of writing he acknowledged the piety to be found in London, and the superiority of the English peasantry to those of Europe which he characterized as 'meer bruits'.

Mather was not alone in making such flattering observations. That the English nation escaped from the political and spiritual mischief of popery, 'under which Nations yet intoxicated with the Popish abominations are pining away', was a cause for gratification and satisfaction, and was due in part to the great lights of the

---

[1] *Pillar of Gratitude*, p. 17.
[2] 'The late revolutions among ourselves has also been attended with some excellent things, whereof we may say, "The finger of God is here". Indeed nothing in the World could more exactly imitate and resemble the late circumstances of our Mother *England* than the *Revolutions* here, in all steps thereof, and this, though we understood not one another. This was from the *Excellent* operations of that God who turns a *wheel* in a *wheel*.' *Wonderful Works*, p. 41; *New England Mind*, pp. 157–8.
[3] *Pillar of Gratitude*, p. 33.

English Church, especially Cranmer and Hooper. Elsewhere was recorded 'the Golden Generation of men in the English Nation' who had none to equal them among the sons of Adam.[1]

In the *Magnalia Christi Americana*, designed to serve the Churches in 'the best island of the Universe', Mather explained how the English nation had been honoured above most of the Protestant and reformed world with clearer discoveries of important points in our Christian religion.[2] In the midst of the War of the Spanish Succession, Ebenezer Pemberton referred to the scores of schools which had been erected and endowed in all parts of the nation where thousands of children of both sexes were freely educated. This, he contended, was 'to the Immortal Honour of our ENGLISH NATION'; it was also 'one of the best methods to advance the work of the Reformation'.

'Nation' was the collective term commonly employed when New Englanders wished to define the wider community to which they belonged. When ministers and writers referred to a separate existence within the nation they frequently used the expression 'people' or the territorial designation 'country': sometimes they spoke of 'the New English'. But Mather occasionally introduced a significant modification into his writing which laid even greater stress on the separate coherence of the New English. In the case of New England, he noted, 'God brought a Nation out of the midst of a Nation.'[3] Although the gloom of Mather is commonly acknowledged it is not surprising that in time of conflict his mood underwent considerable changes. In 1689 he had claimed—perhaps it was wishful thinking—that the whole Papal Empire was near its end 'when none shall help it'.[4] Later he was less buoyant. In a flattering address to the English Churches he raised the question whether New England had not now served its function and whether

---

[1] *Pillar of Gratitude*, pp. 18, 25.

[2] Cotton Mather, *Magnalia Christi Americana* (Hartford, Conn., 1853), ii. 276.

[3] *Pillar of Gratitude*, p. 30. Surprisingly a bishop of the English Church also gave this distinction to New England. Kennet in 1716 explained to Benjamin Colman that the establishment of a colonial bishopric would 'not break in upon your national Rites . . . .' A. L. Cross, *The Anglican Episcopate and the American Colonies* (London, 1902), Harvard Historical Studies, ix. 99, n. 3.

[4] Cotton Mather, *Soldiers Counselled and Comforted. A Discourse Delivered unto some part of the Forces Engaged in the Just War of New-England against the Northern and Eastern Indians* (Boston, Mass., Sept. 1689), p. 36.

the 'Plantation may not, soon after this, come to nothing'.[1] It would be difficult to contend that this mood was not, in important respects, a consequence of the decade of disaster which, for New England, had followed the new dawn of the Glorious Revolution. It was Mather, after all, from whom the name *Decennium Luctuosum* derived.[2] But in holding such sentiments he was not alone. The aged Joshua Scottow, introducing his own modest narrative of the seventeenth century during the mid-1690s, urged that a complete history be laid up in New England's archives before the present generation passed away. 'It was an ordinance of old, to commemorate the Political Birth and Growth of a People; it may not, (we hope) be unbecoming us, to give a small account of the Genesis of their superhuman and really Divine Creation.' Scottow, influenced by the incessant raids upon outlying territories in the north-east, spoke not merely of 'the cropping of branches' but 'the rooting up of the tender plant' and 'the dissolving of the cement'. 'How near New-England now is to its breaking, the All-Knowing One only knows', he lamented.[3] New England's continuance and indeed its identity could no longer be taken for granted.

The rising generation, having observed the collapse of the theocracy in the eighties, were less likely to be impressed by its apparent recovery than by the need, in a world where dramatic change and an uncertain future faced all the colonies, to look about them.[4] But Indian atrocities and the horror of Romist domination gave to all New Englanders a new reason to value the transatlantic foundations of their own culture.[5] There was greater reassurance in

---

[1] Cited in Barrett Wendell, *Cotton Mather, The Puritan Priest* (New York, 1891), p. 159.

[2] See *Narratives of the Indian Wars, 1675–99*. Ed. by C. H. Lincoln (New York, 1913), pp. 186–90. The 'Decennium', contained in this collection, offers a searching inquiry into the occasion and causes of the long war with the Indians which followed the Revolution.

[3] *Narrative of the Planting*, pp. 1, 3.

[4] Palfrey, op. cit. iii. 302. Mather gave them this instruction. See Miller, *New England Mind*, p. 160.

[5] The exclusive attitude of Englishmen toward the commerce of the colonies, as manifested in the wording of the seventeenth-century navigation laws, extended to many other spheres and was practised abroad by English migrants. Endeavour to protect nationals from the exploitation commonly associated with settlement in the New World is to be found in the legal system of several colonies. A Connecticut law of 1650, for example, expressly provided that debtors were not to be sold to any but of the English nation. See Winthrop D. Jordan, *White over Black* (Chapel Hill, N.C., 1968), p. 86.

English roots, and warmth in belonging to a community which transcended township and provincial bounds, at a time when their own corner of the world seemed especially cold and exposed. And when the years of indecision in Europe were replaced by the military ascendancy of the Allied armies, concern for security was overlaid with feelings of pride. Sewall's papers include an address by the clergy of New England to the English Crown, allegedly the first ever made. It dwelt joyfully on the prospect of real peace after decades of war and looked to the time when 'your People like *Israel* of old shall dwell in Safety and be a happy People . . . , and become a quiet and Peaceable Habitation, a Name and a Praise in the whole Earth'.[1] It would be surprising indeed if New England blood had not quickened at the news of Blenheim and the victories which followed, the first of consequence on the continent of Europe since Agincourt. It was not simply in a spiritual sense that the New England clergy, with a fine sense of occasion, informed Anne that the English had now become 'the Head among the Nations'.

New England thought was neither so narrow nor so inward-looking at this time as to lack concern for the spiritual fate of Protestant Europe. Nicholas Noyes said in 1698 'it were infidelity to conclude that God hath done with the Protestant people, and his witnesses in Germany, Bohemia, Hungary, France, the Valleys of Piedmont and many other places in Europe', though he noted that the reformed nations were very much deformed and the spirit and power of the first reformers seemed to die with them.[2] God had raised up a defence of the Protestant religion and interest abroad in a multitude of ways, not the least in the happy accession of King William and Queen Mary. Cotton Mather related in 1689 how some hundreds of people in France were lately fallen into prodigious estates wherein being dead asleep they contended that the late revolutions in England were to begin the deliverance of the Church of God. At the beginning for New England of a long and wearisome war Mather counselled hope. He alluded joyfully to the repeal of

---

[1] *Mass. Hist. Soc. Coll.*, 5th ser. vi. 89. It is significant that a man of Sewall's parochial bent had a reference to this event. In Jan. 1701 he had written:
> Let the transplanted English vine
> Spread further still; still call it Thine:
> Prune it with Skill: for yield it can
> More Fruit to thee the Husbandman. (*Diary*, ii. 393.)

[2] *Duty and Interest*, p. 67.

those laws with which Protestant dissenters had long been harassed and absolved the Church of England from responsibility for a persecution attributable to a knot of ill men.[1] There was reason to rejoice that Protestants had now come to a better understanding of their true interests. 'May the Apples of Strife among them now be removed. . . . May the Reformers have *Peace* among themselves and War with none but Hell and *Rome*.' Mather prayed that the Turkish power which had long threatened Christendom was near its end, but the main fear was the 'Treacherous Grand Seignour of France' who had fettered Europe, 'the most ferocious Tygre in the world'. However, with the forces of three kingdoms now let loose upon Louis XIV he was under attack from every side. It was hoped he would soon perish so that the way would be opened for the liberation of the Protestants in France.[2]

It is scarcely surprising that on several occasions New Englanders produced the rumour that the French king lay dying.[3] There were, of course, grounds for hope in the belief that remarkable and lamentable disasters had pursued the adversaries of New England, an observation made 'a thousand times by more than ten thousand persons.' 'I beseech you' pleaded Cotton Mather 'Read the History.'[4] But New England was passing through a figurative earthquake, not yet over, her position comparable to that of contemporary Hungary.[5] The war had begun with the deliverance from a French force which sought possession of New England.[6] New England was the key to the New World, so New Englanders were told and believed, and if the French king got it into his possession he might soon make himself master of America. Though, after the failure of Frontenac's early projects, Massachusetts and the heartland of New England were never again seriously threatened along the land frontiers and on the sea, the region throughout the two wars remained highly vulnerable. There was no assurance against a future attack on Boston, 'the metropolis of America'. In the spring of 1706 Samuel Sewall was greatly disturbed by a dream in which a vast number of Frenchmen approached him. Though these huddled like a great

---

[1] *Wonderful Works*, pp. 1, 37–9 [2] Ibid., pp. 37–40.
[3] Sewall heard on 6 Sept. 1703 from a Mr. Oakes that Louis XIV had fallen from his horse and broken his neck while reviewing troops going against the Cevennes. Sewall, *Diary*, ii. 88.
[4] *Serviceable Man*, pp. 39–40.
[5] *Wonderful Works*, p. 45.
[6] Ibid., p. 52.

flock of sheep *he* was induced to hide in a thicket. Few New Englanders could have been wholly free of such fears during this protracted period of war, though the thicket they sought may have varied between membership of the English nation, and Protestant industry, and belief in the value attached by God to His own people. The relish of local achievement in war is indicative of the fears that Catholic power engendered. Sewall related with delight how the College at Quebec was burned when Samuel Vetch and William Dudley were there. It set a small chapel on fire which ignited a high cross with a crucifix on it so that it bowed and fell down. He later made verses on the burning at Quebec:

> The bawdy bloudy Cross, at length
> was forc'd to taste the flame:
> The cheating Saviour, to the fire
> Savoury food became.[1]

The people of Massachusetts were not pacifists. The Bay colony initially created to safeguard the Puritan way of life had persisted as an instrument of defence against the Indians and as a means of preserving and advancing the economic welfare of its inhabitants. The inhabitants, accordingly, were expected to sustain this explicit purpose by their own efforts. To this degree the warlike or aggressive character of Massachusetts was unquestionable, and generally speaking the representatives of the people and the clergy revealed few fundamental differences in defining the community's burden and instructing the people how it might best be secured. However, though the virtues of the soldier-citizen could be highly praised for the purposes of war, the political dangers inherent in military strength and activity were never wholly ignored. The problems were clearly brought out in a sermon preached to the Artillery Company in Boston on 5 June 1699. The biblical word *ENOSH*, meaning man of war, but signifying 'sorrowful, sickly, and mortal', was used in preference to *ISH* which implied 'vertue and valour'—not to reproach the calling but to put soldiers in mind of their frailty and to humble them when in their plumes they might be too greatly exalted.

War was regarded as being in its own nature an evil thing. But it could also be unavoidable, and when undertaken not for its own sake but for securing and recovering the public peace and tran-

---

[1] Sewall, *Diary*, ii. 142–3.

quillity, as a means of defence against assault, or offence for
suppressing a molesting adversary, it could be good and necessary
and must be honourable. Christianity was no enemy to soldiering,
for the Christian religion could not otherwise be defended and
secured against unreasonable invaders and aggressors but at the
sword's point and cannon-mouth. This sermon was preached in
time of peace, between the two wars, but the substance of the
doctrine was that peace was never so settled that war may not of a
sudden arise.[1] In the colourful biblical language, with references
to the great battle of Armaggedon yet to come, and to Babylon as
yet unfallen, was drawn a precise picture of the spiritual and political
predicament which faced the New Englanders.[2] Every true Israelite
in the kingdom of God was a man of war. In the visible gospel-
kingdom there were two sorts of men, Israelites only in name and
Israelites in deed. The former were in truth Canaanites, and
Slaves, mancipated to Sin and Satan: but the latter were emanci-
pated by Christ and enrolled in His army. Here there was no
equivocation. The Church under the Kingdom of Grace was
militant, and every Regeneration was born a man of contention.[3]
Those who wished to serve God must be His soldiers: they should
fortify their hearts with an heroic resolution to sustain all the
soldierly virtues—never to flinch from service, nor to desert their
posts, or fly from the colours, nor to love their lives unto the death.
'Be not discouraged if you get a foil, but reinforce the battel, calling
aloud for aid from heaven.'[4]

It had not been the original intention of the people of Massachusetts that others should fight their battles for them. As a
community they were ready to define and to pursue their own

[1] Revd. Samuel Willard, *The Man of War* (Boston, Mass., 1699), pp. 8, 10,
11. 'It is an ill time, when the Trumpet of War is sounded, and Hannibal is
at the gates, for a people to have the Forts to build, their Arms, Ammunition
and Provision to sell, and their Souldiers Untrained. Nor is it less hazardous
when once Peace is proclaimed, for men to let their fortifications fall, hang
up their Arms and let them grow rusty and useless, laying aside their Military
exercises as things superfluous.'

[2] 'Be warned not to fall asleep, because the Sword of War is at present sheath-
ed; remembering that the *Book of the Histories of War* is not yet compleated;
nor will be till the great *Battel of Armageddon* is fought. *Babylon* is not yet
fallen. The Churches Adversaries are still in *their strength*. God will call out his
Armies ere long; and then *Cursed will be he who cometh not forth to the help of the
Lord against the Mighty*.' Ibid., pp. 18–20.

[3] Jer. 15: 10.

[4] *Man of War*, pp. 25, 29.

interests though not above directing the righteous outside of their borders if necessity demanded. Hence the New England confederation which helped to secure the region before the vacation of the Massachusetts charter, which may alternately be seen as an instrument of Massachusetts imperialism or hegemony. The economic pursuits especially in need of protection against an enemy in time of war were the agriculture of the frontier and more importantly the fisheries and the fur trade. And though these possessed a material justification which grew more influential each decade they were also conventionally related to the all-pervading religious purpose which New England had embraced since its earliest days and which, in time of direct and immediate peril, offered a staunch sanctuary against the uncertainties of a future dominated by French power. The primary objective was for the community to walk in a godly way. Defeats and setbacks, evidences of God's displeasure, demanded the renewed hortation of church members and the threat of dire punishment against all who led an unsavoury life. The sanctity of the family and the maintenance of an adequate educational system aided the avoidance of disorder and chaos and facilitated observance of the covenant.

In 1689, however, the peril was neither distant nor manageable. France allied with the Turk had long proved her capacity in Europe: French power stood on the St. Lawrence. Whether as a merchant or a shipbuilder who had gained advantage as a result of—or despite—the navigation system, whether as a town artisan or a farmer with resentments against naval impressments or memories of the Andros land system, whether as a minister who believed as firmly as John Winthrop and the first founders in the City upon a Hill, or as dissident Quakers, New Englanders had few doubts as to the proportions of the French menace. Nor at this date was there reason to represent the hostility of France as resulting from England's selfish pursuit of an interest distinct from that of Massachusetts or of little concern to her. New England, so she believed, had independently rejected James Stuart and identified the enemy with which England was now at war. Her main concern was lest England should lose sight of the purpose—which the colony so readily pursued—or even desert it.[1] As the highest

---

[1] See R. Van Alstyne, *Empire and Independence. The International History of the American Revolution* (New York, 1965), p. 4.

exemplification of the Protestant religion it was inconceivable for her blindly to subordinate her own resources to the purposes of England without betraying a trust. These purposes though framed in a Protestant context were far more equivocal, particularly in the closing years of the War of the Spanish Succession, and earned support only as related to her own special interests for which the empire now formed the main instrument.

Thus in confronting French power on the North American continent both Englands old and New, without a clear understanding of their partnership, sought to manipulate the other. Their designs were facilitated by the extent to which interests coincided, but they were also hindered by a divergence of purpose, less sharp than in the past, but also less readily understood by men unable to perceive how limited was the capacity of the two societies to communicate.[1] For some New Englanders a sentimental attachment to old England persisted. There were those who continued to nourish fond if romantic daydreams of a return 'home' someday. At personal level contacts existed in every sphere though they were not numerous. Samuel Sewall in 1689 moved freely and amiably about southern England grappling with the problems of estate management and enjoying the countryside. Increase Mather maintained close association with the Nonconformists of England, and many New England ministers had likewise corresponded with English dissenters or even visited England. New England merchants had their own coffee-house in London, near Cornhill, behind the Royal Exchange, and also had a reasonable circle of commercial contacts. But in general the theology and ecclesiasticism of New England failed to arouse much sympathy or even much interest in the mother country, in part because of its rigidity. And New Englanders in the capital without the advantage of established connections resented their solitary state more bitterly than the visitor from some remote English county.[2]

The true extent of the distance which now separated these peoples, obscured by the common experience of the revolutions of 1688–9, was not in fact fully apparent until the debacle of the

[1] See *A Brief Relation*, p. 161.
[2] Susan M. Reed, *Church and State in Massachusetts, 1691–1740* (Urbana, Ill., 1914), pp. 14–16, discusses how the dissenters in England had drifted apart from the Congregationalists and Presbyterians of New England. W. L. Sachse, *The Colonial American in Britain* (Madison, Wis., 1956), p. 204.

Walker expedition of 1711 revealed the readiness of each to blame
the other for a failure which cast credit on neither. Not everyone
was blind to this divergence. Richard Coote, Earl of Bellomont,
one of the most successful governors appointed to New England,
perceived the need to strengthen the economic relationship between England and the plantations. 'There's no bond of union',
he averred, 'so sure and lasting as that of interest.' At the turn
of the century a handful of members within the Massachusetts
Council directed vocal criticism at restraining legislation, designed
in the interest of London merchants, which prevented them from
a free trade necessitated by their economic circumstances. The
imbalance in trade for New England was undeniable and Bellomont
reported the inhabitants as very uneasy at the want of returns from
England. It is noteworthy that the Council critics advanced their
case upon the grounds that as they were as much English as those
in England then they had a similar right to privilege as the London
merchants.[1] This was counter to prevailing theory and sentiments,[2]
and the most constructive move considered during this age—the
encouragement of naval stores—had to be promoted by the specious
lie that production would divert New Englanders from woollen
manufacturing.[3]

Most Englishmen, if they considered New Englanders at all,

---

[1] *C.S.P.C.*, 1700, p. 675.

[2] Cf. Edward Littleton, *The Groans of the Plantations. Or a true account of the
Grevious and Extreme Sufferings by the Heavy Impositions upon Sugar and other
Hardships Relating more particularly to the Island of Barbados* (London, 1689),
pp. 23–4, 26. 'Are we not of your own number? Are we not English Men?
Some of us pretend to have as good *English* Bloud in our Veins, as some of those
we left behind us. How came we lose our Country and the Privileges of it?
Why will you cast us out? . . . [The Plantations] are meer Additions and Acces-
sions to *England* and Enlargements of it—[save] that there is a distance and space
between *England* and the Plantations. So that we must lose our Country upon
the account of Space. . . . The Citizens of *Rome*, though they lived in the
remotest Parts of the World then known, were still *Roman* citizens to all Intents.
But we poor Citizens of *England*, as soon as our backs are turn'd, and we are
gone a spit and a stride, are presently reputed Aliens, and used accordingly. . . .
We by our Labour, Hazards, and Industry have enlarged on *English* Trade and
Empire. The *English* Empire in *America*, whatever we may think of it ourselves,
is by others esteemed greatly considerable.'

[3] J. J. Malone, *Pine Trees and Politics, 1691–1775* (London, 1964), pp. 22–3.
Some New Englanders engaged in commerce, such as Thomas Bannister, a
Boston merchant, justified their country in terms of its economic service to the
nation. See Bannister to Council of Trade, 7 July 1715, *C.S.P.C.*, 1714–15,
no. 508.

probably regarded them no more sympathetically than did Edward
Randolph: as disobedient, anarchical, and independently-minded,
a people who substituted arrogance for humility, oblivious of the
favours received through the membership of the English nation and
protection of the English state; who disobeyed imperial regulation
yet claimed every privilege; who persecuted and oppressed with a
sense of righteousness which competed with that of the English at
home. This was the official view, formed over the decades, a product
of the stream of charges poured across the Atlantic by outraged
administrators who had experienced the obstruction or nullification of royal orders.[1]

The superficial interest of a wider public, eager for news of the
Indian troubles which had come to a head in King Philip's war,
had been stimulated by the minor flood from the pen of New
England authors printed in London in the 1670s. *The Present
State of New England . . . Faithfully composed by a Merchant of
Boston and communicated to his Friend in London* was the first of
several publications.[2] These were followed by Mary Rowlandson's
narrative,[3] a dramatic account of the hazards of frontier life first
published in Boston in 1682, reprinted in Boston and London the
same year, and subsequently reissued.[4] This was a personal epic,
but some of the compositions which had preceded it possessed

---

[1] Even Bellomont, a governor more admired by the people of Massachusetts
than their own native Thomas Dudley, thought them more unlawful than any
other plantation. In seeking legislation upon piracy, in conformity with the law
of England, he was told by several councillors that English law had nothing to do
with the people of Massachusetts. But he was critical, too, of other important
features of New England life, including the harsh treatment of the Indians of
Nantucket, said by contemporaries to be 'the soberest, best sort of Indians in
America'. *C.S.P.C.*, 1700, no. 746, p. 180.

[2] These included *A New and Further Narrative of the State of New-England*;
Revd. Increase Mather, *A Brief History of the Warr with the Indians in New
England* (London, 1676); William Hubbard, *A Narrative of the Troubles with
the Indians* (Boston, Mass., 1677), printed in London as *The Present State of
New England*; Increase Mather, *A Relation of the Troubles which have hapned
in New England By reason of the Indians there. From the Year 1614 to the Year
1675* (London, 1677).

[3] *The Sovereignty and Goodness of God . . . being a Narrative of the Captivity
and Restauration of Mrs. Mary Rowlandson. . . . Written by Her Own Hand for
Her private Use, and now made Publick at the earnest Desire of some Friends* (Cambridge, Mass., 1682).

[4] The Liverpool rumour that 10,000 New Englanders had been slain by
Indians before July 1689 may have owed something to an English imagination
enlarged by these writings. See *C.S.P.C.*, 1693–6, no. 2749.

religious and political overtones. One, written by Edward Wharton, a New England Quaker, attributed the war to God's just vengeance on Massachusetts for her persecution of the Quakers, an interpretation at odds with the views of New England's clergy, who considered that lenience towards heretics was a more likely cause, if it was not the moral laxity of the young.[1]

A reading public had thus already been created when the political crises in New England in the 1680s, leading to the overthrow of the Andros regime, brought forth a spate of New England publications, much of it read in London hot from the press. Deacon Nathaniel Byfield's *An Account of the Late Revolution in New England*, a justification of the uprising, was available in June 1689, months before a defence of the Andros regime appeared. Other pamphlets for and against, including four tracts by Increase Mather during his stay in England, placed some of the main issues of New England politics before the literate of the metropolis.[2] The printing of a major work in 1702, Cotton Mather's *Magnalia Christi Americana*, handicapped though it was by diversity of style and clumsiness of method, was received by an English audience already awakened to some of the dominant themes of New England life.

The most damning feature of the New Englander was the extent of his achievement and his evident assurance. What the Englishman was unable to perceive was the accompanying doubts and uncertainties which derived fundamentally from the declension of the mother country. To the New Englander the integrity of England was questionable. It had in the past excelled other nations in the eyes of God and in its regard for the political liberties, so he was told often enough by his ministers, but it had also in the past transgressed and strayed from its highest aspirations. Though the quality of its cultural life was undeniable[3] its overriding purpose could be endorsed in the broad terms of Protestantism only when the menace of Catholicism and the Universal Monarchy fundamentally threatened the future. But not until the allies had gained ascendancy in the War of the Spanish Succession were New Englanders offered any real assurance that this menace had been contained. Until then, and before disenchantment arose from Anglo-

---

[1] See Morison, *Intellectual Life*, p. 184.

[2] Ibid., pp. 199–200.

[3] 'Your books are precious even to the furthest nooks of these colonies: we read you, prize you, bless God for you.' *Pillar of Gratitude*.

American projects for the conquest of Canada, it was a convenient and comfortable mental exercise for New Englanders to limit their adversaries by first seeking to compose differences and then by ignoring the potential menace of Anglicanism. It seems a fair assumption that the New Englander by persistent exposure to sermons of limited theme and content had been conditioned to view himself and the region he inhabited as a special part of God's purpose long after his intellectual commitment to covenant theology had been diluted by other factors.[1]

Irrespective of the degree of secularization or material success which had occurred since the founding generation no people could readily discard a myth of origins and a myth of mission so potent and so effectively propagated as this. Even were it consciously rejected it would still probably linger in the sentiment of every New Englander as a counter to the gross uncertainties which had been faced since 1675. Membership of the English nation, though in the past it had brought threats to the *New England way* as serious as those which at the turn of the seventeenth century stemmed from the French and Indians, was a further haven to which in the face of harsh material realities the merchants had turned several decades before events had converted the theocrats to the wisdom of such a course.[2] We do not know how the common New Englander—the farmer, the fisherman, or the town artisan—regarded the mother country, or how sharply he distinguished himself from his English cousin, but there were many realities in speech, print, and deed to remind him of the relationship and relatively few contacts to sour it before 1709. New England independence was of the sturdiest growth and yet in time of extremity it was natural enough to regard the English nation as an instrument of God, among the highest purposes of which were the welfare of the New English.

---

[1] See Edmund Morgan, 'The Puritan Ethic and the American Revolution', *W & MQ*, 3rd ser. vol. xxiv (1967), *passim*.
[2] See B. Bailyn, *The New England Merchants in the Seventeenth Century* (Cambridge, Mass., 1955).

CHAPTER III

The Nine Years War and Massachusetts Bay, 1689–97

In 1689 New England turned to face the main threat to its future, a force which contrasted significantly with that of its English opponents in the nature of its resources and the form in which they were organized. The French empire, the dominant adversary, was Roman Catholic, autocratic, and largely centralized. Though strikingly inferior in size of overseas population, it made its influence felt over a vast area of the North American continent. 'La France Septentrionale', or New France, centred on Canada where the governor-general resided. Acadia, Newfoundland, and—after 1698—Louisiana, each had separate government. In principle they came within the jurisdiction of the governor-general but direct contact with Canada was not very great. In Canada, the important communities of Quebec, Montreal, and Trois Rivières and the lesser ones along the Richelieu River, politically less sophisticated than their English counterparts, had lost the means they once possessed for communicating directly with the government in France.[1] If the mother country proved sensitive to the needs of its colonists it did so through the exertions of its own representatives.

The French system, inspired by Louis XIV, was cumbersome. Senior officials were instructed by the *Mémoire du Roi*, an annual statement of general policies, which also contained a vast amount of administrative detail concerning decisions taken throughout the colonial empire during the past twelve months. At Quebec the framework of government extended to an intendant, and a council of eight, including the bishop. In France a large and growing

---

[1] Assemblies could not be held without special permission of the governor, nor could petitions be presented without his approval. Forms of expression remaining to the people were protests, complaints, and suggestions to Court or to colonial officials. Earlier practice had allowed three syndics or representatives of Quebec, Montreal, and Trois Rivières, elected by the inhabitants to attend the council and take part in its deliberative functions: Francis H. Hammang, *The Marquis de Vaudreuil. New France at the beginning of the Eighteenth Century* (Bruge, 1938), pt. I, p. 35.

bureaucracy served the colonies under divided control. The minister of marine shared supervision with the controller-general and the minister of foreign affairs. The king, through whom senior appointments were made, probably had the final say in all major decisions of policy. Louis served his empire conscientiously but an impressive industry could not bridge the distance which separated him from his subjects overseas, nor counter the inevitable failings of personal judgement. The French system, minutely organized by comparison with the loose assemblage of English provinces, was, in important respects, self-defeating.

Canada possessed twelve thousand *habitants*, their dwellings scattered for several hundred miles along the banks of the St. Lawrence and Richelieu Rivers.[1] Though few in number by comparison with the Dutch and English communities to the south, they possessed dramatic qualities some of which were a liability to French policy. The vitality of the rank and file was remarked upon by those who governed them; and Lahontan, an experienced traveller, in 1703 praised their enterprise and industry. But energies were squandered. For the young the primitive attractions of the forest and an Indian way of life beckoned strongly, particularly when military service threatened their freedom. The older men, extravagant and over-sensitive, made gambling and drunkenness a serious threat to community stability. Many of the more serious ills derived from the huge importations of brandy, of which only a relatively small amount was sold to the Indians. The region was dominated by 'an infinity of taverns' and Montreal, the centre of the brandy trade, had a reputation on both sides of the Atlantic for drunken orgies.[2] Alcoholic excess brought Frenchman and christianized Indian alike early ruination of health and even premature death. But serious as this problem proved to be it was overshadowed in magnitude by that of population dispersal. A consequence of the fur trade, this seriously stretched the limited resources for defence and hobbled the capacity for aggressive action.[3]

---

[1] Claude de Bonnault, *Histoire du Canada français, 1534-1763* (Paris, 1950), p. 133.

[2] Mack Eastman, *Church and State in Early Canada* (Edinburgh, 1915), p. 246, 274, and 291. Callières, as governor of Montreal, was issued orders in 1699 which described intoxicating drinks as 'the source of the greatest crimes committed in the colony'.

[3] Francis Parkman, *The Old Régime in Canada* (London, 1909), pp. 440-2.

Not only did the French and English empires contrast in religion but in the role of the Church in imperial purposes as well. The Protestant empire of England, though sustained by its religious faith, was divided by the form and aspirations of its churches. The Church of England, which through the Bishop of London maintained a nominal degree of supervision throughout the colonies, when our period begins had little strength on the North American mainland, save in Virginia. For the next twenty-five years, though with decreasing fervour as time progressed, important dissenters and conformists sought to stress their common features and common origins. This muted, though it did not preclude, internecine squabbles. In contradistinction the French empire, monolithic in its essential religious structure, tolerated neither schism nor diversity, save within a very narrow compass. Despite opposition from Colbert, Bishop Montmorency Laval, before his retirement in 1684, had securely established the principle of an ultramontane Church which aimed to determine decisions of state. Laval had striven for stability and Catholic standards which he believed were ensured only by rigid control of the important fur trade. But though successful on paper he had seen his purpose deflected by forces within the colony which contended for an unregulated west. Mgr de Saint-Vallier, whom he selected as his successor, continued his policies. Wealthy and of high birth, Saint-Vallier was initially held in great esteem by the king. At the Council Board he joined forces with the intendant, Jean Bochart de Champigny (1686–1702), to contest expansion for the sake of social standards more closely European. In vitality he equalled Laval but a tactless and contentious nature severely restricted his influence and rapidly disenchanted all with whom he came in contact.[1] State–Church rivalries, canalized into clashes of personality, embarrassed and to a degree weakened New France. But by the 1680s the Church had substantially accelerated the advance towards a more civilized way of life. Thereafter, from the beginning of Frontenac's second administration and under conditions of prolonged warfare, theocratic power diminished. One important cause was a shortage of parish priests. Most parishes lacked a resident *curé* and by

---

[1] See Abbé A. E. Gosselin, 'Mgr de Saint-Vallier et Son Temps', *Revue catholique de Normandie* (Paris, 1899), *passim*.

the end of the century less than seventy served a community of 15,000.[1]

The urge to expansion had been promoted under Colbert who, before his death in 1683, sought the extension of the fur trade to meet the costs of developing the French empire. In 1673 Louis Jolliet, a fur-trader himself, and the Jesuit Father Marquette had explored the Wisconsin River and the Mississippi down to the mouth of the Arkansas. Later under the guidance of another trader, La Salle, the upper Mississippi basin was secured by a series of fortifications built at the mouth of the Niagara River, along the Chicago, St. Joseph, and Illinois Rivers, and on Lake Peoria. Tribes were encouraged to dwell under the protection of the forts which became trading depots through which the Indians passed their furs. In 1682 La Salle explored the lower Mississippi to its outlet and claimed for France the area drained by the great river.

French pretensions were seriously challenged, however, by the Five Nations of the Iroquois: the Seneca, Mohawk, Oneida, Onondaga, and Cayugas, a powerful confederacy whose settlements lay to the south-east of Lakes Erie and Ontario. Backed first by the Dutch and then by the English, after the conquest of New York in 1664, the Iroquois strove for the role of middleman channelling furs from the tribes of the north and west—over whom the French claimed an influence—through Albany and thence down the Hudson River. The enmity of the two peoples was of long standing and extended to the early years of the century. A new phase of the conflict predated the opening of the Anglo-French conflict by almost a decade. For the French colonists it was a struggle for survival which continued without significant abatement for the span of a generation.[2]

---

[1] C. J. Eccles, *Canada under Louis XIV, 1663–1701* (New York and London, 1964), p. 225. The substance of pp. 72–5 is drawn from material published in the *New Cambridge Modern History*, ed. J. S. Bromley (Cambridge, 1970) vi. 484–6, hereafter cited as *NCMH*. Citations from ch. xv of that volume, 'France and England in North America, 1689–1713', by P. S. Haffenden, are printed with the permission of the Syndics of the Cambridge University Press.

[2] See esp. Gabriel Louis Jaray, '*L'Empire français d'Amérique 1534–1803*' (Paris, 1938), p. 188, which describes the struggle as 'the Thirty Years War'. Jaray terms New France 'an empire under siege—poorly fortified and weakly garrisoned, between each front able to communicate only by sea. . . .'

The advantages of the new French fortifications had been compromised by a weakening of the leadership of New France after the recall of Count Frontenac. At the same time, inspired by Governor Thomas Dongan of New York and Lord Howard of Effingham, governor of Virginia, the English secured more effective co-operation with the confederacy. By 1685 English and Iroquois trading parties had reached Michilimackinac at the northernmost end of Lake Michigan. While seeking to breach the alliance, the French, led by Denonville who had replaced La Barre, the successor of Frontenac, countered in 1686 by a move against the English in the Hudson Bay area. Having restricted their establishments at the mouth of the Hayes and the Severn by the capture of the James Bay posts, the French supplemented their success by creating two new centres to the north on Lake Nipigon (1684) and Lake Atibibi (1686). French power extended to a complex alliance system. In facilitating the expulsion of the Iroquois from the St. Lawrence valley France had become associated with a number of smaller tribes counted among their enemies: the Fox, Ottawas, Miamis, and others. But with the highly-organized and dreaded Five Nations on their side the English possessed a tempered instrument of war to add to their numerical superiority, already overwhelming. Yet English preponderance was initially outweighed by the confusion of the Glorious Revolution, and France was presented with an opportunity which superficially she seemed ideally situated to seize.

In September 1689, as successor to Denonville, Count Frontenac returned to Canada bringing news to the colony of King Louis's declaration of war. He was frantically welcomed as *patriae redemptor*, and by his presence infused a new spirit into the colony. The effective manpower at his command, 1,500 *troupes de la marine* and 2,000 or more militia, was scarcely greater than the combined Iroquois warbands. But he was denied the opportunity to employ it decisively. The intendant argued for concentration against the major English trading-post at Albany, believing that its destruction would hasten the decline of the Five Nations. Such a move could also exploit provincial division, for Albany was held by anti-Leislerian forces. The Iroquois would not be directly overwhelmed but in due course might be reduced to submission if French success led to the conquest of New York city. This would deprive them of supplies of firearms, gunpowder, and lead, and through the occupa-

tion of the line of the Hudson River would complete the humiliation of the English colonists, placing them at the mercy of the
French. Capture of the seaport was a tempting project. Apart from
the Leislerian tumult, the colony was rendered vulnerable by its
dispersed settlements and the openness of the principal city to
attack from the sea. But this ambitious plan preferred by Frontenac
required the co-operation of a military expedition from the St.
Lawrence and a naval contingent from Europe. It aimed at the
removal of all colonists who would not swear allegiance to France.
Louis XIV approved of the objectives but long before Frontenac
reached Quebec the time for successful surprise was past.

In abandoning the project Louis may have gambled on the
return of James to the English throne as a client king but it is
significant that the design was never resumed at a later date. During
the course of the war Frontenac repeatedly urged upon Louis the
desirability of forcibly depopulating New York by driving or
transporting the inhabitants into New England or Pennsylvania.
But the requested help from Europe was never forthcoming and
without it the French governor was compelled to defend New
France by other expedients more suited to its limited resources.
He struck in a series of sharp raids on the border settlements:
against Schenectady in New York and against the outlying communities of Maine and New Hampshire. Thus the northern fury
was deflected to New England to an important degree. The French
regained prestige among their Indian allies, lost by the dreadful
massacre of Lachine in 1689. But at a price of relieving pressure on
the Iroquois.

Though sickness scourged the whole Connecticut valley New
England was better prepared in spirit to meet this force than she
was in organization. A direct consequence of the collapse of the
Dominion of New England was a weakening of the defence of the
entire north-east region, the enfeeblement of New England as well
as New York. In place of the systematic purpose of Sir Edmund
Andros was now substituted a mixture of bold plans and parochial
self-interest. One New Englander, Elisha Hutchinson, wrote 'We
are full of troubles and beset with enemies on every side;' yet he
believed that with a little outside help—two frigates and sufficient
ammunition—a major attack on Canada would be possible.[1] The

[1] *C.S.P.C.*, 1689-92, no. 802.

exposed frontiersmen and some of the Indian allies, observant of
the consequences of loss of unified political direction, perceived
more clearly that their own security was undermined. The
Mohawks charged that the government at Boston ate, drank, and
slept much and left the war to the Indians.[1]

As general governor, Andros had built a string of fortifications
to guard the Maine frontier and strengthen eastern Massachusetts
and the Connecticut valley. The furthest protected point eastwards
was Pemaquid on the mouth of the Damariscotta River.[2] Here,
two provincial companies and one regular company, comprising in
all 156 men, were supported by a nearby redoubt holding a garrison
of eighty-four and by strong points at New Dartmouth. The next
line of defence was on the Kennebec, about the lower passage of
which were situated Sagadahoc (Saiodchock), Newtown, and
Fort Anne. Behind, on the Androscoggin River, stood Pojebscot.[3]
180 men defended these positions. Some twenty-five miles to the
south-west, protecting Casco Bay, was Fort Loyal (Falmouth),
garrisoned by sixty men; while further westwards still, within a
day's march of the New Hampshire border, stood the fort on the
Saco River which provided protection for the men and communities of Wells and Kennebunk.[4] New Hampshire's fortification was
situated on Great Island to protect the harbour.[5]

The New England heartland was defended on the line of the
Merrimac River by the local militia and through a fortification at
Upper Plantation; the Connecticut valley by a mixed force of
militia and regulars, reinforced by an independent company. On
the seacoast, north of Cape Cod, where orders had been issued
encouraging the fortification of the ports, Salem was protected by
batteries and Boston by a developed defence-system.[6] The seaborne

---

[1] *C.S.P.C.*, 1689–92, no. 885.

[2] This was in the county of Cornwall, territory between the St. Croix and
the Kennebec River, formerly part of New York but added to the Dominion
of New England in the spring of 1687.

[3] Cf. Barnes, *Dominion of New England*, p. 218, who locates it on the Kennebec.

[4] Two additional forts were alleged to have been at Kennebunk and Wells:
ibid., p. 218.

[5] *C.S.P.C.*, 1689–92, no. 2586.

[6] Mass. Archives, xxxv. 160. For Boston the most important coastal defence-
work was a stone castle situated on an island in Massachusetts Bay, about three
or four miles distant, and commanding the channel by which ships approached
the port. It was equipped with thirty guns and garrisoned with a small force of
men. Boston was further protected by a small fort at its south end mounted

patrol, covering an extensive coastline, consisted of H.M.S. *Speedwell* and H.M.S. *Mary*, aided by two provincial sloops.[1] The forces which garrisoned the various works, 700 men in all, were drawn from what remained of the regular companies under the command of Sir Edmund Andros—two, raised to four when the dominion was extended to include New York—and from the militia of Massachusetts, Connecticut, Rhode Island, and the county of Cornwall, a host totalling some 13,275 men.[2]

In general, militia companies in Massachusetts and Connecticut were organized and armed as were soldiers in England. The standard textbook, widely possessed, was Lieutenant Richard Elton's *The Compleat Body of the Art Military* published in the mid-years of the century. This was later replaced by a work, printed in Boston in 1701 and written by a New Englander, Nicholas Boone, which borrowed heavily from Elton. This was *The Compleat Soldier*. It ran to a second edition only five years after the first printing. By the militia law of 1693 footsoldiers were

with twelve guns but not garrisoned. On the north side of the town, commanding the river as far as Charlestown, was a platform made of stones and turf mounted with two small guns. Elsewhere there were a few scattered forts. Andros had put these in good order and added new fortifications at Fort Hill, in part as a substitute for Castle Island, judged too far away from the town to be effective. This new fort purported to command all avenues of approach by sea and land. The fortifications at Castle Island, generally criticized for their irregularity, were demolished by the distinguished engineer Colonel Romer, sent to New England by King William. In their place was erected Fort William.

Near the end of the war the people of Boston were deeply disturbed to learn that the French were making gigantic preparations to crush English power in America. As the most important community in New England they expected to be the focal point of attack. But when the town fortifications were examined early in 1696 it was found they were very much out of repair and unfit for war-time service. £500 was initially allocated for their repair with a view to voting further sums once the work was in progress. For similar reasons Salem voted £100 and placed its militia in a state of immediate readiness. S. G. Drake, *Antiquities of Boston* (Boston, Mass., 1857), ii. 511, 527; Joseph B. Felt, *Annals of Salem* (Salem, Mass., 1827), pp. 327, 328; Daniel Neal, *The History of New England* (London, 1720), ii. 586, cited Sewall, *Diary*, i. 488; Barnes, *Dominion of New England*, pp. 217–18.

[1] *C.S.P.C.*, 1689–92, no. 912.

[2] Ibid., 1689–92, no. 879. The figures for Maine and New Hampshire are not included in this assessment. Massachusetts did not claim responsibility for New Hampshire but, at the beginning of the war, loaned men and stores of ammunition on credit until the royal pleasure was made known. The shortage of gunpowder was very acute. At one time the fort on Great Island held only one barrel for its ten guns. In 1692 New Hampshire mustered 754 men between the ages of sixteen and sixty. ibid., no. 2586.

armed with firelock muskets and a sword or cutlass for Indian fighting and carried a snapsack with powder, flints, and twenty bullets. After 1700 for the Boston regiment alone the bayonet replaced the sword. Mounted troopers were armed with pistols or carbine and sword. They were obliged to provide a horse of satisfactory quality and size.[1]

Apart from the division of these manpower resources—impressive by French colonial standards—into separate provincial commands, the main consequence of the return of power to the traditional local authorities was the collapse of the system of fortifications. In the confusion, garrisons deserted or turned against their officers and the military frontier rapidly contracted. Massachusetts repudiated responsibility for Sagadahoc, dismissed as a fort erected and then abandoned by the fishermen, while at Newtown and Dartmouth, destroyed as towns by the Indians after the fall of Andros, the protecting forts were deemed to have lost their usefulness. On similar grounds the redoubt in the Damariscotta River was abandoned, as was Fort Anne and Pojebscot. On the Maine frontier in far isolation Fort Loyal and Pemaquid alone were maintained though both were soon to fall, the latter weakened by the loss of its commander, suspected of being a papist. Along the Merrimac River several officers were dismissed and in the Connecticut valley the force was diminished. News of these steps, and the resulting mischief, incensed the Lords of Trade and spurred them to action. Provision was made for the despatch of ammunition and gunpowder and the colony's agents were called upon to give an official account of what had happened.[2] In explaining why certain forts were no longer defended the latter, significantly, made no specific endeavour to justify on military grounds the alternative expedients adopted but implied that the militia was more profitably employed within the frontier-towns than exposed in numerous forts too weak to be of any value.[3]

---

[1] Sylvester Judd, *History of Hadley* (Springfield, Mass,. 1905), pp. 215–22.

[2] Ibid., 1689–92, nos. 912, 913, and 939; H. L. Osgood, *The American Colonies in the Eighteenth Century* (repr. Gloucester, Mass., 1958), i. 69–72. Mass. Archives, lxx. 157, 158.

[3] The number directed by the provisional government under Simon Bradstreet, including Plymouth but not Maine and New Hampshire, was 8,683 foot and 739 horse. With the addition of Rhode Island and Connecticut, under the commission of Sir William Phips (the first royal governor) in November 1691, this was increased by another 3,798 foot and 55 horse.

The Indian adversary facing the New Englanders and guarding New France like a thorn-hedge consisted mainly of the Canibas, inhabiting the Kennebec and its tributaries, the Malicites of the Penobscot and St John River, and the Micmacs of the province of Nova Scotia and New Brunswick. The Sokokis of the Saco River and the Pennacooks of the Merrimac were too diminished in number to constitute any longer much of an independent threat, though the village of Pequawket (Fryeburg), in the heart of the White Mountains and almost inaccessible, was long a source of vexation and weakness to the English.[1]

These Indians who were known to the English by the rivers they inhabited, and collectively called by them Tarrentines, belonged to the fierce Abenaki tribe. Cruelty was a significant feature of their culture and the writings of New Englanders recount the barbarities they inflicted on white prisoners, regardless of age and sex, and on luckless domestic animals as well. And yet kindness and magnanimity were not unknown emotions.[2] Indeed it should be seriously considered whether terror was not employed as a conscious weapon designed to stampede the enemy out of the frontier regions. In any case the Indians aimed 'to drive the pigs to the great sows of Boston

---

[1] S. A. Drake, *Border Wars of New England* (New York, 1897), p. 10.

[2] Cotton Mather tells how James Key, the five-year-old son of John Key of Quochecho, near Salmon Falls on the Maine–New Hampshire border, was horribly tortured and mutilated by his captor before being killed. The 'Decennium Luctuosum' contains a score of incidents recounting similar acts of Indian savagery. See C. H. Lincoln (ed), *Narratives of the Indian Wars, 1675–99*, p. 209. At Methuen, then the western part of Haverhill, prowling Indians came upon a yoke of oxen, cut out their tongues, struck up a fire, and broiled them, leaving the suffering beasts as they were. However, in this same township the Quaker family of Thomas Whittier which refused in time of attack to take refuge in garrison-houses went unmolested, and preserved throughout the period of war a civil relationship with the Indians. Further, the courage of the very young would on occasion provoke respect and forbearance from Indian raiding parties. Four-year-old Jeremiah Moulton of York, who retaliated aggressively after viewing the murder of his mother and father, was allowed to scamper away into the woods, applauded by his enemies. G. W. Chase, *History of Haverhill*, (Mass., 1861), pp. 198, 207, and 216. Generosity to adults was not unknown. During the War of the Spanish Succession Samuel Butterfield of Groton, attacked while gathering in the harvest, killed a sagamore (chief) and wounded another. Unable to decide whether to burn or whip him his captors asked the squaw widow to render them a decision. She replied 'If by killing him you can bring my husband to life again, I beg you to study what death you please: but if not let him be my servant.' This he became during captivity and was well treated. Samuel Penhallow, *The History of the Wars of New England with the Eastern Indians* (Cincinnati, Ohio, 1859), p. 48.

and New York' where they could 'suck them to death': or in other
words to overburden the main cities with refugees so that the
economy collapsed.[1] This endeavour to depopulate the frontier was
only partially countered by the New England government, but
swollen though the larger communities were, and serious as was the
loss of income from the deserted areas, migration never consitituted
a problem of the dimensions envisaged by the more imaginative
Indians.

The pre-eminent New England expedient for frontier security
was the garrison-house. This was an otherwise normal dwelling-
house but better adapted or more favourably situated than its
neighbours and thus designed to serve as a rallying-point in time
of attack.[2] If sufficient warning was given these strong points provided reassuring cover for the inhabitants, though not their property, and could generally concentrate such strength as to discourage
protracted or determined assault. The thick walls of hewn timber
were bullet-proof but offered adequate loopholes for firing from.
In the attack on York in 1692, when between 50 and 100 were
slain by a force of 300 or more Indians, the four or five garrison-
houses escaped.[3] But the existence of havens such as these offered
no more than minimal assurance and could not prevent the disruption of community life which the ever-present threat of attack
produced. Particularly in the early days after the dominion's
collapse Maine settlers charged Boston with incompetence and a
lack of concern for frontier welfare, accusations which were not
wholly justified.[4] Provincial authorities saw the problem from a
narrower perspective than that of the imperial administration in
London or its appointees. The Massachusetts leaders primarily
sought to protect its economic interests and the major centres of
population. For the sake of outlying parts of the province, especially
during the provisional government, they could scarcely dissipate
the limited fiscal resources and ordnance on the maintenance
of costly fortifications, the worth of which they questioned.

---

[1] *C.S.P.C.*, 1689–92, no. 1282.
[2] Local commanders who failed to use these defences were liable to reprimand.
See Mass. Archives, lxx. 336.
[3] *C.S.P.C.*, 1689–92, nos. 883, 885, and 899.
[4] See the petition of 25 Jan. 1690 which blames the insurrection at Boston.
A bill for the relief of the frontier-towns was before the General Court in the
spring of 1690. Ibid., 1689–92, no. 740; Mass. Archives, xxxv. 348.

Bradstreet and the Revolutionary Council had inherited no treasury funds from the overthrown Andros regime, and offensive operations had to be financed by private subscription or other unusual expedients. Stores of ammunition were very low and, despite several appeals to England from October 1689 onwards, it was not until the following summer that the Lords of Trade agreed to their renewal.[1] The garrison-house, properly utilized, offered lodgements of security in time of concentrated danger until more powerful help could arrive. It could not provide scattered settlers with an effective counter to surprise attack;[2] nothing could.

If neglect there was, then it was pardonable in so far as it stemmed from conscious decision not absence of energy. For in 1690 the General Court endeavoured through the appointment of a special committee to systematize its defence policy by designating frontier towns and dividing the male population into two forces, one half to act as garrison, the other to operate as a flying column to aid threatened neighbouring communities.[3] This defensive strategy, supplemented by offensive sallies against the centres of Indian and French power and underwritten by English naval strength and occasional grants of military supplies from the mother country, preserved an inner circle of immunity. Though southern New England was less secure seaward than the eastern seacoast, in the main 'the sows' survived essentially unharmed and some grew sleek[4] Despite the strains imposed by war, slender means were harboured and utilized with such success that a special moratorium of rates was available at the request of hard-pressed frontier communities. Even so the relatively secure inner core of New England was never able to forget that it was engaged in war in which principles of religion and government as well as the maintenance of prosperity were at stake, and that it was threatened not merely by the overseas resources of its main adversary, and the savage auxiliaries which encircled its frontier, but also by a major concentration of power in the St. Lawrence basin, difficult of

---

[1] C.S.P.C., 1689–92, nos. 513, 523, 797, and 939.
[2] C.S.P.C., 1689–92, no. 899. D. E. Leach, *The Northern Colonial Frontier, 1607–1763* (New York, 1966), p. 162, offers excellent pictorial illustration of the character of these buildings.
[3] Osgood, *Eighteenth Century*, i. 94.
[4] Cf. Carl Bridenbaugh, *Cities in the Wilderness: The First Century of Urban Life in America, 1625–1742* (paperback, New York, 1964), p. 175.
N E—D

access and yet uncomfortably close.[1] In this respect, like neighbouring New York, it served the function of a marcher region,
acutely conscious of the alarums and privations of war in a way
denied to the relatively protected communities south of the
Hudson River.[2]

There was no easy answer to the military policy of Frontenac.
Indian sources of strength were located in the remote wilderness,
60–100 miles up the Kennebec and Androscoggin Rivers, protected
by woods and rivers which hindered movement eastwards of any
sizeable force and, since they were human rather than material,
difficult to destroy save through a patient policy of attrition.[3] If
colonial resources could be sufficiently concentrated the short and
most promising solution was to attack the wasps' nest in Canada.
It required no intellectual *tour de force* on the part of the people of
New England to perceive this.

In contrast to King Philip's War, when the English settlements
were confronted with a struggle bearing some of the features of a
civil war, the conflict which commenced in 1689, as a conflict with
the Indians, was waged along a more or less definite frontier no
part of which was ever wholly secure.[4] Yet during the first year
or so of the war Hampshire County and other parts of the
Massachusetts back-county went unmolested while the north-east
coast was exposed to terrifying assault. Dover in New Hampshire,
the first community to be attacked, was sacked on 27 June 1689.

---

[1] The seaport of Salem, for example, panicked in 1690. A number of the
principal men, disturbed by the deplorable condition of the country's defences,
petitioned the governor and Council to lay the state of the colony before Their
Majesties for relief. Others considered a direct appeal to the king and queen.
Felt, *Annals of Salem*, p. 299.

[2] This is not to deny the occurrence of suffering. The Nine Years War
brought to Virginia a severe and prolonged depression, a scarcity of English
goods, and sufficient threat of Indian and French attack to justify the expensive
deployment of Rangers and militia. See J. Hemphill, unpublished Ph.D. thesis,
Princeton University, 1964, 'Virginia and the English Commercial System,
1689–1713', pp. 5, 6; Bruce, *Institutional History of Virginia*, ii. 118, 121.

[3] By the last decade of the seventeenth century the woods were less amenable
to the passage of large bodies of English horsemen or footsoldiers than they had
been during King Philip's War, possibly owing to diminution of Indian cultivation. A Hadley by-law of 1693 obliged every man to work one day a year clearing
bushes from the highways. Judd, *History of Hadley*, p. 98.

[4] James Duncan Phillips, *Salem in the Eighteenth Century* (Boston, Mass.,
1937), p. 8. In King Philip's War the Indians were interspersed among the white
settlements.

Over fifty people were killed or taken prisoner.[1] More importantly, two months later, the distant and now isolated outpost of Pemaquid faced an Indian host of Penobscots led by their kinsman Saint-Castin.[2] Lieutenant Weems, the officer in command, after a token show of resistance, surrendered and the garrison departed without interference. Later the fort would be rebuilt at the instance of the English government, and maintained in the face of sustained criticism from those in Massachusetts who shared the views of Thomas Hutchinson, the province's eminent eighteenth-century historian, that the fort was too remote to fit into any well conceived plan of defence.[3] No doubt this judgement was mature and well founded but loss of the fort permitted French and Indian strength to concentrate on the most vulnerable settlements east of Casco Bay.

With the support of Plymouth and Connecticut counter-measures were set in motion by the Massachusetts Council. Designed to strengthen existing garrisons a force of 600 men under Major-General Swaine relieved Falmouth (Casco Bay) and attempted to clear the intervening country, though they were unable to prevent an Indian assault on Durham, New Hampshire.[4] A second expedition under Benjamin Church later in September helped to beat off an attack upon beleaguered Falmouth and sought to regain some control over the abandoned area eastwards. But it achieved nothing more decisive than the recovery of the heavy

---

[1] This may have related to the settling of an old score with one of the leading citizens, Major Richard Waldron. Cotton Mather asserted that the rise of this war was 'as dark as the River Nilus' and alluded to provocation of the Indians by 'wild English'. *Soldiers Counselled and Comforted.* See also 'Decennium Luctuosum', *Narratives of the Indians Wars*, pp. 186–90.

[2] A Bernais, married to a chief's daughter, he lived on the eastern bank of the Penobscot river and, partly by reason of his forceful personality, exerted a considerable influence over the Indian tribe to which he was related.

[3] Thomas Hutchinson argued that the English ministry was determined to maintain possession in order to prevent the French from claiming Acadie as a derelict country and perhaps taking possession of it as such. For some reason or other this does not appear to have entered into the calculations of the colonists but the English government was at fault for failing to communicate its purpose—if this was its purpose—and thus unnecessarily embittering relations with the New Englanders. Drake, *Border Wars*, p. 51; Hutchinson, *History of Massachusetts*, ii. 51.

[4] *C.S.P.C.*, 1689–92, no. 482; 513. Edward Randolph claimed that a large part of this force—200 men—was not far off at the time of this attack (13 Sept.) on a fort on the Oyster River. See also 'Decennium Luctuosum', *Narratives of the Indian Wars*, pp. 201–2.

guns from deserted Pemaquid: 'the enemy having retired into the howling Desarts where there was no coming at them.'[1] This may have contributed towards the winter respite which now followed until early in 1690, when a major blow was struck at Schenectady by a force of 210 men, almost half of whom were Indian.

The successful surprise of this New York frontier-settlement and the heavy loss of life it occasioned sent a wave of horror through New England.[2] It did not suffice, however, to alert Salmon Falls on the New Hampshire border which, lulled into a sense of security by deep snow, was attacked seven weeks later by a smaller mixed force led by Monsieur Francois Hertel and by Hopewood, a Norridgewock chief.[3] The third assault, more serious for Massachusetts in its immediate consequences, was directed at Fort Loyal, after the fall of Pemaquid the foremost strong point of the English defence system. In the beginning of May between 400 and 500 men, transported by canoes and led by Portneuf, third son of Baron de Bécancour, and by Saint-Castin, fell upon Falmouth. The defenders, short of ammunition, soon quitted the four garrison-houses and congregated in the fort; but after four or five days of heavy losses and the commencement of mining operations by the besiegers they agreed to articles of surrender. The agreement was kept, observed Cotton Mather scathingly, as those that were made with the Huguenots used to be, and many of the survivors were subsequently murdered by the Indians.[4] The fort was now fired to the ground and news of the capitulation served to demoralize the remaining garrisons of the Casco Bay region.[5] Those at Papoodack and Spurwick (Purpooduck and Spurwink)

---

[1] C.S.P.C., 1689–92, p. 203. Cotton Mather believed that the Northern Indians were originally Scythians who had migrated from Asia.

[2] Sixty killed; twenty-seven captured. New York Col. Docs. ix. 408–35; C.S.P.C., 1689–92, no. 745.

[3] The shock for New England was mitigated by the conviction that both communities were the architects of their own misfortune—the result of negligence and internal division. Daniel Allin told Joseph Dudley that those at Schenectady and Salmon Falls ought to have been hanged if they had not had their throats cut. Sewall, Diary, i. 311.

[4] Lincoln, Narratives of the Indian Wars, pp. 219–20.

[5] It had some reputation for strength among the New England people. C.S.P.C., 1689–92, no. 904. The Lords of Trade commended Governor Stoughton for defending Piscataqua and for the measures he took to annoy the enemy after the capture of Pemaquid. But the surrender itself was stigmatized as 'a reproachful action unworthy of Englishmen'—a charge which stung—not least Cotton Mather. Ibid., 1696–7, no. 604, p. 313.

in Cape Elizabeth, and Black and Blue Point in Scarborough, fell back to Saco and thence to Wells, twenty miles to the south-west. Orders from the government to stay put stemmed the tide of refugees from the east and alone prevented the complete loss of the English foothold in Maine. But Governor Bradstreet was convinced that speedy English help was imperative to prevent the complete ruination of New England. The New Hampshire settlements in particular were now more exposed then ever before and raids on Lampereel River (Newmarket), Exeter, and then Amesbury, all in one week, took a further toll of life.[1]

Raids were no new experience for most of the English settlements. Virginia, like New England, had passed through a major conflict with local Indians only a decade and a half earlier, while New York under Governor Dongan had borne an undeclared war with New France. But the immediate effect of the French-inspired attacks was to impel the colonists to look to some form of collective security to take the place of the former Dominion of New England. Both demand and response were directly related to parochial interests and their degree of vulnerability. As yet there was little evidence of wider vision which transcended provincial horizons. However, there was enough of a common mind to produce an inter-colonial conference at New York on 1 May. Leisler, as well as Livingston and his associates in northern New York, feared for the security of Albany. These feelings were shared by Connecticut and Massachusetts. They denied any capacity to offer substantial aid because of Indian depredations yet agreed in conjunction with Plymouth to raise a company for the reinforcement of the town. The New Englanders were especially concerned that the cost of garrisoning their own frontiers as well as the planned expedition

---

[1] Drake, *Border Wars*, p. 54; Lincoln, *Narratives of the Indian Wars*, p. 220; *C.S.P.C.*, 1689–92, nos. 905, 981. Cotton Mather in his accounts of the war more frequently describes his fellow-countrymen as English than as New English. During the raid on Exeter one unfortunate had been appallingly wounded and left for dead. He had been shot nine times and his Indian assailant by two hatchet blows had attempted to sever his head. An 'Irish fellow', so Mather relates, proposed for the sake of humanity to complete what the Indian had begun, but 'the English, detesting this barbarous advice', succeeded in reviving him. He recovered and led subsequently a more vigorous life than the Irishman who as the result of an accident with his gun that same day was made a cripple for life. It is evident that the New Englanders regarded themselves as members of a nation in which the Irish were not included. See *Boston News-Letter*, Monday, 17 Apr. 1704.

to Nova Scotia should be taken up by other colonies. Independently the Leisler government and the Massachusetts General Court approached their immediate neighbours and the Chesapeake provinces of Virginia and Maryland with a view to consultation and a more equitable sharing of burdens.[1] The response was disappointing. Massachusetts, New Plymouth, and Connecticut alone sent delegates. No colony south of the Hudson attended. But a vital decision was taken to attack New France by land and sea. New York agreed to furnish 400 men, Massachusetts 160, Connecticut 135, and Plymouth 60.[2] Rhode Island promised to raise £300 as a contribution to the expenses of the expedition, and Maryland to send 100 armed men. Virginia, under Nathaniel Bacon, the president of the Council, argued an inability to make any commitment.[3]

In the meantime, influenced by the demands of the merchants of eastern Massachusetts, notably John Nelson and Joseph Appleton, that their trading and fishing enterprises be protected from the French, and by desire to counter the charges and designs of Randolph and Andros with actions which would demonstrate a devotion to the interests of the empire, Massachusetts moved independently against Port Royal.[4] Her expedition departed in two sections a few days before the New York conference opened. One part, comprising five ships under the command of Governor Phips, left Nantasket at the southern entrance to Boston harbour on 28 April, and prepared to attack the Penobscot fort before joining with the other—which had sailed from Salem—at Mount Desert. But Saint-Castin was gone and the fort empty, and a few hours after meeting with the Ipswich and Salem companies in their two ships on 5 May, the united force sailed for the Bay of Fundy. Within less than a week it was safely in Port Royal harbour and

---

[1] Osgood, *Eighteenth Century*, i. 80, 81; O'Callaghan, *Documentary History*, ii. 249.

[2] *C.S.P.C.*, 1689–92, nos. 865, 524, and 745.

[3] Osgood, *Eighteenth Century*, i. 81; *New York Col. Docs.* iii. 697–9, 709.

[4] Cotton Mather describes the addition to the English empire of a territory improvable for lumber, fishing, mines, and furs, but this is placed secondary to the purpose of putting an end once and for all to their troubles from 'Frenchified Pagans'. *Pietas in Patriam: The Life of His Excellency Sir William Phips* (London, 1697), p. 31; Miller, *New England Mind*, pp. 160–3. Paul Chrisler Phillips, *The Fur Trade* (Norman, Okla., 1961), i. 315, argues that since the fur-bearing animals of New England had been exterminated by 1689, and Nova Scotia and present New Brunswick were particularly rich in beaver, the expedition against Port Royal received the cordial support of the Massachusetts fur-traders.

had accepted the surrender of a poorly prepared garrison. Two days of looting and plunder were followed by the demolition of the fort and other defence-works and the removal on board ship of all the pieces of heavy ordnance.[1] The inhabitants under duress were obliged to take an oath of allegiance to King William and Queen Mary. Plans were made for the permanent occupation of the region and for its commercial exploitation. A Council was immediately established to lay hands on any French vessels which came within its precincts but also to prepare the foundations of the New England way. Members were instructed to prevent profanity, sabbath breaking, swearing, drunkenness, and thieving. It was hoped that under such guidance the behaviour of the inhabitants would quickly change.

The ships of the expedition arrived safely back in Boston harbour early in the morning of 30 May, just over a month after their departure.[2] An uneventful return voyage had completed a neat and successful operation. If there were casualties or losses through sickness no account of them has survived. Some New Englanders thought a great conquest had been achieved, even if its merit was somewhat lessened by knowledge that the garrison at Port Royal, reduced to eighty-five men, had been without any mounted guns. Others argued that the gains here did not counterbalance the losses at Casco.[3] Mather regarded the event as insignificant in itself, 'only a step towards a far greater action', a view most certainly held by other leading New Englanders. Even before the expedition had sailed Governor Simon Bradstreet informed the Earl of Shrewsbury that its underlying purpose was to encourage the people to an attack on Canada.[4]

To this objective all effort was now bent. *Delenda est Carthago* became the peroration of every speech about defence and the resolution of all New England, as well as New York. In the eyes of New Englanders, Canada was the wellspring of their suffering, the source whence Abenaki savages received their war supplies. The

---

[1] The amount did not defray the cost of the expedition, estimated at £3,000 more than the value of the plunder. See comments of James Lloyd, merchant of Boston. *C.S.P.C.*, 1689-92, no. 1282.

[2] Journal of the Phips Expedition (Boston, Mass., 1690), a copy of which is in the British Public Record Office, NE 5, no. 109; and see *C.S.P.C.*, 1689-92, no. 914.

[3] Ibid., 1689-92, nos. 899, 904.

[4] Lincoln, *Narratives of the Indian Wars*, pp. 214, 797.

main thrust to the north was to be made by sea and Phips was again the leader. But illfortune dogged this ambitious enterprise from the beginning. Delay was occasioned by a shortage of arms and ammunition. Supplies sent for in the spring had not arrived by the following August and on departure the expedition suffered serious deficiency: the flagship had only fifteen barrels of gunpowder and for the fleet as a whole there were perhaps no more than seventy.[1] Difficulties also occurred in raising men. When the inducement to plunder failed to bring in enough recruits, impressment became necessary to provide a force of 2,300.[2] Even so the leaders appear to have done nothing to discourage the belief of the rank and file in easy victory.

The fleet, divided into six squadrons of thirty-two ships, and the soldiers under Major John Walley of Barnstaple, left Boston on 9 August, but encountering adverse winds in the St. Lawrence lost further time in face of a winter already far advanced. In the absence of a single pilot it took three weeks instead of the anticipated three days to get down to Quebec which was not reached until 5 October.[3] Meanwhile on land 1,500 Indians and 500 whites drawn from New York and Connecticut, and led by Colonel Winthrop, assembled for a diversionary attack on Montreal. Hindered by smallpox, lack of supplies, and dissension, the expedition ground to a standstill at the southern end of Lake Champlain.[4] Here, on 15 August, a council of war decided to abandon the campaign, although a small force of whites and Indians, less than 150 in number, pushed on to raid the village of La Prairie and the countryside about Montreal. Relieved from serious pressure, Frontenac was emboldened to transfer resources from Montreal to Quebec, hitherto ill-defended in men and cannon and almost without ammunition.[5] It was claimed by deserters that some 3,000 new men were added to the garrison. Provisions became scarce, the

[1] C.S.P.C., 1689–92, no. 1282; Pietas in Patriam, p. 33.

[2] G. S. Graham, Empire of the North Atlantic (Toronto, 1951), p. 71; Mass. Archives, lxx. 165, 172.

[3] Pietas in Patriam, p. 34.

[4] Channing, History of the United States, ii. 530. G. S. Graham put the New York force at 1,000 excluding Indians. The best account of this expedition, in R. S. Dunn, Puritans and Yankees, pp. 290–2, argues for a three-pronged assault, including a diversionary feint into Maine, designed to prove to William the worth of the revolutionary colonial governments.

[5] Lincoln, Narratives of the Indian Wars, p. 35.

price of wheat was high, and before the siege ended several persons had died of starvation.[1] Thus augmentation brought new problems, though not to be compared with those the English encountered and created. But it is probably true, as Mather argued, that had the diversionary operation fulfilled the expectations of those who had planned it the conquest of Quebec would have been achieved.

Two days after the arrival of Phips the first landing was made, smallpox preventing little more than half the force being brought ashore.[2] The plan was to place the soldiers on a beach about two miles from Quebec, to move as close as possible before nightfall and then encamp—being provisioned and supplied during the dark, preparatory to crossing a small river which separated the expeditionary force from the besieged town. Such ammunition as was initially issued, no more than fifteen to eighteen shot apiece, appears to have been wastefully used. When at midnight the small vessels arrived they brought six field-pieces (useless on the marshy ground) but no provisions and only half a barrel of powder for over 1,000 men. Further, the four ships of war, contrary to orders, instead of mounting a concerted bombardment of the city, employed their cannon and exhausted their resources in random firing against the rocks of Quebec, 'like men in a fright' it was said.[3] Alarmed at the size of the garrison, and at the large force of Frenchmen believed to be approaching through the swamps, and daunted by the fortifications now erected on the river barrier, men began to re-embark. Few lives had as yet been lost, but through negligence and confusion five or six field-pieces were left on shore, as well as drums and colours. On 12 October a new attack was postponed, not surprisingly in view of the lack of adequate ammunition. Demoralization, advanced by the onset of unusually severe autumn weather, was completed by a storm which scattered the fleet and led to the loss of three ships. What had been predicted as an easy victory now became a shameful failure. Losses from military action appear to have been slight but sickness and shipwreck inflated the figure to almost half the original force.[4] For

---

[1] *C.S.P.C.*, 1689-92, no. 1921.

[2] Ibid., 1689-92, nos. 1299, and 1314. Mather argues it was made on 8 October.

[3] Ibid., 1689-92, nos. 1239, and 1314.

[4] Phips gave a figure of thirty (or less) but Sloughter later contended that non-military causes raised this number to 1,000. Ibid, 1689-92, nos. 1282, and 1417; and see Guttridge, *Colonial Policy of William III*, p. 52.

many the consequences were delayed, but it is said that after the survivors arrived back home men 'died up and down like rotten sheep' from smallpox and fever.[1]

Serious consequences for New England, both immediate and long-term, resulted from this disaster, as expected. But New England's maritime expedition had sought to advance the interests of old England as well as her own, and English colonists from beyond the region also predicted the effects of what was undeniably a scandalous reverse on land and sea. Governor Nicholson feared that a lessening of influence over the Five Nations and the military weakness of the Quaker colonies would now permit the war to reach the head of the rivers in Pennsylvania, Maryland, and Virginia.[2] An increased danger to Albany, defended by slender resources of men and ammunition, was inevitable.[3] Voluntary co-operation among the colonies, demonstrably difficult to organize upon a satisfactory and equitable basis, had brought only failure and further discord. Leisler, in arresting the leader of the overland expedition for cowardice, had driven a wedge between the two northern regions upon whose co-operation a satisfactory defence against New France depended.[4] He was reminded that the army which had turned back was no more than a confederate body, a fact of significance which did not escape those critics of provincial government who fervently petitioned England for a restoration of that union they had but recently lost.[5] Upon release Winthrop resolved to give no more assistance until Leisler was superseded by a governor sent from England.

Massachusetts, her treasury empty, had reason to be disturbed at the return of a military force which she had planned to pay with plunder taken from a conquered enemy. Not only had the cost of the expedition added between £40,000 and £50,000 to her provincial debt, but for want of wages the soldiers were on the point of mutiny.[6] They were not disposed to wait for the operation of an act of the General Court designed to levy the necessary money.

---

[1] C.S.P.C., 1689–92, no. 1239.

[2] Ibid., 1689–92, no. 1164.

[3] Ibid., 1689–92, no. 1127.

[4] Ibid., 1689–92, no. 1282.

[5] Address of Several Merchants and others of New England to the King, October, 1690, ibid., no. 1157; Address of divers inhabitants of Charleston, Boston and places adjacent to the King [April], 1690, ibid., 1689–92, no. 1393.

[6] Ibid., 1689–92, nos. 1239, 1282; 1693–6, nos. 110, 273.

Accordingly the debt was paid in paper notes which were to be received as payment for the tax and for all other payments into the treasury. But the notes could not command money nor any commodities at money price, and despite the efforts of Phips to make the scheme work equitably soldiers in the main got no more than twelve or fourteen shillings in the pound.[1] Mather applauded this expedient as 'better than if the mountains of Peru had been removed into these parts of America' and argued that the bills would have kept their value, had not so many people feared that the government would be overturned within six months and their bills of credit converted into waste paper.[2] But to critics of the revolutionary government this was not reparation, and if God's hand was evident in the failure of the Canadian enterprise, New England, for a multiplicity of reasons, remained divided as to its meaning.

The form and character of security were beginning to change. It seems almost beyond doubt that at this moment in the shock of defeat, when the capacity of the enemy seemed terrifyingly enlarged, William could have revised the government of New England in any way he thought fit, short of abolishing representative institutions, without arousing serious opposition. For its people, who by their sense of purpose and reading of history had defended themselves with such skill and resolution in the past, were at last caught with their guard down, bewildered and enmeshed in fear. After 1690 times were not so prosperous in Massachusetts. The revolutions had not directly disturbed the colonial economies but the effect of curtailment of trade with France was more serious. The spread of smallpox, the indiscipline of returned soldiers, and, more importantly, the heavy losses of Boston merchants who had helped to finance the expedition were contributory factors. The gloom of failure permeated every level of New England life.[3]

Provincial expedients seem to have attracted a criticism which might justifiably have been levelled at those who carried them out. Later writers, assessing Phips as a man unequal to the political and military tasks he undertook, have dismissed him as ignorant, brutal, violent, and covetous. Among contemporaries, however, he

[1] Hutchinson, *History of Massachusetts*, i. 341.   [2] *Pietas in Patriam*, p. 44.
[3] *Mass. Hist. Soc. Proc.* (1878), p. 105; *Mass. Hist. Soc. Coll.*, 5th ser. viii. 305; W. B. Weeden, *Economic and Social History of New England, 1620–1789* (Boston, Mass., and New York, 1890), i. 353, 356; J. Belknap, *History of New Hampshire* (Philadelphia, Pa., and Boston, Mass., 1784), i. 263.

escaped serious loss of face. Despite his remaining on shipboard
throughout the Canada campaign, few ascribed failure to the in-
adequacies of his leadership.[1] The reputation for courage was, if
anything, enhanced by his recorded behaviour before Quebec.[2]
Cotton Mather, the scholarly eldest son of Increase, who dedicated
his life to interpreting God's plan for New England, diagnosed
unavoidable disaster in which Phips was not a culpable instrument.[3]

The naval defence of New England, supported by guard ships
of the Royal Navy, was primarily designed against pirates and
privateers. Under General Governor Andros, as has been noted,
coastal defences consisted of the frigates H.M.S. *Speedwell* and
H.M.S. *Mary* and two sloops.[4] No major French assaults had ever
to be contended with, apart from the attacks on Pemaquid fort,
though serious danger never appeared very far distant. In the early
autumn of 1691 news was received at Boston that a fleet, including
two warships, had arrived at Quebec with plans to cruise between
Port Royal and Virginia.[5] This project was scrapped, however,
probably because of the expedition from Albany. But a little later
two French men-of-war were reported off the coast of Nova Scotia.[6]
News of the eagerness of Frontenac to try his hand against the
New England metropolis continued to disturb the whole province.
It was said he had sought permission to take Boston with only
eight men-of-war.[7] And the following year he was rumoured to
have asked Louis for twelve frigates and 2,000 soldiers for a
descent upon Boston and New York.[8]

French seapower remained visibly alert off the coasts of Nova
Scotia and Newfoundland but near her own shores rarely did New

---

[1] *C.S.P.C.*, 1689–92, no. 1313.

[2] See *Mass. Hist. Soc. Proc.* (1901), p. 281. A document, of which John Wise
of Ipswich was probably the author, adds cowardice and indiscipline to the
causes of failure, placing responsibility indirectly on the shoulders of Walley.
Thomas Hutchinson says that he was censured by particular persons but
there was no official inquiry. *History of Massachusetts*, i. 340. 'The Account of
Thomas Savage' denies the guilt of Walley and implies there was endeavour
to make him the scapegoat: *C.S.P.C.*, 1689–92, no. 1314.

[3] *Pietas in Patriam*, pp. 52–3.

[4] *C.S.P.C.*, 1689–92, no. 912.

[5] Ibid., 1689–92, no. 1857.

[6] Ibid., 1689–92, no. 1910.

[7] Ibid., 1689–92, no. 1918.

[8] Ibid., 1693–96, no. 43.

England contend with more than the lone privateer. Solitary French warships were not common: two reported in company in 1692 caused considerable excitement. Yet privateers unaided could do damage enough.[1] They were believed to infest the New York coast, and Salem, an important community north of Boston, is known to have suffered heavily from losses at sea.[2] Injury was widespread during the earlier years of Anglo-French conflict. In the summer of 1690 when the French were particularly active, a privateer, later brought to action, took thirteen ships; New London Connecticut, was fired upon, Martha's Vineyard threatened, and a small raiding-party succeeded in landing on Cape Cod.[3] Later, in May 1695, a small pickaroon captured seven vessels, including one with £1,000 in money aboard, before the frigates were able to get out.[4] But apart from Cape Cod, landings on the seacoast south of the Piscataqua were rare, though islands off the mainland continued to be vulnerable.[5]

Block Island, in southern New England, attacked by the French no less than three times during the course of the war, appears to have been the most dangerous location. The first landing, carried out by a man-of-war and a sloop, was countered by sending two sloops and about ninety men who forced a re-embarkation and chased away the hostile fleet. The following summer the governor of Rhode Island reported that Block Island had again been assaulted and plundered by a privateer which shortly after departure captured three vessels and threatened Rhode Island itself. The third descent was in 1693 when a privateer, subsequently taken by H.M.S. *Nonesuch*, landed parties on the island and seized several

---

[1] Ibid., 1693–96, no. 227.

[2] By the close of the Nine Years War only six ketches remained out of a pre-war total of some sixty odd. Sidney Perley, *History of Salem* (Salem, Mass., 1928), i. 296; *C.S.P.C.*, 1689–92, no. 482.

[3] Cotton Mather noted that in the first two or three years of the war English maritime losses had been assessed at more than £15 millions. No part of the English nation, he argued, suffered so severely as the people of New England whose losses sufficed to make a large fleet. Cotton Mather, *Magnalia Christi Americana*, ii. 671; New England Merchants to the Council of Trade, *C.S.P.C.*, 1702–3, no. 1369.

[4] *C.S.P.C.*, 1693–6, no. 644. Rhode Island's refusal to support the Canada expedition was partly justified by her large unguarded coast which gave her 'no strong bulwark against the enemy'. ibid., 1689–92, nos. 1586, 1593.

[5] Towards the end of the war Martha's Vineyard and Nantucket were each urged by the General Court to spend £150 on fortifications in return for remission of taxation arrears. *C.S.P.C.*, 1696–7, no. 274.

Rhode Island ships. More were later taken by a second vessel. These events were used to justify refusal to contribute towards the landward defences of other provinces. Rhode Island contended that her own seaward frontier occasioned a heavy charge. For Massachusetts the events of the summer were even more alarming when a French corsair landed 130 men at Sandwich on Cape Cod. Fortunately the force was completely defeated. Two companies of militia took the expedition prisoners while the Royal Navy frigate *Nonesuch*, commanded by Captain Dobbins whom Phips himself had promoted, chased and captured the ship. This was Anglo-American co-operation at its most felicitous. Well might Cotton Mather offer special thanks for the protection and strength of the navy. In the last year of the war Portsmouth, Salem, and Boston on more than one occasion observed formidable French squadrons pass by to the southwards and then return frustrated in their intentions. Because of the Royal Navy, it was noted, 'our Lord Jesus hath encamped here'.[1]

For most of the period of war frigates of the navy patrolled the New England coast. Against an elusive enemy they met with varying success. Clashes of temperament and interest between ship's captain and colonial governor, the need to maintain a full complement of men as cheaply as possible by drawing upon colonial sources, and provincial desire to direct the employment of the king's ships for local ends, all provided abrasives to the Anglo-Massachusetts relationship, though with no serious consequences at this stage. Captain George of the *Rose* had been incarcerated and his ship immobilized as a result of revolution against the Andros administration. But to Boston merchants the restoration of this ship to active service was of primary importance.[2] Salem, too, was eager to obtain protection, especially for ketches fishing off Nova Scotia, and requested that a ship of war be permanently available.[3] But following some useful enterprises terminated by the death of her captain, the *Rose* went home in May 1690 and not until the first half of 1692 was she replaced.[4]

---

[1] *Magnalia Christi Americana*, ii. 676, 677. In 1696 the Assembly advised an expedition to Port Royal to destroy several privateers fitting out there: *C.S.P.C.*, 1693–6, no. 2294.

[2] Barnes, *Dominion of New England*, p. 244; *C.S.P.C.*, 1689–92, no. 196, enclosure i.

[3] Mass. Archives, xxxv. 1.   [4] *C.S.P.C.*, 1689–92, no. 985.

The Lords of Trade seem not to have awakened to their responsibilities until the end of 1691 when the Admiralty reported its intention to send the *Conception Prize* to New England after convoy to Virginia and Maryland. Realizing that New England would be defenceless, as it had already been in this respect for eighteen months, the Lords asked the king that a frigate should be sent immediately and supplemented, if possible, by a fifth-rater from Nova Scotia.[1] Presumably the *Nonesuch* was ordered out, for we find her on this coast by July and appearing in company with the *Conception*. But within two years New England was again laid bare when on the order of Governor Phips the *Nonesuch* went back to St. John's and the *Conception* was laid up for a survey of defects. Seizing this opportunity French privateers took five fishing-boats from a province without means of seaborne defence or resources for convoy, save a small boat of seventy tons built by order of the previous Assembly.[2]

By the end of the war, in face of increased French activity on the seas, naval strength was greatly augmented. H.M.S. *Newport* was taken in the Bay of Fundy by Iberville *en route* to capture Pemaquid, but in the summer of 1696 New England had available H.M.S. *Arundel*, H.M.S. *Sorlings*, and H.M.S. *Orford*, a hired ship of thirty-six guns, the *Province Galley*, and a fire ship. This force removed the French garrison on the St. John's River, captured the great guns and other warlike stores recently brought from France, and chased French forces from Mount Desart.[3] Twelve months earlier Massachusetts had asked for naval reinforcements to supplement the two frigates upon the coast, in part to relieve one of them to convoy vessels to the West Indies to load salt for the fishery at Salt Tortugas.[4] Its petition of August 1695 went unread until the following January and not until May 1697 was any recommendation made upon it. Then the Lords of Trade agreed to a fourth-rate frigate undertaking this task, the annual escort convoying the mast ships to New England to have charge of other merchant ships outward and homeward bound. The delay is

[1] Ibid., 1689–92, no. 1998.
[2] Ibid., 1693–6, no. 1089.
[3] Mass. Archives, cvi. 400; *C.S.P.C.*, 1693–6, p. 132; ibid., 1696–7, no. 243; Osgood, *Eighteenth Century*, i. 113.
[4] *C.S.P.C.*, 1696–7, no. 483, enclosure i, 1023.

unaccountable unless the augmentation observed above had been resolved upon prior to the petitions receipt.

Several important factors limited the energy released by war. Personal and jurisdictional conflicts were a pervading feature of colonial administration at all levels. Phips, who as governor developed a personal quarrel with the captain of the *Nonesuch* and ultimately removed him from command, was defeated in an endeavour to use the frigates for defending the coast of Maine during the worst months of the winter. Both the captain of the *Nonesuch* and the captain of the *Conception* feared that ice would damage the vessels and returned them to Boston in November 1692. The need to maintain an adequate crew posed an abiding problem. Seamen's wages were higher than in Europe and men-of-war wintering in New England ports were accustomed to lend out their crews for two to four months to work on shore. This practice increased the landsmen skills of English sailors and fostered and enlarged opportunities to desert. A small vessel endeavouring to sail in the spring might be deficient in crew between forty and sixty men. Impressment was thus regarded as essential and men might be taken at sea while fishing, or on land.[1] In meeting this problem the arrogant conduct of the commanders of His Majesty's ships provoked colonial wrath and in due course restrictive legislation.[2] Hereafter any captain desiring to make up his crew was obliged to apply to the governor or commander-in-chief who, as Vice-Admiral, had sole right of impressment in any of his plantations or in sight of them.[3] The decision to confer such power, taken at the close of the war in October 1696, facilitated the manning of

[1] Weeden, op. cit., p. 369; *New York Col. Docs.* v. 194; Mass. Archives, lxi. 374, 414.

[2] See *C.S.P.C.*, 1697–8, no. 7. At the end of October 1697 Sir Henry Ashhurst reported on the dearth of seamen, which prevented ships leaving Boston harbour. Impressment, though a serious source of complaint, was only one of the factors involved. Members of the press-gang were attacked in broad daylight. Ibid., 1689–92, no. 2283.

[3] Ibid., 1696–7, nos. 604, 721; Mass. Archives, lxii. 161. Jamaica appears to have suffered more severely from this ill than New England. Depopulation was attributed to the activity of the press which drove away seamen and privateers. Migrants were said to be going mainly to the northern colonies. A proposal that merchant ships carry supernumeraries for the supply of men-of-war was turned down by the Admiralty as impractical. The order in Council which eased the problem for the colonies did in fact give captains the right to impress men if governors failed to assist them. *C.S.P.C.*, 1696–7, nos. 48, 97, 101, 233, and 333.

H.M.S. *Falkland* and H.M.S. *Orford*. Probably over half the complement of the latter were New Englanders.[1]

Supplementary to the forces of the Royal Navy were those of local origin. These units were small and frequently hired on a temporary or *ad hoc* basis rather than owned outright by the province. Governor Andros had possessed the provincial sloop *Mary* and the *Speedwell*, a small ketch. The primary purpose of both was to enforce the navigation laws.[2] In September 1689 the *Mary* was ordered to cruise against pirates. Later the *Speedwell* was sent to England to replenish provincial powder supplies, and there was sold to a private buyer by the provincial agents, despite the contention of the Lords of Trade that she belonged to the king.[3] Governor Phips claimed that his locally built yacht of 150 tons was the equal of a sixth-rate, half the expense, and could follow French privateers where larger ships could not go. He proposed that she should release the *Conception* for service elsewhere.[4] After the capture of Port Royal provincial vessels, one of them built through private subscription, were used to patrol Nova Scotian waters. They were again employed in 1690 to search for a French vessel which had landed at Cape Cod. In the winter of 1695 the *Province Galley* cruised between Martha's Vineyard, Block Island, and the Sholes, protecting and convoying coasters and vessels from other provinces. Of shallow draught, she was adjudged much more effective then frigates assigned to this station.[5] Under Captain Cyprian she continued to operate until the end of the Nine Years War, and in 1697 cruised for long periods about the Capes and convoyed Virginian, Pennsylvanian, and Connecticut vessels between Massachusetts, Martha's Vineyard, and Rhode Island. She proved to be of great service and undertook her work without the loss of any of her charges. Another local ship, the *Newport Galley*, was lost while patrolling the Bay of Fundy.[6]

---

[1] *C.S.P.C.*, 1696-7, no. 333; Mass. Archives, lxii. 169, 274. Impressed seamen of colonial origin gained some protection of their interests through the provincial government.

[2] A hired ship—the *William and Mary*—which was discharged from service in 1692 was again hired later in the year because of increased activity by privateer. *C.S.P.C.*, 1689-92, nos. 2234, 2237.

[3] She had cost £211. 6s. 8d. Mass Archives, xxxv. 375.

[4] *C.S.P.C.*, 1693-6, no. 237.

[5] Mass. Archives, ii. 228A; *C.S.P.C.*, 1693-6, no. 176.

[6] Mass. Archives, cvi. 400; *C.S.P.C.*, 1693-6, p. 132.

The burden of keeping provincial ships at sea was a heavy one and induced Massachusetts as the war drew to its close to instruct her sister province in her duty to the English nation:
The advantage that has and will accrue thereby unto the people within your Government in the preservation of their vessels and estates from loss makes it highly rational that they should bear part of the charge as they partake of the benefit; and is no other than what their Majesties justly expect from all their subjects to contribute their assistance and proportionable share of the charge for prosecuting a *national war*.[1]
Connecticut was not very responsive. She did not deny the existence of obligations but argued against assistance till the weather grew warmer. An important part of the problem for Massachusetts related to manning. In this operation many competitors were faced. She complained that men were drawn off to fill out the complement of new ships built in the province by 'strangers' and were thus permanently lost: the needs of the frigates were an additional burden.

In the latter half of 1690 two attempts were made, one theoretical, the other practical, to deal with the immediate problem of securing the Maine frontier. In September Major Church and 300 men set out by way of Casco Bay and Pojebscot fort to attack the principal Abenaki village and fort forty miles up the Androscoggin River. He was accompanied by a further force of 300, under the command of Major Robert Pike of Salisbury, drawn from the eastern garrisons of Massachusetts and including the renowned Indian-fighter Captain Converse of Wells.[2] This large body of men burned the fort but secured only a handful of captives. Its main achievement was to incline the Indians to a truce, established at Wells on 23 November, which provided a brief winter respite.

The assault was renewed at the end of January by an attack on York, a community on the seacoast close to the New Hampshire border with houses stretching for a mile and a half along the river, and carried out in a raging snowstorm. Despite the fate of Schenectady, a warning to all ill-guarded communities, no watch was posted and between 50 and 100 were slain. The four or five garrison-houses escaped untouched, but few inhabitants were able to reach the safety of their thick bullet-proof walls. Later in the summer, under the inspiring leadership of Captain Converse,

[1] Mass. Archives, ii. 228A.
[2] Drake, *Border Wars*, p. 71; Osgood, *Eighteenth Century*, i. 93.

Wells, a straggling village to the eastwards with relatively small manpower resources, beat off a force of 400 Indians and some Canadians led by Baron Saint-Castin, Portneuf, and a few additional French officers. This was welcome instruction that even the more exposed villages could achieve a measure of security. It was a morale-booster in more senses than one, in view of the desperate financial position which led the governor and Council to seek an immediate loan of £1,000 through private appeal in the counties of Suffolk, Middlesex, and Essex.[1]

The consequences of exhaustion were evident enough. Surgeons were reluctant to serve with eastbound forces because of the unlikelihood of being paid. Many recruits were of poor physical quality, ill-armed, and almost destitute of clothing. The Massachusetts authorities without ready resources were obliged to request the regimental majors to beg clothing and provisions for the troops. While they were faced with these anxieties, instructions arrived from the king to begin rebuilding Pemaquid fort. The country was in general hostile to this proposal on the grounds that the fort was neither convenient as a post for any marching parties sent out to discover the enemy, nor for the settlers of the frontier to retreat to.[2] Small though the expense may have seemed to the English, it was a relatively heavy charge for an exhausted community which now bore the additional cost of Indian onslaught threatening south and west of the Merrimac River. In July and August small attacks on families in Lancaster, Brookfield, and Billerica brought home to Massachusetts the extent of her exposure.

Hampshire County had suffered severely in King Philip's War when five towns were broken up. Of these, four—Suffield, Deerfield, Northfield, and Brookfield—were resettled by the mideighties and by the close of the decade this western county possessed ten towns and plantations. But though strict watches and patrols deflected hostile attack four years in succession, the strain of frontier life was nevertheless severe. Recollection of past experiences, and frequent alarms in the present, part of the hazards and difficulties of farming under front-line conditions, were

---

[1] Drake, *Border Wars*, p. 76; Osgood, *Eighteenth Century*, i. 95, 96, 97. The latter claims that the composite force of French and Indians attacking Wells was 500 men.

[2] Hutchinson, *History of Massachusetts*, ii. 51.

coupled unpleasantly with the heaviest burdens of taxation.[1] Small
communities might lose half their families, as did Northfield
through a single attack in June 1689. Here guns were carried to the
meeting-house every Sunday, and wandering Indians proved a
constant source of apprehension.[2]

During 1691 150 Indians arrived from the Hudson and encamped about Deerfield, with their wives and children, being
forced thither by scarcity of provisions. Deerfield nervously
regulated their hunting to no more than five to a party and cautioned
against excessive use of alcohol. But when three or four whites
were killed in 1693 suspicion immediately fell on these 'Albany
Indians' as they were called, though the true culprits were probably Canadian braves. They continued to dwell before Deerfield
and Hatfield until the latter part of April 1697 when they departed
for good, but they had been a source of much disquiet on the
western frontier.[3] Elsewhere in the county, though many people
were taken captive, deaths resulting from assault, twenty-eight in
all, were not heavy. The attack on Brookfield, in July 1693, when
six people lost their lives, seems to have been among the heaviest
blows suffered in this region. Some towns, such as Westfield,
wholly escaped Indian depredations. Hampshire County possessed
a population estimated at 2,500. From this was raised a militia not
far short of 600. As with the Maine communities the burden of
service was onerous but it aroused less complaint than did the
taxation it entailed.

The over-all defence problem faced by the province of Massachusetts Bay was complicated by ambiguous responsibilities.
The commission of Sir William Phips, appointed governor in
November 1691, gave him command of the militia of Rhode
Island, New Hampshire, and Connecticut. Rhode Island contested
this power as contrary to her charter and forbade her own officers,
whom he displaced, to accept dismissal without permission. In
justifying her actions to the Lords of Trade she stressed historical
antipathy to the Bay colony and a superior record of attachment to
the English Crown. Though this did not sway the determination of
the Attorney-General to uphold Phips, the sentiments were a tiny

[1] See ch. iv, pp. 159–60.
[2] Judd, *Hadley*, pp. 248–52.
[3] Ibid., pp. 252, 257; Revd. J. H. Lockwood, *Westfield and its Historic
Influence, 1669–1919* (Springfield, Mass., 1922), i. 266.

counter in favour of the adverse image from which Massachusetts was endeavouring to escape.[1]

With New Hampshire the relationship was equally complex. Tiny resources in manpower offered no comfort for a colony so exposed to hostile attack. The force of 120 men which the Bay province maintained there during the winter of 1692-3 was a highly valued contribution to security, and generally speaking there was no aversion to the continuance of military control by Massachusetts. But the New Hampshire proprietary, if not the Assembly, feared military aid as a prelude to the reassertion of political control. John Ussher, lieutenant-governor and son-in-law of the governor and proprietor Samuel Allen, urged, without success, the sending of an independent company to guard the Piscataqua River. He accused Phips, and was in turn accused by him, of neglecting to provide adequate protection for the people of New Hampshire. Phips charged that nothing had been contributed towards the cost of the war and Ussher complained of under-manned defences, of pleas for help ignored, and of peace made with the Indians without the knowledge of his province. The fears of New Hampshire were most acute during the summer of 1693 when, with 750 men under arms, she faced—as she believed—a threat of imminent assault.[2]

Connecticut, to which New Hampshire had also lodged an appeal for help, had equal if not graver difficulties of her own. Exposed by the Connecticut valley which bisected the colony from north to south, she received demands to aid Massachusetts in Maine and New York at Albany. Moreover, the valley towns outside her borders being more accessible to her own forces than to those of her northern neighbour, to which they belonged, added to her burdens. When in the winter of 1692-3 Phips asked the Connecticut General Court for a quota of whites and Indians to serve on the north-east frontier it was replied that all men were needed for the defence of the valley, a contention which could not be lightly swept aside. However, though promise was made to send £400 in provisions and pay at Connecticut rates, the following year Phips angrily countered that Their Majesties expected the colonies

---

[1] J. R. Bartlett (ed.), *Records of the Colony of Rhode Island and Providence Plantations in New England, 1636-1792* (Providence, R.I., 1856-65), iii. 285-300; *C.S.P.C.*, 1693-6, no. 723; Osgood, *Eighteenth Century*, i. 101.

[2] *C.S.P.C.*, 1693-6, nos. 216, 250, enclosure i; 284, 454, 648.

to shoulder an equal proportion of the common charges of the war. But in May 1693, after a fresh evaluation of the relative importance of the twin thrusts of French power, the Lords of Trade transferred control of the Connecticut militia from Phips to Governor Fletcher of New York.[1]

On the north-eastern or Maine frontier, the rebuilding of Pemaquid fort opened a new phase of the war. Located to cover the Kennebec, Damariscotta, and other small rivers draining the coast between the Kennebec and the Penobscot it was intended to keep the Indians out of the rivers and to encourage the settlers to return to their homes. But remote, exposed, overlooked by a nearby rock, and capable of reinforcement only by sea, it was never garrisoned strongly enough to play more than a defensive role. Many in Massachusetts believed that an important reason for its building was the fashion in fortifications which now influenced Europeans, but more searching opinion grudgingly conceded that while the fort might be ill-situated it served to underwrite a territorial claim to this contested region. Occupied by between 60 and 100 men it was, moreover, a fort of unquestionable power, one of the largest and strongest built by the English during the colonial period, and mounting eighteen guns of which six were eighteen-pounders.[2]

Also part of the renewed effort of Massachusetts under Phips was the despatch in early August of an assault party led by Major Church. This first raided the coast and islands about the Penobscot River, and then penetrated the Kennebec, causing the Indians in despair to fire their own corn and also their fort at Tecconet (Winslow).[3] A more important expedition was mounted the following spring when Phips sent away Captain Converse, with the best officers and men the province could provide. Ranging first in the Wells area, Converse next went to Pemaquid, navigated the Sheepscot River, and then marched through the woods to Teconnet without encountering any of the enemy. This force,

---

[1] Osgood, *Eighteenth Century*, i. 102.

[2] Hutchinson, *History of Massachusetts*, i. 336; Lincoln, *Narratives of the Indian Wars*, pp. 240, 241. Cotton Mather argued that this fort broke the (Indian) enemy's heart. He was, however, critical of the expense entailed when the country was so much impoverished. The Council in 1693 had asked the king to pay the cost of rebuilding. *C.S.P.C.*, 1693–6, no. 100.

[3] Lincoln, *Narratives of the Indian Wars*, pp. 241–2.

however, had effectively kept the Indians on the move and prevented them from assembling for their usual raids on the settlements. In due course the party returned to Saco where, within six
miles from the sea, on orders from the Council, they erected a new
fortification in the form of an irregular pentagon designed to cover
the Saco settlements and, as a trading centre, to act as a counter-
magnet to the French.

The renewed activity of the English, shortage of ammunition,
and the approach of the dreaded Maqua army (that part of the
Iroquois nation reputed to have destroyed two million savages
between the Mississippi and the Atlantic) overwhelmed French
influence at Pentagoët (Castine) and led the eastern Indians to sue
for peace. In early August thirteen principal chiefs, gathered at
Pemaquid, bound themselves in subjection and obedience to the
king of England.[1]

A year's breathing space had now been bought, though the
truce was observed with no more than Indian fidelity.[2] Financial
exhaustion induced Massachusetts to take advantage of the respite
by an immediate reduction of the frontier garrisons. Paradoxically,
this act helped to create an air of false security, despite the killing
of isolated settlers and the capture of others. But a decisive rupture
to the disturbed peace did not come until the attack on Oyster
River (Durham), New Hampshire, in the summer of 1694. It was
swiftly followed by a descent on Groton in northern Massachusetts.
Oyster River, about twelve miles from Portsmouth, was assaulted
by a large force of Indians led by the important chiefs Madockawando and Moxus of the Penobscot. Also included were St. John's
Indians and some Norridgewock of Father Bigot's. The English
community possessed twelve garrison-houses but most of the
people slept in their homes. Losses were heavy. Half of the town-
houses were burned and between 90 and 104 persons killed.[3]
Groton escaped rather more lightly though the military watch had
been ineffectively kept. Here, as in Oyster River, the garrisons held

---

[1] There is record of a highly-organized French attempt against Pemaquid,
plans for which were revealed to John Nelson, then prisoner of Frontenac.
The information being passed to New England beforehand, the garrison was
strengthened. When the two-ship expedition did arrive the fort was judged too
strong to be attacked. Drake, *Border Wars*, p. 88; Hutchinson, *History of
Massachusetts*, ii. 54–5; *C.S.P.C.*, 1693–6, nos. 273, 522.

[2] Hutchinson, *History of Massachusetts*, ii. 55.

[3] Sewall says 90; Mather, 94 or 100; Ussher, 93.

out, but in scattered parts of the village twenty-two people were killed and thirteen captured.[1]

For the next two years, before the dramatic fall of Pemaquid in July 1696, there occurred little that was of significance on the eastern frontier. The year 1695 was generally quiet, apart from scattered slayings about the Pemaquid region and along the Maine coastline. English treachery in the renewed negotiations of February 1696 provoked fresh massacres, and in June and July attacks occurred around Portsmouth and at Dover.[2] The successful assault upon Pemaquid was of a different nature. It comprised two warships, commanded by Le Moyne d'Iberville and Baron Saint-Castin, and a mixed force of Indians picked up at St. John and Penobscot. Captain Chubb, English commander at Pemaquid, had ninety-five men, well-armed, fully provisioned, and equipped to withstand the assault of a much larger force. On hearing news of his capitulation Mather felt that New England manhood was disgraced. Writing as much for an English as a New England audience he lamented: *O merae Novanglae, neque enim Novangli* [O mere New England women, not New England men]![3] But he sought to counter inevitable criticism from outside the province, such as the cutting remarks of the Board of Trade that it was "a reproachful action unworthy of Englishmen", by comparing it to the English surrender in 1695 of St. James's fort in Africa.[4] Chubb, who had given in after only a few shells had been fired, was parolled with his men and sent to Boston, where after a few months' imprisonment and trial for high treason he was acquitted and released.[5]

The advantage was now with the French. 'By land, the Indians being so posted in all quarters that the people could hardly stir out.'

---

[1] Lincoln, *Narratives of the Indian Wars*, p. 254. In response to a plea from the town of Groton the General Court now sent thirty men to protect the frontier in that area and eight troopers to range the ground for Indians about the town: 23 Aug. 1694, *C.S.P.C.*, 1693–6, no. 1256. Total losses during the summer were estimated by the Council and Assembly at more than 150. Ibid., 1693–6, no. 1466.

[2] Lincoln, op. cit., pp. 259–60; Drake, *Border Wars*, p. 105.

[3] Lincoln, op. cit., p. 262.

[4] Mather showed similar sensitivity when describing the failure before Quebec: 'Yet they did not leave Two Hundred men behind them to the mercy of the French, as they who most Reproached New-England, soon after did at Guadalupa.' Ibid., p. 215; *C.S.P.C.*, 1696–7, no. 604.

[5] Mass. Archives, lxx. 307, 336; *C.S.P.C.*, 1696–7, no. 146, p. 144; Osgood, *Eighteenth Century*, i. 113.

But casualties were few, only about half a score of people, picked off at random, mainly while working in their fields. As counter-measures Colonel Bartholomew Gedney moved out with 500 men to strengthen the garrisons, and Major Church was ordered north-east to the Bay of Fundy, as far as Chignecto Bay, where he landed at Beaubassin and plundered and burned. Thence Church joined a third force under Colonel John Hawthorn, who assumed over-all command, to attack the French fort at St. John, 'the nest of all the wasps that stung us'. But the difficulty of the cold season so dis-couraged the New Englanders, as Cotton Mather observed, that after making some few shots 'the Enterprise found itself under too much Congelation to proceed any further.'

Nova Scotia, Maine, the Massachusetts coastline, Rhode Island, Block Island, Connecticut, and the Connecticut valley constituted the main defence ring of the Bay province. Beyond, but related to important strategic and economic interests, was a broader northern arc upon which were Albany, Hudson's Bay, and Newfoundland. In two of these theatres, at various stages of the war, there was direct involvement in co-operative military ventures. On the Albany front the burden of opposing the French and Indians was beyond the resources of New York alone. The degree to which Massachusetts perceived this is not easy to ascertain with any certainty but the concerted attack on Canada in 1690 is some indi-cation that the need to obstruct this gateway to the colonial sea-board was understood in Boston.

This apart, Britain intervened from time to time to direct the employment of colonial resources, although away from the acces-sible maritime regions such action was never more than spasmodic. But in the autumn of 1692 her attention was focused upon the expedient of requisitions. Circular letters were sent to all govern-ments from Virginia northwards, Rhode Island and Connecticut excepted, requiring assistance in men and money on application from the governor of New York, an action which points to the strategic priority accorded to Albany over the Maine frontier, but one which also suggests that the British little appreciated the extent to which Massachusetts had already expended resources on its own various fronts. The size of the contribution was to depend upon the assent of each individual governor.[1] Similar instructions

[1] *C.S.P.C.*, 1689-92, nos. 2533, 2543, and 2547.

to co-operate with New York were sent to Connecticut and Rhode Island the following February; at the same time specific sums of money were requested from Virginia and Maryland. The proposals were without effect but Phips, having declared that he would do his best for the safety of his neighbours, made clear that he intended to co-operate.[1] The British now indicated their conviction that Massachusetts had been contending for local rather than imperial interests by transferring command of the Connecticut militia to the governor of New York.[2]

The interest of the mother country in the problems of the northern colonies culminated in plans to employ a force under Sir Francis Wheler's command which had been sent to the West Indies in the winter of 1692-3. This was to reach New England by the early summer, there to refit in preparation for attack upon Canada. Phips was instructed to organize ships, men, and provisions against the arrival of the expedition and to consult with the governor of New York about the part that province should play.[3] These moves indicated a significant change in emphasis in favour of New England's control and guidance, though the end-product was broadly in accord with the interests of New York also.

Wheler was in New England by early July, but with much reduced numbers. Out of two regiments not more than 650 of all ranks remained, and the fleet had lost more than half its complement. The remainder were in poor health, though the ships were well-provisioned and in good order. Phips who had continued to stress the importance of the conquest of Canada now opposed an assault on Quebec. In his belief 1 July was the latest date for departure which gave any assurance of success. It is likely he recalled the role played by the weather in the earlier fiasco. Furthermore, the force available was much below the envisaged figure of 4,000 men. Half was to be formed from colonial contingents but Phips denied that instructions had arrived in time to gather these

---

[1] Lincoln, *Narratives of the Indian Wars*, p. 216. Governor Fletcher reported that Connecticut sent no answer, Pennsylvania sent good wishes, and East Jersey forwarded £248 with a promise to raise the sum to £400 later. From the rest, he claimed, he had not heard. Phips he dismissed as 'a machine moved by every fanatical finger, the contempt of wise men and the sport of fools'.

[2] *C.S.P.C.*, 1693-6, nos. 92-7.

[3] Ibid., 1693-6, no. 116.

together. Fletcher had received them but he, Phips, had not.[1] As alternative objectives he encouraged Wheler to harass French merchants at St. Pierre and Placentia but was disinclined to co-operate in an assault upon the latter, arguing that Assembly consent was needed to march the militia out of the province and that all available manpower would be absorbed by expeditions against the Indians in Maine.[2]

In the meantime, New York explored ways by which Wheler's resources and the strength of Massachusetts and other colonies might be diverted for the benefit of the Albany front.[3] Though Phips reported to the home government, without comment, the arrival of a representative from the neighbouring province, a request for 200 men fully equipped and paid by Massachusetts provoked his violent anger. He refused to contribute man or money, and declined to send commissioners to New York in October for a projected conference.[4] The outburst was ill-advised but not wholly unjustified. More thought should have been given to supporting the Indian allies of New York who became increasingly hardpressed as the war went on. But the direct dangers to the New York settlements, still shielded by the Iroquois confederacy, were grossly overrated. The resolve of Phips to concentrate his resources on the defence of New England was a reasonable one. Chidley Brooke of New York, who was convinced that the government of Massachusetts was corrupt, felt obliged to concede that the people there were highly taxed. The shortcomings of Phips were obvious and evident, but there is no reason to doubt his assessment of the cost of armed conflict for New England. New York, like other provinces, was ready to accuse her neighbours of avoiding sacrifice comparable to her own but failed to appreciate either their particular problems or the attendant dangers they faced.

The larger colonies were burdened alike by taxation and fearful

---

[1] Ibid., no. 441. No instructions to Phips have survived save a draft letter announcing that Wheler's squadron would arrive in New England in May for an attack on Canada. A copy of this was not received until a few days before the fleet sailed for England, at the end of July. There is no reason to suppose that Phips's disappointment at a lost opportunity was not genuine. Ibid., nos. 136, 545, and 578. See Guttridge, *Colonial Policy of William III*, p. 75

[2] *C.S.P.C.*, 1693–6, no. 475.

[3] Osgood, *Eighteenth Century*, i. 107–8; *C.S.P.C.*, 1693–6, no. 460.

[4] Ibid., 1693–6, no. 486; *New York Col. Docs.* iv. 58.

for their own security: Virginia, no less than her sisters to the north. In the event of overwhelming assault there was no assurance of rescue or restoration: no traditional reservoir of strength to call upon. Provincial survival could not be taken for granted. At least until La Hogue gave England a decisive victory at sea, the capacity and potential of French power was terrifying; the colonial future cold and uncertain. By bitter observations upon the inequality of wartime sacrifice, governors and assemblies acknowledged local interests and revealed the limits of their understanding of the nature of the war. But they also exposed the irrationalities of the political structure which now housed the English nation.

In a tightly-knit community unequal sacrifice is tolerated for the sake of ultimate good. Revolution had created a true community of political interest in place of an uncertain one. War with Catholic France provided more favourable circumstances than peace for its continuance. No British administration, however, perceived or utilized community purpose in any coherent form save in terms of the northern fur trade and the over-all military and economic strength of the empire. Though such concepts were not valueless they did not significantly tighten the bonds of the English nation nor counter the forces of embedded parochialism. No governor, and certainly no assemblyman, confronted with a metropolitan government unwilling to accord overseas Englishmen any but a subordinate or secondary role, can be blamed for first consulting the interests of his own province. With few exceptions colonial assemblies logically organized their resources for the protection of that part of the English nation they represented.[1] If British administrations were unable to clarify strategic priorities in North America and to marshal resources when they were needed, then complaint could not be fairly made against assemblymen who failed to extend their vision beyond mere local objectives.

The difficulties of marshalling the resources of separate provincial governments remained almost insuperable. In the summer of 1693 invitations were issued by Governor Fletcher to a new inter-colonial conference to meet in October. They were accompanied by a scheme for a levying of manpower from the continental

---

[1] See for example the reply of Connecticut in response to a request from New York in 1691. Similarly Maryland and Virginia considered their defence commitments were different in kind from those of the northern colonies. Osgood, *Eighteenth Century*, i. 234, 235.

colonies, based upon an estimate of their male population.[1] This was a lead in the right direction and the Lords of Trade, the next August, followed suit with proposals of their own. Contributions from Virginia, Massachusetts, Maryland, and Rhode Island were doubled, eighty men were ordered from Pennsylvania and specific power was given to the New York governor to command a force from New Jersey not exceeding 700 men. The aim was to provide 2,000 men for the defence of Albany, of which no more than one-tenth were drawn from New York. Yet not one single man was forthcoming and only minute financial aid was received.[2]

Colonists were little-concerned with minor theatres of war where their forces were not immediately engaged. The campaigns of King William in Ireland were too important to escape attention and the vast preparations for war there were duly noted by Samuel Sewall.[3] Major victories were made known through official sources, information being supplemented from incoming ships. The volume of detail about the land war in Europe, given a decade later in the *Boston News-Letter*, suggests that the appetite for news of this order was almost insatiable. While no doubt it was stimulated by an official organ of dissemination it is unlikely that the foundations of this interest were lacking in the 1690s. Some colonists perceived the difficulties and dangers which derived from dependence upon irregular and marginally reliable sources. William Byrd observed 'We are here at ye end of ye World and Europe may be turned topsy turvey ere we can here a Word of it, but when news come we have it by whole sale, very often much more than truth.'[4] But transatlantic news was of a different order from North American. All too often diaries that have survived are silent even about significant events within regions of direct concern to important provincial interests. Not surprisingly the means were inadequate for assessing at all accurately or sympathetically the impact of the conflict upon colonies other than one's own and particularly upon those not involved in its more dramatic occurrences. An egocentric

---

[1] *C.S.P.C.*, 1693-6, p. 173.

[2] Ibid., 1693-6, nos. 1176, 1253, and 2063. Massachusetts Assembly refused permission for the militia to be taken out of the province but granted £50 toward the purchase of gifts for the Indians. Ibid., 1693-6, no. 2075.

[3] Sewall, *Diary*, i. 329.

[4] William Byrd Letter Book, MSS 5, 2B 9965/1, pp. 50, 58A, and 59. Byrd, a Virginian planter, himself published false news of outward-bound fleets in order to raise drooping spirits. 26 Feb. 1692, *C.S.P.C.*, 1689-92, no. 2075.

view of the war, aware only of the narrowest provincial interests, or one conscious of the importance of events in Europe, was commonplace. More sophisticated perception among colonists was rare.

The difficulties of the French *habitants*, though they differed in nature from those faced by the English colonists, were no less severe. If the year 1691 saw Massachusetts out of breath and downcast after her exertions against Quebec, it found New France equally depressed by the weakness of her resources. Among a population swollen by refugees from the Newfoundland fisheries, food and ammunition were so scarce that troops were unable to leave their forts to combat enemy raiders.[1] Without hope of reinforcements from France Frontenac felt obliged to turn the war of skirmishes into a system of assault. Borrowing from the methods of the Iroquois he developed a style of fighting costly in men and equipment, but suited to the Canadian genius and military predicament. Pierre le Moyne, Sieur d'Iberville, member of a gifted family and tactician of great brilliance, added innovations of his own. But this form of warfare could not achieve the reduction of the Iroquois, nor ensure the undisputed control of the fur trade and the fisheries. To Frontenac it remained a second best; for New France on its own lacked resources to destroy New York, and after 1694 French seapower was not available to provide the necessary support.

The greatest French successes were achieved against Hudson's Bay and against English fishing-bases and trading-posts in Newfoundland. Contest for the former, and indirectly for the command of the beaver trade, centred about Fort York. Although in 1693 the English recaptured Fort Albany, which had been lost some time before, a dispirited garrison at York capitulated the following year to Iberville. York was retained for three years, lost, and then in 1697, the ubiquitous Iberville recaptured it for the French. It is doubtful, however, if happenings in remote Hudson's Bay gave New Englanders much cause for concern.

Newfoundland was different. Like the West Indies it was within their economic orbit and hardly less important to them than Nova Scotia. The interest was long established. Fish was sold to English

---

[1] Henri Lorin, *Le Comte de Frontenac* (Paris, 1895), p. 396; Bonnault, op. cit., pp. 142, 143.

merchants who frequented the landing-places, and a market was also developed for agricultural products.[1] French control of the whole island, the primary fear of New Englanders, would bring heavy losses and a grave blow to their region's economy. French settlers were few, according to the census of 1687. Less than 700 were scattered between Placentia, Pointe-Verte, Fortune, Cap Nègre, and l'Hermitage.[2] They were opposed by half as many more English distributed in eleven communities. The latter won an initial success in 1690 when Placentia was surprised by a raiding party from Ferryland—one of the English settlements—consisting of three sixty-gun ships and two smaller vessels commanded by Commodore Williams. Town and port were taken with only trifling bloodshed. Two years later a second attack on the town failed, while a more formidable assault led by Admiral Wheler was turned aside by bad weather achieving no more than the pillage of the island of St. Pierre.

Neither side had the resources to retain their conquests. Frontenac countered first by using French privateers to harry the English settlements. Captain William Holmes at Ferryland beat off an attack in 1694, but during the next twelve months eight large privateers wrought widespread destruction among English vessels and installations; and in 1696 Ferryland fell to an expedition from St. Malo. Then, while Iberville burned the isolated English outposts of the eastern coast, M. de Brouillan, governor at Placentia, assaulted Rognouse, Fermouse, and Forillon, in the south. Together the two leaders destroyed the English forts and turned on their commercial centres.[3] By 1696 England held only Trinity and Conception Bay. On the eastern coast Bonavista and Carbonear alone had escaped destruction. Faced by such a critical reversal of fortune, England resolved to re-establish the Newfoundland communities and revive the fishery. English and New English interests coincided, and the king and Lords of Trade thought it fitting that New England should give all possible assistance to the proposed expedition, by supplying victuals and

---

[1] W. S. Macnutt, *The Atlantic Provinces: The Emergence of Colonial Society, 1712–1857* (London, 1965), p. 4.

[2] Gabriel Hanotaux and Alfred Martineau, *Histoire des colonies françaises et l'expansion de la France dans le monde* (Paris, 1929) tom. i: *L'Amérique*, pp. 90, 91.

[3] Hanotaux, *Histoire*, i. 89.

provisions, and by sending such ships and land forces as might be
spared to join it between Cape Race and Bonavista. New Englanders were roused by fear that completion of the French conquest
would be but the prelude to a major descent upon New England
itself.[1]

The New England diarists carry no observations on events in
Newfoundland. Even the *Decennium Luctuosum* fails to acknowledge that the English had suffered a reverse, possibly because New
England forces were not directly engaged there. Yet the consequences were alarming, and the Board of Trade hastened to warn
Lieutenant-Governor Stoughton that the next step of the French
would be to fall upon New England.[2] The seaboard of Massachusetts, endangered by the critical state of English power to north,
was further threatened by the loss of Fort William Henry, and by
renewed activity on the eastern frontier and at Albany. A general
deterioration in the state of the outer defences explains why
Massachusetts in particular, and the mainland provinces in
general, began to perceive the value of collective security in the
shape of some form of political union.

The ghost of the Dominion of New England was raised by proposals designed to embrace much the same territory that Andros
had once governed, and also designed fundamentally to solve the
defence problem he had once faced. But this time colonists confronted administrators with plans of their own making. England,
for her part, was moving towards acceptance of the need for a
more powerful executive: an important step had been taken in
June 1695 with the decision that the Earl of Bellomont should
succeed Phips as governor of Massachusetts. It was first resolved
that he should be given command of the militia of New Hampshire
and the Narragansett Country, and of the quota of Rhode Island.
During the absence of King William on the continent of Europe
the Lord Justices of England, in pursuing the re-unification of New
York and New England, went even further. They were primarily
concerned to provide a revenue for royal governors, but particularly for the governor of New England, in order to free him from
dependence upon the general assembly. But it was also perceived

---

[1] D. W. Prowse, *History of Newfoundland* (London, 1895), pp. 222, 225:
Graham, *Empire*, p. 76; *NCMH*, vol. vi, ch. xv. pp. 488–9.

[2] 20 Jan. 1697, *C.S.P.C.*, 1696–7, no. 604.

that re-unification would offer both colonies mutual advantages for offence and defence.[1] However, when the commission for Bellomont was finally drafted memorials from several quarters, and not merely that of the Lord Chief Justices, were taken into consideration.

From New England one such representation had been made by the lieutenant-governor, William Stoughton, and his Council in December 1696. This alluded to the experience of 'a wasting war', the advance of the French interest, and the languishment of King William's. Trade between north and south had greatly decayed and the sources of naval stores were threatened; help from Connecticut, New Hampshire, and Rhode Island had been unsatisfactory or nonexistent. For these reasons it was requested that the several governments be joined for the prosecution of the war. Stoughton also proposed that Port Royal and St. John, in Acadia, be settled by the erection of a regular fortification and by the supply of a garrison and stores of war at the expense of the royal exchequer, 'a greater bridle on the enemy than Pemaquid could be'. But the reduction of Canada 'the unhappy fountain from which issue all our miseries' was urged as the foundation for any decision.[2] Unofficial moves concerning the question of re-unification may have taken place behind the scenes in London, for at the end of January, 1697 there was a meeting between the Lords of Trade and 'gentlemen concerned in New England and the neighbouring colonies'. On this occasion the New England agents took a leading part in pressing the consideration of a number of memorials. All were agreed on the necessity of re-uniting New York and New England, but over the form of union there was division.

Three memorials were initially considered. That of the agents of Massachusetts, Sir Henry Ashurst and Constantine Phips, laid stress on the annexation of New Hampshire, 'a chasm in the very bowels of the province', a receptacle for the disaffected and for those who evaded their duty in defence of the province. Twenty-nine other memorialists, including proprietors and northern colonists, lamented the loss of fishing, furs, masts, timber, and peltry trade alike in Newfoundland, New England, and New York. In their eyes, unless the enemy was checked, the subversion of the

---

[1] *C.S.P.C.*, 1693–6, no. 1893; 1964; ibid., 1696–7, no. 800.
[2] *C.S.P.C.*, 1696–7, no. 483, enclosure i.

English mainland colonies loomed as a possibility. Union was the sole remaining means for the protection and preservation of interests. Despite the unfortunate precedents of the Andros regime there was a prevailing conviction that rights and customs could be safeguarded satisfactorily, even under a powerful executive. The third paper, presented by Edmund Harrison, gloomily predicted the separate destruction of each colony as a logical consequence of particularism, a factor which outweighed the English advantage of a larger population over-all. He proposed that the governor of New England should also be civil governor of New York and New Hampshire, and general of the combined forces of all three, together with those from Connecticut, Rhode Island, and the Jerseys. He envisaged not merely a more effective defence but also sufficient offensive power to drive the French from North America. Harrison defended the past behaviour of New Englanders, contending that they had been discouraged by having mean and oppressive persons set over them. Though he believed they should not be obliged to march out of their own territories yet their attendance on Phips indicated a readiness to obey persons of honour and temper. Supported by two allowances which the king was to provide, one for each of the two main provinces, a supply of distinguished men endowed with such qualities would be ensured for the future.[1]

The opponents of these proposals found no difficulty in defending the prevailing system of government despite the exigencies of war. The proprietor of New Hampshire stubbornly urged the independency of that province. More important were the contentions of Connecticut. The Lords of Trade were quick to consult Major-General Winthrop, then in London. Winthrop's opinion was expressed within a restricted parochial frame of reference. Connecticut was accustomed to choose its own leaders, he observed. To impose a governor upon them, with power to demand arms and ammunition and to lead the inhabitants out of the colony without their consent would be a hardship, and contrary to the charter. The importance of retaining power of consent was essential. Moreover, far from favouring integration within a wider union, he drew attention to Connecticut's own claims to the Narragansett country.[2] New York's case was stated at length. It was conceded

---

[1] *C.S.P.C.*, 1696–7, nos. 651–3, Osgood, *Eighteenth Century*, i. 267–8.
[2] Dunn, *Puritans and Yankees*, p. 309; *C.S.P.C.*, 1696–7, nos. 689, 690.

that a single military command could achieve compliance with requisitions, so wanting in past years of conflict. However, sound argument was advanced to the effect that Boston and New York were the metropolitan centres of different systems which could not be bound together politically without leading to the depression of one and the advancement of the other.[1]

The Lords of Trade gave careful consideration to all these proposals and to the specific objections made against them. In their final decision they were primarily influenced by the diverse forms of colonial government which seemed to render any union, save under a military head, impracticable. Failure of the colonies to comply with the regulations of 1694, however, convinced them of the need for a more vigorous executive power. To this end they recommended the appointment of a fit person to be governor of Massachusetts, New York, and New Hampshire, and captain-general of all the forces in Connecticut, Rhode Island, and the Jerseys. His residence was to be at New York although with the right to move to Boston from time to time. Such a system, it was believed, would induce the various general assemblies to recognize their true interests and to enact such laws as would enable a captain-general to execute his commissions.

The Lords had appraised colonial forces and sentiments with some degree of sensitivity. In seeking to mediate between conflicting claims, without sacrificing imperial interests, they had shown a judicious care. The Massachusetts agents appeared to have gained all they had contended for, but they had wrongly assumed that under a combined governorship the resources of New York would be utilized for the defence of the eastern frontier. The commission

---

[1] Ibid., 1696-7, no. 691. More balanced consideration of the interests of New York had been advanced by Peter Delanoy.

'I wish the King would put a General Governor over New England, New York and the Jerseys, so as the Assemblies, Courts and Laws of the respective provinces might be left separate. For our laws and manner of trade differ much, and the distances between us would make it uneasy if the rest of the provinces resort to anyone for common justcie. But a union under one Governor would be very convenient, particularly in time of war, and would be a terror to the French in Canada, who assume boldness purely from our divisions and the piques that are too common among the several Governors.' (Ibid., 1693-6, no. 1892, p. 506.)

Sir Henry Ashurst and Edmund Harrison were both opposed to a union settled by Parliament, which it was feared would create delay and cause a clamour about the people's rights. ibid., 1696-7, no. 704.

of Bellomont made clear that the purpose of New England was to
protect the fur trade and the fishery in Newfoundland and to
help safeguard the Albany front. Since a European peace was
imminent, and the expedient of political union allowed to terminate
upon the governor's premature death, it had little direct effect
upon Anglo-Massachusetts relations. It had, however, revealed the
hollowness of the special relationship, and demonstrated that the
two 'partners' were as unequal in influence as they were in population. The New England helmsman could navigate an imperial
man-of-war independently only when the officers were divided
among themselves and distracted by the dissensions of the crew.
Otherwise his skill was denied, and his steering guided by stars
other than his own.

Peace between England and France was signed on September
10/20, 1697. The settlement of Ryswyck left the boundaries and
outposts of New France substantially unchanged but Newfoundland and Hudson's Bay, theatres of war in which decisive actions
had been fought, were treated as regions in which French influence
predominated. William III, who had made the interests of the
Company a cause of war, was not prepared to risk a peace for their
continued pursuit.[1] Thus in important respects French power in
North America was unchecked, a reminder to New England that
the insecurity, which had loomed large at the end of the reign of
James II, still remained. This was particularly true for the fishery
which faced an awakened French interest. But Cotton Mather,
who spoke complacently of 'the English Continent', welcomed the
tidings of peace as 'the break of Day after a long and sad Night'
and found no cause to criticize their detail. Indeed he seemed to
find its blessings even a little overshadowed.

When the Schools of the Jews delivered, That there were Three Great
Gifts of the Good God unto the world, The Law, the Rain, and the
Light, R. Zeira [Rabbi Zeira, a Palestine *amora* of the fourth century
A.D.] added "I pray let us take in Peace for a Fourth". All these Four
Gifts of God are now Enjoy'd by New-England; but I must now ask,
that our Hope of a Fifth may be added unto the Number; which is a
Governour of Signalized Virtues.

Governor Bellomont was hailed as 'the Greatest Person that

---

[1] For a discussion of those aspects of the Peace related to Hudson's Bay see
Gertrude Jacobsen, *William Blathwayt: A late Seventeenth Century English
Administrator* (New Haven, Conn., 1932), pp. 320–3.

ever set foot on the . . . continent of America'.[1] There was, however, some small reason for rejoicing. An eminent personage carrying powers beyond a mere governorship of Massachusetts promised an improved liaison with England, better, at least, than Phips had been able to obtain. It made thought of a new war less terrifying. In the meantime for the Bay province peace did not bring an immediate end to hostilities. The severest winter in living memory was followed by scattered killings in the summer of 1698. Not until mid-October was a meeting arranged at Penobscot through which an exhange of prisoners was effected.

[1] 'Decennium Luctuosum', *Narratives of the Indian Wars*, pp. 276-70.

CHAPTER IV

The Supports of the Massachusetts Tradition and the Sources of Provincial Wealth

'WE have now languished through ten years which have been the saddest and stormiest that ever we saw.' So wrote Cotton Mather, 'the priest of war', as the seventeenth century drew to its close.[1] The sense of bewilderment and concern evident in Mather's thought is reflected in the many printed sermons which survive this period. It does not solely relate to external factors. The theocratic purpose of Massachusetts Bay had first been seriously compromised by the aspirations of a rising mercantile element which had begun to exert a significant influence in politics during the Restoration.[2] But having looked to England for support and liberation from the restrictive rule of the Puritan theocracy, the merchants had been disenchanted by discovering that more direct monarchical supervision through General Governor Andros was no less narrow and even more threatening to property. The dissolution of the Dominion of New England led to a new division in the emergence of a Patriot or Country Party, led by Elisha Cooke, senior, which, dissatisfied with the charter of 1691, sought a restoration of the 'liberties' and 'independency' enjoyed earlier in the century. But the theocrats, who had negotiated the new charter under the guidance of the Mathers, now sought viability through close co-operation with the Protestant rulers in England and their ministers. In so doing they were better placed to align

---

[1] Mather, *Magnalia*, ii. 658–9, 669.

[2] See Bailyn, *New England Merchants*, pp. 170, 176, 178, 190, and 191. Bailyn argues that, by the time of the Glorious Revolution, New England merchants, well aware of their dependence upon highly-placed individuals in England, had neither desire nor capacity to separate themselves from the English community. Merchants representing a spectrum of interest supported royal governorship—as instituted by the charter of 1691—and sought political influence in the province through representation on the Council. Bailyn denies they were strongly motivated by religion, or closely tied to staunch Puritans, but admits that most of the merchants were closer in mood and sentiment to the sober Samuel Sewall than to the fashion-conscious Samuel Shrimpton who considered himself a member of English society.

their forces with the substantial commercial elements who desired influence within the churches. Yet this assumption of amiable intent could not ensure a return of unequivocal authority.

In important respects the theocratic state would rise again but its foundations had been seriously disturbed and the power of its rulers demonstrably weakened.[1] No one in the mother country had a mind to further the work of restoration. Moreover, the old élite, challenged on many sides—by the growth of the sects, the development and ambition of the Anglican Church in the colonies, the intransigent parochialism of the frontier communities, and a pervasive secularization working particularly upon and through a disturbed younger generation—was itself riven by new 'liberal' currents within the New England Churches.[2] Many of the forces for change—or disintegration—operating within the province of Massachusetts Bay appeared to be singularly potent and antithetical to an educational system designed to safeguard traditional values. But because no alternative destiny under the Universal Monarch of France or his exiled Stuart cousin was conceivable, war served to lessen the impact of internal divergences and to impose a rough but countervailing unity. Further, careful allowance must be made for the resilience and efficacy of institutions and social procedures which were largely able to absorb the energy of internal forces and to survive essentially unaltered the threats and depredations of a terrifying external foe.

The central thread in New England life, in which was embodied the concept of mission, 'the innermost meaning of both nature and economics', was the covenant with God.[3] The gradual decline of spiritual awareness which New England experienced did not suffice to destroy or seriously distort this social elemental. None

---

[1] Cf. Reed, *Church and State*, p. 21. It is here contended that lack of provisions regarding church and state in the new charter of 1691 enabled the General Court to renew the ecclesiastical framework without exceeding the law. Reed further contends that 'in elaborateness of detail and rigid formality the theocratic system reached its highest development in the first quarter of the eighteenth century.' The 'conscience' clause, however, which is recognized as being the only limitation, proved a very serious impairment of theocratic power. See ch. v, pp. 162–7.

[2] See the sermons preached by the Revd. Benjamin Wadsworth: *Mutual Love and Peace among Christians* (Boston, Mass., 1701), which spoke out against the 'great contentions, shameful Strifes, grievous Divisions', cited in Miller, *New England Mind from Colony to Province*, p. 248.

[3] Ibid., p. 403.

but the very strongest-minded individual could consciously reject it, and only a countervailing force of major dimensions, and none was forthcoming, could eject it from the unconscious. Towards the close of the seventeenth century the regard of the New Englander for such a notional view of life was subject to a changing reality in which the intrusion of England's policy of centralization and the threat of outright French success in North America figured largely. Membership of the English nation had assumed a new importance, even if intellectually it posed problems regarding the nature of New England's identity.

Consciousness of the common peril to Protestant values encouraged the Mathers to exaggerate the significance of the United Brethren in England (who by 1690 represented a successful attempt by Congregationalists and Presbyterians to pool their resources), and later ensured a receptive climate for the views of the widely-travelled Francis Makemie that dissenters and Anglicans should minimize their differences and form a united front.[1] The theocratic élite, the Mathers, Benjamin Colman, Solomon Stoddard, William and Thomas Brattle, John Wise and John Leveret, Ebenezer Pemberton, John Higginson, and Nicholas Noyes, to mention the leading protagonists, were each of them, though at odds among themselves, concerned with the need for coherence in face of the threat of disintegration which had been enlarged by the transformed and perilous state of the world external to New England's borders. None was wholly ignorant of this world. Leveret, sensitive to intellectual developments in England, as president of Harvard after 1707 introduced to the college curriculum recent Anglican divinity and Henry More's *Enchiridion Ethicum*. In 1713 he was elected Fellow of the Royal Society. As is well known, Increase Mather spent considerable periods of his life in old England, valued the esteem in which he was held there and, in the face of declining influence in New England, contemplated permanent exile as a hardship not beyond bearing. Benjamin Colman, who during his four-year stay in the mother country in the second half of the 1690s became widely acquainted with the English dissenters, preaching regularly at Bath, enlarged his experience by suffering capture at the hands of a French privateersman and incarceration in a French prison. Thomas Brattle studied abroad and travelled

---

[1] *Truths in a True Light* (Edinburgh, 1699); Miller, op. cit., p. 264.

extensively. Even Stoddard, at the outset of his career, had spent two years as chaplain to the Congregationalists in Barbados and had turned from visiting England only because of the invitation to preach at Northampton in Massachusetts. There are many evidences to indicate that this intellectually purposeful community with its firm sea-going tradition, even if nakedly self-centred in its pursuit of interest, possessed at most levels an extended perspective of the world in which those interests operated.

Nor were the leading theocrats blind to the need to embrace, absorb, and employ the mercantile and propertied element personified by Richard Wharton of the Atherton Company or by the more complex Simon Bradstreet. Men such as these, for the sake of expanding economic opportunities and securing their holdings, supported a simplified Anglo-American purpose which stressed material objectives; provided that purpose acknowledged and underwrote the principles of representative government and the basic political liberties associated with it. But the political world of New England in which the theocrats, hindered by their own divergences, moved during a generation of war was bounded at one extreme by the parochial reactionary Elisha Cooke, senior, who yearned unrealistically for the privileged cocoon of the earlier charter, and at the other by the mature Tory imperialism of New England-born Joseph Dudley, governor after 1702. The latter, reversing the priorities of the theocrats, envisaged an Anglo-American relationship in which the resources of Massachusetts were employed for purposes defined by the mother country.

The growing materialism, for which the provincial religious leaders made allowance in their calculations, also finds expression in their own thought.[1] The value of Protestantism to the English nation could be expressed without embarrassment in pounds sterling. Increase Mather had learned the necessity of reconstructing the relationship with the mother country upon a realistic and viable plane during his mission to England in the 1680s. In partnership with his son, though not without serious concessions to petty objectives and personal considerations, he sought to preserve New England society by a rationalization of Church organization along quasi-Presbyterian lines, and at the same time to strengthen the overseas ties by reconciling local forms with those of

[1] Ibid., p. 397.

the United Brethren. It was not until 1705, however, by which time the United Brethren in London were failing and a renewed Anglican threat to New England was emerging, that delegates from the several associations of ministers in Massachusetts met and drafted *Proposals* of which the Mathers were the chief architects.[1] They were designed to supplement the laws, to prevent scandal, and to avert the breakdown of order. They proposed that each of the five associations be given the right to intervene in local disputes and be able to recommend and vet candidates for particular Churches. Equally important was the recommendation that Churches within an associated area should form themselves into a 'consociation', to consist of both clerical and lay delegates which in turn should erect a standing council to meet at least once a year, and be capable of final determination whether any Church was fitted for communion.

In face of considerable opposition from among the ministers and brethren these proposals were rejected as having a 'prelatical if not a papistical flavour'. But a similar movement in Connecticut, which may have owed something in its inspiration to the achievement of Solomon Stoddard in the Connecticut valley, triumphed in the Saybrook *Platform* of 1708. Here it was justified as part of the oecumenical movement of English dissent.[2] In Massachusetts the opposition had raised a cry that the *Proposals* endangered the liberties of the individual Churches, a principle later to be upheld by the able pen of that same John Wise who had once defied General Governor Andros. Wise's pamphlet, *The Churches Quarrel Espoused* (1713), gave the death blow to the Massachusetts scheme of ecclesiastical centralization. He may conceivably have held his fire until then for fear of exacerbating internal divisions within Massachusetts at a time when external dangers were acute. By 1710 the worst of these dangers were past for the British empire in general and Massachusetts in particular.

Opposition in New England to the provincial leadership of the Mathers had complex roots, though its growth was encouraged by their intellectual arrogance and narrow vision. After the Revolution

---

[1] The first association—'the Cambridge Association'—had been formed from the towns of Cambridge, Boston, and neighbouring communities in Oct. 1689. Four other regions of Massachusetts subsequently formed similar associations. Ibid., p. 216.

[2] Ibid., pp. 266, 267.

a movement, which centred around the Brattles, Benjamin Colman, and John Leverett, sought the use of traditional forms to strengthen the coherence of society. This was not how Increase Mather saw their endeavours, however, when he spoke in 1697 of 'young men apostatised from New England principles'. Thomas Brattle, who had graduated from Harvard in 1676, returned to Boston in 1689 and became Treasurer of Harvard in 1693. His brother William, ordained pastor of the Church in Cambridge in 1696, where he had discontinued formal and public relation of religious experiences as a requirement for Church membership, had ten years earlier been made one of the two tutors at Harvard. Together with John Leverett, chosen fellow and tutor in 1685, these two men for fifteen years deflected the course of college teaching and advanced and disseminated so-called 'liberal' tendencies. To further their ideas and permit the practice of true worship the Brattles, toward the end of the century, invited Benjamin Colman, then in England, to become minister of the new Brattle Street Church. He accepted, and perceiving that the ministers of the other three Boston Churches would not welcome him into fellowship, had himself ordained by the London presbytery in August 1699.

The new Church was not at variance with its sisters in matter of faith, but only in its usages—reading selections from the Bible without comment, admitting all adult baptised members who contributed towards his maintenance to share in choosing a minister, but leaving more discretion than customary in the hands of that minister. These were the innovations which angered Increase Mather, provoked the outburst in *Ecclesiastes*, and paved the way for the abortive movement for religious centralization.[1] To Cotton Mather such practices filled the land with lies and by their ignorance and malice subverted the Churches.[2] No doubt both father and son did fear, though wrongly, that fissiparous forces were gaining strength and disintegration was staring society in the face. There was good reason for anxiety in view of the multiplicity of challenges, but some of the more important fears related to the ministerial élite were misplaced. Colman was no iconoclast and in the long run the objectives of the Brattles were designed to

---

[1] Ibid., pp. 238, 239.
[2] 'Diary', ed. W. C. Ford, *Mass. Hist. Soc. Coll.*, 7th ser. vii–viii (1911–12), i. 325–6, henceforth cited as Mather, *Diary*.

strengthen not to subvert. In this respect they were identical with Cotton Mather's, but the path was different and therefore he adjudged the situation potentially dangerous.[1] By modifying ancient procedures employed since the colony's foundation, they sought to ensure a place within the Churches for the commercial leaders of society. Five of the first twenty-six communicants at Brattle Street, including Thomas Brattle himself, John Mico, and Thomas Banister, were men of wealth, glad to avoid the embarrassment of publicly relating their sins.[2]

On the western frontier Solomon Stoddard had long aimed at a similar target. No transplanted European, even two generations removed, could easily forget the dangers of degeneracy which threatened the unwary colonists. In the exposed Connecticut valley, whither Stoddard had removed, communities needed both strength and guidance to preserve themselves against dissolution and to combat the temptation, among captives of war particularly strong for females and for the young of both sexes, to sink to the primitive savagery of tribal existence, or to embrace the assurances of the Roman Catholic religion. Stoddard, in time of trial, like the Brattles and the Mathers, found the system of Presbyterianism more reassuring than the autonomy which the informal synodical system of Massachusetts tolerated for the individual Churches. Like the Brattles also, however, he aspired to achieve the participation of the whole community: to make town and Church synonymous. 'Stoddardeanism', as it came to be called, allowed professing Christians to take communion and enjoy other privileges of full Church membership, even when uncertain that they were in a state of grace.

Against the Mathers' opposition to this innovation Stoddard defended his view in the *Doctrine of Instituted Churches* (1700), the *Inexcusableness of Neglecting the Worship of God under a Pretence of Being in an Unconverted Condition* (1708), and in *An Appeal to the Learned* (1709).[3] He further advocated a national Church

[1] See W. B. Sprague, *Annals of the American Pulpit* (New York, 1857), i. 236ff., where it is contended that William Brattle's doctrinal opinions were of the strict Puritan sort. But at Cambridge Thomas Brattle had used the Lord's Prayer, had the Bible read as part of the services, and deviated in other particulars from principles of the Cambridge Platform. *D.A.B.* ii. 607–8.

[2] Miller, *New England Mind*, p. 255.

[3] For the roots of 'Stoddardeanism' see Williston Walker, *The Creeds and Platforms of Congregationalism* (rep. Boston, Mass., 1960), pp. 278–80, 282–3.

governed by a synod, argued that the clergy should have more power than had been customary in New England, and in his plan delegated to the laity only the right of electing their ministers. Like Samuel Sewall he was opposed to long hair, wigs, extravagance in dress, and excessive drinking. In the back-country, where by 1700 his influence had become paramount, Stoddard moved steadily towards his ideal of a national Church: given the platform of the annual election sermon in 1703, he warned that the current crisis demanded a rethinking of basic assumptions. But great as his political influence grew to be in the later years of his life, he was unable to extend Stoddardeanism beyond the Connecticut valley.[1] Stoddard was no more a frontier product than were the Mathers, but upon the frontier he proved a great countervailing force, contesting its levelling influences and the dangers of excessive individualism by seeking through a collectivist ideal an ordered and orderly society under the discipline of the ruling Elders. In due course, in repudiation of the concept of local covenants, he organized his area into the Hampshire Association and encouraged it to act like a genuine Presbyterian classis.[2]

In combatting unacceptable aspects of the influence of the Brattles and Stoddard, the Mathers, supported by the conservative Higginson and likewise by Noyes of the Salem Church, directed their attention towards Harvard College, strict guidance for which was essential to ensure the vitality of the Churches and to stave off that Creolian degeneracy which was among their foremost fears. As the chief apostle of conservatism in the colony in seeking to defeat those forces which were prepared to admit the impure to Church membership, Mather recognized the importance of keeping Harvard, 'the nursery, the fountain of the faith', free from contamination.[3] In 1697 the counterattack was marked by the publication of Cotton Mather's 'Life of the Revd. Jonathan Mitchell', primarily an affirmation of the Cambridge Platform.[4] The Brattles

[1] Miller, op. cit., p. 266.

[2] Walker, *Creeds*, p. 281; Miller, *New England Mind*, p. 260.

[3] Osgood, *Eighteenth Century*, i. 323.

[4] The Cambridge Platform of 1648 represented 'the abiding principles of Congregationalism'. It acknowledged the covenanted origin of the local Church, the sole authority of the Bible, and the fellowship of the Churches. It also contained the doctrine that civil authority must restrain and punish corrupt and pernicious principles. For the full preface and text see Walker, *Creeds*, pp. 194–237.

were supported by Leverett, Benjamin Colman, and the gifted
young minister Ebenezer Pemberton. In the immediate issues
Stoddard was not directly involved: the tactics of the Mathers
designed to exclude John Leverett and William Brattle from the
corporation of the college by means of a new college charter aimed
at ensuring the foundations of orthodoxy in the important eastern
seaboard.[1] In 1650 Harvard had been incorporated by an act of the
general court. An attempt by President Mather, soon after the
Revolution, to secure a new charter through the provincial assembly
was frustrated by royal veto. Thereupon he turned his hopes to a
grant from the king similar to the provincial charter. But a draft
placed before the General Court in 1699 which provided that no
person should be president, vice-president, or fellow without
subscribing to the principles expounded by the Founding Fathers
of Massachusetts was vetoed by Governor Bellomont; and his
sudden death headed off a direct approach to the throne.

The temporary successes of Increase in excluding his opponents
from the corporation were gained at the price of added opposition
to his domination of provincial life. Under the administration of
Governor Joseph Dudley the influence of the two Mathers steadily
waned. John Leverett, an old friend of Dudley's now advanced to
legal office as judge of the Superior Court and judge probate for
Middlesex County, was also elected to the Provincial Council, and
before the end of 1707 was used by the governor for two important
missions related to the War of the Spanish Succession. That year,
to the final discomfiture of Increase, Leverett was elected president
of Harvard with the full support of the governor. The latter, having
the cordial co-operation of the legislature, provided for the stipend
of the president and eliminated those fellows hostile to Leverett
by reviving the college charter of 1650.[2]

The contentions of the leading New Englanders are, if not
unsavoury, easily viewed as absurd. But they must be seen not as
petty bickering comparable to those which make tedious the politics
of many contemporary colonies in the New World but as related
to the factors of crisis and uncertainty, and to absorption, conscious and unconscious, in the high and overriding purpose to

---

[1] S. E. Morison, *Harvard College in the Seventeenth Century* (Cambridge,
Mass., 1936), ii. 509.
[2] *D.A.B.* xi. 197–8.

which the province was explicitly dedicated. To the observant English, at best ill-informed, it was impossible to view such contentions in this altruistic light: much of the information which reached the mother country served only to lessen the respect in which New England society was held and to encourage the ambitions of those Anglicans who hoped to bring this important province securely within the establishment.

Though Brattle and Leverett may have introduced in the content of Harvard curriculum some significant modifications which acknowledged more recent European scholarship, and shifted its emphasis, even before the end of the seventeenth century, away from concern with religious forms of polity to preparing students for New England life,[1] the traditional purpose of higher education remained: to provide an educated ministry. The establishment of Yale, encouraged by the Mathers, was primarily designed to ensure that this purpose should not be lost. In part the educational system developed in New England in the seventeenth century was shaped with a view to supplying the college with material already carefully moulded. But the objectives of primary and secondary education went beyond this. The essential determination, inspired by the fundamental belief that faith and understanding were unattainable without an instructed, disciplined, and literate mind, was to combat the manifest dangers of isolation in an American wilderness.[2]

Avoidance of barbaric degeneracy was a cause for constant concern.[3] To this end many European ideals were pursued, some of them conflicting. In part the inspiration was, as Samuel Eliot Morison has expressed it, to prevent 'the flame of humanism being extinguished by the demands of sheer physical living'.[4] But more important was the conviction gained by experience that public

---

[1] Ibid. xi, 198; Morison, *Harvard College*, i. 165; ii. 506–7.

[2] The Massachusetts Act of 1647, sometimes called the Old Deluder Act in recognition of its purpose to combat Satan's intention of keeping men from knowledge of the Scriptures, was explicitly designed 'that learning may not be buried in the graves of our forefathers in Church and Commonwealth. . . .' But see Morison, *Intellectual Life*, pp. 67–70, which seeks to place the preamble to this act in a wider perspective.

[3] See Mather, *Magnalia*, ii. 655; *The Way to Prosperity* (Boston, Mass., 1689).

[4] In 1677 the Plymouth General Court stated that 'the maintainance of good literature doth much tend to the advancement of the weale and flourishing estate of Societies and Republiques', cited in Newton Edwards and Herman G. Richey, *The School in American Social Order* (Boston, Mass., 1947), p. 64.

order, essential for the survival of material, religious, and cultural purposes, demanded underpinning by a system of public education.[1] The aim of the schools was not social levelling nor the development of new opportunities but rather to preserve the prevailing pattern of society in all its essential aspects and standards as brought across the Atlantic and transmitted by the Founding Fathers. Early legislation was cast to achieve this end. The objectives of the state were defined but residual responsibility remained where it had traditionally rested, with the family. If these objectives were not met then children might be taken away from parent or master and apprenticed to someone prepared to carry out the intent of the law.

The Massachusetts Act of 1647, copied by Connecticut in her code of 1650, made compulsory provision for primary and grammar schools. Towns of 100 families or households were to set up a grammar school, to prepare youth for Harvard College, upon pain of fine. Towns of fifty households were to teach reading and writing, to be paid for by parents or masters of pupils, or by the inhabitants in general. In the codification of 1648 it was a duty of selectmen to ensure that children and apprentices should be able to read perfectly the English tongue and thereby arrive at a knowledge of the capital laws. By 1672 all the New England settlements with the exception of Rhode Island had constructed a system of compulsory education. It may be thought that the high standards aimed at were too demanding, even in primary education, for the small farming communities of the region. Evidence of opposition in the form of critical comment by the élite is not lacking.[2] Whether the grammar school provision was enforced it is difficult to say. It has been argued that by 1700 the proportion of towns in Massachusetts possessing a grammar school was as large as it should be. Yet in Middlesex County, for which precise evidence is available, scarcely half the towns with the requisite number of families had endeavoured to meet the law's

[1] For an important discussion of the assumption by the schools of a cultural burden hitherto the responsibility of the family, and of the uses of education as an instrument of deliberate social purpose, see Bailyn, *Education in American Society*, esp. pp. 1–21.

[2] See Edwards and Richey, *The School*, p. 54; Merle E. Curti, *Social Ideas of American Educators* (New York 1935), pp. 4, 5; Bailyn, *Education*, p. 16. In Essex County over a period of forty-four years, six towns were indicted for failure to obey the law, though only one was actually fined.

requirements.[1] One of the most eminent colonial historians contended that the school laws were more honoured in the breach than in the observance and that, when honestly enforced, the results obtained were not noteworty.[2] It is a view that has been vigorously opposed. However several features of the system's operation do raise disturbing questions.[3]

The ideal of the Latin grammar school, at which Latin and Greek were studied for seven years or so, was to teach boys to read, write, and speak Latin as a living language, and to ground them in the rudiments of Greek. No attention was given to mathematics, science, history, or modern languages. By the 1680s, according to one unprejudiced visitor, the standard of Latin among Harvard graduates was deplorably low.[4] This might suggest that the fault lay with the grammar schools. But it is also an indictment against particular schools at Boston, Roxbury, Cambridge, and Charleston which in the last half-century before 1700 supplied a high proportion of those who attended university. During this time some other establishments failed to send a single student to Harvard. One can do no more than speculate on the reasons for this. It was not difficult to observe the letter of the law and yet ignore the spirit. Requirements were customarily regarded as having been met if a town could show it employed a master qualified to teach Latin. The town was not obliged to ensure that boys attended for instruction.[5] Either truancy or indifferent teaching was responsible for the patchy performance of the grammar schools.

After the Glorious Revolution, the attempt of Massachusetts through the act of 1692 to restore completely the system which obtained under the old charter was frustrated when the act was disallowed. Children not being taught to read and write were no longer liable to be bound out, but towns could still be presented to the General Court for failing to establish or maintain schools, and if the charge was upheld, rebuked and fined. Connecticut

[1] Edwards and Richey, *The School*, p. 65; Walter H. Small, *Early New England Schools* (Boston, Mass., 1914) pp. 30–1.

[2] C. M. Andrews, *Fathers of New England* (New Haven, Conn., 1919), pp. 84–5.

[3] Morison, *Intellectual Life*, p. 58.

[4] *Journal of Jasper Danckaerts, 1679–80*, ed. B. B. James and J. F. Jameson (New York, 1959), pp. 266–8. Dankaerts was a Dutch Labadist agent in North America.

[5] Edwards and Richey, *The School*, p. 65.

in 1690, as a concession to such opposition as might stem from practical needs, required that school should be held for no longer than six months each year 'because the Court was mindful of the necessity many parents or masters may be under to improve their children and servants in labour for a great part of the year'.

For the quarter-century before the peace of Utrecht there were many substantial factors modifying the attitude of New Englanders towards formal education. Religion was losing something of its dynamic force. Moreover the Andros administration, having achieved a partial dismantling of the old system, effected a break in continuity which could never be wholly countered. Indian wars and the wider conflict with France imposed a strain on resources, physical and pecuniary, both at individual and at community level. Under circumstances such as these a loss of fervour, a wilting or diminution of effort in face of the need to replace a schoolmaster, or to establish a school, might be expected. The labour of vigorous young hands was deemed more essential for the family unit than for distant or intangible gains from which it would not directly benefit. Persistence of the fervour was testimony to the great strength of New England traditions and ideals.

In sampling the reaction of some of the areas more directly exposed to the face of war—Maine, New Hampshire, northern Massachusetts, and the Connecticut valley—allowance must be made for demographic changes within the townships which posed an additional problem. This factor, the result of over-all population growth and migration, made pursuit of educational objectives a more difficult task. Further, many early New England towns, originally divisions of land between twenty and forty square miles in size containing a village at the centre, in due course experienced a demand from outlying districts or quarters for an effective share in town institutions or for separate institutions of their own. Hence the itinerant schoolmaster, employed by the township but spending only a few weeks or months in each community. In Harwich, for example, 300 schoolchildren were taught by one man at no less than six removes.[1] This was a practical collective endeavour to prevent expenses rising beyond the community's capacity to pay, but save for a few hardy or devoted individuals it could not commend itself to the teaching profession, more

---

[1] Small, *Early New England*, p. 38.

particularly in face of a rigorous climate and, on the frontier, exposure to assault, torture, and death.

In Maine, as in New Hampshire, many of the inhabitants were the descendants of men from Devon and Somerset in England who had migrated not to safeguard religious practices but primarily for economic reasons, to fish and to trade.[1] In the main they were not Puritans and lacked community of feeling or of interest with the settlers to the westward. Here the smallness of the settlements, or dispersal and flight before a ruthless enemy, precluded the establishment of regular schools.[2] So disrupted was the community life at Biddeford, for example, that no town records exist for the thirty years before 1717. After the sacking of Falmouth (Casco) there were no inhabitants in this town for the remainder of the Nine Years War. Not until 1718 was the town incorporated as Portland: and no schoolmaster was in fact employed until 1733.[3]

Kittery had made plans for a schoolhouse and minister in 1669 but these were not carried through, for in 1673 the town was indicted by the General Court for failing to meet the law's requirements. By the end of the next decade the Revd. John Newmarch had probably begun teaching, though it is doubtful if even by then a schoolhouse had been built.[4] The protracted suffering of the Nine Years War reduced the population to extreme poverty here, as elsewhere in Maine, and formal schooling was discontinued for a variety of obvious reasons, one of which being the danger from Indians to which children attending a distant school were exposed.

---

[1] G. Folshom, *History of Saco and Biddeford* (Saco, Me., 1830), p. 38: Everett S. Stackpole, *Old Kittery and Her Families* (Lewiston, Me., 1903), p. 213; C. E. Banks, *History of York, Maine* (Boston, Mass., 1931), i. 13; Nathaniel Adams, *Annals of Portsmouth* (Exeter, N.H., 1825), p. 94.

[2] On 12 Mar. 1694/5 the General Court prohibited the desertion of designated frontier-towns by their inhabitants unless permission was first granted by governor and Council. Eleven such towns were named, including Wells, York, and Kittery. Those who quitted without special licence forfeited their property in land or tenements. The act was justified by the Court on the grounds that the Crown's interest would be prejudiced and the enemy encouraged if any of these posts were deserted or exposed by lessening their strength. It was in force until May 1696. A similar act was passed 22 Mar. 1699/1700, when the number of towns was increased to fourteen. It was revived in June 1702, June 1706, and June 1707. Mass. Archives, lxx. 240: An Act to prevent the defecting of the Frontiers.

[3] William Gould, *Portland in the Past* (Portland, Me, 1886), p. 46; William Willis, *History of Portland* (Portland, Me., 1833), ii. 46.

[4] Folsham, *Saco*, p. 203;

Claims of an improvement in the literacy rate, if justified, suggests that some instruction in writing at least may have been available in private houses.[1]

At Wells and Kennebunk there was no endeavour until 1715 to employ a schoolmaster, and though by the end of the War of the Spanish Succession the town was large enough to require a grammar school no provision was made even for the lowest grade of instruction. Here a whole generation grew to manhood without any form of tuition outside the family. Such evidence as remains suggests that serious cultural interests had disappeared in face of the demanding challenge of war, more testing than anything experienced by the founders of the settlement.[2] But York, the old provincial capital of Maine before the charter of 1691 placed it under the control of Massachusetts, fared rather better, even though the population, a little less than 500 in 1675, had not reached 550 thirty-five years later. In 1698 the community was fortunate in securing the services of the Revd. Samuel Moody, twenty-three years old and fresh from Harvard, a man of great capacity who fostered a revival of religious interest. Under his inspiration, in 1701 the first public steps were taken for the support of a schoolmaster, and a Mr. Nathaniel Freeman was engaged to keep a free school for all inhabitants, with pay of '£8 a year and 3d. per week for teaching to Reade; and 4d. per week for Writing and Sifering and no moor'. He seems to have liked the town and the town liked him for he was re-engaged on an annual basis until 1710 when he contracted for a term of seven years to teach the five-year-olds upwards for seven hours a day in reading, writing, and cyphering. The community in appreciation promised him a substantial dwelling-house.[3]

It is noteworthy that though Massachusetts, albeit reluctantly, was obliged to tolerate a dilution of educational aims in those parts of her *imperium* exposed to the enemy, she was prepared, nevertheless, to shoulder additional financial burden to maintain some semblance of religious life there. In answer to a petition from Samuel Wheelwright, representative in the Assembly for

---

[1] Stackpole, *Old Kittery*, pp. 170, 213, 215, 235, and 236.

[2] It has been suggested that even private schools were lacking. See E. E. Bourne, *History of Wells and Kennebunk* (Portland, Me., 1875), pp. 307, 308.

[3] *Two Hundredth and Fiftieth Anniversary, Georgeana-York, 1652–1902* (York, Me., 1904), p. 53.

both York and Wells, chaplains at these outposts were officially appointed, the provincial treasury providing a contribution of 50s. to their upkeep over and above what was allowed by the local inhabitants. Berwick, petitioning for similar help, also received a hand-out from the court and between them the three communities were given some £200 before 1712 in support of ministers and for the building of meeting-houses.[1] But only garrison-towns or frontier communities made destitute by reason of war or desertion of settlers received direct money-grants and though during this period the influence of the General Court grew at the expense of town autonomy it was never extended beyond the offering of advice to individual Churches.[2]

Much of New Hampshire, as has been seen, similarly suffered the depredations of war; agricultural pursuits were interrupted, provisions became scarce, and the lumber trade was nearly destroyed. But Portsmouth, the leading community, which in 1692 included some 231 families, fortunately escaped serious calamity. Though the inhabitants were kept in continual alarm, and could not avoid hardship, local business was not damagingly interrupted. Interest in a public school seems to have begun as the Nine Years War drew to a close, the town selectmen, Joshua Moody and Samuel Penhallow, being instructed to treat for a schoolmaster as the law directed. However considerable disagreement arose over the salary to be offered and only after its reduction by fifty per cent was a Mr. Thomas Phippis engaged. Even so, additional payment was required from fathers and masters: 16s. for readers, 20s. for writers and cypherers, and 'Lattiners' 24s. By 1701 Phippis, who had been on a yearly contract, had left and a Daniel Grenlefe was hired in his place.

There remained the problem of finding a suitable schoolhouse, but a satisfactory temporary arrangement was made to keep school 'as near ye tower fort as may be' until the schoolhouse was fitted up. By 1703 the town was once more in need of a teacher, and the following year boldly empowered the selectmen to 'call and settell a gramer scoll . . . for ye advantage of ye youth of ower

---

[1] Reed, *Church and State*, pp. 64–5.

[2] Ibid., pp. 51, 53. It was regarded as the duty of the General Court to appropriate funds for the support of religious worship where poverty made independent maintenance difficult. This was justified as essential to the good morals of a town and hence the province as a whole.

town to learn them to read for ye primer, to wright and sypher
and to learn the tongues and goodmanners'. The appointee,
William Allen of Salisbury, lasted only six months, at the end of
which time Nathaniel Freeman was called in from York to help
out.[1] A few years later, using land which in 1700 had been donated
by the widow Mrs. Bridget Grafoot, out of love and affection for
her birthplace, the town took steps to build a schoolhouse and
engaged Freeman to teach all the town children he should judge
capable of reading, writing, and spelling.[2] Of the other significant
communities Dover may have avoided serious[3] obstacles in seeking
to provide educational facilities at primary and secondary level,
while Exeter, equipped with a primary school during the second
half of the seventeenth century, had so grown by 1700 as to require
by law a grammar school. During the War of the Spanish Succession
a schoolmaster was hired and preparations made to build a substantial schoolhouse.[4]

On the northern frontier of Massachusetts over and against
New Hampshire some communities suffered severely. Haverhill,
a frontier-town for nearly seventy years and particularly vulnerable,
was surrounded for much of this time by immense and mostly
unexplored forest. Early in the wars, in March 1690, an important
meeting was held to resolve whether security could be adequately
improved by requesting outside help or whether it was preferable
to abandon the town completely and seek safety elsewhere.
Haverhill had been rebuked in 1681 for failing to keep a schoolmaster according to the law, but when James Chadwick was
appointed toward the end of 1685 he was ordered to instruct
not only children in writing, reading, and ciphering but also
adults of any age. By 1695 Haverhill was again without an instructor
and ordered to conform to the law, but the following year a
terrible massacre laid low some of its most promising citizenry.[5]

A few years later, in 1700, the town struggled to erect a general
utility building which might serve the purpose of a schoolhouse

[1] Adams, *Annals of Portsmouth*, pp. 99, 128; Ralph May, *Early Portsmouth
History* (Boston, Mass., 1926), p. 208. Charles W. Brewster, *Rambles about
Portsmouth* (Portsmouth, N. H., 1859), p. 77.

[2] May, *Early Portsmouth History*, p. 204.

[3] See John Scales (ed.), *Historical Memoranda of Ancient Dover, New Hampshire* (Dover, N. H., 1900), i. 44.

[4] C. H. Bell, *History of the Town of Exeter, N.H.* (Exeter, N.H., 1888), p. 286.

[5] Above, p. 106.

but during the War of the Spanish Succession her response to the law's demand for tuition was obstructive or apathetic. The law of 1700, a statute of revision, demanded that every town of fifty families and upwards should be constantly provided with a schoolmaster and every town of 150 families furnished with a free grammar school 'as may fit them for admittance into college'. But in November 1705 the impoverishment occasioned by the Indian wars led the General Court to lower its demands again and to exempt for three years from the stipulation for higher education all towns of less than 200 families. In September 1701, after debate, Haverhill resolved that it lacked the necessary number of households or families to justify a grammar school but disbursed a small sum of money to a schoomaster, probably hired on a temporary basis. The following year, having been fined by the General Court, it engaged a Mr. Tufts on an annual stipend of £34. But for some reason or other this agreement terminated in 1703. In the summer of 1703 three meetings were held to consider the issue of education in July, August, and September respectively, and on each occasion there was hot debate. No decision was arrived at until the third meeting when it was resolved that the sufferings of Haverhill justified ignoring the legal requirement to find a replacement for Tufts.

Following the attack on Deerfield the town petitioned the Assembly in 1704 for an abatement of the year's taxes. But toward the end of the war, at the annual meeting of 1711 when pressure from the enemy had lessened, selectmen were ordered to hire a grammar school master who should move quarterly, as directed, to diverse parts of the town. Yet even at this date Haverhill was hardly a tempting post for the pedagogue and six months were expended in a fruitless attempt to engage a teacher. Accordingly sights were lowered and subsequently it was proposed to pay a teacher £6 to keep school for a quarter-year at the village schoolhouse.[1] Inhabitants living at a distance from the village centre refused to contribute even to this small sum, for instruction not readily accessible to their young, and some successfully sought an abatement of their rates. But others here, as elsewhere on the

---

[1] During this time Haverhill was not wholly without instruction. Local records show that Obadiah Ayer kept school for half a year in 1710 and 1711. He was paid £15 annually for this service. G. W. Chase, *History of Haverhill* (Haverhill, Mass., 1861), p. 209.

frontier, were deeply concerned at their children being denied the benefit of learning and petitioned the town-meeting to provide better educational facilities. They did not succeed. Once again Haverhill came under fire from the General Court for being destitute of a schoolmaster and representatives were summoned to Salem to answer the charges. But the town proved obdurate, convinced that its suffering justified special consideration.[1]

In Hampshire County, in the Connecticut valley, a region which escaped serious harm during the Nine Years War, there was no effort lacking to meet the Assembly's will and the needs of the young. Springfield in 1690 offered £20 or more for a schoolmaster and ten years later made provision for a grammar school which was to have two locations during the course of the year.[2] Northampton in 1692 instituted a free-school system and voted £40 a year for a schoolmaster, though this met with considerable opposition from prominent citizens. Parents were obliged to furnish fuel for his use, each scholar on pain of fine being ordered to bring one load of wood, even if attending no more than two months in a year. Scholars at grammar school grade, if from other towns, were charged tuition fees.[3] Hadley, less than twenty miles north along the valley, commenced a free school in March 1697 to be maintained exclusively by town rates, but the arrangement did not long continue. Those who had no children of school age objected and the town in 1699 made a revised recommendation that half the cost of tuition should be borne by the parents of scholars. This stipulation remained in force for the duration of the War of the Spanish Succession.

The first schoolhouse in Hadley, twenty-five feet in length, was built in the summer of 1696.[4] Hatfield, one of the northernmost communities, took advantage in December 1706 of a lull in hostilities to erect a new schoolhouse of similar dimensions. Here under a Dr. Hastings, and subsequently his son Thomas, schools were regularly maintained throughout the period of conflict. At Westfield the town selectmen in 1696 voted to settle a school-

---

[1] Chase, *Haverhill*, pp. 135, 152, 205, and 209.
[2] H. M. Burt, *The First Century of Springfield* (Springfield, Mass., 1899), ii. 75.
[3] Lockwood, *Westfield*, i. 280; J. R. Trumbull, *History of Northampton* (Northampton, Mass., 1898), i. 426–7.
[4] Judd, *Hadley*, p. 37.

master for half a year and to pay a *pro rata* salary for reading and writing. All families with boys aged seven to fourteen contributed towards the cost of education, whether the children went to school or not. Westfield experienced difficulty in securing a schoolmaster, though in 1702 a contract was made with Isaac Phelps whereby he was remunerated in rye and corn. The following year a stormy town-meeting occurred when the rate for 'writers' was lowered to 3*d.* a week and for 'readers' to 2*d.* a week. This distressed some of those present but the poverty of the people perhaps made many reluctant to contribute towards the cost of schooling enjoyed by another man's children. However the principle of paying outright for the children of the poor seems to have been accepted from the first.[1]

No community in the valley suffered as severely as Deerfield which was shattered by the onslaught of 1704. Here under the direction of a school committee a large schoolhouse was built in 1698. Hitherto schools such as Mrs. Beeman's had been kept in private houses. Now, all heads of families possessing children male or female between six and ten years were to pay by poll, whether they sent their children to school or not. Children below the age of six and above the age of ten might attend school but paid according to the time they attended. The town voted £20 per year towards maintaining the school for twenty years. Within a short time, however, it was evident that such a levy was beyond its resources and in 1701 it was unanimously voted to void the former act and substitute an allotment of £15 for seven years. John Richards, who began teaching in Deerfield in this year, was contracted on a salary of £25, one-third of the sum being paid in barley and the other two-thirds in corn, peas, or rye.[2]

Clearly there was greater activity in Hampshire County than in

[1] Lockwood, *Westfield*, i, p. 279.
[2] George Sheldon, *History of Deerfield* (Deerfield, Mass., 1895–6), i. 273. Deerfield in the past had received various sums for the support of the ministry. In 1705 the General Court resolved to send a chaplain to replace John Williams, taken prisoner by the French, and twice voted £20 for six months' tenure. In the course of five years £100 was defrayed. Other towns in the interior were similarly helped. Lancaster, which lost its minister in the Indian attack of 1697, petitioned for financial aid to help attract a replacement. Brookfield, maintained as a garrison town for many years before acquiring township privileges, received a total of over £200 before 1714, and Northfield received substantially more. See Reed, *Church and State*, pp. 66, 67.

Maine, where the educational provisions under the direct impact
of war had all but collapsed. The limited nature of the evidence
presented does not justify sweeping conclusions. With the exception of Deerfield the valley suffered less direct damage than Maine,
though the expenses of war were high there. Another factor lacking
in Maine was the strength of the Puritan tradition. But it must
not be assumed that the creative activity of the Connecticut valley
was simply a response to the stimulus of war, an instinctive endeavour to maintain standards threatened or lowered by barbarous
assault. It is evident that many communities showed less concern
to ensure that children attended than that educational provisions
were financed in a way which met the requirements of the General
Court. This may reveal a sensitivity to the dangers incurred by
unaccompanied children on their way to or from school, or it may
signify a general lowering of aspirations.

It is noteworthy that in the act of 1701 the Massachusetts General
Court showed grave concern at the neglect of earlier laws which
was 'tending greatly to the nourishing of ignorance and irreligion'.
Many towns it was alleged had preferred a fine rather than fulfil
their responsibilities: others employed a schoolmaster for a short
time while the court was in session or employed the local minister,
a practice forbidden by the law.[1] But this fault should not be attributed to sheer wilfulness on the part of townships narrowly
concerned with cheese-paring. The experience of Andover is
instructive:

This may certify to whom it may concern, that the selectmen of the said
town have taken all the care and pains they could for to procure a
schoolmaster for our town for the year last past but could not obtain
one; first we agreed with Mr. Obadiah Ayers of Haverhill for $\frac{1}{2}$ a year,
only he expected liberty if he had a better call or offer, which we thought
would be only for the work of the ministry, but, however, he was pleased
to take it otherwise and so left us; whereupon we forthwith applied
ourselves to the college to the president for advice, and he could tell us
none, only advised us to the Fellows to ask them; and they advised a
Mr. Rogers of Ipswich, for they could tell us of no other; and we
applied ourselves to him and got him to Andover. But by reason our
Rev. Mr. Bernard could not diet him, he would not stay with us, and
since we have sent to Newbury and Salisbury and to Mistick for to hire
one and cannot get one; and we do take the best care we can for to

---

[1] Edwards and Richey, *The School*, p. 105.

bring our children to reading by schooldames, and we have no grammar school in our town as we know of, and we are now taking the best care we can to obtain one, and therefore we pray that we may be favoured so far as may be, for we cannot compel gentlemen to come to us, and we do suppose they are something afraid by reason *we do lie exposed to our Indian enemies*. Pray consider our great extremity in that regard and we shall do our uttermost to answer to the true intent of the law in that behalf.[1]

The obvious difficulties, in this instance the product of human fears, are sometimes the most readily overlooked. Conflict with a terrifying, destructive, and seemingly ubiquitous enemy was a major obstacle to New England's educational intent for twenty-five years or more before Utrecht. Under circumstances such as these the supply of stout-hearted teachers properly qualified, perhaps already limited at source by other factors, may have proved insufficient for competing needs.

It is difficult to make any constructive comparisons with the New England experience from among the English colonies during the period under review. No other province possessed what might be called a system or had defined its objectives so clearly, though New Yorkers in the seventeenth century showed a zeal for education comparable to that of the New Englanders.[2] But in 1691 and 1696 bills designed to promote public education there failed. Enlightened and ambitious plans in Pennsylvania, to make education universal throughout the province as a contributory means to the unification of government and society, also withered in face of opposition to the act of 1693 and the complexities of governing a mixed and divided population.[3]

Virginia offers a few useful points for comparison though they are scarcely very close ones. Two long wars may have encouraged certain expenditure upon educational facilities, but contrariwise diminution of Virginian fortunes might have been responsible for the failure of the free schools to increase in number significantly. In any case the impact of the conflict was largely indirect

---

[1] Cited by Small, *Early New England*, p. 38. The italics are those of the present writer.

[2] A. C. Flick, *History of the State of New York* (New York, 1933), ii. 393; iii. 23, 71; L. B. Wright, *The Cultural Life of the Amercian Colonies, 1607–1763* (New York, 1957), p. 106.

[3] See James P. Wickersham, *History of Education in Pennsylvania* (Lancaster, Pa., 1886).

and there was no public system of primary and secondary education to be stimulated or discouraged.[1]

In important respects a more useful comparison may be made with the purpose and limitations of New France. Here the vitality of educational resources owed much to the zeal of the Jesuits and Recollets and to outstanding leaders of the Church such as Laval and Saint-Vallier. The extent of the primary system, still wholly within the hands of the Church, is difficult to determine. In the lower town of Quebec, Bishop Laval had founded a primary school sometime before 1700. Hitherto the Jesuit school had sufficed to meet the needs of the population. A school for girls was established as early as 1691 and in 1700 a further elementary school for boys, under priests from the seminary, was begun in the upper town. Endowed by the bishop for eight years in the first instance, its financial support was subsequently taken over by the king. It continued to exist until the end of the *ancien régime*. The needs of the countryside in the Quebec district were met by the school of St. Joachim, which by 1690 had some forty boarders, most of whom were paid for by their parents. Bishop Laval, its founder, awarded six scholarships annually after 1693 for country children of good morals to train up to the age of eighteen in piety, reading, and writing.[2] Other endowments followed, and by the end of the century St. Joachim's was said to be in a flourishing condition. A Latin school was shortly added to it, but soon transferred to Château-Richer.

Other schools in the province were at Pointe Levis, where the *curé* in 1695 opened a boys' school at his own house, taking pupils from Trois Rivières as well as Quebec, at Sillery, at Ste. Foy, and at Ste. Famille on the island of Orléans. Montreal was reported to have two schools. Fort Frontenac, La Prairie-de-la Magdeleine, Lachine, Pointe-aux-Tremble, and Boucherville each had establishments. However, it is difficult to say with any certainty whether elementary education was general in the country districts of New France at this time. The evidence is conflicting. The intendants Raudot, Vaudreuil, and Bégon commented, as

---

[1] Cited in Bruce, *Institutional History*, i. 335–6, 339, 383, 390, and 399; L. G. Tyler, 'Education in Colonial Virginia', *W & MQ* (Apr. 1897), vi. 78, 221.

[2] Abbé A. E. Gosselin, 'Education in Canada under the French Régime', *Canada and its Provinces*, ed. A. Short and A. C. Doughty (Toronto, 1914), xvi. 330–2.

representatives of the Crown, on the absence of schoolmasters in
the rural areas; but historians in this century have regarded the
number of ordinances on elementary education issued by the
bishop of Quebec as significant evidence to the contrary.[1]

For girls, educational opportunities until the 1690s rested in
the main on the Ursuline congregation of Notre Dame, founded
in 1659, which by the end of the century had twenty-five sisters
and the assistance of an endowment from Saint-Vallier. In 1697
Saint-Vallier had also founded an Ursuline community at Trois
Rivières, partly for the education of girls. The colonists contributed
towards its upkeep. Finally, the Sisters of the Congregation
held a mother house in Montreal, and a number of convents in the
surrounding region, and these devoted part of their time to teaching. It is true that the character of instruction offered was generally
very restricted and meant little besides the manual arts regarded
as suitable for the female sex, but the education of girls at primary
level was not seriously neglected. Outside the St. Lawrence valley
instruction for both sexes was less promising. In Acadia, schools
had long been established at La Hêve and at Port Royal. At the
latter there were two seminaries, one for boys and one for girls,
but these suffered severely from fire and pillage in the Nine Years
War, although the convent school of Notre Dame survived until
the fall of Port Royal.[2]

Throughout all these schools the books used were those used in
France: the *Small* and *Great Alphabet,* the *Psalter,* and *Christian
Thoughts.* As in France, religion formed the foundation of education, although to this were added some elements of Latin and
grammar.[3] In secondary education also, French practice was
closely followed and at the Jesuit college, the only completely
organized secondary school, the methods of La Flêche were adopted
in their entirety. Here were classes in grammar, the humanities,
rhetoric, philosophy, and theology. A science course was provided
lasting two years, and physics and mathematics were taught as
part of philosophy. Lahontan described the college as a 'for-
saken nursery' but its superior, probably not without just pride,
held a high opinion of the industry of the students and thought its

---

[1] Gosselin, loc. cit. xvi. 347.
[2] Abbé L. Groulx, *L'Enseignement français au Canada* (Montreal, 1933),
ii. 11–12.
[3] Gosselin, loc. cit. xvi. 359–60.

achievements better than many French colleges. By 1699 it is
estimated to have contained between 130 and 140 scholars.[1]

In addition to the Jesuit college there existed Latin schools,
situated in various places, as well as the Little Seminary at Quebec
which through religious and moral training prepared boys for an
ecclesiastical life. Despite two fires early in the eighteenth century
the latter was observed to be in a flourishing condition in 1705.
Some schools of Arts and Trade had been formed, although
these were not numerous, and facilities declined during the wars.
In 1685 twelve of the thirty-one pupils at St. Joachim were occupied in trades, and for five years—from 1691–6—the gifted sculptor,
Jacques Le Blond de la Tour, headed the workshop of wood-
carving, and trained pupils who contributed to the Church work
of New France. At one time St. Joachim's also offered hydro-
graphy, mathematics, and probably painting as well, but by 1705
only instruction in agriculture was available. At Montreal, Father
de la Chauchetière, maintained by the king, taught navigation,
fortification, and other branches of mathematics. Beyond the St.
Lawrence valley in Nova Scotia, Isle Royale, and Isle St. Jean,
there were no facilities for disciplined advanced study at all.
And generally speaking, secondary education was less well-
developed than in contemporary France, despite the excellent
special facilities which were available from time to time. Save for
Acadia, the experiences of war neither directly impaired the
quality nor unduly restricted the opportunities open to the youth
of New France. In fact, owing to the vigour of the Church, this
proved, in contrast to New England, to be a period of unprece-
dented growth.[2]

The leaders of New France were seriously concerned with the
inadequate moral fibre of the young, their readiness to slip into the
forest to avoid military service, the ease with which they adopted
Indian practices, cohabited with Indian squaws, and shed the
attributes of Christian civilization. Although New England
ministers were alarmed at the number of English captives who
in face of physical danger and moral pressure shed the Puritan
way of life, this problem, in proportion to the percentage of
population involved, loomed less large for the English colonies.

---

[1] Gosselin, loc. cit. xvi. 363, 365, 367, and 370.
[2] N.C.M.H. vol. vi, ch. xv. pp. 496–7.

Even so there is reason to suppose that those who grew to manhood in time of protracted war constituted a severely disturbed generation.

It is not proposed here to attempt an extended analysis of the highly complex phenomenon of the Salem 'witches' of 1691 and 1692 and the trials and executions which followed. In important respects this cast an unfavourable reflection upon almost all levels and ages of society. Generally decried as the darkest page in New England's history, it has been used by some writers as an instrument through which to attack the Puritan theocracy. Neither the supposed appearance of the witches nor their hanging was an experience novel for New England. Between 1647 and 1662, Massachusetts and Connecticut executed between them some fourteen people. But Massachusetts alone was responsible for only six sporadic cases before 1692.[1] Blame has been heaped upon the heads of the two Mathers in particular and the leaders of Massachusetts society in general, the former for having precipitated the outbreak, the latter for having done so little to control and extinguish it. No one in high position was wholly free from blame. Those opposed to the domination of the Mathers sought their discredit for the part they had played. But New England in pursuit of its prejudices was no worse than many other western countries in the seventeenth century and less harmful than some. Allowance should be made for the environment which, by reason of its heathen Indians supposed by the English to be devil worshippers, conditioned the communities to a very real fear of their spiritual vulnerability. Belief in a plot by Satan to destroy New England sprouted readily from such foundations. Tested by King Philip's War and frayed by the Andros regime, the nerves of New Englanders had no time to recover before the strains of a new war were thrust upon them. Malice and teenage hysteria spread like ink upon blotting paper to involve the adult population, undermining the remnants of traditional steadiness and common sense. But the madness was localized and the recovery swift. The subsequent recantation of judge and jury, a unique event, did something to atone for the community's excess by helping to expedite the cause of reform in England. But the English at home in general viewed

---

[1] George Lyman Kittredge, *Witchcraft in Old and New England* (Cambridge, Mass., 1929), pp. 338, 367, and 368.

the executions, and remembered them, as further evidence of the
religious imbalance of New England.

Religion was still a vital factor of life, if for some colonists no
longer a central one, but could not completely counter the influence
of a prolonged period of conflict upon moral standards and behaviour. By 1690 crime was already a major problem for the colonies
and each sizeable community was obliged to make some provision
for nocturnal security. The seaports suffered most seriously.
In the Nine Years War Boston and New York alike were protected
at night by a military watch, whereas Charleston, lacking any such
institution until 1703, fined its civil watch-keepers 40s. if found
asleep or 'Tyed [them] neck and Heales ye Next Morning'. In
Newport, after 1707, privateersmen were the main disturbers
of the civil peace; the watch in Charleston on occasion was
attacked and beaten by sailors, sometimes from the Royal Navy,
though there is no record of Boston having suffered in this way.
Added to the traditional upheaval of war were disorders arising
from immigration, and from the migration into the older settlements of people from threatened frontier areas. A marked increase
in the number of thefts was a major consequence. Boston suffered
between 1704–7 from a wave of petty thefts caused by 'the flocking
in of the disorderly poor'. New York in the later years of the War
of the Spanish Succession was unable to protect its Churches,
to the scandal of the local population.[1] Both northern ports had
come to know violence and rioting against administration and
customs. By 1720 Boston, still regarded as the best-governed
town in the colonies had a reputation for riots in which both sexes
participated.

Drunkenness was a universal vice, despite the numerous laws
designed for its discouragement and the thundering denunciations
of Solomon Stoddard, Samuel Sewall, and the Puritan ministry.
In the seaboard areas drunken sailors seriously aggravated the
problem of maintaining law and order as did the readiness of the
local population to welcome pirates or free them from gaol, if
need be. The younger generation was probably more deeply
affected by the disturbed times than any other segment of the
population. Before the witchcraft scandals broke, early in 1692,
provincial equanimity was shaken by an outbreak of juvenile

[1] Bridenbaugh, *Cities in the Wilderness*, pp. 217, 220.

delinquency in which the Sabbath was profaned.[1] By 1699 illicit relationships were no longer uncommon. During the War of the Spanish Succession, when for the first time the colonial populace experienced widespread contact with European soldiers and sailors, a marked increase in adultery and illegitimacy was observed. The sabbatarian code of 1692 in time was openly flouted and the law of 1700, which provided harsh punishment for 'Adultery and Fornication', failed as an effective deterrent. Cotton Mather spoke of a 'wicked, stupid, abominable generation: every year growing worse', and promoted private organizations to combat 'the leprosy of sin'.[2] But although membership of these organizations grew rapidly, the tide was running strongly against a strict code of behaviour once widely honoured.

While the wars stimulated as well as hampered colonial development, many aspects of colonial life, as indeed many regions, were little affected by their occurrence. If Maine communities were learning to live without books, Boston, which had possessed an active printing press continuously since 1639, was by 1690 the second-largest printing and bookselling centre in the British empire. In September New England enterprise was responsible for a monthly newspaper 'designed to counter false reports'.[3] Rigid censorship prevented a second issue but in 1704 there began a regular journal, *Boston News-Letter*, under the supervision of the governor's Council. Libraries developed substantially in all the colonies, despite the cost of transporting goods across the Atlantic. Cotton Mather's held 4,000 volumes, a number equalled in Virginia by that of William Byrd II. Others, such as those of Ralph Wormeley and Richard Lee, were smaller but nevertheless significant collections. In Maryland Dr. Thomas Bray established libraries in nearly every parish and in Charleston founded an impressive library, regarded by dissenters as an instrument of Anglican propaganda, from which each inhabitant had the right to borrow books.[4]

---

[1] Charles M. Fuess, *Andover: Symbol of New England* (Portland, Me., 1959), p. 113.

[2] Bridenbaugh, *Cities in the Wilderness*, p. 226. Cf. Morison, *Intellectual Life*, p. 173.

[3] Bridenbaugh, *Cities in the Wilderness*, p. 133.

[4] David D. Wallace, *History of South Carolina* (New York, 1934), i. 196. This right was probably the cause of its ceasing to exist after a short space of time. L. G. Tyler, 'Education in Colonial Virginia', pt. iv, *W & MQ* (Oct. 1898), ser. i, vi–vii. 69.

Compared to the activity of the Puritan press and the growth of colonial libraries, the cultural vitality of the French settlements might seem impoverished and more directly dependent upon European infusions. There were no poets to place against New England's Edward Taylor. Personal collections of books were very modest in size and no match for contemporary New England or Virginia. Jean Deshayes, hydrographer to the king, possessed volumes on mathematics, cosmography, and the nautical sciences in 1706 but in all he held no more than forty books.[1] None but ecclesiastical bodies owned libraries worthy of the name, and the *habitants*, unlike the New Englanders, rarely possessed written works of any sort. However this was partly a consequence of the absence of a printing press in the French settlements and did not necessarily indicate a lack of interest in the written word. Both for pleasure and instruction, reading had an important role throughout the community and books circulated freely from hand to hand, though under Saint-Vallier the Church sought to confine the interchange to permitted texts. The publication of major works describing the country and its expansion, such as Le Clerq's *Premier establissement de la foi dans la Nouvelle France* (1690), and Fr. Louis Hennepin's *Nouvelle découverte d'un trés-grand pays, Situé dans L'Amerique* stimulated reflection. But until conquest by the English half a century later New France was without a literature of its own.[2]

By contrast the literary output of the English colonists during this time, the product of a much larger population, was substantial and interesting. Commentary on most colonies appeared in some form or other—*An Historical and Geographical Account of . . . Pennsylvania and West New Jersey* (London, 1698) was written by Gabriel Thomas, a Welshman who had spent fifteen years in North America, and *A New Voyage to Carolina, containing an Exact Description and Natural History of that Country* (London, 1709) by John Lawson who met an untimely death at the stake, killed by his Indian captors. But the two main focal points of all writing were Chesapeake Bay and New England. At a time when belief in the certainties of New England was beginning to dissolve

---

[1] Antoine Roy, *Les Lettres, les sciences et les arts au Canada* (Paris, 1930), p. 64.

[2] *NCMH*, vol. vi, ch. xv, pp. 495-7.

in men's minds, the productions of Virginia display a novel assurance and with it an incipient identity. In 1697 Henry Hartwell, James Blair, and Edward Chilton submitted a report to the Board of Trade, published a generation later, entitled *The Present State of Virginia and the College*. Shortly after there followed an important political tract by an unknown American (reputedly William Byrd): *An Essay upon the Government of the English Plantations on the Continent of America* (1701). Finally, as a corrective to the inaccuracies of Sir John Oldmixon's *British Empire in America*, came Robert Beverley's *The History and Present State of Virginia* (1705): the first major historical work. The quality of these writings is undeniable. Though of a different order they bear comparison with Cotton Mather's 'Decennium Luctuosum', which appeared in 1699, or may be placed alongside the unique *Magnalia Christi Americana* (1701). Virginia, like Massachusetts, had her diarist: William Byrd as opposed to Cotton Mather and Samuel Sewall. But what distinguished New England and continued to nourish her self-awareness was the printed sermons which, despite their modified significance in colonial life, poured forth from the Boston press.[1]

Whatever suffering and anxieties the wars brought upon New Englanders, whatever strain was imposed upon their resources by costly expeditions, there yet developed after 1689 a period of marked economic activity and growth in many spheres. Loss of property through enemy assault, diminution of labour resources due to emigration or to forced or voluntary service outside the province, and the dislocation of exposed communities contributed a severe check to prosperity. But despite the heavy burden of debt with which peace was faced after the settlement of Utrecht, it would be wrong to describe Massachusetts in 1713 as a province ruined by war.[2] Even so, considerable exertion had been necessary on the part of her people to prevent a serious decline in wealth.

The failure of the Canada expedition of 1690 had a direct effect upon provincial business, especially in Boston. The seaport's merchants had subscribed heavily to the venture and the disappointment which accompanied its losses deepened a gloom settling

[1] Morison, *Intellectual Life*, pp. 167, 173–6.
[2] See below, pp. 158–60, 274–80.

on every side.[1] The disorders and political uncertainties which had
characterized the months since the collapse of the Andros
regime and the serious curtailment of trade with the Mediterranean,
a direct effect of the French war, had already discouraged commerce
so severely that nothing short of a major reversal of fortune could
be expected to revive it.[2] Under Governor Bellomont, who in
writing home stressed the economic value of Massachusetts to
England,[3] the continued trade depression and the sharp decline
in the price of cod inspired a recommendation that naval stores
should be produced as a contribution towards recovery.

Yet the maritime wealth of Massachusetts in 1700, though
curbed, was still impressive. Bellomont estimated that Boston
had, in craft above the size of herring-boats, more bottoms than
all Scotland and Ireland combined.[4] Since 1676, however, the
number of ships had declined. There were twenty per cent fewer
vessels employed of over 100 tons in Massachusetts—sixteen in all,
of which thirteen were from Boston—and the total over-all had
fallen dramatically to a little more than a third of what it had once
been.[5] If Edward Randolph's figures for the earlier date are
correct, a great number of small craft had been lost, sold, or had
departed from New England in the intervening years. After 1700,
however, losses were rapidly replaced, significantly by ships of a
larger average tonnage.[6] An increasing number of these were
registered at Boston. Privateering and other captures also helped

---

[1] Fitz-John Winthrop placed the figure at £6,000. See Weeden, *Economic
and Social History*, i. 353.

[2] 'Bullivant's Journal', *Mass. Hist. Soc. Proc.* (1878), p. 105. Throughout the
New England colonies seamen's wages were higher than in Europe, a factor
which encouraged desertions from British warships stationed on their coasts.
Ordinary seamen received £1. 15s. to £2. 15s. a month. Common labourers
could earn two shillings a day and craftsmen twice as much. Even so, periodic
dislocation of trade and accompanying hardship drove men from time to time
into British military service and even to enlist on English ships. *New York Col.
Docs.* iv. 502, 871; v. 194.

[3] *C.S.P.C.*. 1700, no. 466, pp. 181, 678; ibid., 1701, p. 182.

[4] Bernard and Lotte Bailyn, *Massachusetts Shipping, 1697–1714. A Statistical
Study* (Cambridge, Mass., 1959), p. 21. Boston in 1702 with 6,443 registered
tons was outranked in England as a port by Bristol and London alone: *New
York Col. Docs.* iv. 790.

[5] Weeden, op. cit. i. 363; Bailyn, *Massachusetts Shipping*, pp. 18, 81.

[6] Ibid., pp. 42, 45; *New York Col. Docs.* iv. 790. Cf. Weeden, op. cit. i. 364,
who argues that a fall in the number of vessels over 100 tons continued, but
that a slight increase took place in the number of smaller vessels.

to fill the gaps. In exceptional years, 1702, 1703, and 1711, ten per cent of the total tonnage of newly registered Massachusetts vessels came from this source which added sixty-five vessels (5,991 tons) in all.[1]

At no time was shipbuilding at a standstill. In the 1690s the Barstows began building in Hanover; a shipyard opened at Braintree and another at Gloucester. Before the end of Queen Anne's reign facilities had developed considerably, particularly in Massachusetts and Rhode Island. In part this was to meet a demand from buyers outside New England. According to Governor Dudley a fleet the size of that based on Boston was built every two years for sale to the merchants of London and elsewhere. In one year alone (1709) England ordered more than fifty ships.[2] Almost one-third of the 75,267 tons known to have been built in Massachusetts between 1697 and 1714 eventually passed to home ports in Britain or its possessions outside the mainland colonies. It is likely that much of this was built on orders from British buyers.[3]

Prices relative to the earlier period were low, resting in 1697 at about sixty per cent of what they had been in 1676, rising to eighty-five per cent in 1700 and falling back to seventy-five in 1712.[4] But there is no suggestion that wages fell also, so that either profit margins were reduced or efficiency increased. Between the close of the Nine Years War and the end of the War of the Spanish Succession, Boston, and neighbouring Charleston, and Cambridge built 484 registered vessels of 36,492 tons; Salem and Scituate a little more than 6,000 tons apiece; and all other Massachusetts towns between them 16,222. In the same period Maine produced fifty-six vessels of some 4,430 tons.[5] By and large this expansive

---

[1] Bailyn, *Massachusetts Shipping*, pp. 43, 51.

[2] *C.S.P.C.*, 1708–9, no. 391; Curtis P. Nettels, *Money Supply of the American Colonies* (Madison, Wisc., 1934), pp. 92–3. Costs of building merchant ships in Boston were 40% lower than in England. *C.S.P.C.*, 1700, no. 953.

[3] Bailyn, *Massachusetts Shipping*, pp. 53, 55. The hiring of Boston registered vessels was also a profitable source of income. See Nettels, *Money Supply*, pp. 70–1, n. 5.

[4] Weeden, op. cit. i. 366–7. For the earlier period other evidence suggests that prices remained stable at £4. 5s. a ton in New England money between 1695 and 1701. See Mass. Archives, lxii. 74, 397.

[5] Nettels, *Money Supply*, p. 69. The figures for Salem show a steady decline from 1700 onwards. The fall in tonnage produced at Scituate was even more dramatic.

building was financed by the people of Massachusetts. Relatively little British capital was involved in replacing or developing the provincial sea-going fleet: a more significant contribution came from the remainder of New England. Not only did merchants and shipmasters finance and own many of these ventures but also an equal number of ordinary investors were involved and shared their risk. A high proportion of these were Bostonians.[1] 'The shipping inflation', a consequence of war, helps to demonstrate, if demonstration is needed, that early eighteenth-century Boston was no provincial backwater. It scarcely suggests a community impoverished or overburdened by the strain of defending and sustaining the frontier-towns. Boston, in association with neighbouring Charleston, cleared 1,000 ships annually and held facilities to load and unload fifty vessels at a single time. Marblehead, Salem, despite its decline in shipbuilding, and Ipswich were likewise said to be commercially flourishing.

Provisions of all sorts were reported to be plentiful in the seaboard area, although prices were very much higher than at home: between 150 per cent and 225 per cent.[2] In the Nine Years War a scarcity of East India goods had sent the prices of some commodities rocketing, and muslins of the best sort were sold for £10 a piece. Shipping charges helped to keep the cost of things high. In 1693 one consignment was rated at 13·5 per cent of the English value of the goods. Freight rates were heavy, as might be anticipated, and insurance ranged from £8 per cent to 16 guineas during 1690–9. Wartime prices encouraged the manufacture of cloth.[3] At the turn of the century, spinning, weaving, hemp and flax culture, hitherto neglected, now commenced on such a scale that homespun industries made considerable progress. Spinning spread throughout eastern Massachusetts and by the end of the War of the Spanish Succession several kinds of weaving were carried on at Nantucket. Caleb Heathcote and Lord Cornbury both commented

---

[1] Nettels, *Money Supply*, p. 70. The Bostonian element made up almost 70% of this number: Bailyn, *Massachusetts Shipping*, pp. 31, 61, 62, 90, and 91.

[2] 'Captain Uring: Notices of New England. 1709', *New Hampshire Hist. Soc. Coll.* iii. 142; *New York Col. Docs.* iv. 871; v. 194. Clothing and drink were double the price in England, and reached a peak of 225% of the prices in the mother country in 1706. *C.S.P.C.*, 1714–15, no. 508.

[3] T. W. Higgison, *Letters and Journals*, ed. M. T. Higgison (Boston, Mass., 1921), p. 209; Mass. Archives, lxi. 361–2, cited in Nettels, *Money Supply*, p. 74; Weeden, op. cit. i. 369; *C.S.P.C.*, 1708–9, no. 391.

on the presence of woollen and linen manufactures. Fulling mills for finishing hand-woven woollens were reported from Colchester and Dorchester in Massachusetts, as well as from Stamford, and Guilford, Connecticut, in the first decade of the eighteenth century. Forges at Hanover and Rehoboth, a slitting mill and mining at Dorchester, testify to the diversification of the economy taking place in Massachusetts, as in Connecticut, during the War of the Spanish Succession.[1] Before the war ended it was calculated that this process had lowered the import bill by £50,000 (New England money).[2] Save for the frontier areas, there is little evidence of serious privation comparable to the sufferings of Virginians in the 1690s, or of New France, in 1705, reduced to serious want through the loss of a single ship laden with goods.

From the turn of the seventeenth century various expedients enabled New England to pay for imports annually averaging £103,500.[3] In so doing she furnished business for some sixty London merchants. Annual exports averaged less than £40,000.[4] Part of the imbalance was accounted for by sales to Newfoundland settlers, who in 1691 were already buying some 300 tons of rum, lumber, provisions, tobacco, sugar, pitch, and tar annually. In the view of one English official, sharp practices by the 'Saints' kept the islanders in economic bondage, permitting them to monopolize the trade of the settlements and to use their location

[1] Weeden, op. cit. i. 392, 393, and 397. The lumber trade was sufficiently prosperous for the New Hampshire executive to judge it capable of bearing an additional tax in 1704. Encouragement to naval stores, though development was less than anticipated, further helped the economic diversification which counter-ed the early Anglo-French wars. *Documents and Records relating to the Province of New Hampshire*, (Concord, N.H., 1867) iii. 291; *Mass. Hist. Soc. Coll.*, 5th ser. vi. 207.

[2] Thomas Bannister to Council of Trade, 7 July 1715, Essay on Trade of New England, CO 866, f. 225. Buttons, stuffs, kerseys, linseys, woolseys, shallbones, and flannels were listed as products of the husbandmen and house-holders designed to counter the high prices of English imports. If the figure cited is an accurate one it more than offset the cost of wartime insurance. Nettels, *Money Supply*, pp. 73–5. See also Malone, *Pine Trees*, p. 153.

[3] Figures for the inter-war years were close to this. From 1702 to 1706 they fell to an average of £62,750, but in the second half of the War of the Spanish Succession this figure doubled to an annual average of £120,000.

[4] Whale products, ship timbers, naval stores, and furs were the most import-ant. The sale of ship-masts reached a peak income of £6,000 in the final years of conflict. The West Indies were regularly supplied by New England. Nettels, *Money Supply*, pp. 73–4; Malone, *Pine Trees*, p. 48.

as a mart for selling fish to visiting European vessels.[1] Provisions, lumber, and rum were traded for Newfoundland fish, which in turn might be exchanged on the other side of the Atlantic for European goods or, preferably, specie. Dried or salted fish dominated the highly profitable trade with Portugal, 'the Streits', Spain, and Italy, and formed an important item of the commerce with the Azores and Madeira.[2] In addition the islands imported beeswax, and pipe staves, in return for wine shipped by the New Englanders to old England.

Within the mainland colonies the Massachusetts port of Boston dominated as an entrepôt for European goods and as a clearing stage for bills of exchange.[3] Connecticut farm produce, tar, and turpentine together with much of New Hampshire's lumber, was channelled through this source. Valued at a rate fixed by the Massachusetts legislature, the foreign coin from Rhode Island's important trade with Curacao and Surinam drained away to the New England metropolis to pay for English goods.[4] The port of New York was a poor competitor. In the second decade of the eighteenth century Boston received five times as many sailings from London in a year and sent three times as many ships to the English capital. Its hinterland stretched effectively into the Hudson valley, furnishing West Indian products, rice, and European goods in exchange for wheat and other provisions. Maryland and Virginia, as well as the Carolinas, formed part of its extended orbit. During the course of two wars, as Boston's grip upon the tobacco trade strengthened, sales of salt, sugar, molasses, rum, lumber, fish, earthenware and European goods almost doubled. By 1700 Boston held a commanding position in the trade of the Carolinas. As from New England and New York, so from these southern plantations and farms, coin and bills of exchange drained away to the Bay province where they eased for the 'Saints' the imbalance of trade with the mother country.

---

[1] Report of Capt. Hawkins, 1691, CO 1/68, no. 92, enclosure i; Report of Commodore Graydon, 13 Mar. 1701, CO 195/3, p. 6, cited in Nettels, *Money Supply*, pp. 73, 76, 77, and 78. See especially CO 390/5 for export and import figures. The carrying trade was almost an exclusive New England preserve.

[2] See Governor Dudley to Lords of Trade, 8 Apr. 1712, CO 5/865, f. 467.

[3] Salem alone shared this role to a limited extent. No other New England port carried on significant outside trade.

[4] Governor Cranston of Rhode Island alleged that £20,000 in money was sent each year to Boston.

A substantial legal trade was carried on with the southern plantations. Rum, molasses, salt, and sugar, derived from the West Indies, and wine and cider were exchanged for pork, Indian corn, and wheat, some of which was taken north to the Newfoundland fishery. But the foundation of New England's commerce was the trade with the West Indies. During the first part of the War of the Spanish Succession this was so seriously disturbed by the French that Boston merchants threatened withdrawal unless it were better protected. Horses, lumber, fish, and a variety of provisions, were sold to Jamaica, the Leewards, and Barbados, to Dutch Surinam, and the Spanish colonies. Sugar, molasses, and rum figured importantly in the exchange with the sugar islands, as did the bills drawn on English merchants.[1] But the most valuable item in countering the imbalance of trade with England was the Spanish money acquired in Jamaica, Barbados, and Curacao. Freight charges and profits—prices in the West Indies were half as high again as in the northern towns—were the final item which freed the New England provinces from an economic domination of the mother country such as was experienced by southern mainland colonies.[2]

There are no certain figures relating to the degree of illegal trading, and many historians of the colonial period have felt obliged to leave opinion open on this subject.[3] But in February 1704 the opportunities for legal trade were extended when, in

---

[1] Precise figures of this trade are difficult to come by but Massachusetts appears to have owned 80% of the shipping engaged in the sugar trade. Nettels gives the names of twenty-one Boston merchants engaged in the West Indian trade between 1693 and 1714. *Money Supply*, pp. 82–3, n. 75. See also Mass. Archives, lxi. 345–6, 425, and 426; CO 5/848, ff. 3, 7, 11, and 17.

[2] Weeden, op. cit. i. 386; Curtis P. Nettels, *The Roots of American Civilization* (New York, 1963), p. 261.

[3] In 1700 it was charged that at Boston, as at New York, fully one-third of the trade was against the law. Bellomont regarded the regulatory machinery as negligible. Jahleel Brenton, the Collector, was absent for two years. His deputy was a merchant, assisted by two waiters who also kept a public house. There was little to stop the determined merchant from trading illegally. *New York Col. Docs.* vi. 776, 792. Robert Quary later reported that the impoverishment of war made Bostonians more amenable to control, though Rhode Island and Connecticut remained centres of illegal trade. See T. C. Barrow, *Trade and Empire* (Cambridge, Mass., 1966), pp. 68–70. Governor Dudley listed disposition, constitution of government, and intercourse with Rhode Island, as the three factors most responsible for illegal trade. *C.S.P.C.*, 1703–4, no. 611, p. 374.

face of the Dutch supply of the colonial subjects of Philip V
through Curacao, the English were given permission to trade
freely with the Spaniards.[1] Before the end of 1706 French pressure
in the West Indies lessened and the worst hazards for New
England traders were over.[2] However the consequences of enemy
action were not easily countered. Robert Quary commented
two years later that Boston's trade was only a third of what it
had been[3]

There were other sources of wealth, some of which directly
helped to offset the shortage of specie. Save for the extreme
north, fur-bearing animals in New England had been rendered
all but extinct before the Glorious Revolution. Yet the trading
interest remained in being. The Port Royal expedition of Sir
William Phips was in part designed to advance the aspirations of
the fur-traders: success in the Quebec campaign would have
opened the way for control of the fur trade of the St. Lawrence.
After the Nine Years War had closed, Massachusetts made a
resolute effort to recover the trade of Maine, voting £300 for this
purpose in 1699 and again the following year. In 1701 it was agreed
to appropriate annually treble this sum to finance a trade centred
on Casco Bay.[4] For their part the Indians, in an attempt to play
off English against French, argued for cheaper prices and urged
the building of a more convenient trading post located at Pemaquid.
Some such move was necessary to bring the trade from Port
Royal, whither it had shifted after the destruction of Pemaquid,
nearer to the centres of English power. Saco, in Casco Bay,
proved too far southwards for Indian liking. Upon this issue
several conferences were held between the two races at the beginning of the War of the Spanish Succession but though the Board
of Trade, backed by Governor Dudley, supported the project
for reasons of its own, the Massachusetts Court effectively resisted
it on grounds of cost, buttressing their case with the seemingly
untenable argument that Pemaquid was disadvantageously far

---

[1] Nettels, *Money Supply*, pp. 32–3.
[2] Wesley F. Craven, *The Colonies in Transition, 1660–1713* (New York,
1968), p. 309.
[3] Board of Trade to House of Commons, 19 Nov. 1707, CO 389/19, pp. 181–
298; Quary to Board of Trade, 10 Jan. 1708, CO 323/6, no. 62.
[4] *C.S.P.C.*, 1699, no. 437; ibid., 1700, nos. 129–30, 143; ibid,. 1701, no. 19;
Phillips, *Fur Trade*, i. 316.

from the main Indian routes.[1] Not until the capture of Nova Scotia in 1710 were the main difficulties facing the Massachusetts traders effectively removed.[2]

Although the cost of financing the several expeditions against New France—including the wasted preparations of 1710—were heavy, the province of Massachusetts gained not inconsiderably from the provisioning of British forces engaged in the colonial theatre of war. Over £57,000 in bills of exchange were forwarded from Boston in the last three years of the war.[3] A less respectable source of gain, but lucrative, nevertheless, was the treasure and specie brought in by pirates. By the turn of the century all the New England colonies had acquired a bad reputation in the mother country for their amiable attitude towards piracy, if not for its outright encouragement.[4] But the worst practices, which the act of 1696 sought to counter, were facilitated by the uninhibited behaviour of Rhode Islanders.

The notorious Thomas Tew, after his adventures off the coast of Africa, retired unmolested at Newport. Application for a new privateering commission was refused by the Massachusetts government, but in Rhode Island he acquired one easily enough for £500. Following a second profitable voyage, he returned there again to disperse his loot of gold and diamonds, settling down temporarily to a tranquil and 'civilized' life. In the autumn of 1694, making no secret of his intentions, he prepared a third expedition from Newport and sailed to capture Moorish booty worth £180,000.[5] Yet the Earl of Bellomont, who captured Captain Kidd, charged that most of the pirates were from Massachusetts, where the ships were built and where the money they acquired circulated without questions asked. Under Governor Dudley, if not before, in support of British policy, the government adopted an uncompromising attitude to these men officially regar-

---

[1] Ibid. i., 316; *C.S.P.C.*, 1702–3, no. 687.

[2] Dudley reported in the spring of 1709 that all trade was increased save the fur trade. *C.S.P.C.*, 1707–9, no. 391, p. 236.

[3] Some of these may have originated as payments drawn on New York. See Craven, *Colonies in Transition*, pp. 309–10.

[4] As a consequence of the sack of Vera Cruz in 1683 Boston is alleged to have been enriched by the sum of £80,000 brought in by the pirates. *C.S.P.C.*, 1681–5, p. 598, no. 2042; ibid., 1689–92, p. 47.

[5] G. F. Dow and J. H. Edmonds, *The Pirates of the New England Coast 1630–1730* (Salem, Mass., 1923), pp. 92–3.

ded as a scourge to the community and a force for disorder. To ensure a conviction for the captive John Quelch, the court, presided over by the governor, permitted a questionable latitude in the testimony by the prosecution, calling upon interested witnesses and disregarding prevailing rules of procedure. Quelch and a number of his crew were sentenced to death. The captain was from England, as were most of his crew; but some among them were New Englanders. The endeavour of the town ministers to bring the prisoners to repentance produced a result that was not anticipated. From the gallows Quelch, his last words turned in irony, warned the people to 'take care how they brought money into New England, to be Hanged for it'.[1] He was aware that in advancing his own fortune he had also performed a valuable service for the colonists.

Parliament's act of 1699 paved the way for the suppression of piracy, and during the War of the Spanish Succession the specie contribution from this source diminished. A further avenue whereby Massachusetts, in competition with other colonies, sought to attract foreign specie by overvaluing it in terms of sterling, was substantially barred by royal proclamation in 1704 and statute in 1708.[2] Henceforth standard rates operated for foreign coin circulating in the colonies. At the beginning of the long struggle with France Massachusetts had taken precise steps to meet the problem of an inadequate circulating medium by the issuance of paper money. Primarily to meet the cost of the Canada expedition money to the value of £40,000 was printed.[3] Three-quarters of this sum still remained in circulation by the early autumn of 1691, and taxes designed for collection in 1693 and 1694 were levied to cover its redemption. Similar procedures carefully regulating the amount in circulation were followed throughout the Nine Years War. At the end of the short peace, however, as much as £5,000 still remained in use and with the renewal of hostilities the amount increased steadily, the time set aside for redemption being gradually extended. Until 1707 the ceiling was held at £28,000, about 25 per cent above annual taxation; but thereafter the figure rose sharply. By 1710 it stood

---

[1] Ibid., pp. 110, 113.
[2] Merrill Jensen, 'American Colonial Documents to 1776', *English Historical Documents*, ix. 425–9.
[3] Below, p. 263.

at £89,000 and bills issued that year could not be redeemed until 1715. Then in two further years, inflated by the £50,000 in private credit advanced through those merchants who supplied the Walker expedition of 1711, it almost doubled. The growth was accompanied in New England by a steep rise in prices for all commodities.[1] But in Governor Joseph Dudley's view, had the government not mortgaged its revenue this way it could neither itself have subsisted nor yet clothed the forces which defended the colony.[2]

During the second war the burden of taxation was particularly heavy. Taxes were levied upon polls and on estates, real and personal. In May 1704 the sum assessed from these sources was raised sharply to £22,000, at which figure it remained for the rest of the war.[3] An import duty brought in rather more than £3,000; and tonnage and shipping, and excise accounted between them for well over a further £1,000. The grand total for 1710–11, the twelve months in which the war for Massachusetts was reaching its peak, came to £27,027. 9s. 11d. On average, expenses were £30,000 per annum, but for the year of the Walker expedition they were forecast at £50,000. The poll tax was particularly burdensome, and by the beginning of the second decade of the eighteenth century bore heavily upon a generation which had grown to manhood knowing no other state but war. The consequences are not easily assessed with any degree of accuracy.[4] Thomas Hutchinson noted how by 1713 the provinces of Massachusetts and New Hampshire had failed to equal the growth of other colonies, which in a quarter-century had doubled their population. The war burden in terms of taxation, he granted, had been heavy, and for this reason the stoicism of the people of the day deserved a tribute from posterity. He conceded that high taxes may have induced emigration to other provinces, but unlike some contemporary observers he did not consider this to have been exceptional. Those that did attributed flight to a desire to avoid being

---

[1] Nettels, *Money Supply*, pp. 257, 258, n. 31, 32.

[2] Cited in Craven, *Colonies in Transition*, p. 325.

[3] This figure was double that of twelve months preceding and quadruple the figure at the beginning of the war.

[4] Governor Dudley to Lords of Trade, 8 Apr. 1712, *C.S.P.C.*, 1711–12, no. 375. The population at this date was estimated at 75,102. Separate figures for the poll tax are not given.

called forth to service, as well as to escape the tax collector.[1]
A further cause of lost manpower was *going abroad by sea*, 'few of
them returning home again'. But whatever the reason it was
generally concluded that the population of Massachusetts had
been significantly diminished.

In Hutchinson's view this decline had mainly come about
through death at the hands of the enemy or by distempers contracted in the service. In this way, since 1675, 5,000 or 6,000 of the
youth had perished who in forty years might have raised the
population by almost 100,000. Such are the speculations of an
historian writing later in the eighteenth century. However, in
many respects the gloom evident in 1700 did not deepen in the
decade that followed. If tax burdens were heavy, manpower
depleted, and certain sections of the economy seriously disturbed,
there was also much evidence of vitality and healthy growth.
Signs were not wanting that the more acute dangers stemming
from Catholic France were receding. No major blow had been
struck at Boston, or its immediate hinterland: no cherished
principles had been sacrificed since the compromises of 1691.
If under the pressure of war and the influence of widening horizons
the nature of the Massachusetts tradition and the character of its
supports were changing, an important measure of continuity had
been preserved; there was no abrupt break with the revered past
such as had been experienced during the 1680s under the last
male Stuarts.

In looking back from later decades, influenced by the startling
failures of imperial co-operation, provincials would be inclined
to overlook or minimize the value of England's contribution
to their security. But before disappointments such as these soured
a relationship, which had seemed so promising when the eighteenth
century began, men from the sheltered eastern region, who had

---

[1] The Secretary of Massachusetts reported to the Plantations Secretary in
1696 that men were removing to the southern plantations for these reasons. It
was a repeated complaint of Governor Dudley. In the first five years of his
administration 200 left; later movement may have been greater. Few departed
from New Hampshire but there was a similar outward migration from New
York to Pennsylvania and Connecticut. For Massachusetts emigration may have
been offset by immigration from Newfoundland—handicraftsmen, seamen,
and fishermen who came thither in expectation of high wages. *C.S.P.C.*, 1693–6,
no. 611; ibid., 1696–7, no. 243; ibid., 1703, no. 1399, pp. 856; ibid., 1708–9,
nos. 391, 392; ibid., 1711–12, no. 123.

watched the growth of maritime strength and shared in its prosperity, must have paid unconscious tribute to the forces which underpinned it. During the years 1708–11 alone England spent £220,000 in protecting the trade of New England and New York and in organizing the convoys upon which it rested. No New England minister, however persuasive, could deny that the exertions of British naval strength were essential to the well-being of Massachusetts or that the splendid victories of British arms were helping to remove the worst uncertainties which overhung the English settlements in North America.

CHAPTER V

The Face and Purpose of the Adversaries: a survey of the fields of battle and the debatable ground

FOLLOWING the granting of the 1691 charter a revised ecclesiastical system was constructed in Massachusetts to replace the one dismantled in the inter-charter period. It rested on legislation, passed during the next four years and, subsequently, on the important act of 1706. The primary provisions obliged each town to provide an 'able, learned, orthodox minister', selected by members of the Church with the concurrence of the town, to whose maintenance all inhabitants and rateable estates contributed. His support was drawn from land set aside for the minister but rested mainly upon an actual salary provided out of the rates.[1] By a law of 1692 town officials failing to uphold the fiscal requirements of the province were liable to fine or imprisonment by the Court of Quarter Sessions which might then impose a 'competent allowance'. A ministerial council, established in 1695, acted as arbiter where disputes arose between a town and its Church over the choice of ministers.[2] But in the mid-1690s, ministers convening at Boston were alarmed at the many parts of the country which existed without a settled ministry, having failed to take any steps to provide for one. Moreover, difficulties persisted where town communities opposed the wishes of their Church without offering

[1] The various administrative terms were admirably clarified by Susan Reed, *Church and State*, pp. 51, 53. The township, originally a grant of land to persons who intended to settle a town and gather a Church, had a territorial sense which was distinct from a town as a civil organization. Precincts, or, as they were sometimes called, parishes or districts, were divisions of a town. Villages or hamlets were a group of homesteads, but these terms denoted no civil organization. New precincts, which in due course might become a new town carved out of a former township, were formed on the basis of religious needs. In ecclesiastical law the precinct was composed of inhabitants attending a single meeting-house, was a separate tax unit, military unit, and also, in supporting a separate school, usually became a school district. Men frequenting a meeting-house outside their precinct might be taxed by both congregations.
[2] Ibid., pp. 61, 62; Goodell, *Acts and Resolves*, i. 62, 216.

an adequate explanation. Finally, during the reign of Anne, in an effort to meet this unsatisfactory situation, provincial powers were extended. Henceforth delinquent towns were liable to be taxed by the General Court to provide a necessary maintenance.

In the exercise of its ecclesiastical powers, raised to their highest point by the law of 1706,[1] Massachusetts faced severe problems. Not only had control of Maine and Plymouth given her an *imperium* which proved a mixed blessing to the theocrats, but the religious homogeneity of Congregationalism, in its outworks, if not elsewhere, was crumbling before increasing Quaker strength and the potential menace of Anglican growth. In times of continuing uncertainty, and while seeking to create a novel relationship with the mother country, she was confronted with forbidding internal enemies, in former times expelled from the colony but now within the gates and seemingly possessed of an alarming capacity to harm her interests. Increase Mather, in offering thanks to King William for the ending of formal hostilities, found little to distinguish these from the forms of threat which still remained. In his writing he turned naturally from the molestation of one enemy to that of another:

If the Indians have chosen to prey upon the Frontiers and Out-Skirts, the Quakers have chosen the very same Frontiers and Out-Skirts, for their more Spiritual Assaults; and finding little Success elsewhere, they have been Labouring incessantly and sometimes not unsuccessfully, to Enchant and Poison the Souls of Poor people, in the very places, where the Bodies and Estates of the people have presently after been devoured by the Salvages.

Mather's identification of cause and effect is not always directly instructive but he was factually correct in stating that the Quaker faith, which had been a thorn in the side of the Puritan theocracy since the earliest days of Massachusetts Bay, was to be found particularly in the border counties.[2] There were an estimated 3,000 Quakers in the three new counties created when the former

---

[1] Reed, *Church and State*, p. 32.

[2] Reed, *Church and State*, provides detail for the period 1689–1713 about the location of the Quaker communities and their political activities. Apart from this work there is no satisfactory history. The best—Rufus Matthew Jones, *The Quakers in the American Colonies* (London, 1923)—is highly selective for New England and does not attempt to chart the growth of Quakerism. James Bowden, *The History of the Society of Friends in America* (London, 1850), does not extend its inquiry into Massachusetts beyond the 1670s.

colony of Plymouth lost its separate identity. These were concentrated in the region of Buzzards Bay, especially Falmouth and
Sandwich, on Cape Cod, and in Bristol County on the Rhode
Island border.[1] Rhode Island, a province where creeds were to
be numbered in their thousands, was itself under Quaker government.[2] Quakers also constituted one-third of the Piscataqua region,
which embraced the New Hampshire towns and villages, and
formed part of the communities of the Maine coast. Within Massachusetts proper they were to be found in Salisbury, Jamaica,
Newbury, Haverhill, and in the region round Scituate.[3] In
Boston, after severe persecution, they were enabled to build their
first brick meeting-house in 1694, but away from the metropolis
they were strong only where the established order was weak. But
for Massachusetts the most dangerous concentration of dis-
affection was in the protected area adjacent to Rhode Island, not
in the exposed frontier of the north where the inhabitants, though
sustained by itinerant preachers from Salem and Lynn, were
indifferent rather than favourable to Quakerism.

The new provincial charter of 1691 had granted formal religious
toleration, a feature to which Increase Mather frequently alluded
in emphasizing the comparability of old and New England. In the
election sermons of 1692 and 1693 he offered reassurance to
provincial dissidents by stressing their advantages: 'Your religion
is secured to you. Now you need not fear being sent to Prison . . .
You may Worship God and no one may disturb you.'[4] But others,
such as Samuel Sewall, were less happy about the consequences
for God's people which might arise from a deflected purpose.
And in Quaker eyes, if in the eyes of no other, it seemed that
the theocracy had changed only its coat and not its character.
Subsequent legislation appeared to testify to the clarity of their
vision.

Quakerism was a challenge to established authority, and in this
respect appealed especially to the younger generation, and to
individualists of every age angered by exclusion from political

---

[1] Reed, *Church and State*, pp. 16, 28, and 36.
[2] See 'An Account of the State of Religion in the English Plantations in
North America', by Col. Dudley, Governor of New England, *Prot. Episc. Hist.
Soc. Colls.* vol. i, pp. xiv, v.
[3] Reed, *Church and State*, p. 46.
[4] Ibid., p. 21.

and ecclesiastical influence.[1] Yet it employed, as one of its most effective assets, a highly integrated form of organization which was beyond the power of the Congregationalists to emulate. Quaker unity derived from regular meetings, held monthly and quarterly, and from the great yearly meeting which Friends from all over New England flocked to attend. In addition it drew strength from the exceptional power of the English Quakers, who similarly supported a developed system of centralization under the London Yearly Meeting, and who numbered among their members influential men such as William Penn, Thomas Ellwood, John Field, and others. These men were aided by an effective parliamentary lobby.[2] Quaker persistence, thus sustained by a system of support which breasted the Atlantic, and operating through an extended network of influence, not only helped to reveal the divergences between New Englander and Englishman but also served to deepen them substantially.

Quaker manipulation of English colonial administration contrasted with the blundering vacillations and petty bickering of a divided Puritan élite. Having previously worsted the theocracy under the covering power of General Governor Andros, influential Quakers skilfully advanced once more to test the power of the restored theocrats. In January 1698 the Lynn monthly meeting complained to London against a system whereby they were taxed to maintain the established Massachusetts Churches. However, though vigorously supported in England, they were obliged to rest content with the ruling that laws passed by representative assemblies and confirmed in England could be repealed by those assemblies alone.[3] Efforts by the London meeting to join forces with English Presbyterians and Independents in combatting legislation hostile to the principle of religious toleration failed twice: in 1703 and in 1705. But the revival in 1703 of an old Connecticut law against heretics helped to prepare the ground for future success.

[1] It did not always directly weaken military effort. Quakers in the protected region along the Rhode Island border remonstrated with Friends in Hampton and Dover who refused to pay public taxes, the proceeds of which would be used for war. Ibid., p. 90.

[2] Ibid., p. 96; O. M. Dickerson, *American Colonial Government* (Cleveland, Ohio, 1912), pp. 20–57; I. K. Steele, *Politics of Colonial Policy. The Board of Trade in Colonial Administration, 1696–1720* (Oxford, 1968), ch. iv, esp. pp. 71–6.

[3] Reed, *Church and State*, pp. 92–4.

Dudley was firmly convinced that London Quakers confused Massachusetts with Connecticut, or in their thinking regarded the two provinces as one. In the *Boston News-Letter* a passage, believed to be officially inspired, indirectly accused them of misrepresenting the Bay colony in England. But the attempted defence by the governor failed and Massachusetts was rebuked by the Board of Trade for 'Creating of heats and Animosities amongst her Majesty's subjects'.[1] This was a heavy charge against Dudley, a governor dedicated to the need for unity in wartime. It was also deeply disturbing to Cotton Mather. He was incensed that the 'wicked spirit of Quakerism', having vilified his country, should find support among Congregationalists and Presbyterians in London who chose to reject the testimony of their New England brethren.[2] It was particularly to be regretted as revealing a new and more serious check to the movement for unity among the Non-conformists which Increase Mather, while negotiating in England for a new provincial charter, had done so much to advance.

In 1691 the 'Heads of Agreement' were framed under the inspiration of Mather, the Presbyterian leader John Howe, and Matthew Mead, Congregational pastor of a large Church at Stepney, only to collapse three years later when the English Congregationalists seceded from the Union. Nevertheless, in New England hopes of an abiding union were retained, especially by the Mathers. Cotton, on receipt of a copy of the *Heads of Agreement*, preached on them at once to his Boston congregation. They were printed and circulated widely in 1692, and included later in *Magnalia Christi Americana* as the ideal exposition of Congregationalism.[3] For Massachusetts, however, they led locally to the abortive *Proposals of 1705*, while in England they failed to become the foundations for a new attempt at transatlantic unity. When, under Queen Anne, in face of the dangerous aspirations of the High Church Tories, 'The Body of the Protestant Dissenting Ministers of the Three Denominations in and about the City of

---

[1] *C.S.P.C.*, 1702, no. 966; Council of Trade and Plantations to Governor Dudley, 4 Feb. 1705/6, CO 5/912, pp. 119–20.

[2] *Mass. Hist. Soc. Colls.*, 6th ser. vii. 571.

[3] Carl Bridenbaugh, *Mitre and Sceptre, 1689–1775* (New York, 1962), pp. 32–4; Walker, *Creeds and Platforms*, pp. 441–52; Neal, *History*, ii. 656–63.

London' was formed, co-operation with New England never advanced beyond occasional correspondence with the Mathers and with Benjamin Colman.[1]

The repercussions of the law of 1706 further revealed the degree of isolation towards which the New England establishment was moving once again. Local Quaker defiance was reported from many of the communities of northern Massachusetts, including Salem and Haverhill, and from Bristol County. Instead of rallying to the support of the Congregationalists the English Independents volunteered to write and remonstrate against the spirit of the new legislation.[2] In an endeavour to justify its actions and rehabilitate its standing the Massachusetts General Court prepared a lengthy memorial. But it is questionable whether the reputation of the New Englander, which had already widely suffered as a result of the running battle with the Quakers and, in a long-term sense, from the political obduracy of the past, was not further impaired by a stiff and sententious apologia of orthodoxy.[3] In retrospect, the purposes of both Quaker and Congregationalist are defensible and readily understood, but their conflict dramatically reveals how the New England tradition, even diluted as it was by the passage of time, was steadily becoming a thing apart from the rest of the English nation. If the leading English dissenters found more common ground with the ranks of dissent in New England, the Quakers and the Baptists, than with the established order, which still persisted in observable forms and conventions, what hope had that order of engaging the understanding, let alone the support, of the Anglican Church and the English establishment? In religion a clash of interests, though initially muted and accidentally delayed, was unavoidable and foreshadowed the shattering blow to the Anglo-Massachusetts military *entente* which came from the failure of the Walker expedition of 1711.

By the early 1690s the Anglican Church had become established in all the mainland colonies from Maryland southwards. Yet it was not the Church of the majority of the colonists, save in Virginia, and even there vestry control was already limiting the power of the clergy. In Maryland radical sects predominated; in North

---

[1] *Blessed Unions* (Boston, Mass., 1692); Bridenbaugh, *Mitre and Sceptre*, pp. 35–6.

[2] Reed, *Church and State*, p. 107; Mass. Archives, xi. 279–80.

[3] Reed, *Church and State*, p. 111.

Carolina, as in Pennsylvania and the Jerseys, Quakerism was the dominant faith. Moreover, new types of immigrants, notably Huguenots, added to the religious diversity that was already a marked feature of colonial life before the Revolution. But despite the practical value of religious toleration as an aid to peopling the colonies, and despite its embodiment as a principle in the parliamentary legislation of 1689, the potential resources of the Anglicans were rendered less alarming only by the overshadowing threat from Rome. The New Englanders were conditioned to an awareness of such dangers; the recent experience of the establishment of King's Chapel under General Governor Andros was only partially erased by the abdication of James and the assurances of William.[1] The old enemy inside the gate, even though bearing the badge of alliance, was not entirely to be trusted. Between Revolution and Peace few—if any—fears were expressed that it might ever reassume a hostile garb or re-acquire its former power but, as the Anglican revival under Anne gained strength, speculative fears were aroused at the purpose of weapons of spiritual warfare which appeared to be directed not at the common foe but rather inwards to the central New England bastion. New Englanders became alarmed, though not with undue precipitancy, at the aspirations of the Society for the Propagation of the Gospel in Foreign Parts, and at the specific desire, included among these aspirations but receiving forceful support from independent sources, to erect a colonial bishopric.

The S.P.G., as it was commonly known, was founded in 1699 to promote missionary work in the colonies.[2] For New England ears references in the charter to the danger from 'Popish superstition and Idolatry' were pleasing, as were some of the early sermons preached before the society in which the more effective missionary zeal of the Roman Catholic Church was alluded to as a reproach to Protestantism.[3] But under the presidency of the Archbishop of Canterbury and in co-operation with the Bishop of London, until 1713 the vigorous Henry Compton, the S.P.G. was well

---

[1] Barnes, *Dominion of New England*, p. 130.

[2] David Humphreys, *An Historical Account of the Incorporated Society for the Propagation of the Gospel in Foreign Parts* (London, 1730); Charles F. Pascoe, *Two Hundred Years of the S.P.G.* (London, 1901), i. 4–8.

[3] E. B. Greene, 'The Anglican Church in the American Colonies in the Early Eighteenth Century', *American Historical Review*, xx (1914–15), 70–1.

suited to co-operate closely with the political arm of British colonial policy.[1] An express aim was the instruction of colonists 'in the principles of true Religion', and in a statement of priorities, presented by the Bishop of Lincoln at the first anniversary sermon in 1702, it was made plain that the settlement of religion among *our own people*, in those regions where an established ministry already obtained, was to take precedence over conversion of Indian and negro and the spreading of the gospel to the frontiersman. Thus correction of error was raised above the more simple expansion of Christian influences

This was a clumsy challenge to the New England 'Saints', overlooked even by the more perceptive Congregationalists until after its modification in 1710. It implied objectives not precisely identifiable with those of the founder, Thomas Bray.[2] Bray, though deeply disturbed by the atheism of Rhode Island, expressed respect for the established dissent of Massachusetts and Connecticut. 'My design', he declared, 'is not to intermeddle where Christianity under any Form has obtained Possession.' The execution of policy by missionaries in the field was initially faithful to this object. Their limited activity was confined to areas of religious apathy in the south-east of Massachusetts and on Cape Ann. Anglican Churches at Swansea and Little Compton were formed at an early date, but elsewhere achievements were slight. At Braintree a small vociferous minority appealed to the governor, and later to the Bishop of London, against taxation for the support of a Congregational minister. Active nuclei also developed at Marblehead and at Newbury.[3] But during the very early years of the War of the Spanish Succession there were a number of other noisier challenges.

In far-off Carolina, Governor Nathaniel Johnson in May 1704, by a close vote, procured the passage of a bill which excluded dissenters from the House of Representatives and imposed Anglican

---

[1] See Bridenbaugh, *Mitre and Sceptre*, pp. 26, 57. Dudley was a member of the S.P.G. and a supporter of its aims, but for the sake of provincial peace he played an important role in modifying Anglican demands. See esp. Reed, *Church and State*, p. 168.

[2] It was Perry Miller's belief that New England's reaction in the 1700s to the aims of the S.P.G. showed more bewilderment than anger. *Province to Colony*, p. 464.

[3] Reed, *Church and State*, pp. 154–6, 160, and 163.

usages upon the province. This fact was hardly made more palatable by the unfavourable reaction to it of the S.P.G.[1] Nearer home, Governor Cornbury sought to advance the power of the Church by denying Dutch ministers entry to the province of New York and filling all Dutch benefices vacated by death with Anglican clergy. In New England itself, George Keith, a former Scottish Presbyterian, sometime leader of the Pennsylvanian Quakers, and now converted to Anglicanism was the centre of a religious storm. His clamorous progress raised fear and anger, even if it did little to increase the number of Anglicans. Keith crossed swords with Increase Mather and President Willard of Harvard, and, like Cornbury, perceived the advantage of attacking the New England heart at Cambridge as a means of reclaiming New England 'from its evil ways'.[2] His proposal, not accepted, was that pious and able divines from Oxford and Cambridge in old England should be sent thither. Hardly less fundamental, though equally unsuccessful, was the project to use the bishops suffragan of Colchester, Dover, Nottingham, and Hull, for direct episcopal supervision in North America.[3]

Yet not until almost the end of 1712 did the fears of Congregational ministers find open expression, when Benjamin Colman informed White Kennet, Dean of Peterborough, that the purposes of propagating the gospel were being perverted. Though Kennet was placatory and had no mind to worsen the relationship with New England, there was no easy reconciliation of the legitimate grievances of the Congregational ministers and the legitimate aspirations of the Anglican missionaries.[4] Understandably the latter were resolved to establish a colonial bishopric, since without an episcopal system it was believed the Church could not achieve an important part of its meaning. Kennet and Compton had both urged and supported such a move in the past, and during the reign of Queen Anne circumstances in its favour seemed to be steadily increasing. Only the death of the monarch prevented a plan, prepared by the S.P.G. and backed by the Anglican hier-

---

[1] Cross, *Anglican Episcopate*, p. 35.

[2] Greene, loc. cit., pp. 68, 70, and 76. Keith described dissenters as at their best 'Christians of a decidedly inferior type and at their worst as hardly better, or even worse than, the infidels themselves'.

[3] Cross, *Anglican Episcopate*, p. 100.

[4] See Bridenbaugh, *Mitre and Sceptre*, pp. 57–9.

archy, from being submitted to Parliament in legislative form.[1] In face of the visible growth of Anglican political strength in England and the express animosity towards English dissenters, it is surprising not that New England ministers reacted but that they failed to react more sharply. For in 1711 following earlier unsuccessful attempts, the High Church Tories passed through Parliament the occasional conformity bill, a sacrifice by the Whigs of the principles of religious toleration.

The hostile demonstrations by the populace against Nonconformists and their property, inflamed by the sermons of Dr. Sacheverell which accompanied these measures, marked a decisive stage in the return to influence of High Church doctrines. Sacheverell had violently attacked both Nonconformity and Latitudinarianism from the pulpit of Oxford University before he turned to confront the Whig doctrine of the right of resistance and the comprehension scheme of 1689, in his famous sermon at St. Paul's Cathedral on 5 November, 1709.[2] His trial began in Westminster Hall at the end of February, 1710, and though he was voted guilty by a majority of sixty-nine to fifty-two, which included seven bishops, almost as many bishops had voted for his acquittal. In an outburst of fury against dissenters, Protestant refugees, and the influence of the great London merchants who desired the continuation of the war, mobs in London and Westminster assaulted dissenting chapels, half a dozen of which went up in flames. Whigs and dissenters were attacked in town and country and a call for the closing of dissenting schools was raised. The cry of the crowd to Queen Anne, 'We hope your majesty is for the Church and Dr. Sacheverell', must have chilled all those New England hearts which revered the covenant, and have warned even the most sanguine that the England of the Stuarts, defeated by the landing of William of Orange at Torbay, still lived.[3] Though the High Churchmen were not Jacobites, from 1710 onwards they included

---

[1] Cited in ibid., p. 27; Cross *Anglican Episcopate*, pp. 92–101.

[2] Tories and High Churchmen believed that the Church of England was in danger of being destroyed by 'unlimited toleration'. See George Every, *The High Church Party* (London, 1956), p. 126.

[3] I. S. Leadam, *The Political History of England, 1702–60*, ix. 160–9; G. M. Trevelyan, *England under Queen Anne. The Peace and the Protestant Succession* (London, 1946), iii. 55–8. But see Sheldon S. Cohen, 'The Diary of Jeremiah Dummer', *W & MQ*, 3rd ser., vol. xxiv, no. 3 (July 1967), pp. 398, 408, and 409.

a significant Jacobite wing consisting of non-juring priests and laymen who had returned to the Church of England. The bright hopes raised by the Glorious Revolution were now rapidly darkening as the associations of Massachusetts debated how best to meet the future.[1]

Upon reflection, the events of 1710 and the years remaining to Queen Anne could be represented as an advanced stage of a continuing assault upon the forces of colonial dissent. Earlier events could now be seen in a more sinister light. In 1701 the anticipated fall of the Quaker colonies of Pennsylvania and Rhode Island, as proprietary and charter institutions, had been linked in the minds of English Quakers with the efforts of Dr. Bray, Edward Randolph, and Jeremiah Basse to secure a provincial structure of government which would support an established Anglican Church. At home their own governor, in his pursuit of the reconciliation of conflicting interests within the province for the sake of wartime unity—a delicate and demanding task, had contributed importantly towards allaying suspicion and fear. But his success in this role was by no means unqualified. In 1701 he had himself contributed a paper to the S.P.G. on the state of religion in the plantation and, as governor, had made the bad-tempered and damaging observation that the people of Massachusetts were an angry people unable to bear either the government or the Church of England among them.[2] He remained throughout his life a staunch prerogative man.

Dudley, and two out of the three other governors who headed the Massachusetts executive between the Glorious Revolution and the Settlement of Utrecht, were New England-born. In this respect each had an advantage over the administrator of British birth in an initial insight and experience of local politics. However, experience also meant involvement which, though no serious liability for Stoughton and Phips who held office in the 1690s, proved a serious hindrance to Dudley. His record included service under the Stuarts, an unpalatable fact which could be countered only with difficulty. As president of the Massachusetts Council after the vacation of the charter in 1684 he was distrusted by many New

---

[1] Every, *High Church Party*, pp. 27–8; Bridenbaugh, *Mitre and Sceptre*, pp. 62, 66.

[2] Osgood, *Eighteenth Century*, ii. 127; Palfrey, *History of New England*, iii. 270, 271; Dudley to Sec. Hedges, 26 Nov. 1704, CO 5/751 f. 59.

Englanders, and *persona non grata* to some.[1] His candidature as the
successor of Governor Phips, following the death of the latter in
1695, was effectively opposed by the provincial agents Constantine
Phips and Sir Henry Ashurst. William III was aware of the extent
of provincial opposition to his appointment and embarrassed by
the parliamentary move to reverse the attainder against Jacob
Leisler, in which Dudley had played a leading part. Otherwise it is
likely he would have been given the post, for he had powerful
friends in England, including William Blathwayt, the Earl of
Portland, Lord Cutts, the Duke of Leeds, and Lord Sydney, and
claimed, though with some exaggeration, that most of the people
of Massachusetts were for him.[2] He retained the friendship of
Cutts, who as governor of the Isle of Wight had Dudley made
his deputy, a position he held for nine years. By industry and
intelligence he shaped himself for the task he desired, becoming
Member of Parliament for Newtown, Isle of Wight, in 1701,
wooing the leading ministers among the English dissenters and
cultivating the Mathers, who at one time had been his foremost
opponents. So successful were his manoeuvres that he gathered
the Nonconformist weight behind him in his second candidature
and induced Constantine Phips to revise his personal estimation.[3]

The support of the English dissenters proved decisive, a significant milestone in view of the alienation evident only a few years
later. Against the stresses and strains of war it is difficult to argue
that over-all Dudley's appointment was not a success, particularly
if it be conceded that the most important task for a royal governor
of the Bay province was to secure the Anglo-Massachusetts
relationship upon an even keel. He advanced a surprising way
towards achieving this while managing to protect the queen's
prerogative from serious damage. Though an avowed imperialist
and a staunch Church of England man, he was by no means

[1] Joseph Dudley was born at Roxbury, Mass. in 1647, the son of Thomas
Dudley, second governor of the colony. He held office continuously from 1673,
when he first became representative for Roxbury in the General Court, until
the fall of the Andros regime. The historian James Truslow Adams estimated
that by 1689 he was the most hated man in New England—'a title for which
at the time there was no slight competition'. His role as Chief Justice in Leisler's
trial even further damaged his reputation. *D.A.B.* v. 481–3.
[2] Palfrey, *History of New England*, iii. 150; Everett Kimball, *The Public Life
of Joseph Dudley* (London, 1911), pp. 66–8.
[3] Palfrey, *History of New England*, iii. 179.

ill-equipped to pursue such complex and demanding evolutions. If his administration lacked spectacular achievements, or more complete success, this is less a commentary on his own shortcomings than on the men who headed English affairs in the closing years of Queen Anne's reign.

Among those who preceded him Phips had neither the intellect, the background, nor the personality to perform the service Dudley aspired to. As the darling of the Mathers, holding office during the honeymoon period of the Anglo-Massachusetts relationship, Phips had great advantages, but he lacked the political sophistication and patronage which Dudley had acquired in England. At his best he was but 'coarse homespun' and in striking contrast to the quasi-viceregal grandeur of Sir Edmund Andros. In this he was a token that Massachusetts was to be wooed and not coerced to an imperial purpose. He was not altogether politically guileless. Having joined the North Church of Boston in March 1689, as a means of laying the foundation for his political ambitions, he carefully avoided compromising participation in the revolutionary disturbances.[1] But as governor his crude control of the General Court was achieved at a cost of alienating both those who advocated and those who opposed a return to the old charter regime. For the Mathers, who wished to re-unify the province by a moderate policy which accepted the permanence of the royal administration yet continued to pursue through this framework the liberties lost in 1684, his period of office was a disappointing failure.

When Phips died in England in 1695, having been recalled to defend charges levelled against him, William Stoughton, who had been his lieutenant-governor since 1692, continued in office as temporary governor of Massachusetts, a post he held until his own death in 1701, save for the period between May 1699 and July 1700 when the Earl of Bellomont was in Boston. A more subtle and complex politician than Phips, Stoughton was in close sympathy with the ideals of Joseph Dudley, perhaps the only man for whom he had affection and deference. Having been educated at Harvard

---

[1] After leading the successful Port Royal and the abortive Canada expeditions of 1690, Phips revisited England early in 1691. He was appointed governor at the end of the year, having urged upon William III the necessity of an aggressive policy in North America and the importance of the fur trade and the New England fisheries. V. F. Barnes, *DA.B.*, xiv. 551.

and New College, Oxford, he had begun a varied and extensive political career in 1671, at the age of forty, as an assistant in the General Court, an office he held for fifteen years. Though later he served in both the provisional council of Dudley in 1686 and under Sir Edmund Andros, he cleared himself of this taint in 1690 by co-operating in a denunciation of the acts of the Andros regime. As Chief Justice of the Court of Oyer and Terminer, he played a leading role in the Salem witchcraft trials which preceded the arrival of Phips in the colony, and was openly criticized by the governor for his conduct.[1] Later, rejecting the confession of error made by Samuel Sewall and other notables, he refused to repent of his use of spectral evidence, an attitude which did not appear to jeopardize his influence within the province at all seriously. His consistent firmness and resolution won him respect, and helps to explain why (shortly before his death) the Council in Assembly asked that he be made permanent governor.

An Irish Lord, Richard Coote, the Earl of Bellomont, preferred in 1697 before Dudley, was the only non-New Englander to serve Massachusetts at this time. As joint governor of New York and New England between 1697 and 1701, he spent scarcely more than one year in Massachusetts. However, during this brief period his frankness, sensitivity, and concern for the people created a bridge of goodwill between the English government and the New Englanders that augured well for the future.[2] Part of Bellomont's success stemmed from his alliance with Elisha Cooke senior, his friendship with Ashurst, who held him in great respect and with Constantine Phips who remained a political power in the province, and, perhaps above all, from his express distrust of

---

[1] Phips to the Earl of Nottingham, 21 Feb. 1693, *C.S.P.C.*, 1693–6, p. 30; Sidney G. Morse, *D.A.B.* xviii. 113–4. The English historian A. J. Doyle described him as 'a man of narrow mind and harsh temper'. In the view of Morse he is 'proud, cold, and obstinate'. The most severe criticism against him, penned in the nineteenth century, stresses his behaviour in the Salem witchcraft trials. See especially Emory Washburn, *Sketches of the Judicial History of Massachusetts from 1630–1775* (Boston, Mass., 1890), and C. W. Upham, *Salem Witchcraft* (Boston, Mass., 1867). J. G. Palfrey argued that he excelled in being 'churlish, wilful and obstinate' but concedes he had 'dignity, assiduity, and a sense of duty'. *History of New England*, iii. 178.

[2] A Whig lord whom Thomas Hutchinson described as professing 'the most moderate principles in religion and government'. *History of Massachusetts Bay*, ii. 84, cited in W. Kellaway, *The New England Company 1649–1776* (London, 1961), p. 261.

Dudley. But the foundation of his successful stay at Boston was a
shrewd use of natural assets. The deference which New Englanders
frankly accorded him, as the first nobleman who had ever headed
their government, he returned by respecting their more hallowed
traditions as well as the leading persons of church and state. When
the General Court adjourned to attend the weekly sermon the
governor accompanied it. He played upon the emotions of all
classes and cultivated their prejudices by damning the Stuarts as
aliens who had never defended English interests in battle and who
had parted with Nova Scotia and its lush fisheries to serve the
ends of popery. By such devices he created a favourable climate in
which his manipulations of the Council passed without notice and
a rewarding harmony prevailed between all parts of government.[1]
The General Court demonstrated its favour in no uncertain way
by liberally granting him £2,000. But he may yet have been
fortunate in his death, for in urging the English government not to
employ native New Englanders in the king's service he rejected an
essential component of that partnership which his own actions
during a short administration had seemed designed to favour.

The circumstances under which Massachusetts Bay was governed
changed permanently with the vacation of the charter in 1684, and
no amount of wishful thinking or skilled diplomacy could re-
establish the trappings or deceits of provincial sovereignty.
William III, and more gently Queen Mary, had spelled out to
Increase Mather the limits under which a special relationship
might operate. This did not, however, prevent the Court attempting
to test its powers under the new charter. Its first act in October 1691
was an assertion that 'no aid, tax... or imposition whatsoever'
should be 'levied on any of their Majesties subjects or estates, on any
pretence whatsoever, but by the act and consent of the Governor,
Council and Representatives of the people assembled in General
Court'. This was disallowed by the Privy Council; and thereafter
the contentions of the legislature were rarely diametrically
opposed to the main aims of English policy. But the traditions of
half a century of quasi-independence upheld by biblical sanction were too strongly embedded for the General Court ever to
become a mere ratifying body of Parliament or Crown, even under
an admired and trusted king. Each issue of common concern was

[1] Hutchinson, *History of Massachusetts*, ii. 106–9.

judged separately upon its merits and no inch of privilege and no right was ever yielded gratuitously by men whose forefathers had created a new and separate commonwealth when Charles I was king. The underlying problem which governed this relation with the sources of English power, as that between provincial assembly and governors who pursued with a greater or lesser degree of understanding and resolution the objectives defined by London, was the coercing of an autonomous past to conform to an imperial present, 'of conforming... inherited institutions to the new orders of things.'[1]

Since 1691 the role of the governor had been forcibly changed. He was no longer an elected head amenable to the people but a royal appointee, the direct servant of the Crown and the main instrument through which king and Parliament made known their aims and objectives. The promise of the Glorious Revolution, and a monarchy which rapidly established its integrity by aligning the English colonies against France, facilitated the acceptance of a new institution in the abnormal circumstances of war. Merchants and ministers were one in acknowledging the value of a new and closer relationship with this reformed England, and the choice of New England men for governor was a wise concession to a proud people conscious of their own importance. But it was not always enough. In the case of Dudley, a prerogative man who had compounded his early Toryism by an overlong stay in England which changed both his style and his manners, the governor was long seen by the nervous and by the politically vengeful as a hostile reminder of an old England from which New England wished to be freed.

Within this framework the governor could become, as Dudley for a while appeared to be, an enemy within. But throughout the period there were major issues of contention between governor and Assembly over the governor's salary, his expenditure of defence moneys and the selection of his council, and over various assembly rights, especially the selection of the Speaker. Over these issues a battle raged in which the people contended for their ancient autonomy and the governor sought to defend the royal prerogative.

The administration of Sir William Phips, the first post-revolu-

---

[1] Palfrey, *History of New England*, iii. 126. Randolph constantly charged that they held fast to anti-monarchical principles spread among them by the English republicans, Sir Henry Vane and Hugh Peters; *C.S.P.C.*, 1689–92, no. 482.

tionary government, was a clumsy attempt to unite the political forces in New England, despite the best endeavours of the Mathers. Phips was not without gifts, as is testified by his own spectacular rise from obscure origins, the influence he exercised in England until his death, and his able termination of the witchcraft prosecutions; but a fiery temperament and a readiness to employ the crude and abusive expressions, to which he had become accustomed in his earlier career at sea, scarcely fitted him for the delicate task of knitting together the diverse and divergent political elements of Massachusetts. Predictably, he was not readily acceptable to those within the province who retained hopes of a restoration of the charter of 1629— 'the ungrateful sheep' in Cotton Mather's *Political Fables*. Nor could he perceive a way to work amicably with them.[1] In May 1693, at the first election of councillors conducted by the General Court under the new charter, Phips refused Elisha Cooke, senior, membership of the Council.[2] Cooke was a formidable enemy and the main pillar of the old charter party. He had been elected deputy to the General Court in 1681, had become Speaker the following year and had provided intransigent opposition to surrendering the charter then under attack from London. Randolph had singled him out for special disfavour for his leading role in the overthrow and imprisonment of Andros and Dudley and for his membership of the Council of Safety. As colonial agent in London from 1690-2, he firmly opposed the new provincial charter, for which reason he had become particularly odious to Increase Mather. By the mid-1690s, however, as one of the wealthiest men in Boston, Cooke was possessed of widespread influence and able to pursue with considerable success his opposition both to clerical control and to royal prerogative. He was to the forefront of the faction whose hostility to Increase Mather's designs for Harvard ultimately led to his relinquishment of the presidency: in 1694, while Phips was away in England, he was again elected to the Council and held his seat during the administration of Bellomont with whom he achieved a cordial relationship. Not surprisingly he was to prove a thorn in the side of Joseph Dudley.

As has been noted, circumstances had changed decisively for the General Court since the imposition of the new charter. A

[1] Miller, *New England Mind*, pp. 170-1.
[2] Palfrey, *History of New England*, iii. 129-30.

return to the untrammelled autonomy which had been obtained before 1684 was no longer possible. In all important respects the Massachusetts General Court was indistinguishable from any other English colonial assembly in the western hemisphere. Though it might take a prolonged period of readjustment before this were accepted by the people of Massachusetts in any profound sense, if it were ever accepted at all, the formal language of political address paid recognition to an altered situation. In June, 1692, with the convening of the General Court, the speaker of the deputies, William Bond, prayed the governor that 'the accustomed privileges of an English Assembly (which he expected as their due)—that is freedom of debate, free access to the governor, and security of arrest for themselves and their servants', might be allowed. The Court adjourned after enacting that all such laws of Massachusetts and Plymouth as were not inconsistent with the new charter of English law should be revived and continue in force.

Much was achieved. Laws for the administration of towns, the support of ministers and schools, and for sabbatarian observance were passed without hindrance. The blue law of 1692 prohibited on pain of fine Sunday work, games, travel, or entertainment, save for guests or strangers at public houses.[1] The judicature was substantially revised by the creation of J.P.s and the erection of Courts of Session and Courts of Common Pleas, and by the institution of a Superior Court with original and appellate jurisdiction.[2] Acts to establish the main features of the former representative system were introduced in the early 1690s but an important innovation was that of 1694 which decreed that representatives must be freeholders and residents of the towns by which they were elected.[3] The purpose of this measure was to prevent Assembly domination by commercial Boston, in the main, adverse to Phips, by preventing a practice whereby complacent

---

[1] See R. E. Brown, *Middle Class Democracy and the Revolution in Massachusetts 1691–1780* (Ithaca, N.Y., 1955), p. 106. Thirty-eight of the laws passed were subsequently confirmed. Eight were disallowed, including the Act for continuing local laws, *C.S.P.C.*, 1693–6, no. 1874.

[2] Palfrey, *History of New England*, iii. 127.

[3] Brown, *Middle Class Democracy*, p.63; Hutchinson, *History of Massachusetts* ii. 59; Sewall, *Diary*, i. 386. Hutchinson regarded this as a salutary measure in that it opposed a pernicious practice, but at the same time he saw it as an abridgement of liberty.

N E—G

or distant back-country towns trimmed expenditure by using
Bostonians to represent them. Within the House it was opposed
as contrary to English custom and as a violation of the charter.

From these contentions there arose a clear conflict of principle
between the executive and legislature over judgement of returns,
when six non-residents representing Bristol, Marblehead, Springfield, Oxford, Chingford, and Swansea, presented themselves
before the Assembly of 1694 for swearing in. Phips prevented this,
though he did so without a single element of finesse. Of the six,
only two were Bostonians of political importance: Samuel Legge,
elected for Marblehead was one; he had been a member of the
Committee for War appointed in 1692 and was later one of the
four named by the Commissioners of Customs to make a preliminary examination of the charges against Phips. Nathaniel Byfield
was the other.[1] Both Legge and Byfield contended that the members
of the House of Representatives, and not the governor, were the
proper judges of their own returns. Byfield was chosen as spokes-
man to represent, before governor and Council, the views of the
rejected members, following which meeting the governor stormed
down to the House without his hat to bully the representatives into
submission.

Byfield, an admirer and close confidant of Dudley, connected
to Stoughton by the marriage of his daughter, made Speaker of
the House in 1698 and member of the Council the following year,
was to bear the charge of Wait Winthrop that he hazarded and
undermined hallowed political traditions for the sake of a closer
dependance upon England and in order to safeguard personal
interests.[2] Though Byfield's connections with the prerogative
'party' are undeniable, Wait Winthrop's political judgements do
not necessarily command respect, albeit he was the grandson of
the illustrious founder of Massachusetts Bay. Byfield's opposition
to the bill, which he implored Dudley to have disallowed in
England, was on the grounds that it would permit an unscrupulous

---

[1] The remaining four were Captain Davis for Springfield, Captain Disley for
Oxford, Timothy Clarke for Chencford (Chingford), and Ebenezer Thornton
for Swansea. Byfield said that Phips also refused to administer the oath to
Francis Foxcroft, a Boston merchant, churchwarden of King's Chapel and
friend of Francis Nicholson: *C.S.P.C.*, 1693–6, p. 294; Bailyn, *New England
Merchants*, p. 192.

[2] Dunn, *Wynthrop Dynasty*, pp. 268–73, 276, and 282.

governor to pack an assembly with his own men. In his mind the treatment of the Assembly by Phips was unparalleled in the English nation, and so strongly aroused were his feelings that he claimed himself ready to quit the province of Massachusetts Bay, which would lose its value as a place of residence if the law were confirmed.[1]

Earlier, in November 1693, Byfield, as Speaker of the House, had been dismissed by Phips on the grounds that he had been the occasion of sundry disorders committed in the House. The Representatives were peremptorily instructed to choose another Speaker, and a deputation which questioned the governor's right to such action failed to bring redress. The Assembly, however, did acquire some countervailing reassertion of powers as the administration of Phips drew to a close. On one occasion when accounts were challenged by Byfield the governor excused his own actions by rashly placing the blame upon England; 'a Whitehall stroke', as he called it. A more positive step was taken when, in December 1693, the House passed a resolution upholding the right of Representatives to ascertain to what use money was to be put before they voted it. Early in 1696 proposals were made, ultimately to become a bill, requiring the Treasurer to lay his accounts annually before the General Assembly.[2]

For five years under Lieutenant-Governor Stoughton a calmer period ensued in which men by degrees became somewhat more reconciled to their new charter status. In part this was no more than an inevitable process, though Stoughton as the head of the government may take some credit for its peaceable realization. He had been involved in each Massachusetts administration of the revolutionary crisis yet avoided making serious political enemies until the end of his life. Increase Mather himself had named him lieutenant-governor to Phips and he had been warmly praised in England as the only man in the Bay colony who put king before country.[3] In due course, however, his political associations and his

---

[1] *C.S.P.C.*, 1693–6, p. 294.

[2] Ibid., 1693–6, nos. 688, 717, and 1103; p. 294; ibid., 1696, no. 2289; Osgood, *Eighteenth Century*, i. 317.

[3] *C.S.P.C.*, 1693–6, no. 133. Osgood describes him as 'an educated gentleman of the Boston type, regular and orthodox in all his doings and connections, a genuine Massachusetts man, though of unquestioned loyalty to Britain'. It is an important subject for speculation whether Cooke or Stoughton, in their political ideals, better represented the men of Massachusetts.

loyalties obliged men to divide in their opinion of him both in old and New England. He was distrusted by Sir Henry Ashurst in London, and the Whiggish Earl of Bellomont treated him coldly as one of Dudley's committed men. In the eyes of Wait Winthrop he was no better than a Jacobite instrumental in ruining the ancient liberties of Massachusetts.[1] This did not, however, mark a serious decline in the esteem in which he was held throughout the province, for on the death of Bellomont the House of Representatives dismissed a council recommendation of Winthrop for restoring former charter privileges and proposed addressing the king that Stoughton, though visibly ailing, should be promoted to full governor. The way was now open, however, aided by the growth of Tory strength in England, for Dudley's accession to power and the imposition of elements capable of protracted abrasive action upon those provincial forces resistant to change.

Dudley's candidature was not uncontested in New England. Within the province of Massachusetts Bay support for him was increasing but strong opposition remained within the General Court. The first move of his opponents, under the guidance of Elisha Cooke, was to promote Wait Winthrop, a popular man of modest talents, grandson of the first governor of Massachusetts and son of the first royal governor of Connecticut, to a position of influence. He was preferred before Increase Mather to represent the people's interests in England, ostensibly to draw attention to French claims to the country east of the Kennebec and to an exclusive fishery upon the seacoast. But before he could leave Boston news arrived that Dudley was already appointed governor.[2] Cotton Mather's letter to him that 'there was not one minister nor one of the Assembly but were impatient of his coming' was little more than a pleasantry but on arrival he was given a cordial and respectful welcome by the Council, among whom were Winthrop, Cooke, and Peter Sargent, and other of his most bitter opponents, aware of the need for closing ranks in face of a threat of renewed war with Louis XIV, now seemingly inevitable.[3]

There were worse choices for governor than a New Englander

---

[1] Dunn, *Wynthrop Dynasty*, p. 270.

[2] Richard Dunn observes that Winthrop had taken the field 'only to find that he had no troops', ibid., pp. 275–7. Cf. Palfrey, *History of New England*, iii. 178–9.

[3] Hutchinson, *History of Massachusetts*, ii. 100–2.

with powerful patrons in the mother country, as his initial address to the Council, which he allowed to be printed, suggests. He alluded to the dangers of war—news of the declaration of which arrived three days later—and the devotion of Queen Anne to the Protestant religion; he instructed them in the threat to the balance of power in Europe and awakened their sensitivities to the religious past by allusions to the reign of Queen Elizabeth and the comparable menace then posed by Catholic Spain.[1] With an end to encouraging the production of naval stores and strict observance of the navigation laws he reminded members bluntly that they were not immediately profitable to the Crown, as were the southern and island colonies, but he flattered their pride by asserting (what the Mathers had always wished to believe) that the province was particularly favoured by the new sovereign as by the old and that for this reason, if for no other, their more ready obedience was to be expected, particularly in establishing a civil list. He raised the vexed question of the rebuilding of Pemaquid, a bone of contention between mother country and colony which was still unsettled, reminding them that compliance here might induce the queen's government to assume a share of the onerous burden of defending the frontiers.[2] In short he showed a readiness to bully as well as to woo, whichever seemed fitting and most likely to achieve the carrying out of his instructions.

Dudley held strong views on the need of the governor to dominate the composition of his Council, and in pursuit of this he achieved considerable success. He later complained to the Lords of Trade that the election of councillors had been scandalously used to affront 'every loyal and good man that loves the Church of

---

[1] 4 May 1692–24 June 1706, *Council Records*, pp. 290–1.

[2] The queen's Order in Council for the raising of Pemaquid was dated 24 August 1702. It included instructions for the raising of a battery on the next point of land 'in case of attack by sea', and the construction of a redoubt or round tower in St. John's Island. In addition there were orders for a new fort in Piscataway River on the site where a fort (Newcastle) was already standing. The justification of this was the growing trade of the river. Dudley supported Massachusetts footing the bill for this fortification, which stood on the boundary between Maine and New Hampshire, because of the poverty of the neighbouring province. But the Massachusetts Assembly took exception to his argument. It considered its contributions to the defence of New Hampshire in other respects were already a one-sided form of aid. *C.S.P.C.*, 1702, no. 896; ibid., 1702–3, nos. 30, 315, 433, 687, and 1201; Hutchinson, *History of Massachusetts*, ii. 112–3.

England and dependence on her Majesty's government'. The
right to refuse a nominee of the House of Representatives was
indisputable though it had been exercised on only one occasion
since the charter was granted. The first clash occurred in the
elections of May 1703, when Dudley complained to the Speaker
and the House that the names of several gentlemen of ability and
known loyalty had been omitted. He raised pointed objection to
five names—Elisha Cooke, Peter Sargent (who had married the
widow of Phips), Thomas Oakes, John Saffin, and John Bradford—
all known supporters of the old charter. The House argued and the
Council concurred that every person chosen councillor of the
province ought to have the support of the major part of the elec-
tors, but Dudley successfully countered that this method was
contrary to precedent and the need of the Crown.[1] He prevailed,
despite Cook's long tenure as a councillor, his wealth, and extensive
connections.[2] Cooke and Peter Sargent were again elected the
following year. But once more the governor applied his veto, and
against Cooke a third time in 1706. In 1708 two more men were
rejected.

Dudley's vetoing of five councillors in 1703 considerably diminished the esteem in which he was held by the people of Massachusetts, and two years later, possibly by reason of prudence in
which there was embodied an element of statesmanship, he
accepted defeat of an attempt to influence the choice of Speaker.
When Thomas Oakes was selected he informed the House that he
disapproved and directed them to proceed to the choice of another.
Oakes, a 'known Commonwealthman' unable to accept the charter
of 1691 and deeply dissatisfied with the royal government that had
followed, though negatived as a councillor in 1703, retained his
seat in the House and probably increased his influence there as a
consequence of his rejection.[3] In defiance of the governor the

---

[1] *Council Records*, pp. 384, 385, and 387; and see Kimball, *Dudley*, pp. 89, 90.

[2] Hutchinson, *History of Massachusetts*, ii. 101, 111. Cooke had married a
daughter of former Governor Leveret and was said to have a better estate than
Dudley himself, who had made possession of 'little or mean estate' one of the
criteria of rejection.

[3] It seems fairly certain that Dudley, whose familiarity with English political
life was first-hand, used the term 'Commonwealthman' advisedly. Within a
short time of taking up office he had observed: 'Not a person fit in all the Province
for a Secretary'; and of the Council ' . . . so many of them are Commonwealth's
men and do so absolutely depend for their stations upon the people that they

House contended that it alone held the right of choosing the Speaker, which was secured by that law which named it the sole judge of the elections of its members. Dudley gave little fight. He accepted not only Oakes but the complete list of councillors which the House had moved to name without instructions from the governor. He did so, he explained, because of the pressure of war and of public business, a tactical surrender which received the approval of the Board of Trade.[1] It was not to be expected that his record of service to James II and his known devotion to the prerogative would endear him to the governed, whom he described as an angry people difficult to keep steady to the acts of parliament, but concessions such as these helped in time to ease political tensions and made possible the degree of provincial consensus achieved in the later stages of the War of the Spanish Succession.

In seeking the establishment of fixed salaries for the governor, the lieutenant-governor, and the judges, Dudley achieved little real satisfaction. On 1 September 1702 he had read to the Assembly the queen's letter urging a settlement of salaries for high officials. The Assembly parried with the plea that the war having occasioned notable absences in the gathering it was not prudent to proceed with a matter so momentous. A running battle then ensued, with the House appearing to make concessions by lateral movement but in fact yielding not an inch of important ground. Well might Dudley observe two years later that the people were unreasonable to expect stores of war furnished at the queen's expense while they alone of all colonies refused to settle a salary on Her Majesty's governor and other officials there. The charge, untrue, was no more effective than were letters from the queen, another of which

dare not offend them. And so H.M. has no manner of service from them, nor countenance to H.M. affairs, which makes my station very difficult and prevents everything which looks like an expense, which the poor country Representatives obstinately withstand, and are glad of any countenance from the Gentlemen of the Council therein.' 10 Dec. 1702, *C.S.P.C.*, 1702–3, no. 31. Caroline Robbins offers the following definition: 'The Commonwealthmen within the terms of their age, their class and their education, asserted liberty, talked about equality, and assumed the possibility of progress at a time when most Englishmen thought of the constitution as sacrosanct, and change as dangerous if not sacrilegeous.' *The Eighteenth Century Commonwealthman* (Cambridge, Mass., 1959) pp. 4, 5, 57, and 91. But see also W. Paul Adams, 'Republicanism in Political Rhetoric Before 1776' *Political Science Quarterly*, vol. lxxxv, no. 3 (1970), pp. 402–3.

[1] Osgood, *Eighteenth Century*, ii. 136; Board of Trade to Dudley, 4 Feb. 1705/6, *C.S.P.C.*, 1706–8, no. 85.

arrived in September 1704. Earlier Anne had warned that failure
to comply might lead to withdrawal of royal favour and bounty.
From time to time, however, the governor was mollified by
annual grants; three-fifths in the spring, the rest in the autumn;
though even these were variable in amount,[1] and not infrequently
accompanied by political sermons on 'the native privilege and right
of English subjects to raise and dispose of money according to the
present exigency of affairs.'[2]

Such rights and privileges were stoutly defended. In November
1703, the Assembly had voted that appropriation for other uses
by the governor of moneys granted for the fortification of Boston
was one among many grievances: they were answered by rebuke
and prorogation. After the close of this stormy session Dudley
wrote to the Secretary of State in England 'that the people of
Massachusetts loved not the Crown and government of England,
to any manner of obedience.' He believed they meant to put 'a
slight upon her Majesty's government'. It is unwise, perhaps, to
read too much into these statements.[3] Dudley was seeking to
justify his limited success in carrying out his instructions. If his
language was bold and dramatic in describing the political behaviour of the people of Massachusetts, and it was so on a number
of occasions, it was because he sought to explain that they were
not docile sheep stampeded mindlessly by English resolution.
They contended, as they had ever done in the past, for the fullest
autonomy possible. And yet in his choice of words there is indica-

---

[1] In July 1708, for example, instead, of the customary £300, £200 was
offered. An attempt to raise this sum failed and the governor prorogued the
Assembly. A compromise was arranged the following November. Palfrey,
History of New England, iii. 299.

[2] In mid-Nov. 1703, the House answered a speech by the governor in the
following words: '*As to perpetual salaries*: It hath been the privilege from Henry
III and confirmed by Edward I, and in all reigns unto this day granted, and now
is allowed to be the just and unquestionable right of ye subject to raise when
and dispose of how they see cause any sums of money by consent of Parliament,
the wch. privilege we H.M. loyall and dutiful subjects have lived in ye enjoyment
of, and do hope always to enjoy ye same under our Most Gracious Queen Anne
and Successors, and shall ever endeavour to discharge the duty incumbent
on us, but humbly conceive ye stating of perpetual salaries not agreable with
H.M. interest in this Province, but Prejudicial to H.M. good subjects.' 16 Nov.
1703, *C.S.P.C.*, 1702–3, no. 1266. In using Parliamentary procedures to obstruct
Assembly wishes Dudley was inadvertently encouraging comparisons between
the rights of Parliament and those of the General Court. See p. 187, n. 2.

[3] *C.S.P.C.*, 1702–3, nos. 1266, p. 814; 1317; 1344, pp. 853–4; 1398.

tion that the relationship between governor and governed was
rapidly deteriorating from distrust to outright political conflict.

Both sides gained victories. On the question of the salary
neither was it fixed nor was it adequate by comparison with the
grants made to his predecessor.[1] Defeated on this issue, Dudley
had conceded to the Assembly determination of its Speaker, first
contended for in 1693, but gained acceptance of his right to control
composition of the Council. However, he also failed to triumph in
key matters of defence. Over raising a fort at Pemaquid the
Assembly had proved obdurate and had addressed the queen
against its construction without informing the governor of its
intentions.[2] In Dudley's view the Assembly of May 1703 was
especially chosen to keep out anyone likely to meet royal wishes
over the fortifications or salary issue. Later in the year he took a
committee of the Assembly with him to Pemaquid which reported
on the reasonableness of the queen's demands. But the Lower
House refused a conference with the Council on this matter until
Dudley threatened dissolution. The conference proved in-
effectual.[3] In due course the governor was moved to consider
holding the Maine frontier region by means of a new settlement of
English or Scottish planters, the province regarding itself too hard-
pressed financially to give way merely to please the Crown of
England.[4] Even if, on balance, it could be shown that the bestowal
of stores outweighed expenditure, representatives in the General
Court would still have had a difficult time justifying to constituents

---

[1] Governors Phips and Bellomont had each received substantially larger
sums. See *Acts and Resolves*, i. 174, 188, 395, and 437, cited in Osgood, *Eighteenth
Century*, ii. 132–3.

[2] Conflict between executive and legislature raged just as fiercely over proced-
ural practices. On 15 Nov. 1703, Dudley requested a copy of the Address.
He afterwards directed the Secretary and one John Foster to carry the same
message, and withal to intimate to the House the usage of the Houses of
Parliament, viz. that when the House of Lords desired to inspect the Commons
Journal then the Clerk of the House attended their Lordships with books, but
that when the Commons desired to inspect the Lords Journal they did it by a
committee; and that he only expected either a copy, or their Clerk to attend and
read the same out of their books. The Speaker and the House refused to bring
up the Journal contending that it lay open on the table of their own House
and that this was what they understood to be Parliamentary practice 'and the
usage in this country'. 13 Nov. 1703, *C.S.P.C.*, 1702–3, p. 814.

[3] 10 Dec. 1703, *C.S.P.C.*, 1702–3, no. 30; 10 May 1703, ibid., 1702–3, no. 673.

[4] Dudley to Board of Trade, 1 Feb. 1705–6, *C.S.P.C.*, 1706–8, no. 69. For
further discussion of this issue see ch. vi, p. 220 n. 1.

their approbation of the reconstruction of Pemaquid, which was considered militarily undesirable, or the erection of a new fort on the Piscataqua, which was opposed in principle.

During this difficult earlier period of Dudley's tenure of office his fiscal integrity remained fundamentally unshaken, even if the Assembly harassed him from time to time for the authorized issuance of moneys and the violation of English liberties. Members were not easily moved by his pleas and arguments, however well-founded they might seem. To those who retained a clear image of the original theocratic purpose of Massachusetts, who regretted the loss of past autonomy and who feared outside influences immune to local control, Dudley was a feared enemy. Few men sympathized with Increase Mather who, contending in 1708 against the election of John Leveret to the presidency of Harvard, was rudely told to keep his station and permit his ministerial equals to have a share in the government of the college. Yet it was not possible to ignore the seemingly overwhelming resources of the English crown which through its most important representative had the potential if not the immediate intention to shape Massachusetts to a religious and political form at variance with the past and less favourable than the present. Not all men opposed change, provided the means by which it was effected implied an element of partnership and not mere subordination.

It is not surprising, therefore, that strenuous efforts were made to bring about the recall of Dudley and the substitution of a governor more closely aligned to these sentiments prevailing within the province. Moreover, the accusations levelled against him that he traded with the enemy angered the assemblymen of 1706, many of whom had first-hand experience of Indian fighting or the consequences of Indian attack and wanted neither trade nor truck with the French. Dudley was saved from removal by powerful friends in London—the Bishop of London, Blathwayt, Nottingham, and the Massachusetts agent, Constantine Phips.[1] After this crisis, from 1708 onwards, the cleavages in polity and society narrowed and governor and Assembly joined in close co-operation for a decisive blow against the common enemy outside the colonial frontiers.[2]

[1] G. M. Waller, *Samuel Vetch; Colonial Enterpriser* (Chapel Hill 1960), pp. 86, 95.

[2] Palfrey, *History of New England*, iv. 301.

English policy, in so far as it aimed at any precise objectives, sought wealth, security, and efficiency, probably in that order, according to the customary mercantile guidelines. Centralization and uniformity of colonial governmental structure were seen only as a means to this end and never acquired sufficient weight in any individual mind, with the possible exception of Edward Randolph's, to be regarded as ends in themselves. The search for effective means provided opportunity for a handful of resolute administrative officials to play a leading role in the shaping of policy: Edward Randolph, though with diminishing influence as his life approached its end in 1703, and Robert Quary among those primarily in service in North America; William Blathwayt, the gifted plantations secretary, and the better-informed Treasury men, especially Lord Godolphin. In the mid-1690s the movement for administrative reform and political uniformity still retained something of the momentum it had gathered under the Restoration, if it was not in fact acquiring additional force as some believed. Before the Nine Years War ended, and while the French diverted their energies in North America to plans for expansion, the English undertook two important acts relating to the administration of their colonial empire: the framing of the great Navigation Law of 1696 and the establishment of a Board of Trade to succeed the ailing Lords of Trade.[1]

English commerce since 1689 had undergone considerable expansion, but despite evidence of this and the great expectations aroused by the victory of La Hogue, trade was believed to be in decay and the future uncertain. Two factors were thought primarily responsible: organized defiance of the navigation laws and the widespread activities of Scottish interlopers. Already before 1695 the outports of Bristol and Liverpool had petitioned Parliament for the support of legitimate trade. A year earlier the Customs House had alleged that £50,000 in revenue had been lost through trade illegalities.[2] Edward Randolph, whose single-mindedness and narrow vision had contributed significantly to the failure of the Dominion of New England, anticipated that the magnitude of the alleged infractions would advance his own plans for the political

---

[1] The establishment of the Board of Trade was precipitated not by the needs of colonial administration but by a crisis in trade and finance. The new body was not expected to survive. See Steele, *Politics of Colonial Policy*, p. 17.

[2] Hall, *Edward Randolph*, p. 156.

reorganization of the empire. He contributed to, but was not primarily responsible for, the resolve to improve the working of the old colonial system. In January 1696 the Customs Commissioners, who blamed the proprietary and corporate colonies for many of the difficulties under which this system laboured, admitted to having prepared a bill to reinforce the existing acts of 1660, 1663, and 1673. During the winter of 1696 the question of reform was examined by a committee of the whole Privy Council but it rejected as too radical, as the Customs Commissioners had done, Randolph's proposal for the restructuring of the proprietary and corporate colonies.

The outstanding merit of the Act of 1696 was that it clarified the intention of earlier legislative acts, established new administrative rules and penalties, and placed greater stress on the governor's responsibility for seeing that the law was enforced. In addition, by extending the Statute of Frauds to America, it systematized the customs organization for the colonies. Of great importance also was the decision to establish Vice-Admiralty courts with jurisdiction over the penal clauses in the Navigation Acts.[1] To facilitate the exercise of the Crown's extended powers a new institution was created in the Board of Trade. This replaced the Lords of Trade, a Privy Council committee which until the later years of its existence had proved to be the most efficient organ of colonial administration yet produced by the English. Some measure of continuity was achieved through the personnel of the new body. The first president of the Board was the Earl of Bridgewater; another member was William Blathwayt, while the esteem and influence of Edward Randolph remained substantially unchanged. The function of the Board as a consultative body was extensive. But unlike its predecessor it lacked executive power and save for its very early years was dominated by the Treasury under Godolphin and by the Secretaries of State.[2]

With a single-mindedness which was an abiding characteristic of the man, Randolph accompanied his firm successes, expressed by the passing of the great Navigation Act, with renewed efforts to achieve the nullification of the corporate and proprietary charters

---

[1] Hall, *Edward Randolph*, pp. 162–4.
[2] Steele, op. cit., pp. 86, 92–100; Channing, *History*, ii. 233–6; *NCMH*, vol. vi. ch. xv. pp. 490–1.

which he ever regarded as an impediment to administration securely loyal and profitable to the Crown. Blathwayt's vision was wider, his devices less rigid. Unlike Bellomont he was convinced of the wisdom of employing local men for imperial ends whenever possible, though a number of considerations combined to make those of a military background preferable to others. He had learned from the break-up of the Dominion of New England that a political combination of New York and Massachusetts was impracticable not only because of the great distances involved but also because their governmental ethos was dissimilar.[1] His absences from England after 1692, when as Secretary at War he accompanied William to the war front in the Netherlands, gave him a more acute awareness than Randolph could ever possess of the impact of the European conflict on colonial administration and its objectives. He was essentially a practical administrator, dazzled by the achievements of the French and their administrative techniques, a Tory in politics but too sensible to believe that the prerogative could be effectively pursued at the expense of the representative principle, committed to consolidation and opposed to expansion. It was he who selected Dudley as governor of Massachusetts, having for years firmly believed in his suitability for the post.

Not surprisingly New Englanders regarded Blathwayt as a dangerous enemy: he had once described them as 'a mean and mechanical sort of people'. This judgement may have been partly a projection, for within his own nature there were some elements of the mechanical. The administrator who perceived that political dissimilarities substantially divided New York and New England lacked sufficient insight or profundity to draw instruction from this fact. To him colonies were not emergent political entities, historically conscious and selfpossessed, they were mere economic adjuncts of the mother country given over to fruitless squabbling and absurd posturing. But in seeing them thus he was no more blind than the overwhelming majority of his contemporaries.

The colonies had no single imperial master but the most important governing influence in England was probably the Treasury. (Blathwayt, despite his nominal power, had not a single office at his disposal.)[2] Under William III it had lacked sufficient power to

---

[1] Jacobsen, *Blathwayt*, p. 310.
[2] Ibid., p. 343.

do more than protest when opposed to Board of Trade plans for expenditure, but during the following reign Treasury influence grew rapidly as the Board of Trade declined in significance.[1] The two bodies clashed in particular over the use of Crown revenues in the provinces. Whereas the Board of Trade preferred to leave them for local uses wherever they were raised, the Treasury wished to employ them for non-American purposes. The inconsistency of this practice is evident, for it was part of Treasury policy that the provinces should be self-sufficient and, save in extreme cases of hardship, wholly independent of the Crown. But lacking a clear and coherent policy the monarch missed such opportunities as arose to control land grants effectively.[2] Shifts in political power in England between Whigs and Tories, personal clashes such as that which occurred in 1711 over the Canada expedition between Henry St. John as Secretary for the Northern Department and Oxford as head of the Treasury, the loss of vigour following the tenure of Godolphin, and inconsistencies in the practices of even the clear-sighted and dedicated Blathwayt help to explain why nowhere in the English colonial world, with the qualified exception of Virginia, Maryland, Jamaica, and Bermuda, was a permanent civil list obtained.

Even primary objectives could be cancelled out and lost sight of as a consequence of conflicting party aims, or ignorance, petty jealousy, and the spite of small men wielding large power. Under circumstances such as these the temporary successes—Dudley's dogged defence of the prerogative, for example—stand out as major achievements. Only a firm conviction, in which Randolph and Blathwayt joined, that corporate and proprietary charters must be vacated before an orderly and purposeful system could emerge gave any real sense of coherence to British policy in the years following the creation of the Board of Trade.[3] And even this, the combined product of faith and personal ambition, once before

---

[1] Even policies for improving royal control of colonial government were sometimes sacrificed if they conflicted with the interests of the Exchequer. See Dora Mae Clark, *The Rise of the British Treasury* (New Haven, Conn., 1960), p. 4.

[2] Ibid., pp. 30, 33.

[3] Alison Gilbert Olson argues that there was a distinct Parliamentary interest which aimed at developing a stronger Westminster-directed mercantile empire. 'William Penn, Parliament and Proprietary Government', *W & MQ*, 3rd ser. xviii (1961), 183.

checked in full flood, was now robbed of its full tidal force by a multiplicity of small but effective devices which served as break-waters.

At the end of the seventeenth century the power of the colonial proprietors remained considerable, as the failure of Randolph to impose Crown-appointed attorneys-general on all the colonies indicates. The Lords of Trade in 1691 had advised bringing the overseas plantations into closer dependence upon royal power but at that time the king was unable to give the proposal much heed. In 1697, however, under the leadership of Randolph's patron, the Earl of Rochester, a committee of the House of Lords appointed to consider England's trade concentrated its attention for more than a month upon those colonies which possessed a considerable degree of practical independence.[1] At this date, it will be recalled, Virginia, New Hampshire, and New York alone of the mainland colonies were royal. Randolph, called before the committee and eager to implement to the letter the Act of 1696, recommended that government of all the proprietary provinces should be invested in the king. For the remaining years of his life the attainment of this end became his overriding concern. Despite strenuous efforts, however, he was unsuccessful. Letters were sent to Rhode Island, Connecticut, and Pennsylvania in April 1697 threatening for-feiture of charter and patent but it was understood that the govern-ment of the chartered colonies could not properly be assumed save by Act of Parliament or due process of the law.

Bills for the destruction of some or all of the colonial charters, designed to counter piracy and illegal trade and to ensure the creation of effective Vice-Admiralty courts, were subsequently introduced into Parliament upon five occasions before the Peace of Utrecht. They aimed in general to set the plantations 'upon a more equal foot'.[2] The earliest attempt came nearest to success. This was backed in England by Anglicans, both lay and clerical, supported by influential administrators, such as Governor Nichol-son and Robert Quary, who later succeeded Randolph as surveyor-general of the customs, and endorsed by a number of leading colonial figures. Dudley, seeking appointment to the governorship

---

[1] Cf. H. E. Egerton, *A Short History of British Colonial Policy, 1609–1909* (London, 1920), pp. 116–7.
[2] Hall, *Edward Randolph*, p. 171; *C.S.P.C.*, 1701, no. 473.

of Rhode Island and Connecticut as well as Massachusetts, and
Jeremiah Basse, intent on obtaining the governorship of New
Jersey once the proprietary there was dissolved, joined forces
behind Edward Randolph. But the charter colonies were skilfully
defended, the Carolinas by the Earl of Bath, Pennsylvania by
members of the Penn family, and Rhode Island, Connecticut, and
Massachusetts by Sir Henry Ashurst.[1] The role of William Penn
may well have been critical despite the great claims of influence
among the Lords which Ashurst made. In 1702 a second bill,
advanced in a Parliament dominated by Whigs, was modelled on
the first and framed to meet the exigencies of renewed war with
France.[2] Proposals were put forward for the appointment of a
commander-in-chief for the colonies, the re-uniting to the Crown
of all military power, and improved superintendence of the
customs. All other civil authority was to remain unchanged. The
Board of Trade was less than satisfied with such limited revision
but it was the king's death which prevented the final sanction.[3]

Under Anne the attack on the charters continued but now as the
Board of Trade's influence ebbed that of William Penn singularly
improved. Yet it was difficult for New Englanders to assess the
situation accurately or to ascertain whether the most serious danger
was yet passed. Resumption had failed to attract the critical
attention of English politics or to divide the parties in Parliament.[4]
Further, despite the support of important Anglicans abroad,
surprisingly backed by some members of the New England Company, a rival to the S.P.G., the project faced opposition from a
number of Church Tories. Only the Board of Trade was vitally
concerned. Yet Dudley in Massachusetts and Cornbury as governor

---

[1] See House of Lords MSS.: N.S. IV, 318–55; Osgood, *Eighteenth Century*,
i. 216–28, offers a very full account of this struggle; and see Olson, loc. cit.,
esp. pp. 189, 190.

[2] 18, 20 Feb. 1701/2, B.T. Journal, CO 391/14 pp. 335–7.

[3] Steele, *Politics of Colonial Policy*, pp. 77. Steele makes William Penn
the author of this plan and observes that the dissatisfaction of the Board of
Trade was related to fear of creating a series of charters like the current one for
Massachusetts, which had proved a considerable obstruction to imperial policy
in the decade since it was granted. See also 18 Feb. 1701/2, CO 5/1289, p. 383;
L. P. Kellogg, 'The American Colonial Charter', *American Historical Association
Report for 1903* (2 vols., Washington, D.C., 1904), i. 291; *NCMH*, vol. vi,
ch. xv, p. 491.

[4] See Steele, op. cit., pp. 79, 80. Cf. Olson, loc. cit., p. 191, who seeks to
demonstrate the strength of Penn's Tory support.

of New York made strenuous efforts to keep the issue alive, aided by the adverse publicity which the military delinquencies of Rhode Island attracted.[1] In 1706 a new bill was prepared under the guidance of Secretary Hedges and William Blathwayt only to be rejected by a vote of fifty to thirty-four. Its defeat on second reading is partly explained by the excessive powers which the Board of Trade proposed should be conferred on the queen. This would have given Anne the right to appoint governors, councillors, judges and all other administrative officers, and sole power and authority to govern the plantations.[2] In effect the colonial *status quo* had been protected by conflicts inherent in the English constitutional framework, but the sources of attack emanating from the colonies were themselves crumbling. Randolph was now dead, Cornbury was discredited and soon to be recalled, and Dudley faced charges of trading with the enemy levelled against him by his own assemblymen.

The efforts of those who had striven to abolish the independent governments were not entirely void. William Penn yielded all his political power, as did the proprietors of East and West New Jersey, and Maryland remained in the hands of the Crown until Anne's death. This was a poor substitute for the centralization envisaged by the Lords of Trade under the Restoration, but at least royal governments had now become the rule and not the exception on the mainland of North America. But for Massachusetts her sense of charter security and permanent special rights had been shaken. Quary, as Admiralty Judge, had advocated to the Lords of Trade the eradication of the distinguishing features of the New England governments, such as the elected Council of the Bay province, to bring them into line with all other royal governments. His main aim was to protect the latter from republicanism and commonwealth notions which operated unhampered in Rhode Island and Connecticut, and were believed to be on the increase there.[3] Even so the New England charters remained

---

[1] Kellogg, loc. cit. i. 300; *Rhode Island Recs.* iv. 12; 7 Feb. 1705/6 CO 5/3, nos. 24, i, 27. In the autumn of 1705 there was a belief current in Massachusetts that Governor Dudley sought to undermine the moral, religious, and political system of the Puritans. He had stated in a private letter to his son Paul that the country would never be worth living in 'for lawyers and gentlemen' until the charter was 'taken away.' Hutchinson, *History of Massachusetts*, ii. 140.

[2] CO 5/3 no. 27; *Journals of the House of Commons*, xv, 151, 168, 180, 181, 183.

[3] Cited Brown, *Middle Class Democracy*, p. 122.

intact: the autonomy of Rhode Island and Connecticut stayed unchanged, the Massachusetts charter of 1691 undisturbed.

It was questionable however, whether survival offered sufficient grounds for reassurance or self-congratulation. Allies had come from some surprising quarters but few of these were friends. As yet there was no consolidated enmity to New England but shoots of distrust sprouted in every direction rooted in past aspirations of autonomy, infractions of the trade laws—how many Englishmen, even in high office, could effectively distinguish between Rhode Island and Massachusetts?—and the persistence of Puritan practices and modes which seemed a mixture of the quaint and the sinister. In viewing New England Englishmen saw some of the less appealing features of their own past. They did not find the spectacle attractive, let alone heroic: what was not amusing was looked upon with contempt.[1] But the prevailing attitude was neither amusement nor outright hostility but rather indifference. In the end this combination of moods, against which there were few positive countervailing forces, would wreck the endeavours of New Englanders to achieve a special relationship with the mother country.

While the English empire groped towards administrative reforms to counter the impediments of Assembly government and provincial-mindedness, while Blathwayt counselled consolidation, and the Carolinian traders and soldiers registered staggering gains of territory and influence on the southern borders of the English mainland colonies, New France, guided by Louis, abandoned its irresolution and adopted a new forward policy, dramatically extending its field of operations. The French empire had not escaped serious internal divergences though their nature, dependent to a considerable degree upon personal animosities, differed from those of its English adversary.

Religion and the fur trade, though sharing an interest in the frontier regions, for long pulled in opposite directions.[2] Saint-

---

[1] See Edward Ward, *A Trip to New England* (London, 1699). Ward particularly commented on the absurdity of the laws, the lack of an acceptable business ethic and love of material possessions, sexual laxity, idleness, and excessive indulgence in sensual pleasures—particularly tobacco, uncleanliness, and religious hypocrisy.

[2] Donald Creighton, *Dominion of the North*, (Boston, Mass., 1944), p. 92, and above, p. 74.

Vallier, who defended the purposes of the Church for ten years against Frontenac's expansionist aims, was recalled to France in 1694 where the king sought unsuccessfully to induce him to resign. Yet his policy, which accorded in important respects with that of Colbert, was officially in the ascendant, for in 1696 the king and the minister of marine, Louis Phélypeaux de Pontchartrain, ordered the abandonment of the western posts, and the concentration of the fur trade at Montreal. The *coureurs de bois* were directed to return to the colony. Under Frontenac's successor, Louis Hector Chevalier de Callières, purposeful efforts were made to enforce these orders and it seemed at last as though Colbert's aim of consolidating French power on the St. Lawrence was to become a reality.

However, French power had by now established a further foothold on the North American continent through the enterprise of Pierre le Moyne d'Iberville. Following the death of La Salle and the collapse of his attempted settlement in 1684, French claims to the Mississippi mainly rested on the presence of the fur-traders and a few isolated individuals such as Michel Accault, living among the Illinois Indians. But in 1689 the land between the Mississippi and Lake Michigan was formally occupied in the name of King Louis. In the upper reaches of the river temporary forts were erected such as Bon Secours built in 1695 on Lake Pepin. Desire to substantiate French claims to the lower reaches was revealed within the French government by Pontchartrain and his son Jerome, who succeeded him in 1699. Both were aware of La Salle's warning to the Marquis de Seignelay that New France would fall if the Mississippi were not held. Yet it is doubtful if these factors significantly influenced the French case at Ryswick.

Louis XIV was not stirred to decisive action until the publication in Holland of the edition of Hennepin's *Voyages*, which invited William of Orange to seize this vast territory.[1] The representation of Argoud and Rémonville, the latter an associate of La Salle, seeking aid for a joint-stock company charged with colonization and settlement in this area, also drew attention to the menace of expanding British power and to the necessity of defending the exposed Ohio valley. Fear of British intervention there already alarmed French merchants and officially it was hoped that the

---

[1] M. Giraud, *Histoire de la Louisiane*, (Paris, 1953), i. 5, 13.

commerce of the Mississippi would soon be opened up. Shortly after the submission of Argoud's *mémoire*, spurred on by news that in England Dr. Daniel Coxe was urging the settlement of French Protestants in the Gulf of Mexico, Pontchartrain took the first step towards preparing an expedition by selecting Iberville as its leader.[1]

From the outset Louisiana faced difficulties in attracting the right sort of colonists. Canadians predominated in the tiny initial force which occupied the coast. Many found the climate hard to bear, while the *coureurs*, better accustomed to the heat, regarded the discipline of a sedentary life as insufferable. Population dispersal, which had undermined New France in the seventeenth century, Iberville hoped to counter by banning the fur trade and by skilful design of settlement and site. To raise the population rapidly immigrants were recruited from among the French poor and out of the families of garrison men. Iberville's aim was to stabilize the tiny colony's boundaries and to protect them by military posts on the Arkansas and Missouri. But with war threatening again in Europe, French merchants would not risk committing their resources in this distant project, and the plans for establishing two colonies of between 200 and 300 persons around Mobile were abandoned.[2]

By 1702, the population of Louisiana, thinly extended between the Mobile and the Mississippi, had increased to no more than 140. Iberville was deeply critical of the failure of the French people to support his venture but this only partly explains why Louisiana did not show convincing growth. More serious was the faulty appreciation of climatic problems and the inadequate attention given to the question of food supplies. Livestock was scarce and some of the vegetable crops were destroyed by heat or by heavy rainfall. Inability of many settlers to adapt to their natural environment led to disillusionment and desertion. Shortage

---

[1] For the colonizing projects of Coxe see V. W. Crane, *The Southern Frontier, 1670–1732* (repr. Ann Arbor, Mich., 1956), pp. 48ff. Other Englishmen had warned of the consequences of successful French colonization in this region. The propagandist Charles Davenant wrote 'Should the French settle at the disemboguing of the river Meschasipe they would not be long before they made themselves masters of that rich province, which would be an addition to their strength very terrible to Europe.' Cited in *Cambridge History of the British Empire* (Cambridge, 1929), i. 325.

[2] Giraud, op. cit. i. 86–8.

of skilled labour caused the miscarriage of plans for the cultivation of sugar and bananas. Iberville's vigorous lead brought some solid achievement but after 1702 even this began to falter. Within three years he was dead and Louisiana, robbed of its one source of strength, was reduced to isolation for long periods by the insufficiency of the French navy.[1] Throughout, however, the colony's fortunes had fundamentally rested upon the king's mood and Louis, concerned at the size of his wartime budget and unwilling to offer the financial support necessary to put the enterprise squarely on its feet, blamed the colonists for its shortcomings. The possibility of abandonment long persisted, although effectively countered by Pontchartrain who regarded the colony's strategic value as of more immediate concern that its questionable economic worth. Through him succour was brought to Louisiana in 1709 and 1710 and in the closing years of the war Louis became reconciled to its continuance.

Uncertain as was its growth, plagued as it long was by the fear that Louis would withdraw his support if it did not speedily demonstrate its material worth, Louisiana nevertheless played an important role in the development of French policy immediately before the commencement of the War of the Spanish Succession. The struggling colony offered an alternative source of trade goods to New France and an alternative outlet for the fur trade. So serious was the diversion that French officials and merchants on the St. Lawrence claimed that Canada faced ruin. Despite efforts by Callières and Champigny it was soon realized that the policy of returning the *coureurs de bois* to New France must be abandoned. With the taking of this step, facilitated by the European ambitions of Louis XIV, the *coureurs* were transformed into valued instruments of French imperialism.[2] For at the beginning of November 1700 the ailing Charles II of Spain had at last died, having previously named Philip, Duc d'Anjou, a grandson of Louis, as his successor.

Before the month was out Louis had accepted the will and was morally committed to defend the Spanish Empire in the New World, the claims of which were extensive. The restraints which hitherto had held back a French forward policy in North America

[1] Ibid. i. 103.
[2] Eccles, *Canada under Louis XIV*, pp. 245, 247–8.

were now effectively broken. In the spring of 1701 the French king gave unequivocal support to holding the Illinois and Ohio country and the centre of the continent from Hudson Bay to the Gulf of Mexico. This new and decisive move was celebrated by the establishment at Detroit in July 1701 of a fortified post, designed to block the route to the west for English traders, while creating a guarded line of communication between Canada and the region of the Miami and Illinois Indians.[1] In support of the forward policy the missionary resources of Catholic France could now be largely turned, still dissipated by fruitless quarrels, but increasingly employed for the political, military, and commercial purposes of the state.

The religious frontier of the French mainland possessions extended in a wide arc from northernmost Maine westwards to the Illinois country and south to radiate locally in the lower Mississippi basin from the new and struggling settlement. Activity in the north-east posed a sustained threat to the security of the New England frontier. In 1688 France had retained only a precarious hold in Maine at Pentagoët (Castine) and Governor Denonville, who preceded Frontenac's second administration, aware of the peril which Canada faced if the English gained control of the Abenaki, favoured the creation of Jesuit missions from the Kennebec northwards to the St. John River. The Jesuits had first gathered the Abenakis at Sillery but soon moved them (in 1683) to St. Francois de Sales, on the Chaudière, south of Quebec, and then later revived their mission in Maine with the erection of a chapel at Narantsouac (Norridgewock) on the Kennebec River.[2] Jesuit effort secured the Kennebecs, Etechemins, and Penobscots for the Roman Catholic religion and in 1699 the order moved to take over the parish at Pentagoët, hitherto administered by the Sulpicians, their chief rivals. To counter the disturbing success of this mission-work within its own boundaries Massachusetts twice peacefully attempted, in 1698 and 1701, to persuade the Indians to send their French mentors away. When war came again, an expedition under Major Church was sent to ravage the village on the Penobscot, while another under Colonel Hilton reached Fr. Râle's mission at Narantsouac and burned the Church there.

---

[1] Gustave Lanctot, *A History of Canada* (Toronto, 1964), ii. 147.
[2] Eastman, *Church and State in Early Canada*, p. 242.

Jesuit work among the Iroquois produced mixed results. In the quarter-century before the English Revolution ceaseless endeavours had led to the establishment of a community of converts at Sault St. Louis, south of Lachine. These made up about half of the christianized Indians residing in New France. They were never effectively assimilated by the French but proved valuable auxiliaries until the peace of 1698, losing heavily during the course of the war.[1] But within the territory of New York Jesuit influence among the Five Nations was negligible. In 1689 only a handful of converts were known to exist and the sole priest, Fr. Peter Milet, was a prisoner of the Oneida. Yet the English in New York in particular feared its revival as a prelude to the sundering of a valued alliance and in the Iroquois negotiations with the French in 1700, from which they were excluded, Fr. James Bruyas, well received by the Indians though unable to gain christian converts, played an important part in securing the Iroquois commitment to neutrality in future war. In 1702 the Iroquois cantons requested the restoration of the Jesuit mission which survived until its destruction by Colonel Schuyler in 1709.[2]

The more spectacular achievements of the French took place in the upper Mississippi basin. By the close of the War of the Spanish Succession Vincennes had been founded on the Wabash and missions created among the Kaskaskias, Miamis, and Pottowattomies. At these locations settlement slowly developed with some intermarrying between the christianized Indians and the French.[3] Further missions were planned by the Jesuit leaders to the Illinois tribes of Cahokia and Tamarois and to the Osages and the Missouri. But the Sulpicians, backed by Saint-Vallier, resolved to share in the conversion of the western Indians, and also established missions among several tribes, including the Arkansas and the Tonicas. On the lower Mississippi Jesuit industry began to bear fruit. A Father Du Ru in 1700 began visiting Indians in the proximity at Port Biloxi, erected by Iberville, moving to Mobile when the post was abandoned. In the same year a chapel was constructed among the Oumas. The missionaries sent out by the

[1] Lanctot, *History of Canada*, ii. 204; Eccles, *Canada under Louis XIV*, 224.

[2] J. Dawson Shea, *A History of the Catholic Church within the United States* (New York, 1886–92), i. 593–4, 597, 609.

[3] J. Winsor, *The Struggle in America between England and France, 1697–1763* (London, 1895), p. 84.

seminary had less practical success though they had survived an
attempt by the Jesuits to obtain exclusive direction of the French
settlements in Louisiana. Ill-health and incapacity combined to
wreck their endeavours: English aggression added to their difficulties. A Church near the fort on Isle Dauphine was destroyed
in 1710, only a year after it had been built. The Tonica mission
threatened by English and Indian war parties was withdrawn to
Mobile in 1708. Alone of the seminary missions the station at
Tamarois (Cahokia) showed any real signs of vitality.[1]

It is unlikely that the New Englanders knew very much of the
personal squabbles and uncertainties which characterized French
imperial activity after 1689. From a multitude of sources, including
English captives, they were well-informed of the state of the St.
Lawrence communities and of some of the projects hatched by
their leaders for attacking the English settlements. After the
publication of the *Boston News-Letter* there was available more
precise and certain detail of the European conflict than could
possibly reach their ears about the hazards of early Louisiana or
the movements of solitary French missionaries. But their situation
was changing and in 1700, as the French struggled to gain a footing
on the Gulf of Mexico, and Louis resolved to commit French
resources to a Spanish empire under a Bourbon king, the spectre
of the Universal Monarchy hung over the North American continent threatening to drive the English from the coastal plains or
to destroy them. Chills of apprehension traversed the spines of
perceptive individuals long before they were recorded in Assembly
discussion. As the War of the Spanish Succession led into a series
of significant British victories, awareness of the real limitations of
French power dawned on New Englanders as it did on Europeans.
But for much of the war, and certainly through to 1706 when the
threat to the Massachusetts charter seemed serious, it was apparent to many that the promise of 'the Happy Revolution' of 1689
and a sense of partnership with England in a common war had
been diluted, whereas the dangers which they alone faced had
increased and multiplied.

Thus in their harsh but revered corner of the Atlantic seaboard
the New English perceived they were exposed to a hostile world in

---

[1] Shea, *Catholic Church*, i. 549, 551, 554; Giraud, *Louisiane*, i. 220, 309,
NCMH, vol. vi, ch. xv, pp. 498–501.

which even the dissenters, their traditional friends who helped bridge the gap in communications which separated them from the old English, seemed cold and alienated. Religion remained a more important feature in their lives than it was in contemporary England,[1] but something of the certainty which sustained the Founding Fathers, and the succeeding generation, in their isolated environment had departed or was submerged. As yet the substitute forces, which the Mathers in particular had evoked to adjust the sense of community and purpose to a changing world, had failed to produce clearly visible advantages.

[1] Bridenbaugh, *Mitre and Sceptre*, pp. xiii, 55-6.

CHAPTER VI

Massachusetts Bay in the War of the Spanish Succession

NEW England had gained no immediate cessation of hostilities with the signing of the Peace of Ryswick, a humiliation which separated her from the rest of the English nation on both sides of the Atlantic. Sensitive New Englanders felt the gibe heard in London and in foreign lands that the 'Saints' were on bad-terms with heaven. Indian raids had dragged on into 1698 as the decade of woes lumbered mournfully to its close.[1] But serious as were the hardships suffered by the colonists they were probably light in comparison with the distress of the Five Nations of the Iroquois. Though Frontenac's endeavours to crush this powerful enemy had not met with direct success the English could claim little credit in the eyes of the Indians. They had failed to succour them with men and money and in time of famine were unable to send adequate supplies of corn. The inutility of the alliance was laid bare. Despite Governor Bellomont's overtures to Count Frontenac the European settlement excluded them; nor had it any acknowledgment by the French of the English claim of sovereignty. Until the end of the Nine Years War loyalty to the English alliance was not in doubt but now, reduced to 1,300 warriors, the Mohawk nation almost extinct, and apprehensive lest the French and English combine against them, the Iroquois felt obliged to open separate negotiations with Quebec.

Upon Frontenac's death in 1698 it was left to Governor General Callières to conclude successfully the protracted preliminaries of the treaty finally agreed to in 1701.[2] By this the Iroquois accepted defeat of their aim to wrest control of the western fur trade from the French. In return for a French promise to respect their

---

[1] *Magnalia*, ii. 673. When the Judges of the Superior Court came up from Boston to Deerfield in 1698 to try a case of infanticide they were escorted by twenth-six troopers. Judd, *Hadley*, p. 261. See also the comments of Governor Stoughton on the effects of prolonged warfare. *C.S.P.C.*, 1697, no. 1354.

[2] See Eccles, *Canada under Louis XIV*, pp. 242–4.

neutrality they promised to remain aloof from future wars in which the English were involved. That same year, dramatically renewing friendship with the English by placing large portions of their hunting grounds under the protection of the king of England, they endeavoured to maintain a profitable economic relationship in that quarter without being obliged to contribute by force of arms to an English supremacy which in the long run could only undermine their own territorial claims.[1] In relieving pressure on the St. Lawrence valley and in paving the way for the practical neutrality of New York province, which persisted for all but the final phase of the war, the defection of the Iroquois ensured the release of French resources for concentration against New England.

The acute apprehension which New Yorkers possessed of the machinations of the French among the Five Nations was reflected by the New Englanders' fear for the eastern Indians and graphically commented upon by the colonists' joint governor, the Earl of Bellomont. French influence had been increased by the widespread rumour, difficult to discount effectively save by the gift of guns and ammunition, that the English intended to disarm their allies. English prestige lay under a shadow. The forts at Albany and Schenectady, where the garrisons totalled less than half their requisite strength, were deplorably weak and held in contempt by those natives who felt menaced by the newly-built French fort at Cadaracqui.[2] Indian esteem was further diminished by the visible state of the soldiers at Albany—their want of clothes and other necessities. By July 1700 many had deserted: the remainder had received no pay for over two years. Bellomont urged the sending of more men from England to bring the four New York independent companies up to full strength, and the building of a sod fort in the country of the Onondages, the Iroquois nation closest to the new French fortifications at Cadaracqui.[3] Robert Livingston, Secretary of Indian Affairs, even more alarmed than Bellomont at the dejected and 'staggering condition' of England's principal allies in North America, argued that their integrity could be ensured only by creating a 'system' of fortifications. Meanwhile the strengthening of Quebec and Montreal was rapidly pro-

---

[1] Leach, *Northern Colonial Frontier*, p. 117.
[2] *C.S.P.C.*, 1700, no. 167, p. 92.
[3] Ibid., 1700, nos. 307, 346, enclosure xii, 357, enclosure, i.

ceeding, if not already complete, and in the fevered imaginings of the English the Jesuit was omnipresent in the back-country.

Nervous endeavours on the part of New Englanders to maintain peace with the eastern Indians absorbed considerable energy at this period. In June 1701 when the latter's representatives were warned that peace might be broken by the French at any time they asserted their desire to be free (of both European nations). But in an endeavour to create a tie the English promised to send an armourer from time to time to mend their broken rifles. Closer relations were hindered by a long-standing grievance of the Indians which to the English seemed a matter of relatively small moment. Two Indian children, John and Robin, given as hostages during the time of Governor Phips, had never been return-ed. One had since died but the other had gone to England and, according to the Indian commissioners, refused to return. The Indians were highly suspicious of the explanation given by the English, complaining that they themselves on such occasions had always forced hostages to return to their own people. Again and again, whenever representatives of the two nations met, the case of John and Robin was revived.[1]

The Jesuits did their best to widen every difference and used their influence with great skill. They promised that France would never relinquish her claim to a frontier on the Kennebec River and told the eastern Indians they were fools to tolerate the English to the westwards of it.[2] They kept them fully informed of the wavering of the Five Nations and were partly responsible for their decision to send observers to the negotiations conducted at Albany.[3] Dudley, to delay their co-operating with the French, for there was little real hope of establishing an abiding peace, had a further meeting in August 1702. At Pemaquid he confronted Moxus and eight sagamores representing all the eastern Indians from as far away as the St. Croix and the Penobscot. They were accompanied by 140 braves.[4] Trade relations were discussed and the Indians were advised not to enter the English settlements lest their intentions be regarded as hostile. This they accepted but

---

[1] *C.S.P.C.*, 1702, 10 Mar. 1702, no. 184, p. 120; no. 810.
[2] *C.S.P.C.*, 1702, no. 642.
[3] Ibid., 1702, no. 801, p. 571; no. 966.
[4] Ibid., 1702, nos. 805, 966.

disliked being obliged to frequent the trading factories at Casco and Saco, in part because of the dangers in crossing Casco Bay in winter, and asked for a trading-house at Pemaquid which was closer to their own communities.[1]

Rumour of renewal of the French conflict was current in New England and indeed throughout the mainland and West Indian colonies for more than twelve months before the actual outbreak of war.[2] Requests reached England from every quarter for advance notice of the formal commencement of hostilities in order to lessen the chances of surprise attack and the complete collapse of provincial defence. New York feared assault by land, Virginia by sea, and the Leewards a rising of the Irish papists on Montserrat who, augmented by the immigration of the settlers' relatives from Ireland and elsewhere, continued to outnumber the Protestants by twenty to one. Few colonists who made their voice heard had any illusions that if war came the dominions would be deeply involved from the outset.[3] At Williamsburg and in the surrounding countryside in mid-August the blessing of Almighty God was requested for the Protestant religion, and a Day of Fasting, ordered by the governor and Council, was subsequently extended throughout the whole province. New England's anxieties were added to by the build-up and concentration of French strength associated with the arrival of Brouillan in Acadia. The Nova Scotian governor, in proposing an initial suspension of arms, warned that he had instructions to prevent Englishmen from fishing within sight of

---

[1] Trade supplies not exceeding £200 were ordered to be sent in the *Province Galley* to Sagadahoc.

[2] *C.S.P.C.*, 1701, nos. 320, 401, and 423.

[3] Ibid., 1701, nos. 431, 471, 613, and 622. In the case of Virginia this does not appear to have been an abiding fear. At the end of the year Nicholson reported that not only were assemblymen unable to perceive the necessity of assisting the exposed province of New York with men and money but also denied that Virginia was under any danger of attack either from land or sea. Nicholson ascribed this 'insularity' to the overwhelming preponderance among the settlers of men born in the province. Few of these had either read much or been abroad in the world. He believed that this effectively prevented them from forming any idea or notion of the nature of foreign military power though he admitted it did not hinder their management of plantation affairs nor their flair for trade. Nicholson examined the possibility of securing a place for shipping at moderate cost at Tyndall's Point and on the York River. But to guard against the very real danger of destruction of the tobacco crops between the months of April and October he requested from the Council of Trade a powerful squadron to secure all the mainland colonies. Ibid., 1701, no. 1040.

his territories.[1] Massachusetts had no desire to take the initiative in re-opening the conflict. She agreed to the proposal, pending advice from the king, but rejected the fishery claims as contrary to the Peace of Ryswick.

Steps taken to advance provincial security mainly rested upon the prudent stationing of available naval units. This best secured the larger seaboard towns but for the colonists was also the cheapest form of defence. Few held the complacent Jamaican belief that the French and Spaniards would not attack first, but northern composure was rudely shattered by the sighting of a French squadron late in October. As in the Chesapeake, convoy procedures were immediately resumed. H.M.S. *Arundel* was held at Boston fourteen days to escort ships to England, and H.M.S. *Gosport* ordered out on a twelve-day scouting cruise to report upon the movements of the French.[2] In addition the home government was precisely instructed upon the subject of local fortifications: the necessity of a small fort at Casco Bay, fifty miles to the eastward of any settlement, as a base for the Indian trade, and the requirements of Salem, Marblehead, Gloucester, Plymouth, and Hull, 'so many avenues by which the Enemy might make an impression'.[3] Stores of war in need of replenishment were listed as '1000 good fuzils, and bayonets, flints, balls, lead and mould and 100 barrel of gunpowder'.[4]

Notification of the declaration of war was sent to New England for despatch to the continental and West Indian plantations on 5 May. The following day a circular letter was prepared by Nottingham, the Secretary of State, to the same effect. But as late as mid-June, when Governor Dudley made his initial address to the Assembly, certain news of the outbreak of hostilities had not yet arrived. When it did, three days later on 19 June, it was immediately passed to H.M. ships in port and to those outward-bound. H.M.S. *Gosport* was ordered out on a ten-day patrol

[1] *C.S.P.C.*, 1701, nos. 785, 785, enclosure ii.
[2] Ibid., 1701, nos. 814, 889, 893, 901.
[3] Ibid., 1701, nos. 1061, enclosure ii, pp. 664–5.
[4] Ibid., 1702–3, no. 238. Governor Stoughton had earlier stressed the absolute necessity of stores from England to stimulate the people to 'stand their ground and expose their lives . . . otherwise their difficulties will be so insupportable as will necessitate them to draw in'. *C.S.P.C.*, 1701, nos. 320, 373; ibid., 1702, no. 544.

between Cape Cod and the North Shore and Cape Ann.[1] Despatches were also sent eastwards to the forts at Casco Bay and Saco instructing commanders to inform the Indians, and to fishing vessels at the Isles of Shoals, Richmond's Island, Cape Newaggin, Pemaquid, Monegin, and even to Cape Sable, the westernmost point of Nova Scotia. The chief officers of each county militia and the captain of the *Province Galley* were among those officially advised that the long-expected conflict had at last begun. Dudley was primarily concerned to organize and employ resources with such efficiency and spirit that the Crown would be moved to supplement any serious deficiencies which became evident.[2] Even so the highest administrative standards could not aspire to make every settlement safe. The length of exposed frontier rendered this impossible. As in the previous conflict outlying communities were obliged to hazard life and property for the sake of provincial welfare. Maine suffered severely, sharing the brunt of the enemy assaults with the Connecticut valley, further opened to attack by the unfavourable shift of power along the Hudson.[3]

As has been seen, by creating fortifications at Detroit and Michilimackinac, France was extending her hold on the interior. In addition she was committed, though none too firmly, to the new and struggling colony of Louisiana. But in many important respects this war was to be a repetition of the earlier struggle. The French grand design aspired to the conquest or destruction of New England as a prelude to the occupation of New York. Le Moyne d'Iberville foresaw that the English, unless checked, would overrun by natural growth all the land to the east of the Mississippi. He welcomed the union of France and Spain under the House of Bourbon as providing the means for driving them off the North American continent, and bombarded his king, Louis XIV, with proposals suggesting how this might be brought about.[4]

---

[1] Ibid., 1702, no. 679.

[2] Massachusetts Council in Assembly, 16 June 1702; ibid., 1702, no. 608.

[3] Official recognition of this was given by the decision to hold the Inferior Court of Common Pleas and Court of General Sessions for the County of York at York instead of Wells. The main reason for this was the danger of travelling eastwards in July and October when the sessions were held. *Acts and Laws*, p. 263.

[4] Osgood, *Eighteenth Century*, i. 400: *New York Col. Docs.* ix. 725, 729, 735. Iberville appeared to have little respect for the New Englanders whom he regarded as poor and dull-witted soldiers. He preferred to launch his project

He planned to seize Boston by surprise with a force consisting of 400 regulars aided by an equal number of Indian auxiliaries and 1,000 Canadians.[1] From the Chaudière River they were to cross the mass of lakes and rivers of northern Maine to the settlement of Norridgewock on the Kennebec, the place of rendezvous from whence this force, laying waste the countryside as it went, was to fall upon unsuspecting Boston. Once Boston fell, it was believed, New York would be fatally weakened.[2] This project, which involved co-operation with a small maritime force was, however, abandoned, as similar proposals had been in the previous decade, in favour of stinging raids—the limited objectives of which were better suited to the resources at the disposal of New France. This signified, however, no more than a shift in intent. For the northern colonies the war on land was slow to start. Neither was there the frightening roar which marked the immediacy of Armageddon or the far-off din of scattered slayings. Not until August 1703, after an uneasy summer, did the first blow fall.

Nerves were strained during the preceding winter to keep the eastern Indians at peace, and in November Dudley informed the Council that if need be he was ready to leave Boston to confer yet again with them.[3] He was hindered from so doing by preparations for the Jamaican expedition, yet despite persistent and widespread Jesuit activity he was enabled to report in the New Year that the Indians as far as the Penobscot were quiet and eager to continue the peace. An important reason for this was not difficult to find. New England privateers had captured nineteen French vessels in the early months of the war, including three bearing clothes and provisions from Quebec. This threw the Indians into a temporary but direct dependence upon the

in winter when the vessels which frequented the coast had returned to Europe leaving 'only mechanics who are illy qualified for fighting and fancy themselves in security because they cannot imagine us in a condition in Canada to form designs of that magnitude, especially in a season so rigorous as that of winter'. Nellis M. Crouse, *Lemoyne d'Iberville. Soldier of New France* (Ithaca, N.Y., 1954), pp. 225–7.

[1] The European component was to sail from France to the Penobscot or Kennebec, and thence to march overland to Quebec observing on the way which would be the best trails for an army moving southwards, visiting *en route* Baron de Saint-Castin and endeavouring to enlist Indian allies. Ibid., p. 227.

[2] Iberville, like Frontenac, regarded Boston as key to the mastery of North America. See *C.S.P.C.*, 1700, no. 641.

[3] *C.S.P.C.*, 1702, no. 1172; ibid., 1702–3, no. 13.

English. Dudley and his councillors were asked at the conference to supply both necessities.[1] In the meantime, as a precautionary measure, the Assembly had agreed that every fourth member of the militia should be clothed and ready to march within twenty-four hours of notice. Scouts patrolled the frontier daily.[2]

In the spring, evidently surprised that peace had lasted so long, Dudley again met those Pennacook sachems (or supreme chiefs) known to be friendly, with a view to regulating their supplies and obtaining speedy notice of the movements of any Indians who had committed themselves to the French.[3] But the phase of peace-like war was soon to end. At the beginning of March scouts from Dover, New Hampshire, surprised what was thought to be a war-party in the woods at Cochecha. Troops in Dover were readied to enlarge the search, and a company from the Essex Middle Regiment was alerted with a view to strengthening the eastern part of the province.[4] The governor proposed sending these two companies (100 men in all) to march between Wells, Saco, and Casco Bay and thence to the head of the frontier at Haverhill to secure the English and protect those Indians whom the French had failed to win over. Later, disturbing news came in from some of the scouts that the Pennacook sagamore, Watanu-man, and his men had withdrawn from their village, having made no preparations for planting that year. They had gone to Paquasset, a place within two or three days' journey from Quebec, where they were determined to settle.[5]

In a final attempt to maintain the uneasy peace Dudley prepared to go eastwards yet once more.[6] At the end of June he was to be found at Casco Bay, dallying in expectation that the eastern Indians would come in to meet him as they had agreed to do. He had gained useful information from the sachems Moxus and Bomazeen that a large French ship had come into Mount Desart and that a party of Frenchmen accompanied by Cape Sable Indians were preparing to open hostilities against the English. This was confirmed by Lieutenant-Colonel Tyng at Dunstable who had been

---

[1] Ibid., 1702–3, nos. 30, 269, and 315.
[2] Ibid., 1702–3, no. 30.
[3] Ibid., 1702–3, no. 432.
[4] Ibid., 1702–3, no. 413.
[5] Ibid., 1702–3, no. 625.
[6] Ibid., 1702–3, no. 768.

informed independently of this by Watanuman's sister and by
two Indian men from Pegwocket.[1] Dudley considered his trip a
success. He had met with all the sachems of the Penobscot and
with the chiefs Moxus and Adiwando, presenting them with
gifts to the value of between £400 and £500. But on this occasion
the governor had found that the superficial cordiality had gone:
the Indians had replaced it by a sullen mood. Accordingly precautionary measures were intensified. The Massachusetts government had 200 men out scouting, divided into two parties twenty
miles distant from each other and interchanging ground every
two days to prevent the enemy from coming between them. While
one party, drawn from the Essex and Middlesex militia, was on
the line of the frontier from Marlborough to Haverhill, the other
ranged from Haverhill to Saco, seeking out the enemy or observing
his movements. A company of militia was also at the ready on
the Connecticut River.[2] The defence-system was soon to be
fully tested.

In August, for 'six terrible days', 500 French and Indians under
Sieur de Beaubassin attacked the exposed Maine villages still en-
feebled from their hammering in the previous war.[3] Boston was
alarmed by unofficial reports that the number of slain was very
high. Kennebunk, Cape Porpoise, Winter Harbour, Scarborough,
Spurwink, Purpooduck, and Falmouth were each assaulted.
At Winter Harbour thirty-five persons were reported killed or
taken when the stone fort fell: Spurwink (Cape Elizabeth) suffered
twenty-two casualties, and Purpooduck thirty-three. Fort Mary at
Winter Harbour, Scarborough, and Falmouth (Fort Casco) held
out but at the latter, saved from complete disaster only by the
arrival of the provincial galley, some 130 persons were either killed
or captured.[4] Maine reeled under these blows, and horrified in-

---

[1] *C.S.P.C.*, 1702–3, nos. 863, 898, and 969.

[2] Ibid., 1702–3, nos. 969, 996.

[3] *New York Col. Docs.* ix. 756.

[4] This was not Fort Loyal. Casco Fort built in 1700 by the provincial government was 250 ft. long and 190 ft. broad with bastions at all four corners. It was
built near the shore on the eastern side of Casco Bay, supported on the shore
side by a block house and with timber walls more than 1,000 ft in circuit enclosing
several buildings and a magazine. Its purpose was to supply and trade with the
Indians and to encourage settlement. There was an important meeting here
with the Indians in 1703. Benjamin Church's recommendation the following
year that it should be abandoned was rejected. Gould, *Portland*, p. 158; Mass.
Archives, xx. 51.

habitants in the more sheltered communities of Massachusetts speculated on the consequences if the north-east frontier collapsed. For along this entire border only a few isolated garrisons now remained intact.[1]

Vaudreuil, successor to Callières, had sought to counter Abenaki dependence upon English weapons and utensils by committing the tribes to ferocious raids designed to provoke retaliation where New France was least vulnerable. To a degree he was highly successful. Dudley reacted speedily.[2] The governor of New Hampshire was ordered to send immediate help to the stricken communities, a levy of 150 men was raised from the southern regiments of Massachusetts, and volunteers were called for from Middlesex and Essex counties. Before September had come, at a cost to the province of £3,000 a month, the governor had put not much less than 1,000 men under arms, half of which force was quartered in garrisons.[3] His vigour and calculation brought forth unstinting praise from the Council of Trade.[4] But he had failed to create an effective *force de frappe*.

Two expeditions, representing the best of the combined resources of Massachusetts and New Hampshire, sent against the Indians in October, failed even to make contact with the enemy. Nor did the large number of men under arms suffice to avert an attack on Black Point early in the month, nor prevent killings in the York and Berwick area. With the approach of winter, Dudley, in an effort to create a new offensive screen, emulated the French by sending out small parties equipped with snowshoes and stimulated by the promise of high bounty money for every scalp

---

[1] Drake, *Border Wars*, p. 160. It would be wrong to regard this terror as necessarily widespread or sustained. Lt.-Gov. Usher of New Hampshire visiting the out-garrisons in mid-February 1704 found that families had abandoned them to return to their respective houses 'secure as if no war, notwithstanding the enemy hath twice made attacks at garrisons in several places, killed and carried away many English'. *C.S.P.C.*, 1704–5, no. 120.

[2] Osgood, *Eighteenth Century*, i. 406–7; Drake, *Border Wars*, p. 163. The Indians had been instructed that there was virtue in murdering the English who had crucified Jesus Christ, a Frenchman. Perley, *Salem*, i. 36.

[3] *N.H. Documents and Records*, ii. 403ff.

[4] 16 Feb. 1704, *C.S.P.C.*, 1704–5, no. 110. In view of the failure of the governors of Connecticut and Rhode Island to provide help to Massachusetts, the Council of Trade urged the queen to write to them. Also, because of arms shortage, they advised that 400 firearms be sent to the governor of Massachusetts. Ibid., 1704–5, no. 109.

secured from Indians above the age of ten.[1] But it is indicative of
the relative impotence of such punitive measures that the killing
of a dozen Indians by one such body should be inflated to the
dimensions of a real victory. It may have reassured the faint-
hearted on frontier and coast to know that the patrols were out in
strength, but others were acutely aware of the strain imposed on
provincial resources during the winter months by maintaining
the large force raised at the end of the summer. Some questioned
whether this was value for money.[2] However, the flurry of military
activity which Dudley had organized should not be lightly discounted. Towards the end of January Berwick was attacked and
then Haverhill, alarming the whole of Essex County. As far down
as Salem the militia turned out. Thereafter for the first time
French military pressure switched from the eastern frontier to
the Connecticut valley.

In February 1704 remote Deerfield, long apprehensive by reason
of its exposed and northerly position, was caught in a night attack
with its watch asleep and without snowshoes enough for the
survivors to pursue and possibly destroy 'a drunken, loaden,
tyred enemy'.[3] In the spring, pressure on the towns in the north-
east of the valley was increased by the creation of an Indian
strongpoint at Cowassic. An attack on the garrison of Northampton
swiftly followed. Connecticut's understanding of her responsi-

---

[1] On 10 Nov. Council resolved that £10 should be paid out of the public
treasury for every scalp of the enemy killed in combat that was 10 years of age
or more, taken or brought in within the following four months. A few weeks
later the House proposed that the figure should be raised to £40. In the spring
of 1704 the figure was again raised substantially—this time to £100. *C.S.P.C.*,
1702–3, no. 1344; ibid., 1704–5, no. 260; Mass. Archives, lxx. 653.

[2] Dudley rejected the proposal of the House that winter marches should be
avoided and the mobile forces stand down, on the grounds that this was precisely
the time to harry the enemy. In this he was supported by the lt.-gov. and Council
of New Hampshire. One of his problems was to keep the marchers provisioned.
They were obliged to carry provisions in their 'snap-sacks', as the way was
impassable for packhorses. *C.S.P.C.*, 1702–3, no. 1409; Drake, *Border Wars*,
p. 170.

[3] The Deerfielders defended themselves tolerably well against an enemy
which had entered the palisade surrounding forty of the houses. Within
twenty-four hours 300 men from Springfield and Hatfield were in the town
but unable to pursue the attackers through want of snowshoes. Deerfield
lost twenty men and seventy women and children carried away. The enemy
left behind thirty dead. *C.S.P.C.*, 1704–5, p. 100; Sheldon, *History of
Deerfield*, i. 288ff.

bilities for this region, the fate of which was important to her own safety, was fortunately influenced more by the enlightened perspective of Governor Fitz-John Winthrop than by the suspicions of Sir Henry Ashurst, her agent. To frustrate Dudley, Ashurst counselled against sending soldiers beyond the provincial boundary. Winthrop, however, who saw the two colonies as 'brethren, under one Crowne, one Religion, one intrest, and assuredly under one affection', promised the fullest help. By midsummer Connecticut, having made unsuccessful attempts to cover Deerfield and the upper valley, had placed between 600 and 700 militia in service patrolling outside the colony's border. These destroyed the Indian post at Cowassic but failed to satisfy Dudley who contended, unsuccessfully, that officers serving on Massachusetts soil should bear that government's commission and not their own. He remained highly critical of Connecticut's contribution to the defence of New England and urged that it should be raised to one-third of the cost shouldered by Massachusetts.[1]

On the eastern frontier large scouting-parties out on snowshoes in the second half of March and early April had no better success in locating the enemy than had been gained during the winter. It was believed that the Indians were gone from the Penobscot, probably having left some four months earlier. If so, then the exercise had been largely fruitless, having little justification beyond demonstrating to English and Indian alike that the English could bear the frost and travel in winter as well as they. But there was now no standing down of men. Dudley organized a force of about 700 to range the coast from Casco Bay to St. Croix, the object being to keep the Indians from fishing and planting, and so disrupt the trade with the French that they would lack support the following winter.[2] If the opportunity seemed favourable, Norridgewock was to be destroyed. Dudley would have welcomed an assault against the contraband trade centred on Port Royal,[3]

---

[1] Dunn, *Puritans and Yankees*, pp. 338, 339.

[2] *C.S.P.C.*, 1704–5, no. 451; Governor Dudley to ?Nottingham, 10 May 1703, Mass. Archives lxx. 673.

[3] His enemies accused him of illegal trading with the French. See *C.S.P.C.*, 1702–3, pp. 297, 373, 410, and 665; Kimball, *Dudley*, p. 112; Hutchinson, *History of Massachusetts*, ii. 115ff.; Benjamin Church, *History of the Eastern Expeditions of 1689, 1690, 1692, 1696, and 1704 Against the Indians and French*, ed. Henry M. Dexter (Boston, Mass., 1867), pp. 128ff.

which Colonel Church the leader of this ambitius raid continued to urge; but without the explicit support of the home government, first approached in 1703, he refused to give his sanction to this additional venture.[1] While Church ranged in the north served by a force of twenty sloops, which were to attend him with provisions, 600 more men were to garrison the towns and forts from Marlborough to Wells.

Dudley thus hoped to keep the war at a distance but he was not so optimistic that he would be able to root the enemy from the swamps and waters of eastern Maine and Nova Scotia. Church, the old hero of King Philip's War, who carried with him the governor's hopes, was at sixty-five well past his prime and so stout that when on the trail of Indians, so it was said, he was accompanied by a burly sergeant whose duty it was to hoist him over fallen trees.[2] The force he commanded included a sprinkling of Plymouth Indians with each company of whites. Church boasted that all were volunteers, a statement of doubtful accuracy. The New Hampshire men, in particular, fearing to leave the security of their exposed communities in hands other than their own were inducted largely through impressment.[3]

Church left Portsmouth, New Hampshire, on 15 May, accompanied by two armed vessels of the Royal Navy and the fourteen-gun *Province Snow* sailing under the provincial flag. He proceeded to sack French habitations in the Penobscot Bay, at Mount Desert, Machias Bay, and Pemasquoddy (Eastport), and took a few families prisoner *en route*, including the daughter of Saint-Castin and her children. Later Church burned down Grand Pré (Minas) and destroyed the settlement of Chignecto (Beaubassin) at the head of the Bay of Fundy. Port Royal was visited, though in keeping with the governor's instructions the invaders lay off in the basin out of range of cannon shot and restricted their activity to

---

[1] J. T. Adams, *Revolutionary New England*, p. 69.

[2] F. Parkman, *Half Century of Conflict* (Boston, Mass., 1892), p. 114.

[3] Osgood, *Eighteenth Century*, i. 413; Goodell, *Acts and Resolves*, 1703–4, VIII, 338. The difficulties of raising soldiers is indicated by legislation of 1702. 'Whereas it has been found by often Experience, that when warrants have been issued for the Detaching or Impression of Souldiers for the defence of the Country, the ablest and fittest for service have absconded and hid themselves from the Impress.' Further Act for Levying Soldiers, 27 May 1702, *Acts and Laws*, (Annual Supplements to 1706), p. 229. The two men-of-war were the *Jersey* (forty-eight guns) and the *Gosport* (thirty-two guns).

idle demonstration. Norridgewock, on the Kennebec, was not attempted.[1] It is not easy to judge this expedition a failure, as so many writers have done.[2] It had achieved its stated objectives, demonstrated to New France and its Indian allies the vulnerability of all French settlements on the eastern mainland, and exposed the nakedness of Port Royal.[3] With limited objectives spectacular success was not to be anticipated. Yet even so it must have persuaded New Englanders that emulation of the military exploits of New France had revealed that the French had far less to lose in this sort of warfare, both in men and property, than had the English.

In the meantime, while the valley gained a respite, the northern frontier of Massachusetts was hit in July at Lancaster on the Nashua River by a force of 400 French and Indians. The force was heavily engaged and with some luck, in Dudley's opinion, defeated before it withdrew. Groton, Amesbury, Haverhill, and York were harassed and then small attacks were made on Exeter, Oyster River, and Dover in New Hampshire.[4] The Indian foe was reported everywhere in this quarter, but in small parties and largely inactive. Later the governor could write 'we have lost nothing to the enemy this summer'. Dudley was succeeding in keeping the war at a distance but the cost was high.[5] By midsummer his forces were raised to 1,900 men, excluding those in vessels guarding the sea coasts. This was more than double the number of twelve months earlier. As all were agreed it was an insupportable burden for the province to bear alone, Council and Assembly joined in petitioning the queen to this effect.[6]

Maine, which had not yet recovered from the previous war, was already suffering grievously the effects of the renewed conflict.

---

[1] See Hutchinson, *History of Massachusetts*, ii. 107–9; 'The Deplorable State of New-England, By Reason of a Covetous and Treacherous Governour and Pusillanimous Counsellors', *Mass. Hist. Soc. Coll.*, 5th ser. vi (1879), 126–7; 'A Modest Enquiry Into the Grounds and Occasions of a Late Pamphlet, Intituled, A Memorial of the Present Deplorable State of New-England', ibid., pp. 65–95.

[2] See Hutchinson, *History of Massachusetts*, ii. 107–9.

[3] Dudley contended that this expedition had prevented a major descent upon Newcastle and another upon the upper towns of the Connecticut River. 13 July 1704, *C.S.P.C.*, 1704–5, no. 455.

[4] Drake, *Border Wars*, p. 208.

[5] 10 Oct. 1704, *C.S.P.C.*, 1704–5, no. 600.

[6] Humble Address of the Council and Assembly of Massachusetts Bay to the Queen, 12 July 1704, *C.S.P.C.*, 1704–5, no. 451.

Francis Parkman painted a gloomy picture of a half-barbarous
people, some with log cabins no better furnished than wigwams,
beset by social jealousies run wild—the product of evil-tongued
women—and cursed with shiftlessness and intemperance, the
consequences of an excess of New England rum.[1] It is debatable,
if the conditions were as represented, whether this was a reflection
on the decadence of the inhabitants who tolerated such a society
or whether it resulted from the protracted and excessive strains
to which that society had been exposed. At the end of 1704 Wells
petitioned that a third of its inhabitants had gone including the
minister—who had left for want of a convenient dwelling-place—
and that those remaining were impoverished or significantly
diminished in resources. Such money as had been laid aside during
the half-decade of peace to build meeting-houses and mills was
quickly used up. Wells begged remission of taxes and was granted
an abatement by the General Court of half the £80 levied the
previous year. York raised a similar plea, complaining that her
inhabitants were unable to raise one-tenth of the bread corn
necessary for their subsistence. Its inhabitants requested one of
three things: either a direct grant of money, abatement of the
provincial levy, or permission to remove from their posts. The
last-mentioned related to their confinement to garrison-houses
which left estates neglected and cattle unprotected. Kittery made
a similar case, pithily observing 'the seat of war is with us'.[2] Well
might each of the townships have used the words employed by
Massachusetts in 1709 in her representation to the queen: 'We
have stood our ground and not been driven in.' But it was also
true that these communities were legally obliged to stay put.

The three towns of Maine were included in the enumeration
of a Massachusetts law in 1699 designed to prevent the desertion
and collapse of the provincial frontiers. In addition Amesbury,
Haverhill, Dunstable, Chelmsford, Groton, Lancaster, Marlborough,
Brookfield, Deerfield, Mendon, and Woodstock were likewise
defined as frontier settlements. None could be broken up or
voluntarily deserted, save on pain of forfeiture of estate or a
substantial fine. The General Court and Council reserved for
itself the power to decide whether 'drawing off' might or might

[1] Parkman, *Half Century*, p. 39.
[2] Mass. Archives, iii. 405–9.

not be allowed. Also named in law as being particularly open to attack by the enemy, although not governed by the above conventions, were Salisbury, Andover, Billerica, Hatfield, Hadley, Westfield, and Northampton.[1] Like the Maine towns Groton, which had ten years earlier petitioned the General Court for an abatement of taxes, again in 1704 requested relief. On this occasion it was allowed £20 out of the public treasury to assist in procuring another minister and £10 to be divided among those who were the greatest sufferers in the late attack.[2] The town petitioned once more in 1706. But suffering extended beyond mere destruction of property or restriction of earnings. Marlborough, about twenty miles westward from Boston, 'a sort of way station for families bound for towns further in the interior', endured constant alarms. In the summer of 1704, like so many inland towns, it was harassed by Indians and in August 1707 experienced scattered attacks. Beyond this it had little first-hand experience of the war, yet its classification as a frontier community and its garrison organization reminded it, if reminders were necessary, of the continuance of hostilities. Along the Connecticut valley, where more soldiers were now to be seen than at any time since King Philip's War, persistent rumours of an approaching enemy kept the country in a continued state of alarm.[3]

The expense of maintaining or strengthening local defences bore heavily on a provincial treasury upon which so many demands were being made. Had not the cost been so excessive it is unlikely that the Assembly would have adopted the intransigent stance that it did in refusing to rebuild Pemaquid, risking its reputation in the eyes of the queen and the Board of Trade. Dudley's contention that failure to recognize royal commands had interrupted the course of supplies to the province was a matter to be taken

---

[1] 13 Mar. 1699/1700, *Acts and Resolves*, viii. 402. Dracut, Concord, Stow, Sherborn, Framingham, and every town within the county of Hampshire were additionally named in the Snow Shoes Act (1704), ibid. viii. p. 547.

[2] Mass. Archives, lxxi. 107, 108; and see S. A. Green, *Groton during the Indian Wars* (Groton, Mass., 1883), p. 89. Individuals might also be recompensed: e.g. Henry Seager, who by the death of one son and the capture of another had lost arms valued at £5, horns, powder, bullets, and a snap-sack, in the public service, was voted by the House of Representatives forty shillings from the public treasury. Ibid., p. 93. There are many petitions and grants of this order to be found in Mass. Archives, lxx, lxxi.

[3] Trumbull, *Northampton*, i. 464; Mass. Archives, lxxi. 454.

seriously.[1] But in contrast to Pemaquid, over which the governor, pressed by the home government, laboured in vain, the defences of Boston were the focal point of Assembly attention.[2] This is readily understood. Since it was the place and port of greatest consequence in New England, the direct advantage of expenditure in this quarter could easily be comprehended by members: further, in this instance the estimated cost bore a realistic relation to provincial resources. A committee consisting of Elisha Hutchinson, Captain Timothy Clarke, and Thomas Brattle was established in mid-July 1700 to order the laying out of money for Castle Island.[3] A report by Colonel Wolfgang Romer, a royal engineer, stationed temporarily in North America to survey colonial fortifications, confirmed that the defences needed to be enlarged.[4] Romer was given the task of supervising the rebuilding. Hutchinson planned that the fort should house 100 pieces of ordnance and possess a standing garrison to be raised to 120 officers and men. An additional 700 men, including 400 'muscateers' and 300 matrosses or gunners, were to be available on first call of alarm.

---

[1] The cost of the previous fort—as yet unpaid for—was £80,000 (Mass. Archives, xx. 51). As the ground was already trenched and the foundation in good repair the cost of rebuilding was estimated at very much less than this: about £12,000, £7,000 of which was for repairs, and as near as much again for lodgings or furnishings within; but this was still too much to justify a provincial commitment. Mass. Archives, xx. 103, 132; Palfrey, *History of New England*, iii. 274. Colonel Romer requested that the fort should be supplied from England with fifty cannon, two mortars with ammunition, 4,000 hand grenadoes, 600 firearms, and 400 heads for half-pikes. These arrived in the charge of two master gunners and one bombardier. *C.S.P.C.*, 1702, no. 32.

[2] Before hostilities commenced Governor Stoughton, contemptuously dismissed by Edward Randolph as no military man, had expressed concern at the attention given to the fortifications on Castle Island which served 'only for the defence of Boston when other avenues lie open to the enemy'. *C.S.P.C.*, 1701, no. 208, pp. 105, 106, 155, no. 373.

[3] Mass. Archives, lxx. 479. Earlier in the year, as Commissioner of War, Hutchinson had been appointed to take account of all artillery, gunpowder, and stores belonging to the province. Ibid. lxx. 575; Drake, *History of Boston*, ii. 527.

[4] Mass. Archives, xx. 65. The decision to proceed brought approbation from the Board of Trade. 'The province can do no better for its reputation than advance defence works.' Ibid. lxx. 535; *Council Records*, 1692–1702, p. 319. In addition to the money voted for Castle Island, a grant of £1,000 was to be laid upon the batteries of Boston and £400 for a powder-house to be constructed arched, to prevent it being burned by a bomb. The lines between the batteries were in a dangerous state of disrepair. 11 Mar. 1703, Council Records, *C.S.P.C.*, 1702–3, no. 433.

To supply them 100 barrels of gunpowder and enough provisions to last 1,000 men for twelve months were to be lodged in the castle. For the building and furnishing of the fortifications men were pressed from the garrison.[1]

From the beginning the British engineer clashed repeatedly with the Assembly watchdogs. Romer blamed the committee for the dilatory or insolent behaviour of some of the workmen. He found difficulty in getting his instructions carried out and believed his position was undermined by constant meddling. The inexpertness of much that was done he blamed upon Captain Clarke. Romer himself may have given less than adequate attention to the influence of local climatic factors upon the execution of the work and the materials to be used.[2] At the very least his undue sensitivity posed a barrier which made communication with craftsmen and assemblymen unduly difficult.

Under such circumstances it is hardly surprising that the work of construction dragged on well into the war and that its cost was widely underestimated. In April 1702 Dudley had forecast to the Lords of Trade that the Castle would be completed in two months. But by midsummer, though much had been achieved through Romer striving for a deadline which would enable him to meet Cornbury at Albany in June, there was still considerable platform-work to be finished and the south-east platform had not even been laid. The initial grant for the fortifications proposed by the Council in February 1702 was £1,500. Thirteen months later a further £500 was voted. But this supplementation proved insufficient. In July 1703 £700 was set aside for discharging debts already contracted and for finishing the gun-platforms. But though a new boat and boat-house were built from these funds, much to the disgust and anger of the House, completion was not attained and before the final allocation £250 more was voted by the representatives in the spring of 1704. That summer the House asked for the precise sum necessary to bring the work to a close and established an *ad hoc* committee for this purpose. The figure reported was £313. In reply the Assembly bluntly voted '£300 and no more'.[3]

[1] Mass. Archives, lxx. 564.
[2] But see Colonel Romer's report, Mass. Archives, lxxi. 170.
[3] Ibid. lxxxi. 33, 58, 59, and 170.

By the early autumn Dudley sanguinely judged the Castle defences to be in perfect form 'and not inferior to any of Her Majesty's newest fortifications in England'.[1] However, in less than two years further expenditure was thrust upon the province. Colonel Rednap, a royal engineer who had succeeded Colonel Romer, in reporting on New England fortifications drew attention to the weakness of Boston neck and the shore defences. He recommended a considerable enlargement of the North Battery and repair of the South Battery, which were both on the south-east of the town. The House speedily accepted most of his suggestions, proposed an even greater enlargement of the North Battery, and allocated a substantial sum for fortifying the neck. In less than a week the town-meeting, moved by the 'imminent danger the said town is in, which is the head of the province for trade and navigation', granted £1,000 to carry out the recommendations of the Assembly. On the same day a message was sent to the Council affirming that any town could, with the governor's approbation, raise sums of money for their fortifications or defence without further allowance or sanction from the Court.[2] There was, however, a constitutional conflict brewing over this issue.

The sturdy readiness of Boston to provide cash may have inclined the Assembly to be less ready to assume fully the burdens of other ports such as Salem, Marblehead, Plymouth, and Gloucester. Massachusetts compared her lot unfavourably with that of New York: 100 miles of vulnerable coast, a longer land-frontier, and no royal garrison to call upon such as New York possessed. In the case of Salem and of Marblehead, as for Charleston, misapplication of funds in the past strengthened the provincial assembly's unwillingness to allocate its slender resources. Accordingly it was resolved that those fortifications which could not be maintained by the province should be supported by the towns. Before the War of the Spanish Succession commenced Salem had received £100 towards repairing her fort on condition that the town matched this grant with an equal sum and kept the fort

---

[1] 10 Oct. 1704, *C.S.P.C.*, 1704–6, no. 600.

[2] Mass. Archives, lxxi. 220, 221–5. The small town of Gloucester, by reason of its scattered dwellings and poverty, complained that it was too poor to undertake its own defence. It asked for the erection of a small fort so situated as to command the harbour. Petition to Governor Dudley, 10 Mar. 1702/3, Mass. Archives, lxx. 620.

in good repair. Marblehead had been given a smaller grant on similar terms. Salem was also allowed her own powder levy, 12*d*. per tun or one pound of good gunpowder on every non-provincial ship entering harbour. Hitherto this levy had been entailed for the use of Castle Island, Boston. Marblehead, on application, was granted a comparable privilege.[1] However, the provincial treasurer was also reimbursing Salem for the expenses of maintaining ten men at Salem fort and one gunner at Marblehead, although this had not received the approval of the House. Though the governor and Council in November 1706 ordered that no more sums were to be paid without the consent of the House, payment appears to have continued and was classed as a grievance of the House. In mid-1707 a resolution was passed that the sums paid out, £141. 7*s*. 1*d*. in the case of Salem and £46. 9*s*. 7*d*. for Marblehead, should be added to the annual provincial taxes levied on the two towns.[2]

The difficulties of a defence-system which operated on three tiers, metropolitan, provincial, and town, without any clear demarcation of responsibilities is evident enough. Here was a fruitful source of continued and complex constitutional conflict between all three bodies. Salem had held a stormy town-meeting on 24 June 1706, at which fortifications were the central issue. After a considerable debate it was resolved not to comply with a request from the governor that substantial repairs should be undertaken. The main work, Fort Anne, situated on Winter Island two miles from the body of the town, was the queen's—so it was argued—and ought to be a charge on the province. It was acknowledged that great danger existed from the seaward approach to the port and that the fort was of value, being stronger than any on the Massachusetts coast, with the exception of Boston. But Salem pleaded, not without justification, perhaps, that 'poverty and decay' occasioned by the war was so great that the town could do little to provide for its upkeep. It had, however, kept in repair a stockade 200 feet long and two block-houses, in which there were several guns. This was at the end of the town, about a mile from the fort. Here was maintained a nightly watch. In 1708 the Council, presumably with the approval of the Assembly,

---

[1] Ibid. lxx. 529, 581.
[2] Ibid. lxxi. 235, 271, and 349.

offered to put soldiers in the fort if the people of the town would undertake repairs.[1]

At the entrance of the important Piscataway River, on the boundary between Massachusetts and New Hampshire, stood Newcastle fort, subsequently named Fort William and Mary, boasting thirty-one guns. It was considered the only suitable place in the province for a major fortification. Away from the sea the country was so wide and woody that the enemy could easily avoid such strong points which would thus waste provincial resources. But at the fort half of the guns were only demi-culverin and the carriages and platforms of many were in need of repair. Although well-located, however, it was inadequate for the protection of the growing trade of the river, according to Romer. He advocated a strengthened system by the erection of a strong tower on the point of Fryer's Island, and batteries on Wood Island and Clark's Island respectively.[2] Dudley's hopes that the inhabitants might be induced to carry these out themselves was met by the customary plea of poverty.[3] However, commerce coming down the river was charged a considerable duty which went towards the cost of the fort and in 1703 the province was able to grant £500 towards revamping the fortifications of Great Island, an act which brought from Governor Dudley fulsome praise which he used at the expense of Massachusetts.[4]

In the summer of 1704, six months after Romer's gloomy comments that progress was nil and would not be achieved without a royal grant, it could be reported that the Piscataway was 'in a very good posture of defence'. Dudley had supplemented the Assembly grant by employing every man in the province to give his labour to the fortification unpaid.[5] However, there was still wanting 'men, arms and ammunition'. And beyond the Piscataway the permanence of fortifications was even less certain. Nine leagues to the eastwards lay the Saco River. It was small and not well suited for navigation. About six miles from the mouth on the western side near the falls stood a stone fort and a tower in the

---

[1] Felt, *Annals of Salem*, p. 345.
[2] Mass. Archives, lxx. 489; *C.S.P.C.*, 1702–3, no. 1425, enclosure ii, p. 919; ibid., 1702, no. 544.
[3] Mass. Archives, xx. 132.
[4] *C.S.P.C.*, 1702–3, nos. 543, 1398, p. 882.
[5] *C.S.P.C.*, 1704–5, no. 3; ibid., no. 417.

form of an irregular pentagon. By 1700 both of these had fallen into disrepair and Colonel Romer marked out a place two miles nearer the mouth for the security of the fishery. Colonel Rednap also recommended that a new fort be built in place of Saco, to be erected at Winter Harbour. Although the House gave its approval in November 1705, orders to put this proposal into effect were delayed until the summer of 1708.[1] Further eastward still, the village of Falmouth and the stone fort of Casco had, like Pemaquid, been destroyed in the late war. For Casco Massachusetts ordered a new fort to be built.[2]

Inland the fortifications were much less impressive. Many towns, like Wells and York on the coast, relied for safety on the little garrison-houses which had been used in the previous war. At Dunstable under Tyng's supervision in 1702 a large fortified trading-house was erected, which was used to supply the Indians of Penncook. The village of Deerfield had been protected by a stockade. This had not sufficed to avert the massacre, however, and the summer of 1704 was a testing time for the defences of the Connecticut valley. Each river-town had taken steps to improve its fortifications. In the previous autumn Deerfield had estimated that the rebuilding which it wished to undertake would cost £320 and had asked the General Court for help. Northampton, Hadley, and Hatfield had each laid out considerable sums and looked to the public exchequer for a dole. Hatfield organized its labour resources carefully but when an inventory was taken of its ordnance and supplies it was found that they had been allowed to run down badly. In the whole town there was no more than one full barrel of gunpowder, and flints and lead were scarce. Six new guns were ordered.[3] For the towns of the Connecticut valley the summer of 1704, following the destruction

---

[1] Mass. Archives, lxxi. 167–9; 457.

[2] Mass. Archives, lxx. 489; lxxi. 427; C.S.P.C., 1706–8, no. 511; ibid., 1708–9, no. 391. In 1707 it was ordered to be abandoned, yet in March 1709 Governor Dudley reported to the Council of Trade that it was still in being.

[3] Supply of powder was a recurring problem for all colonial communities. In Massachusetts it was the duty of the town's selectmen to see that the stock of powder was renewed from time to time. One barrel of good powder, 200 bullets, and 300 flints for every sixty listed soldiers were to be held in stock on pain of a £5 fine for the town and a fine of 20s. for the selectmen. Acts and Laws (Annual Supplements to 1706), p. 48. From time to time community supplies were raised or augmented by a powder levy. Marlborough was granted this right in Oct. 1702. Council Records, 1692–1706, p. 326.

of Deerfield, was a time of anxiety and fear. At the time it was not at all clear that this frontier could be held.

The New England coast during the War of the Spanish Succession was exposed not merely to the danger of large-scale attack—in the early stages of the war Bostonians understood well that in any French attempt to crush New England Boston would be the focal point[1]—but to the persistent threat of offensive action by privateers or French ships marauding singly. In the summer of 1703 a French privateer falsely flying English colours cruised near Sandy Hook and captured at least two ships, one from Boston, the other from Antigua, before being driven away by English sloops.[2] The same vessel may have taken the briganteen *Society* off Milford, Connecticut. The more powerful English ships of war, H.M.S. *Gosport* and H.M.S. *Jersey*, had failed to sight any privateers at all, although the latter had cruised at Rhode Island and Block Island, locations particularly favoured by marauding corsairs.[3] But the continuing vulnerability of New England was especially shown in the spring of 1704 when the French fitted out a private shallop of twenty-seven men to intercept the southern trade as it came northwards laden with provisions. Fortunately the vessel was wrecked on Plymouth's shore. Had its venture succeeded it would have supplied the needy forces of the French and their Indian allies, and have broken Dudley's blockade.[4] Bad weather would sometimes favour the enemy by forcing ships into their hands. Three ketches were lost in this way at Cape Sable in 1702, and a fourth four years later. Whatever the cause, shipping losses were never light in any year but they were heavier in the second half of the conflict when vulnerable tonnage was gathered for campaigns against Port Royal and Quebec.

[1] Drake, *History of Boston*, ii. 527.

[2] Perley, *History of Salem*, i. 296; *Boston News-Letter*, xvi, 31 July–7 Aug.

[3] Ibid. xix, 21–28 Aug. The *Jersey* accompanied the New England forces to the West Indies, leaving the *Gosport* without support from any other Royal Navy ship. Dudley complained to the Council of Trade that this was by no means a security for a large coast of 100 leagues (300 miles).

[4] Dudley had information in the spring of 1703 that a considerable number of Frenchmen had lately arrived at Port Royal for the manning of privateers to 'infest and annoy' the New England coast. He also learned that two men-of-war had been fitted and set forth from this coast. 20 Mar. 1703, *C.S.P.C.*, 1702–3, no. 488. A petition of New England merchants to the Council of Trade about this time claimed that the French seldom had less than two men-of-war (fifty guns each) off the north-east coast.

Enemy privateering on any part of the Atlantic coast gave concern to the whole seaboard. Hence news of the arrival of frigates in the Chesapeake or at New York was regularly printed in the *Boston News-Letter* as a feature of abiding interest, particularly for the commercial element. During the summer of 1705 there were full reports of privateers, who had cruised off Sandy Hook, landing in East New Jersey and burning a country house. Others chased into New York a vessel from North Carolina. From Virginia came news that the man-of-war *Strombula* had scared off a solitary enemy. Convoys for the trade with Europe were usually large and well-protected.[1] On 18 July of that same summer, the *Deptford*, a fourth-rate ship, and nine other men-of-war, including the *Lowestoft*, a fifth-rater, brought into Boston a fleet of 120 sail. Some of these had now reached their destination but others were bound for New York, Virginia, and the West Indies.[2] The *Deptford* dropped out of the protective screen and henceforth remained at Boston as guardship. For similar reasons the *Lowestoft* was left at New York. Large outward-bound fleets, also under convoy, left North American shores though more frequently from the Chesapeake region than from the north. The Virginia fleet in August 1705 consisted of about seventy-six sail escorted by H.M.S. *Oxford*, H.M.S. *Litchfield*, and H.M.S. *Strombula*. This was the customary guard for the Virginia traders, some of which were large vessels. It was augmented for passage up the English Channel by cruisers especially located off Land's End. Because of the increased complements and improved firepower which accompanied a growth in the dimensions of the French ships such precautions were essential. Two or three frigates of from twenty to thirty guns apiece were insufficient. Under Cabinet direction the Admiralty had become more sensitive to the interests of English commerce.[3]

As in the previous war, coastal commerce and the fisheries expected protection from the English guardships, but local forces often supplemented their patrols or from time to time were obliged to act as a substitute for them. Because no clear system of distributing guard-ships was applied no governor was ever certain of

---

[1] See J. H. Owen, *War at Sea under Queen Anne* (Cambridge, 1938), p. 60.
[2] *Boston News-Letter*, lxvi, 16–23 July.
[3] Owen, op. cit., pp. 30, 107, and 109.

the naval resources at his disposal for very long. H.M.S. *Gosport* was at Boston when the conflict with France was renewed but Dudley was less than content with the armament this disposed. Repeatedly he requested from England additional aid in the shape of a fourth-rater which would help the blockade of stores for Canada and Port Royal. In the previous conflict New France and especially Port Royal had lived off the spoils of captured New England coasters. Dudley also wished to free his privateers for more aggressive work. Then in the late summer of 1703 the situation took an all too familiar turn when the *Gosport* made ready to leave before there was even the promise of a relief from England. She was prevented from sailing by lack of a full crew but this was no real solution to a very serious problem. The absence or incapacity of the *Gosport* meant an alarming diminution in security.[1] But provincial forces alone could from time to time bring off spectacular success. In 1706 a Connecticut master chased by a French privateer ran his boat aground in Rhode Island and warned the colony of the enemy's presence. Within a few hours 100 well-equipped volunteers had been gathered by beat of drum and placed on board two sloops. The French ship *en route* for Port Royal, but with orders to cruise first off the New England coast, was captured intact along with its crew of thirty-seven men. Yet local defences also had their failures, and obvious limitations. In 1704 the *Essex Galley* was beaten and forced ashore after an wholly unequal battle.[2]

As the war progressed, the menace from privateers seriously worsened. By the spring of 1705 it was estimated that 140 sail of ships had been lost. Three years later the British official, Colonel Quary, spoke of 'the great trade of Boston' as a thing of the past and estimated that it was reduced to a third of its former size. He predicted that the country would be utterly ruined and the fishery destroyed unless a speedy and effective remedy was found: the New England economy alone had not the strength to bear the cost of a provincial navy large enough to protect its fishing fleets. Francis Nicholson and Samuel Vetch, similarly alarmed at the volume of losses, especially heavy in the summer of 1709, petitioned the Earl of Sunderland about the urgency of taking Port Royal,

---

[1] Dudley to Lords of Trade, 5 Aug. 1702, *C.S.P.C.*, 1702–3, no. 996.
[2] Penhallow, *Wars of New England*, p. 42; Felt, *Annals*, p. 56.

the main source of New England's ill 'for unless this place be reduced', they claimed, 'this country must be abandoned as to its trade'.[1]

By 1710 French ships were taking almost a daily toll of captures and on a single day in August the following year a privateer off Rhode Island took three sloops and forced a fourth ashore.[2] Special measures were invoked to deal with this intensified threat. From the last week in August, and for the next three or four months, the *Province Galley* was joined by a second sloop of sixty to seventy men, which was not to be withdrawn from patrols against corsairs without express permission from the Assembly.[3] French privateers were doing particular damage to the coasting trade, and the implication appears to be that the earlier convoy-system round Cape Cod had broken down or had been discontinued.[4] Part of the French success was a consequence of vessels of the Royal Navy failing to perform their recognized duty. One captain in particular was charged with exercising a petty tyranny against the fishermen of Cape Cod. In place of chasing privateers he commandeered local labour for personal purposes, threatening force if his will was not complied with. Another, Captain Matthews of H.M.S. *Chester*, in defiance of his

---

[1] To Council of Trade, 10 Jan. 1708 *C.S.P.C.*, 1706–8, no. 1273; ibid., 1708–9, no. 794; 15 Mar. 1704–5, *Cal. Treas. Papers*, p. 327.

[2] Waller, *Samuel Vetch*, p. 171. Their depredations continued into 1711: *Boston News-Letter*, nos. 381, 382, and 383.

[3] The *Province Galley* continued as the main source of local strength. A new vessel built during the years of peace was by 1705 considered too small and decayed. £2,000 was allocated by the Assembly for rebuilding a ship of nearly 200 tons with a crew of sixty and carrying eighteen guns. Augmentation from time to time was drawn from whatever sources were available. At the beginning of the war the *Greyhound*, owned by Jeremiah Dummer and carrying a crew of seventy was equipped and fitted out initially for one month only. Later the Council ordered two sloops—the *Anne* and *Mary*—to be commissioned. *C.S.P.C.*, 1702–3, no. 488; Mass. Archives, lxiii. 193.

[4] 'French privateers lying at Holmes Hole, or other Harbours thereabout, so easily surprize our Coasters in their passage that there may be adjustable signell made from Gayhead and a suitable place at the last end of Martha's Vineyard, by the inhabitants, when they perceive any of the enemy, to prevent any vessels passing either way from falling into their hands.' Proposed by House of Representatives, 5 June 1711, Mass. Archives, lxiii. 181. Proposals were also made that Connecticut, Massachusetts, and Rhode Island should combine to secure the trade to the south of Cape Cod during the vulnerable summer months. Ibid., p. 160.

orders to guard the coast, sailed to the Banks of Newfoundland
in search of lucrative prizes.[1]

The General Court of Massachusetts was particularly sensitive
to the need for fishery protection. In 1700 the Dukes of Shrewsbury
and Bedford had been petitioned about the encroachments of the
French and a plea had been made for protection in peacetime.
The Lords of Trade had recognized that the fishery deserved
the utmost encouragement.[2] Repeatedly provincial directives and
resolutions stressed its value both as a direct source of wealth and
as a means of making returns to Great Britain. Yet much of the
naval protection given was either partly or wholly financed
from private sources. Thus in 1707 a private guard-ship, under
the command of Captain Pickering and with a crew of between
twenty-five and thirty soldiers and sailors, escorted 'out and home'
and gave protection in eastern waters about Cape Sable.[3] By
1710, however, French and Indians in and about the coast of Cape
Sable and other fishery grounds led to fear of their being lost altogether. Gloucester, Manchester, Piscataqua, Boston, and Salem,
the latter through seven petitions, requested provincial help.
It was given in the shape of a six-gun sloop of fifty tons and with
a complement of thirty to forty men, but the commander was
empowered to impress one or two men out of each fishery vessel
in case of need. It was also proposed by the Massachusetts House
that some suitable vessel from the Canada expedition should
frequently visit and help guard the fishery at Cape Sable, and
that this device might help provide serviceable intelligence for
the escorting fleet.[4]

It should be borne in mind, however, that New England produced her own corsairs in substantial numbers. At the beginning
of the War of the Spanish Succession the Massachusetts governor
had sought to encourage merchants to equip privateers. Mariners
and soldiers who enlisted were freed from all impresses for other
services. Some privateers were retained for provincial purposes

[1] Ibid., lxiii. pp. 158, 185.   [2] Mass. Archives, xx. 32, 44–6.
[3] Mass. Archives, lxiii. 90; Perley, *Salem*, i. 296. Apparently the fishing fleet
often arranged for a convoy of its own. The masters or owners pooled resources
to employ an armed vessel to take them to the Banks and stand by while they
fished. See *Essex I.H.C.* xlii. 164, 165, cited in Felt, *Annals*, p. 56.
[4] Mass. Archives, lxiii. 168. The *Province Galley* had been impressed to
assist the expedition against New France.

but the practice was otherwise frequently a means whereby men
were lost temporarily or permanently to the province. Boston,
if not other ports, did not enthusiastically support the governor's
action.[1] Early in the war selectmen were instructed to request
the governor to prevent men from privateering on the grounds
that every man was wanted at home as a counter to the ravages
of the Indians and French.[2] In the first year of the war there were
six privateers out of Boston but the ultimate drain through which
manpower was lost was Rhode Island. Newport replaced Boston
as the more convenient base.[3] Impressment was a further source
of losses, men being taken by the Algerine pirates as well as by the
Royal Navy.[4] When H.M.S. *Swift* arrived in July 1702 with
expresses of the declaration of war she stripped some of the ships
in Boston harbour clean of men. But she was fired on, prevented
from passing the Castle, and her captain suspended. Regulation
of intake to the navy was now officially under the supervision
of the governor, and seamen, moreover, were prevented by legislation from defecting from one ship to another, or from incurring
debts which could lead to imprisonment.[5]

The War of the Spanish Succession confirmed what the Nine
Years War had already revealed: that a colonial consensus which

---

[1] By 1706 Governor Dudley was boasting that he had equipped more privateers
'than all the Queen's governments on the [North American] Continent'. Yet
he claimed not to have taken away too many men from the land service 'which
has been very pressing', nor to have robbed all the merchant men. He admitted,
however, that he had had many complaints from the latter. *C.S.P.C.*, 1706–8,
no. 511, p. 237.

[2] Drake, *History of Boston*, ii. p. 526.

[3] *C.S.P.C.*, 1702–3, no. 1094, p. 691; ibid., 1704–5, no. 1407, enclosures
ix, xii.

[4] Migration quickly became a problem, as it had been in the previous war.
The governor complained that men removed to those colonies where there was
land to be settled, in order to be quit of taxes and service. Many, it was alleged,
went to Rhode Island. Ibid., 1702–3, no. 1399; ibid., 1702, no. 1135. New England
seamen in particular went thither. Every day, so Dudley told a London cor-
respondent 'they fly from us both out of HM ships and our privateer merchant-
men.' Ibid., 1702–3, nos. 673, 1094, p. 691: Phillips, *Salem*, p. 91. Losses to
Algiers were presumably modified by the treaty with Algiers, 17 Aug. 1700.
Mass. Archives, lxi. 311.

[5] The number of petitions from the relatives of men taken from the fisheries
by the royal frigates is considerable. Dudley would not have been able to
regulate intake outside his province. Ibid. lxi. 169, 274, 374, and 414. This
was offset, in part, by English desertions to New England ships off Newfoundland. *C.S.P.C.*, 1702, no. 768.

endorsed the principles of Protestantism and representative government while repudiating Stuart legitimacy did not necessarily open a path to united war effort. There was no means of compelling recalcitrant assemblies to aid with men and money those North American provinces threatened by the enemy, and for many assemblymen the first duty was to guard the interests of constituents and husband their resources. Remoteness from the pulse of empire, which of itself imposed many hardships and burdens, was justifiably valued from time to time for affording a compensating, albeit temporary, security. Moreover want of an imperial machinery, which could apportion contributions equitably, induced few assemblies to hazard their slender means for the sake of questionable ventures or gains which might later be sacrificed at a European peace table. Such was the consequence of a federally inclined system which possessed no federal framework of government. It remained for the colonial governors and a few perceptive and far-sighted individuals to urge the necessary economy of co-operative effort which through the fullest exploitation of resources could lead to the swift destruction of French power in North America.

In the meantime, and before this rationale could take effect, the exposed provinces sought by diplomacy to lessen the unbearable strains of war and to create an immunity from attack. Rendered vulnerable by the defection of the Five Nations, New York for two-thirds of the war gained terms from the enemy acceptable to her. Massachusetts, in turn hard-pressed by the neutrality of New York and her Indian allies, proved unable to follow suit, though she had sought at one time to do so. But despite a temporary adherence to such aims, which at this stage in history the colonial possessions of conflicting empires might pursue without offending the rules laid down by metropolitan governments, Massachusetts in the War of the Spanish Succession proved the best overseas partner England possessed.

For several reasons the Board of Trade showed particular concern for New England at the beginning of the conflict. In early 1703 the Board urged a royal gift of powder, firearms, and cannon to encourage the colonists to rebuild Pemaquid and strengthen the Newcastle fort. Eighteen months later the Board backed Dudley's request that cannon should be supplied for Boston Castle. Massachusetts, alone of all the continental colonies, received as a 'gift' a substantial proportion of the ordnance required, though she had to meet the costs of shipment.[1] In contrast Virginia, which received but a small proportion of the small-arms asked for, was obliged to purchase outright.[2] The exposure of New England to direct attack was doubtless the main reason for this attention though it was conceivably facilitated by the particular relationship which obtained between Secretary Blathwayt and Joseph Dudley. Blathwayt also secured a special concession for New England in the Spanish American trade, and advised the purchase of provisions there in preparation for an expedition under Lord Peterborough.[3]

Alone of all the continental colonies Massachusetts was selected to supply men for service in the West Indies in the defence of Jamaica. These men were to be raised as volunteers and furnished with supplies and transportation. There were obvious attractions which Dudley publicized as best he could: hopes of plunder from the Spanish, a special grant from the Crown, and expectations of a bounty from the Jamaican Assembly. None of these things was secured, however, nor were the men kept under their own officers, despite promises to the contrary and a warning from some of the Council that this was likely to happen. Under the lead of Captain Walton in New Hampshire and Captain Larrimore in Boston two companies were raised and provision made for a third.

Aware of the sensitive issues involved Dudley expressed fears lest this opportunity for Anglo-American co-operation should be mishandled:

They are the first men in armes that ever went out of this Province or from the shoar of America, and if at first they meet with discouragement I am sure I shall never send from hence one file of Volunteers more. I therefore humbly pray on their behalf that they may be kindly dealt withall and provided so that I may have a good account of them to be made public here.[4]

---

[1] Account of Ordnance Stores, 30 May 1706, *C.S.P.C.*, 1706–8, no. 349; Wm. Lowndes to Mr. Blathwayt, 15 Jan. 1705, *Cal. Treas. Books*, xix. 462; Report of Wm. Blathwayt to Lord High Treasurer, 22 Jan. 1705, *Cal. Treas. Papers*, xciii. 316. The cost of this consignment of stores, which included 20 great guns, 100 barrels of powder, and 500 small arms, was £3,283. 8s. 11d.

[2] Steele, *Politics of Colonial Policy*, pp. 93, 94.

[3] Blathwayt to Nottingham, 19 June 1702. B.M. Add. MS. 29588, f. 492; cited in Steele, op. cit., p. 93.

[4] Min. of Council of Jamaica, 11 Feb. 1703, *C.S.P.C.*, 1702–3, no. 319.

Dudley had observed to the Council of Trade that no colony on the American coast was further from Jamaica than Massachusetts, and had stressed the problems of an inland frontier with the Indians of more than 200 miles of open villages, and a seacoast of such length that in the previous war single French privateers had ravaged the shoreline with impunity. He used the occasion to direct attention to the need for a joint attack on Port Royal, the destruction of which nest would release New Englanders for service abroad. Predicting greater obstruction to the West Indies project than in fact arose, Dudley took this opportunity to criticize the degree of autonomy which the Council had been given by the charter of 1691, and its sensitivity to popular control.[1]

It is conceivable that the initial proposal for such a project emanated from Dudley himself, for its success could advance his purpose and indirectly aid the province, particularly if he were allowed to tailor the shape of New England's contribution to fit provincial susceptibilities. An earlier writer has suggested that the scheme was imposed as a penalty because the continental colonies were not so serviceable as their island counterparts.[2] If this were so, there remains to be explained why Massachusetts was chosen and not some other province less open to the ravages of war. Such invidious distinction runs contrary to the consideration shown by the Board of Trade to the need of strengthening the province. But whatever the source of the design little thought was given in England to its execution. Despite the advice of Dudley the volunteers were treated with indifference and put on the lowest English establishment. Their pay was markedly inferior to the remuneration they might have received in New England for less risk and was without any of the financial compensations promised. Before the return home the men were taken without adequate clothing or sufficient food to Newfoundland where many of them sickened. Their sole gain was the summary praise of Admiral Benbow and a view of distant parts.[3]

Neither the treatment the men had received nor the management of the campaign could be expected to promote the right spirit

---

[1] 17 Sept. 1702, *C.S.P.C.*, 1702–3, no. 966; 10 Nov. 1702, Dudley to Council of Trade, ibid., 1702–3, no. 1135.

[2] Osgood, *Eighteenth Century*, i. 401.

[3] Ibid. i. 401; *C.S.P.C.*, 1704–5, no. 1297.

for future co-operation.[1] It may, however, have helped to broaden the New England view and contributed toward the compassion expressed for St. Kitts after that island had been ravaged by the French.[2] In April 1706 the attention of all charitable and disposed christians within the provinces of Massachusetts Bay and New Hampshire was directed towards the deplorable circumstances and distressing wants of 'their said Xtian brethren and fellow subjects and exciting them to put on bowels of Xtian compassion and charity for the relief of the pinching necessities of their distressed Friends and Countrymen'.[3] Town ministers were directed to publicize this appeal and to stir up their people, notwithstanding their deep poverty, to a cheerful and liberal contribution. The money collected was to be put into the hands of Samuel Sewall and Andrew Belcher and invested in provisions forwarded under the supervision of the governor and Council.

Concern with the tide of battle in Newfoundland, a region important and familiar to maritime New England, may well have been stimulated by the unfortunate experiences of the companies of Captains Larrimore and Walton after their return from the West Indies.[4] But New England's interest in this theatre needed no extensive publicization to make it understood. Here at the commencement of the war the English had taken the initiative and under Captain John Leake, the governor, had captured twenty-nine merchant- and fishing-vessels and destroyed the French establishments at Trepassey and Saint Mary's. But in 1703 Admiral Graydon had refused to risk a force, designed primarily to protect the West Indies, by attacking the French base at Placentia, which Dudley believed equalled Port Royal as the source of New England's ills.[5] Two years later the French counterattacked in force from this Newfoundland port with 600-700 men led by Governor Subercase against St. John's.

---

[1] See W. T. Morgan, 'Some attempts at Imperial Co-operation during the Reign of Queen Anne', *Royal Hist. Soc. Trans.*, 4th ser. x (1927), 177; J. Burchett, *A Complete History of the Most Remarkable Transactions at Sea* (London 1720), p. 598; *C.S.P.C.*, 1702–3, no. 319, pp. 159, 187, and 192.

[2] See above, p. 56.

[3] Mass. Archives, ii. 625A.

[4] Osgood, *Eighteenth Century*, i. 402; Hutchinson, *History of Massachusetts*, ii. 121.

[5] *C.S.P.C.*, 1702, no. 966.

Despite impoverished resources the town withstood a siege of five weeks, and the frustrated French turned aside to destroy Ferryland and ravage northwards to Conception Bay, Trinity, and Bonavista.[1] But before this, in the summer of 1704, about 144 French and Canadians in two sloops and canoes endeavoured to surprise Bonavista harbour. Three English ships were taken but to the delight of New Englanders a small New England ship of fourteen guns avoided and fought off a whole French force which had turned the guns of the captured ships against it. This inspired the inhabitants who had fled to the woods to appear as a body in arms; whereupon the French departed. Without this intervention the French must have completely destroyed Bonavista.[2]

Only slowly did the British Cabinet realize what issues were at stake in Newfoundland and how the English interest had rapidly declined, but Massachusetts evinced no desire to undertake responsibility for securing bases, and further Anglo-American enterprises do not appear to have been contemplated.[3] A British project in 1708, proceeding direct from Ireland and designed to seize control of the island and take the French post at Placentia, was frustrated from the start by administrative blunders and bad weather. No consideration had been given to co-operation with New Englanders.[4] Thus unhampered the French were enabled to make a successful descent upon St. John's in which the governor was captured and the English fortifications destroyed.[5] Subsequent raids were undertaken against Carbonear and Ferryland. The French, led by Sieur de Saint-Ovide, nephew of Brouillan, in despair of holding St. John's and its two forts for long, abandoned their captures the following summer. But the severe check received by the British in Newfoundland was of some value

---

[1] Graham, *Empire of the North Atlantic*, p. 87; *C.S.P.C.*, 1701, no. 549; ibid., 1702–3, no. 479. *Boston News-Letter*, no. 56, 7–14 May 1705, in a statement purporting to come from St. John's, says there were between 600 and 700, including French soldiers, inhabitants, and fishermen from Placentia, Acadians from Passamaquoddy and Port Royal, Canadians from Quebec and places adjacent, and fifty New England 'Eastern Indians'.

[2] *Boston News-Letter*, no. 25, 21 Sept. 1704.

[3] Graham, *Empire of North Atlantic*, p. 89.

[4] Byng Papers, *Navy Records Society* (1930–3), ii. 159, 206, 212.

[5] Samuel Sewall had no illusions about the repercussions of the event, 'like to prove a great and surprising Evil to this place'. 29 Apr. 1709, Sewall, *Diary*, ii. 254.

for it served to publicize the significance of the war in North America.[1]

The conflict in Newfoundland was real enough but on the mainland, apart from the aggressive activities of the Carolina traders, Massachusetts, Rhode Island and New Hampshire alone of the English colonies were in effect at war with the French and Indians. The rest enjoyed a practical neutrality, in the main because of their fortuitous location.[2] Against this background there was nothing sinister in the tentative moves by New England to share an immunity which twenty years before had formally embraced the whole of North America.[3] By 1705, partly owing to the sheer exhaustion of the principal combatants, the conflict upon land had ground to a halt leaving a considerable number of prisoners in the hands of both sides.[4] The initiative for an exchange came from the Massachusetts legislature and led to the Sieur de Courtemanche, an emissary from the French government, visiting Boston in June.[5] He was cordially received by Dudley and returned to Quebec accompanied by the governor's son, William, and by Samuel Vetch. The English representatives, after a protracted stay, arrived back in Boston in November bringing with them proposals for the return of all prisoners without exception, and proposals for a truce and the cessation of hostilities.

Louis's ministers, conscious of the demands on French strength in Europe, sought at all costs to preserve the pacification of the Iroquois, who themselves feared that the Abenaki raids on New

[1] *C.S.P.C.*, 1708–9, nos. 543–50. Samuel Penhallow in his eighteenth-century history of the wars of New England devoted considerable attention to Newfoundland.

[2] Hutchinson, *History of Massachusetts*, ii. 104.

[3] The Treaty of Neutrality signed between Louis XIV and James II in 1686. In 1701 Governor Brouillan of Nova Scotia had proposed to the governor of Massachusetts that with the consent of their masters the two provinces should make a treaty of neutrality. Parkman, *Half Century of Conflict*, p. 4.

[4] Captain Samuel Hill, a prisoner paroled by Vaudreuil, claimed there were 117 in French hands and seventy more scattered among the Indians. Boys and girls were kept apart from their parents to work, either as domestics or at other occupations. New Englanders were greatly concerned at the number of captives who had become converted to Catholicism. This was more detested than a relapse into barbarism. The most notorious was Esther Wheelwright who, carried away from Wells when a child, rose to become Mother Superior of the Ursulines of Quebec. Some children had to be 'kidnapped' by their relatives and carried off. Drake, *Border Wars*, p. 210; *C.S.P.C.*, 1706–8, no. 69.

[5] Waller, *Samuel Vetch*, p. 80; *Acts and Resolves*, viii. 120, 134.

England would ultimately force New York to take an active role in the struggle. To avoid this Pontchartrain was prepared to recommend a strict and pervasive neutrality, short of destroying the alliance with the Abenaki.[1] But Louis did not intend that any treaty should be made which recognized Anne as queen of England. Generally French officials, aware of the strength of provincialism within the English empire, sought to exploit the petty allegiances which appeared to divide Englishman from Englishman. But in this instance, nervously focusing upon their own needs, they made excessive demands, the execution of which assumed capacity for concerted action which just did not exist. The plan, which protected the shipping of each party from capture and sought recognition of French claims to Acadia, threatened New England's fishing rights and required also the concurrence of all the English colonies. After taking preliminary steps to communicate the French proposals to New York the General Court primly rejected Vaudreuil's overtures, being resolved that reduction of Canada was a more desirable solution to New England's problems than a perpetuation of the sources of conflict. But the temporary truce was a useful breathing-spell, and Dudley was accused by the French of prolonging negotiations and spying on Canada's fortifications without the intention of achieving agreement.[2] Both Pontchartrain and Vaudreuil had hoped that if the plan was rejected this would, in a war-weary people, provoke animosity against their administration in Boston and also against London. In fact it had no perceptible influence in this respect and served rather to demonstrate the unity of purpose possessed by the English nation.[3]

One of the consequences of the negotiation for an exchange of prisoners—an objective which was popularly supported throughout Massachusetts because of the number of families who had lost

[1] Waller, *Samuel Vetch*, p. 81; *New York Col. Docs.* ix. 755; Hutchinson, *History of Massachusetts*, ii. 114–5; Drake, *Border Wars*, p. 210.

[2] Hutchinson, *History of Massachusetts*, ii. 114–15; Charlevoix, *History of New France*, v. 176. To the Council of Trade Dudley denied that he had need of any such Truce but 'can well enough defend myself'. He alleged that with four ships and mortars from Her Majesty, he was ready to go over to the offensive and remove the French from Canada and Port Royal. 1 Feb. 1706, *C.S.P.C.*, 1706–8, no. 69.

[3] In England the queen's government confirmed the rejection of the French offer. Sec. Hedges to Dudley, 1 Aug. 1706, *C.S.P.C.*, 1706–8, no. 456; Mass. Archives, ii. 595, 604; *Mass. Acts and Resolves*, 1703–7, viii. 149–50, and see Waller, *Samuel Vetch*, p. 82, n. 25.

members to the French—was the growth of trade with the enemy. Dudley himself had issued a proclamation denouncing this practice in August 1703 and was supported by the royal enactments of 1704 and 1705 prohibiting all trade and correspondence with the enemy.[1] In 1706, however, William Rowse, under a flag of truce, sailed a small vessel to Nova Scotia for the ostensible purpose of bringing home English prisoners. Despite a prolonged visit he returned with only seventeen. Being sent a second time, he brought back another seven though many more were expected. In due course he was formally charged with having used these occasions to trade with the enemy, supplying them with ammunition and other stores. The storm which now arose in the province, in part the product of internal political tensions, involved other important traders, including John Borland and Samuel Vetch, and before long enveloped the governor, who was charged with manipulating the trial of the accused, countenancing an illegal trade with the French, and supplying them with ammunition.

Feelings ran high.[2] During 1705 hostilities on land had almost totally ceased but the renewal of outrages in the early summer of 1706 had come as a severe shock to New Englanders.[3] About 300 Indians in three troops fell upon the frontier from Wells to Deerfield. Either they were singularly inept in their assault or Dudley, who called out 1,500 men, was singularly efficient in countering them, for the damage inflicted was negligible. Even the smallest villages attacked, such as Dunstable, escaped largely unscathed. After losing a score of men the war-parties returned with no greater trophies than the scalps of half a dozen women and children. But the fear and anger they aroused bore no relation to their achievement. The elections of 1706 brought into the General Court many new men, 'resolute rustics' who, like the warhawks of 1812, had personally suffered from the effects of war and were in no mood to temporize with the foes of the province. They were resolved to destroy a trade which 'put knives into the hands of those barbarous infidels to cut the throats of our

---

[1] Waller, *Samuel Vetch*, p. 82.

[2] *New York Col. Docs.* ix. 779; Waller, *Samuel Vetch*, p. 83.

[3] Above, p. 251. Penhallow, *Wars of New England*, p. 31, observed that the frontiers 'were greatly infested' but gave notice only of the attack on Spruce Creek in Kittery, during which five were killed and five were injured.

wives and children'.[1] They were supported by popular clamour
within the province as a whole and not least within Boston itself.
Also influencing the general mood was resentment against the
immunity of New York which freed enemy Indians for attacks
against western Massachusetts, and suspicion that Albany traders,
in return for plunder, were furnishing war supplies to the enemy.[2]
But Dudley had a political career to safeguard and unless this
was firm he could not secure the interests of the province nor
prosecute the war effectively.

It seems likely that as a means of protecting those directly
accused from the worst excesses of popular resentment, while
preserving his support among the mercantile elements, Dudley
encouraged the General Court itself to conduct the trial. In so
doing he ensured his own influence, which would have been
destroyed had the men charged been sent before a court of
justice.[3] As it was, all were found guilty of high misdemeanour
and received heavy fines. Rowse was also debarred from public
office. There are few or no grounds, however, for supposing that
Dudley had ever been guilty of pursuing narrow economic profit
at the expense of the people of Massachusetts. Trade with the
enemy was not an end in itself. Even the sensitive conscience of
Samuel Sewall had to concede that Dudley, if seeking to gratify
the merchants, had not intended to harm the interests of the
province.[4] The Board of Trade ultimately dismissed the charges
against him as 'frivolous'.[5]

If the affair is seen not simply as an endeavour to advance
charter rights and traditional privileges against the governor's
skilled assertion of the prerogative, which is how it ultimately
emerged, but additionally as a society testing its soundness in
time of stress, then the response had been reassuring. Samuel

---

[1] *Mass. Hist. Soc. Coll.*, 6th ser. iii (1889), 333–6, cited in Waller, *Samuel
Vetch*, p. 83.

[2] Waller, *Samuel Vetch*, p. 86; *Mass. Hist. Soc. Coll.*, 6th ser. iii (1889),
335; Osgood, *Eighteenth Century*, i. 422; *C.S.P.C.*, 1706–8, nos. 773, 832,
enclosure iii; *Mass. Acts and Resolves, Private Acts*, 1692–1780, vi. 63–8.

[3] Kimball, *Joseph Dudley*, p. 119, rejects such a notion but Waller, with
considerable evidence to support him, has no doubts that Dudley managed
the trial procedure. See *Samuel Vetch*, p. 89.

[4] Nov. 1707, Sewall, *Diary*, ii. 200, 201, 202–4; Mass. Archives, xx. 111.
As father-in-law of Joseph Dudley's son, Sewall's position was an extremely
delicate one.

[5] Kimball, *Joseph Dudley*, p. 189.

Vetch, closely related to the Albany magnates, was a focal point of provincial anger. But then Vetch was a Scotsman and an outsider. Dudley, though he had recharged his Englishness by political service in the mother country, was not. Nor was he another Sir Edmund Andros, though both men were essentially servants of the Crown. No political reverse could negate the fact that his association with New England was deep-rooted and complex. Despite endeavours to remove him from office, the homogeneity of the province in its confrontation with the French had been dramatically demonstrated to the discomfiture of Vaudreuil. This was possible because the principles of old and New England remained broadly in accord and their objectives still essentially one.

In Europe in 1704 and 1706 English arms had contributed to the striking victories of Blenheim and Ramillies. The jubilation expressed by colonials on receiving news of the former is easier to observe for Virginia than for New England. Here there was wild rejoicing. For New England 1704 was a gloomy year. In February, Deerfield had been assaulted and in the spring the detailed European news now available for the first time in the *Boston News-Letter* at first did little to lighten spirits. Account of the serious losses at sea during the great storm of November 1703, fourteen ships and 1,523 seamen off the English coast from Yarmouth to Spithead, were described in one of the letters printed by the paper as an instance of God's judgement.[1] Colonists learned through the queen's address to Parliament of the general European situation and, in reading of the excessive price of coal in England, had the means of understanding the vexations to which the people there were subjected by the war. But the very first number carried alarming news that numbers of papists were at large in Scotland and Ireland, as a prelude to a threatened French invasion. They were reminded that the ruination of the Protestant interest and the fruition of Universal Monarchy was sought through the aspirations of a Pretender—'a stated Enemy to our Liberty and Religion'—under obligation to the French king. If the three nations of the British Isles, the English, Scots, and Irish, were embroiled in a civil war, then old and New England within the English nation must form the core of the Protestant cause. The shape and dramatic impact of this printed news,

---

[1] 29 May, *Boston News-Letter*, No. 7; 5 June, ibid., no. 8.

following so shortly after the experience of Deerfield, must have impressed on New Englanders anew how closely their destiny was interwoven with that of England and how uncertain the future still remained for them.[1]

In midsummer, the opening of trading facilities within the Spanish dominions offered the first glimmer of an improving situation. Official news of the preliminaries of the battle of Blenheim appeared in early September but it was nearly two months more before information of the European victory celebrations were printed. At the end of the first week in November Governor Dudley decreed that the twenty-third of the month should be a Day of Thanksgiving (London's had been Sunday 7 July), which should include good harvests and diverse other instances of favour towards the province of Massachusetts Bay, of which the European victories of the past summer formed only one part. Thus neither the brilliant success at Blenheim nor the capture of Gibraltar were accorded separate rites. In England Blenheim, as the first decisive victory over the hereditary foe for nearly three hundred years, brought a great upsurge of patriotism. It would be surprising if something of this sentiment was not shared by the colonists. But the celebrations lost the element of spontaneity which would have made them meaningful. As a leaven the new feelings of national pride may thus have taken several years to work, if work they did, finding expression in the enthusiastic preparations for the Anglo-American assault upon Port Royal and then Canada. But first Massachusetts mounted her own endeavours to destroy the privateer nest which had contributed importantly to the grave losses she was incurring at sea. However, in this venture she failed dramatically and, in so doing, demonstrated again to all New Englanders her dependence upon the mother country, which alone possessed the assured capacity to rid her of the threat of destruction.

---

[1] Scares arising from the Pretender's intentions continued throughout the war. After the threatened invasion of Scotland, earlier in 1708, the Council and Assembly sent an address to the queen:
We adore the divine Providence . . . preventing that wicked and insolent attempt having any other effect than the shame and confusion of the impious projectors and contrivers thereof.
20 Oct., *Boston News-Letter*, No. 216; Mass. Archives, xx. 114.

CHAPTER VII

Against Port Royal and Quebec: Anglo-Massachusetts co-operation and the aftermath of failure, 1707-1713

THE summer of 1706 was a time in which the landward defences held firm against widespread attack. It was followed by an equally successful winter in which the forces of Massachusetts and New Hampshire were enabled not only to discourage any assault upon their towns but also to harass the enemy so that his supplies dwindled. Parties of twenty and thirty, sometimes under a French officer, ranged the woods of Maine but with little effect. At least one of these parties was completely wiped out. In laconic mood Dudley could complacently explain that the snow-shoes worn by his men were better than those of the enemy. Twenty brigantines and sloops kept the eastern Indians from their winter fishing and in the spring, when between 200 and 300 English scouted the woods, they were prevented for the fifth year in succession from planting in their customary areas of settlement near the coast. In face of such sustained pressure the Abenaki moved westward to the cover of Quebec and the centres of French power.

Encouraged by his growing record of achievement Dudley confidently addressed English administrators about the degree of provincial accord he had behind him and of the good spirits with which the heavy charges of war were borne: 'in their General Assembly and everywhere [the people] say they are well defended and supported and are easy under the Government.'[1] Such optimistic comment underplayed the recent rifts occasioned by the bitter charges of trading with the enemy[2] but they were in marked contrast to the complaints made earlier in the administration about the difficulties of governing Massachusetts Bay. Moreover now that the military problems on land had temporarily abated there

---

[1] *C.S.P.C.*, 1706–8, no. 947.
[2] For a thorough discussion of this issue and the involvement of the governor see Waller, *Samuel Vetch*, pp. 79–93.

was sufficient lessening of provincial discords to reveal the foundations for a more spectacular offensive spirit. The dimensions of the threat to the very existence of Massachusetts caused by the havoc of French privateers helped to create a new mood and a new purpose.

In March 1707 Dudley laid a proposal before the General Court for an expedition against Port Royal. In due course a committee of both houses reported favourably on the project, recommending that the governor be empowered to carry it out. Dudley sought help outside Massachusetts from the other New England provinces. New Hampshire, which was under his government, furnished a single company and Rhode Island, similarly alarmed by the war at sea, agreed to press forty-eight men and to provide facilities for seventy to eighty men. She also offered to supply an armed vessel of not more than eighty tons. Connecticut refused help. Her governor returned a cynical reply which underestimated the difficulty of capturing Port Royal and questioned the value of a conquest which he believed would certainly be negated by British diplomacy during the peace negotiations. The Connecticut Assembly was, if anything, even more intransigent. The overwhelmingly preponderant contribution was thus from Massachusetts which resolved to provide a force of 1,000 men, to be filled by impressment if insufficient volunteers were forthcoming. Colonel John March, a former commander of Fort Casco, was put in charge of the force and Colonel Redknap was instructed to accompany it as the engineer. The fleet, consisting of fifteen transports and eight open sloops, and defended by the guard-ship *Deptford* and the *Province Galley*, left Nantasket on 12 May. Massachusetts had filled the ranks of her two regiments with volunteers and had augmented them with 100 Indian auxiliaries.[1]

The expedition anchored off Port Royal a fortnight later. The main objective was a fort of four bastions about seven or eight miles away. It was well-protected by thirty-eight guns and two mortars, amply supplied with ammunition, and provisioned to support 500 men for one year. The English had great superiority in numbers and took the enemy by surprise but the garrison had been critically augmented by the arrival of sixty Canadians just

---

[1] Osgood, *Eighteenth Century*, i. 425; Beamish Murdoch, *History of Nova Scotia* (Halifax, 1865), i. 288–9.

before the landing. The French commander, Governor Daniel d'Auger de Subercase, a man of resolution and courage, had vowed to make Louis master of New England. It was unlikely that he could be tricked into an easy capitulation. The artillery resources of the attackers were manifestly inferior to those of the French and scarcely adequate for the task they had in hand.[1] They carried only eight field-pieces and two small mortars, a testimony to the optimism of Governor Dudley.

Difficult terrain of thick woods and swampy marshes separated the fort from the landing place and it was ten days before the invaders were able to bring their limited armament into play. During this time March, with three-quarters of the men, advanced from the south shore of the Port Royal basin while a subordinate commander brought up the remainder from the north shore. As soon as the troops were in position realization of the strength of the fortifications which were stronger than anticipated led to a prudent decision to turn aside to the destruction of the enemy's settlements and property. Houses were burned over an area of twenty miles from the fort, some 150 in all; 1,000 head of cattle and all the sheep and swine in the vicinity were also destroyed. The corn and pastures were drowned by cutting the sea-dams. This having been accomplished, it was decided by a council of war to re-embark. The force withdrew to Casco Bay for further instructions.

Redknap had denied that the vociferous and organized sense of outrage at the failure of this expedition was anything save the work of a few 'insolent spirits', Dudley's enemies, who designed to exploit his discomfiture and Boston's disappointment that the privateers' nest had not been destroyed. Had similar havoc been wreaked in the neighbourhood of Boston these few would have raised an outcry that their own province was undone, he observed. It was Redknap's opinion that the force had had the best officers available in Massachusetts.[2] Moreover Captain Stukely, who commanded the *Deptford*, notably refrained from criticizing the leaders, an unusual if not unprecedent act by a Royal Naval officer at this period: opportunities for outspoken comment on colonial ineptitude were rarely overlooked. Stukely, however, had

---

[1] Hutchinson, *History of Massachusetts*, ii. 123, confines himself to saying that 'the fort was to insulted if practicable.' The successful expedition of 1710 used the guns of its ships to bombard the fort into submission.

[2] 20 Feb. 1708, *C.S.P.C.*, 1706–8, no. 1347.

nothing but contempt for the armchair generals, 'the *fighting* men at Boston' as he scathingly described them, who had written so many scurrilous and vilifying letters without the courage to sign their own names. To his mind it was not to be expected that raw volunteers could take well-fortified and well-defended forts. In fact, Dudley had taken a gamble which might have come off if the fort had been poorly defended and the levies brilliantly led: it had failed, however, and the leaders and men were allowed to become the scapegoats.[1]

In these circumstances to send them back for a second time when the odds against them would have lengthened was an act which had little to commend it in military terms. The erstwhile volunteers, now well apprised of the difficulties to be encountered, had lost confidence. A round robin was signed against making a second attempt but when the ringleaders were discovered the incipient mutiny collapsed.[2] Dudley, however, concerned only to justify the expense of raising the expedition and to silence his critics, failed to draw the obvious instruction from this event. Indeed later he foolishly claimed that the men were sent to Port Royal a second time 'rather to show their obedience'. To make matters worse March, the unsuccessful commander, was now lumbered with a three-man commission, one of whom was Leverett, a former Speaker of the House. The other two were Colonel Elisha Hutchinson and Colonel Penn Townshend. As a military expedient this would have been a difficult move to justify under the best of circumstances, and where used in history has more often than not helped only the enemy. It had no other value than to broaden responsibility in the face of renewed failure.

[1] There are two highly unfavourable accounts of the expeditions of 1707 against Port Royal but both pay tribute to the courage of the rank and file in the earlier assault. One anonymous tract—'The Deplorable State of New-England, By Reason of a Covetous and Treacherous Governor and Pusillanimous Counsellors'—aimed directly at Dudley. He was charged with designing to avoid capture of the fort for the sake of continuing a nefarious trade with the enemy. The other—the Autobiography of the Reverend John Barnard, *Mass. Hist. Soc. Coll.*, 3rd ser. v., 189–96—was written by the chaplain of the forces. It is highly critical of the leadership of John March and assumes a want of spirit, without examining in any detail the practical difficulties faced and the deficiencies of military equipment. Many disappointed Bostonians (and Col. Quary) accused the troops of cowardice. The criticism of March is repeated by the near-contemporary account of Samuel Penhallow, pp. 42, 43. The choice of him for leader is said to have been a concession to the demands of the Boston mob.

[2] Hutchinson, op. cit., ii. 152–3.

It is notable that the accompanying armament for the second expedition had not been improved and, although fresh blood was brought in by the addition of 100 new recruits, the army which left Casco Bay in mid-July was diminished to two-thirds of the size of the first expedition through desertion and sickness. Before many days were passed sickness also removed March from nominal command, and Wainwright, the former second-in-command, himself an unwell man, took over. Rarely could any enterprise have begun under less auspicious circumstances. In this instance the French garrison, reinforced by the crew of a French frigate under the command of M. de Bonaventure, were better prepared. Employing the lessons taught by the first expedition's movements, and taking advantage of the dilatory disembarkation of the English, they had barred the way to any landing on the south side of the basin. Accordingly the English, obliged to disembark on the opposite side of the fort, were in every respect more disadvantageously placed than on the previous occasion. Now even their base was under fire and had to be abandoned. Fires along the river prevented bringing up the artillery by water. Moreover the climate had turned against them. Although this was mid-August the nights were growing colder and men sickened readily with the flux and swellings in the throat. Morale must have been appallingly low. As Thomas Hutchinson has said, most of those that were not sickened in body were sickened in mind Their final demoralization occurred when a small party of plunderers—less than a dozen—which separated itself from the main body of troops was skilfully set upon and cruelly cut to pieces. The end was inevitable. After ten days of futile effort the expedition withdrew and returned to a savagely hostile Boston. Arrangements were made for a court martial which in the vagueness of its findings was even less military than the behaviour of the troops it sought to assess. In the mild general censure no man was singled out for disgrace.[1]

Whilst these forces were employed against the French in Nova Scotia the Indians in small troops of twenty to forty each continued their harassment of the frontiers. Oyster River, Exeter, Kingston, and Dover in New Hampshire and Berwick, York, Wells, Winter Harbour, and Casco sustained small losses. Of the inland towns, Marlborough alone was attacked. Dudley claimed that all of these

---

[1] Osgood, *Eighteenth Century*, i. 426; Hutchinson, op. cit. ii. 127.

parties were well met and received greater injuries than they delivered. At Wells a large party of sixty canoes, with four of five men in each canoe, was badly mauled by an audacious fishing-shallop which killed or wounded about twenty. Six troops of horse and 100 footsoldiers, which by a forced march covered the 100 miles to Winter Harbour in two days, sufficed to scare the Indians away.[1]

If the palpably absurd charges that Governor Dudley sought to limit the successes of the 1707 expeditions for personal profit be dismissed, then the over-all failure stands out as an object lesson that Massachusetts alone was not only too feeble to protect her commerce from French privateers based in the New World but was also no longer capable, as she had been in 1690, of reducing that stronghold unaided. But Port Royal, though serious enough in itself, was in effect not the source of the threat to New England which was rooted at Quebec on the St. Lawrence. During two decades of war many colonial officials had observed that the destruction of French power in North America was a strategic necessity if the existence and growth of the British settlements was to be assured. Each New York governor from Dongan to Cornbury had pressed that this be undertaken, while in Massachusetts Dudley had become a convert as early as 1704. Samuel Sewall observed that conquest was the solution voiced by many intelligent persons and indeed for Massachusetts its advantages were so obvious that even the governor's enemies dared not risk obstructing projects for its attainment or the taking of any steps which might discourage English support. For if it was now questionable whether the colonists alone could subdue Acadia it was unthinkable that they should consider the conquest of Canada without substantial support from the mother country.

The instrument of this new aggressive policy which stretched beyond the mere provincial or even regional boundaries of New England was primarily the Scotsman, Samuel Vetch. Vetch's economic interests and political vision enabled him to perceive how the enlargement of the French dominions in the interior was 'hemming in' every English colony from the Carolinas northwards.[2] It also facilitated his representing in terms acceptable to

[1] Hutchinson, *History of Massachusetts*, ii. 128.
[2] Waller, *Samuel Vetch*, p. 102.

the British the value of preserving a New England which, with Nova Scotia, formed a potential source of naval stores and which, by its sale of fish to Europe, its consumption of manufactured goods and its export of specie to England, could be seen as a prized possession of empire. Though he failed to understand in any profound sense the nature of the religious gulf to be bridged before more fruitful co-operation could be achieved between old and New England, he sought instinctively for the empire as a whole a return to that unity of purpose which the English in particular had shown at the time of the revolutions of 1689.[1] Outside New England the designs of Vetch gained momentum through his own tenacious resolve and the endorsement of important administrators such as Robert Quary, and George Vaughan, the agent for New Hampshire.[2]

The Board of Trade with whom Vetch initially made contact moved unhurriedly to consider his proposals through the summer and autumn of 1708. Because of the absence of Sunderland, Queen Anne was approached by means of Secretary Boyle. But in face of royal irresolution no progress could be made until Sunderland's return, though in the meantime Dudley added his written support to the contentions of Vetch. Like Vetch he stressed the threat of encirclement by trade and discovery which affected every English settlement from Massachusetts to Virginia. He pointed to the growth of Catholic influence among the Indians and to the territorial aggrandizement which every year made the prospects of successful conquest less easy. Time was not on the English side.[3]

It was not until November that Vetch, joined by Francis Nicholson with whom the Board consulted on colonial matters, was able to discuss his military problems in any detail. He envisaged a colonial force of 2,500, three-fifths drawn from Connecticut and the middle colonies, to march overland from Albany against Montreal. A smaller force, comprised of Massachusetts men, was

---

[1] 'Canada Surveyed or the French Dominions upon the Continent of America briefly considered', 27 July 1708, C.S.P.C., 1708–9, no. 60. Vetch's developed argument looked to the direct advantages to be drawn from the natural resources of the conquered country which would also provide a place of settlement for North Britons. He stressed the economy of ending at one blow the source of hostile power in North America. Ibid., 1708–9, no. 196; CO, 324/9, 221–46.

[2] Col. Quary to Council of Trade, 10 Jan. 1708, C.S.P.C., 1708–9, no. 1273.

[3] To Council of Trade and Plantations, 10 Nov. 1707, C.S.P.C., 1706–8, no. 1187.

to combine with the two battalions of British regulars and six men-of-war. Though there was no question but that the over-all command must be British, he strongly urged that the colonial levies should be under their own officers. The commissioners of trade listened with respect and then adopted Vetch's reasoning to present his proposal to Sunderland. Inevitably New England's own suffering figured importantly in what they had to say. Vetch was fortuitously supported by the arrival of a letter from Governor Cornbury of New York which gave independent support to his objectives and flattered his judgement by closely matching the assessment he offered of French power.[1]

The evidence of Samuel Vetch's capacity to influence people in high and low places through insight into human behaviour, personal charm, and well-placed bribes, is overwhelming. But he was also helped by the aspirations of Whig leaders and the threats to their ascendancy. From Harley, Vetch had little to fear, while Sunderland had good reason to applaud objectives which, pursued by Scots and English alike, could serve to cement the Act of Union and by the successful planting of a new Scottish colony obliterate the memory of ill-fated Darien. Such objectives could also strengthen his hand with the queen against Harley's growing influence. As a dissenter who revered the power of the legislature and valued the importance of trade, Vetch was aided by an exceptional vision which enabled him to engineer a confluence in which Scottish, English, and New English interests could mingle and flow.

The force of New England enthusiasm for the project was visibly expressed by the revived vitality of Massachusetts. Energetic measures were adopted by its General Court to ensure that the chances of success were not blighted by an ill-advised leakage of news.[2] Such fervent support, qualified by the resolve that local men should serve under local officers, had its counterpart in the quasi-independent colonies of Connecticut and Rhode Island, the latter staggering Vetch by its surprising zeal for his proposed enterprise.[3] But in the colonies southward of the Hudson River

---

[1] 31 Aug. 1708, C.S.P.C., 1708–9, no. 107, cited in Waller, *Samuel Vetch*, p. 113.

[2] 30 Apr. 1709, Sewall, *Diary*, ii. 254; Mather, *Diary, Mass. Hist. Soc. Coll.*, 7th ser. viii. 8; Mass. Archives, lxxi. 527, 529.

[3] The zeal is less surprising when the losses to Rhode Island shipping by enemy action are considered.

interest in the Canada project was lukewarm. Though important figures grasped the advantage of the removal of French power many traders perceived that unfavourable consequences might arise from the unqualified triumph of the British.

Quaker opposition in New Jersey and Pennsylvania came as no surprise to New Englanders. In the former, the contrived defeat by opponents of the Quakers of a proposed system of volunteers financed by the Assembly led Vetch and Nicholson to urge that henceforth Quakers be excluded from colonial assemblies. Only belatedly was an objective, which concerned the English community as a whole, enabled to triumph over the factional disputes of local politics. After an extra session the New Jersey Assembly finally made provision to pay for volunteers. In Pennsylvania the support of Governor Gookin, a majority of the Council, and most of the men of note in Philadelphia, was countered by the opposition of entrenched Quaker power in the Lower House. These men were prepared to contribute no more than a token sum of £500 as a present to the queen and even then reluctant to consent to the money being used to buy provisions for war.[1]

But however desirable it may have been in the long run that all the mainland colonies should recognize their community of interest with the provinces to the north, and Vetch has been faulted for his failure to sell to the British a scheme which included the Chesapeake colonies and their southern neighbours, in the short run the delinquencies were more than compensated for by the zeal of Massachusetts, subject to the careful supervision of committees of the House. This brought forth almost double the number of volunteers requested.[2] It was a matter which, in the words of Cotton Mather, had been effectively 'spread before the Lord'. It did indeed quickly become the Lord's purpose to free the Bay

---

[1] Waller, *Samuel Vetch*, pp. 135–8; *New Jersey Archives*, iii. 465–73, iv. 36–8, xiii. 371–2; *New York Col. Docs.* v. 78; *Pennsylvania Col. Records*, ii. 460, 479, and 481–6; *C.S.P.C.*, 1708–9, nos. 579–86; E. Armstrong (ed.), *Correspondence between William Penn and James Logan and Others, 1700–1750* (Philadelphia, Pa., 1886), ii. 349.

[2] Not without complaints from the House of Representatives about the acute shortage of manpower, worsened by a mortal fever raging in Boston and neighbouring towns. Mass. Archives, lxxi. 513. Manpower quotas for the overland expedition were New York 800, including its four independent companies; Connecticut 350, New Jersey 200, Pennsylvania 150. 1,200 men were expected of Massachusetts and Rhode Island. Britain promised 500 marines. Waller, *Samuel Vetch*, p. 139; Osgood, *Eighteenth Century*, i. 429–31.

colony from the severe pressures which for so long had threatened its townships. But whoever might claim credit on earth for forging the instrument its nature remained essentially a combination of the dominant elements of the English nation. And New Englanders at all levels by their willingness to serve paid tribute to the rightness of the cause and their faith in the success of an enterprise which had the backing of the mother country. Vetch, in minding to surpass the conceptions of Marlborough, struck a note which appealed to New England esteem, though New Englanders were probably less interested in his plans to match the imperial power of Spain by taking Florida and the Spanish island adjacent to the British Caribbean colonies. It was questionable whether God's purpose directly embraced such a project.

However, the English government had decided by the end of May not to send their contribution to the expedition. Instead they diverted it to Portugal. In bringing this about Sunderland showed no consideration to the colonial governments whatsoever. A month passed before the Admiralty was even instructed to carry the news to America, and the summer was almost over before any ship was made available for this purpose. Nor did Sunderland consider himself obliged to explain to the colonists the reason for the fleet's diversion. Hence it was not until 11 October that a ship arrived from England with the advice that forces originally intended for New England were ordered elsewhere.[1] It also bore instructions to consult whether the forces already raised, and for the sake of which the Massachusetts government had applied such stringent regulations on the community as a whole, might not be employed against Port Royal, supported by the ships of war of which there were several at Boston.

Vetch had earlier pointed out that failure of the English to provide their promised support would render all the colonies 'much more miserable than if such a thing had never been projected or undertaken'. Colonial sacrifices, occasioned by the marshalling of resources left idle from May to November, and by the consequent disruption of trade, were of concern to the more outspoken critics of the Massachusetts administration even before

---

[1] Godolphin to Marlborough, 31 May 1709 B.M. Add. MS. 9105, f. 63; Sunderland to Admiralty, 24 June 1709, ADM 1/4093, f. 78; *Penn–Logan Correspondence*, ii. 357.

news arrived of the diversion of English forces.[1] The decision to turn aside from Canada in 1709 might be justified on grounds of strategy or diplomacy, if the preliminaries of peace envisaged a return of all conquests, but the manner of proceeding, though perhaps a logical expression of the subordinate importance of colonies in mercantile thought, was, by reason of its indifference, an insult to colonial endeavour and sacrifice. Administrative sloth alone does not explain the decision to burden the ship bearing news of the British resolve with a routine patrol in the Atlantic, lengthening its westward crossing to nine weeks. Had instead news of the changed plans been hastened to Boston, the proposal that the assault should be redirected to Port Royal would have made good sense to men unaware that the preliminaries of peace required the restitution of all captured colonies.

But the blow to colonial pride was accentuated by subsequent events. Sunderland followed his letter of 1 July with a second written to the more important colonial governors requesting that they should co-operate in the recovery of the Bahamas Islands. The justification for this project was the security of 'Her Majesty's Dominions in America'.[2] If such a proposal made any sense at all it suggested that Sunderland was less well apprised of the situation in the island, where there were no permanent French lodgements, than were the colonials he sought to instruct, and that he was prepared to demonstrate beyond any shadow of doubt that he valued the vitality of the northern colonies only as a sword to protect threatened English interests. Subsequent rejection by naval captains in Boston harbour of the revived Port Royal project underlined Sunderland's slighting inferences about priorities. Two of the frigates whose normal station was New York sailed immediately from Boston without taking leave of any provincial official. The commanders of the remainder, with the exception of the captain of the H.M.S. *Chester* guard-ship at Boston, explicitly

---

[1] Waller, *Samuel Vetch*, p. 151; 21 July 1709, Sewall, *Diary*, ii. 259–60. Sewall was particularly incensed at the entertainment of British officers at the expense of the province, while the merchants were resentful at the prices for provisions established by the Court. But even the heavy expenses incurred by the colony in this futile exercise produced no serious criticism of Dudley nor of the purposes of the project. Kimball, *Joseph Dudley*, p. 126.

[2] Waller, *Samuel Vetch*, p. 155; Godolphin to Marlborough, 20 Apr. 1710, *The Private Correspondence of Sarah, Duchess of Marlborough* (London, 1838), ii. 423; *C.S.P.C.*, 1708–9, no. 658.

refused to consider convoying colonial transports to Nova Scotia. Such decisions which may have been influenced by the sailors' expectations of honour and profit were at bottom a consequence of muddled or superficial deliberation in England, which the colonial leaders proved powerless to counter. Sunderland's earlier assurances that the naval ships would remain available for use in northern waters were valueless. The enterprise had cost Massachusetts a year's revenue, well over £30,000, without a single advantage accruing.[1]

The revival of the Canada project came through the representations of Jeremiah Dummer, whose influence was enlarged by his appointment as colonial agent for Massachusetts late in January 1710, through the stream of forceful letters which Vetch penned from Boston, and from the activity of Francis Nicholson in London. A conference at Rehoboth, the previous summer, designed to salvage as much colonial unity as possible from the abandoned campaign against New France, produced few positive consequences but it did utter a firm resolve to impress the nature and importance of the major colonial objectives upon the English mind. An outstanding feature of the awareness of the value of propaganda was the proposal to send representatives of the Five Nations to England but Nicholson, not waiting for the considered implementation of this scheme, had precipitately left North America about the end of October.[2] Accompanied by Peter Schuyler, who had been second-in-command at Wood Creek, the Indians, three of whom were Mohawks, subsequently arrived in England to back the efforts of Nicholson. Vetch had engineered that Major Pigeon should aid Schuyler because of his lack of familiarity with Europe. In so doing he aroused criticism from members of the Massachusetts Council who were not consulted about this step. There was fear that the interests of the Bay province might suffer in face of the enlarged representation of New York.[3]

What these interests were was well enough understood by the

[1] Gov. Dudley, Col. Nicholson, Col. Vetch, and Capt. Moody to Earl of Sunderland, 24 Oct. 1709, f. 110; idem to idem, 25 Oct., f. 113; Gov. Dudley, 24 Oct., f. 120, CO 5/9; Kimball, *Joseph Dudley*, p. 125.

[2] See esp. R. P. Bond, *Queen Anne's American Kings* (Oxford, 1952), p. 36; B.M. Egerton MS. 929, ff. 119, 120, and 121.

[3] 4 Feb. 1710, Sewall, *Diary*, ii. 273; Sewall to Dummer, 13 Feb. 1710, *Mass. Hist. Soc. Coll*, 6th ser. i (1886), 389.

provincial leaders and, in the main, by the clergy. In 1710 Ebenezer Pemberton, in an important election sermon which influenced ministers throughout the colony, cautioned that all earthly power derived from God, who governed not by unaccountable will but by stable measures. He argued that earthly rulers should likewise govern by unalterable principles and fixed rules according to the laws and established constitution they were under. However, the design of the sermon was not primarily the affirmation of political rights but the avoidance of anarchy. Pemberton warned that though he was not ignorant of the extravagant height to which the doctrine of submission to rulers had been carried there was danger in the contrary extreme of depressing it to a mere nullity. Lawless anarchy and sullen tyranny were comparable perils. Pemberton refused to concede that 'a God of Order' invested men, who lacked civil office but possessed the demagogue's skill, with 'a lawless power' which on a pretence of public mismanagement could damage the interests of the state and overturn the foundations of government.

If ever the cohering force of community seemed important, after William had been settled on the throne, it was in the closing years of the War of the Spanish Succession. But Pemberton was no politician, and failed to perceive the more subtle interests to which a man like Sewall was alive. Later in the year he quarrelled with Captain Martin, commodore of the fleet which was destined to take Port Royal. He bitterly criticized Sewall as a Justice of the Peace for not proceeding against Martin and also for having invited him to a formal dinner. Sewall's justification was unanswerable:

The Fleet was a chief Mean of Taking Port Royal... A personal Resentment of what had pass'd before the going to Port Royal, ought not to make a Balk in a Publick Invitation after God's granting Success; which had been so much and Publickly pray'd for; and Thanks to God Return'd. And if the Justices had sent for Capt. Martin I cant tell what could have been made of the Offence. Tis difficult medling with the Captains of Frigats. Reasons of State require the overlooking of many grievous Things.[1]

On 18 March 1710 Francis Nicholson was granted a commission to reduce Port Royal 'or any other place in those parts of America'. He was given command of an Anglo-American force, the colonial

---

[1] 28 Nov. 1710, Sewall, *Diary*, ii. 291–3.

component restricted to the region of New England: a regiment of marines supplied by the British were to be supported by four colonial regiments; two from Massachusetts, commanded by Massachusetts men Sir Charles Hobby and Colonel Tailer, one from Connecticut under Colonel Whiting, and a fourth made up by the men of New Hampshire led by Colonel Walton. The composition of the naval element was likewise divided but the more powerful fighting ships were from the mother country. The British provided three fourth-raters, the *Dragon*, the *Chester*, and the *Falmouth*; two fifth-raters, the *Lowestoft* and the *Feversham*, and the star bomb (a small vessel used for carrying mortars) *Rochfort*. The *Chester* was already stationed at Boston but the *Lowestoft* and *Feversham* were guard-ships at New York. The other two ships escorted Nicholson back to New England from London. Supporting this fleet was the *Province Galley* under the command of Cyprian Southack, fourteen transports in the pay of Massachusetts, five of Connecticut, two of New Hampshire, and three of Rhode Island. In all, there were thirty-six vessels.[1]

To stimulate provincial enterprise the colonists were offered preference in the land and trade of the region to be conquered but it was made clear to them that alternative demands upon British resources prevented an assault upon Canada in 1710. However, resumption of hostilities and a change in political circumstances in England temporarily altered this decision. In the spring Godolphin, Lord Treasurer and leading minister of Queen Anne, informed the Duke of Marlborough that the Cabinet Council were inclined to renew the large design of the previous year, five regiments of troops being now available for this purpose. The declining power of the Whigs, the fall of Sunderland, and his succession by Dartmouth helped to advance the project.[2] Marlborough had his own uses for the additional soldiers, including a possible attempt on Calais. He objected to the expense of the expedition against Quebec which he believed would do little to advance the peace and serve only to ruin well-trained regulars. But he was loath to come out into open opposition lest he be charged by his political enemies with undermining or destroying the project. Under the command

---

[1] Hutchinson, *History of Massachusetts*, ii. 164–6.
[2] Waller, *Samuel Vetch*, pp. 173, 174, and 178; *Sarah, Duchess of Marlborough*, ii. 423; Bond, *American Kings*, pp. 47–8, and n. 124.

of Viscount Shannon preparations were pushed ahead until late July when, with the troops encamped on the Isle of Wight, they were discontinued because of the lateness of the season.[1]

Colonial opinion, however, was influenced little, if at all, by this resolute but transient military flourish in Britain. The General Court, having learned from the bitter experience of the previous year to expend its resources with caution, made no serious move to get things ready until the British ships and marines arrived with Nicholson in mid-July,[2] though under Commissary-General Andrew Belcher supplies of clothing and provisions had been gathering at Boston.[3] Castle William, the North and South Battery, and the forts at Salem and Marblehead, were ransacked for stores and laid bare. Culverin and demi-culverin were taken from several places, and Boston South Battery so stripped of shot that the re-mining guns had nothing left to fire. Only now did the General Court prepare to raise the militia, offering to volunteers a coat worth thirty shillings, one month's wages in advance, and ex-emption from the impress for three years. From the ranks of the militia the best remaining men were next drawn off and one commissioned officer sent by the Crown was attached to each com-pany to supervise the working up of discipline. Quotas were effectively met though not renewed without complaint of the drain on manpower resources.[4]

The English fleet left Nantasket on 18 September. Apart from delays off the Maine coast the voyage was uneventful until the arrival at Port Royal six days later. On this occasion aided by overwhelming superiority in numbers, the English were enabled to

---

[1] Marlborough to Godolphin, 10 July 1710, Godolphin to Marlborough, 2 May, B.M. Add. MS. 9109 ff. 155, 15; H.M. Commission to Richard Viscount Shannon, *C.S.P.C.*, 1709–10, no. 301; Autobiography of Revd. John Barnard, *Mass. Hist. Soc. Coll.*, 3rd ser. v. 209; B.M. Add. MS. 9109 f. 180; cf., 'The Walker Expedition to Quebec, 1711'. Ed. by G. S. Graham *Publications of the Navy Records Soc.* (London, 1953), xciv. 11, where it is claimed that five regiments were embarked at Portsmouth on 14 Oct. and not until several weeks later was the project abandoned.

[2] These were lodged in barracks on Castle Island built the previous year at a cost of £144. 3s. charged to Her Majesty. Mass. Archives, lxxi. 644, 773.

[3] Arms set aside by Britain for the expedition of the previous year were available in 1710. Ibid. lxxi. 651.

[4] Mass. Archives, lxxi. 513, 648, 651, 660, 666, 668, 669, 719, and 733; CO 5/9 f. 156; Osgood, *Eighteenth Century*, i. 436–7; *C.S.P.C.*, 1710–11, no. 396; Waller, *Samuel Vetch*, p. 180.

mount their cannon overlooking the fort. They were opposed by a garrison of less than 300.[1] In the first few days of the siege, which lasted only a week, there were small English losses from sporadic firing outside the fort but on 29 September the governor sent out a flag of truce.[2] The ostensible justification for this was the desire of Governor Subercase to pass some of the French ladies to the shelter of the English camp but shortly after, the English having realigned their artillery to provide a formidable bombardment, the French agreed to lay down their arms. The articles of capitulation were generous. The garrison were allowed to retain possessions, arms, even a number of their guns, and offered transport to Rochelle or Rochefort. Transport was also promised for privateers, while inhabitants within cannon-shot of Port Royal (that is, within three English miles) were permitted to remain in possession of their estates for two years before taking an oath of allegiance to Queen Anne. If they wished to evacuate to Canada or Placentia in New-foundland they were to be allowed to do so within twelve months.[3]

The surrender at Port Royal was followed by the submission of all the other settlements about the Bay of Fundy. A mixed garrison was now established of 200 marines and 250 New England volunteers. The remainder of the force divided and went home, the New Englanders reaching Boston on 26 October. Their reception was predictably enthusiastic and the General Court passed an address to Queen Anne exulting over the increase of wealth, strength, and territory, and the improved protection for the eastern frontier. Samuel Sewall was so touched that he wrote a Latin poem honouring Francis Nicholson and sent to him a personal letter of gratitude. However, such euphoria did not inhibit Massachusetts from claiming as its special privileges fishing and whaling rights in the seas off Nova Scotia and use of the necessary shore facilities for drying fish and extracting whale oil. Request was also made for permission to dig and transport coal without tolls or duties.[4]

---

[1] Hutchinson, *History of Massachusetts*, ii. 134–5; Osgood, *Eighteenth Century*, i. 438; *New York Col. Docs.* ix. 928; *C.S.P.C.*, 1710–11, no. 897.

[2] Twenty-six men were drowned when the transport *Caesar* went aground on the south-east side of the Gut of Port Royal. Mass. Archives, lxxi. 750, 754.

[3] Hutchinson, *History of Massachusetts*, ii. 136; Articles of Capitulation, 2 Oct. 1710, *C.S.P.C.*, 1710–11, no. 412.

[4] Waller, *Samuel Vetch*, pp. 188–90; *C.S.P.C.*, 1710–11, nos. 503–5; Samuel Sewall, *Letter book*, i. 399–400. The cost of the expedition was £862. 6s. 2d. Mass. Archives, lxxi. 774.

As in 1690, so twenty years later, the taking of Port Royal was viewed by New Englanders as merely the prelude to the more important conquest of Canada, and in the autumn of 1710 Nicholson crossed the Atlantic once more to promote this vital enterprise.[1] In England the political climate was growing ever more favourable to its promotion as Englishmen became increasingly familiar with its broad features and objectives. Jeremiah Dummer, agent for Massachusetts in England from January 1711, added his voice to that of Nicholson and—despite the resistance of Harley— Henry St. John, Secretary of State for the Northern Department, adopted the design as his own and advanced preparations for a strike at Canada in 1711.[2]

In the meantime, New England by her offensive action had not dissuaded the enemy from making minor incursions. York was attacked in the spring of 1710 but ably defended. The following June a party led by Colonel Hilton of Exeter suffered several casualties including the death of its leader. Shortly afterwards Exeter itself fended off an unsuccessful attack. The defeated enemy inflicted a handful of casualties on Waterbury and Simsbury while moving away from the coast, and thence struck at Brookfield, Marlborough, and Chelmsford. Winter Harbour was assaulted by a party of fifty Indians at the beginning of August causing some loss of life and the capture of prisoners; but the fort remained intact. Again, in October, the settlement suffered lives lost and prisoners taken but the fort proved too strong for any assault to be considered. After the return of part of the Port Royal expedition Massachusetts was enabled to enlarge the forces upon her threatened frontier, and towards the end of the year nearly 200 men under Colonel Walton scoured the eastern country. But throughout much of the summer the manpower resources of Massachusetts were stretched to the full when 17,000 men were under arms to the detriment of the Massachusetts economy. Of these 700 were in the garrison-houses and towns of the eastern frontier and 1,000 more were stationed at Port Royal.[3]

As governor of Nova Scotia Samuel Vetch sought to persuade

---

[1] 11 Nov. 1710, *C.S.P.C.*, 1710–11, no. 482, 435, 503, and 505.

[2] Oxford's account and Edward Harley's 'Memoires of the Harley Family', H.M.C., *Portland MSS.*, v (Harley Papers, iii), 464, 655; cited in Waller, *Samuel Vetch*, p. 209.

[3] Gov. Dudley to Council of Trade 15 Nov. 1710, Mass. Archives, lxxi. 491.

Massachusetts to pay for the men he commanded but he was reminded of the original agreement that soldiers in the queen's service should be paid by Her Majesty. Similarly, appeals to the Massachusetts General Court for reinforcements, couched in flattering language which compared it to the 'present British Parliament', were ignored. Weakened as she was by a generation of war Massachusetts showed no inclination to stretch diminished resources beyond essential limits or to extend her *imperium* where English power could be employed. The primary aim remained the prosecution of hostilities until the menace to the fisheries and commerce was firmly removed and the sources of frontier devastation controlled or destroyed. The essential problem was to harness imperial power to this end.[1] In this view she was supported by the other New England colonies and by New York, all of which provinces could reap immediate gain by the removal of the French presence.[2] But to achieve her objective Massachusetts had to influence the will of English politicians whose field of vision was obscured by domestic complexities and by the proximity of the European battlefield.

Allied successes in Europe since 1704 had done something to lessen colonial apprehension of a future in which the Universal Monarchy was triumphant, but circumstances had not so changed as to hold prospects of a major reorientation of New England thought. This was what the optimists in New and old France hoped for, as a forlorn means to undermine or divert the anticipated assault. French agitation led to the mission of La Ronde Denys in an endeavour to convince the 'Bastonnais' that the ultimate design of the British was to impose the yoke of Parliament on the northern colonies. M. de Costibelle, governor of Placentia, and Pontchartrain were both convinced of the value of such a move.

The readiness to negotiate with the 'Bastonnais' as an independent people, and to offer exemption from French hostility, was a calculated, if predictable, move to divide old and New England. But if the French, including La Ronde Denys, a former resident of Boston, were alive to the underlying tensions which divided the

---

[1] By the spring of 1711 captives from twenty northern and western communities—little short of 100—were held in Canada. A quarter of these were from York and Wells. Roll of English Prisoners in the hands of French and Indians, 5 Mar. 1710/11, Mass. Archives, lxxi. 765.

[2] *C.S.P.C.*, 1710/11, nos. 491, 503–5, and 583.

two parts of the English nation, they had no positive evidence that any new wave of parliamentary imperialism was imminent.[1] Attempts to revoke colonial charters had been made in the recent past and, given the nature of the old colonial system, there could be no firm assurance against renewed attempts in the future. But the people of New England were experienced in defending their rights as Englishmen and could count on powerful allies in the mother country. And there is no indication that English statesmen looked to the conquest of Canada as a means to facilitate the enslavement of the English colonies. It was scacerly a situation in which New Englanders could be expected to change sides or forego an opportunity to destroy their main enemy. However, there is little doubt that, at a less serious level, distrust between New Englanders and the English leaders was rising. The fear of the Bostonians was not that the mother country might use the conquest of Canada for sinister political designs but that once again she would decide to put aside this project.

A contributory cause of this suspicion was the veil of secrecy which overhung preparations for the Canada expedition.[2] Not until 8 June 1711 did Colonel Nicholson, sent on in advance with two men-of-war and two transports, arrive in Boston to provide the people there with the first precise information of the intentions of the home government. He carried orders to the several governments of New England, to New York, the Jerseys, and to Pennsylvania, to have their quotas of men in readiness for a fleet expected to arrive within a short space of time.[3] What was even more disturbing for Massachusetts was the sudden request for ten weeks' provision for the English army. It was questioned whether this could be met at such notice, for the fleet was due within little

---

[1] Parkman, *Half Century of Conflict*, i. 150ff. Osgood argued that the French view represented the underlying truth of the situation, *Eighteenth Century*, i. 441.

[2] St. John desired to prevent the French obtaining knowledge which would lead them to reinforce Quebec. Concern with secrecy may even have led to withholding information from Navy and Ordnance Boards.

[3] *C.S.P.C.*, 1710–11, nos. 701, 850; Sewall, *Diary*, ii. 313–14. The quotas for the land expedition were 600 from New York, 300 from Connecticut, 200 from New Jersey, and 240 from Pennsylvania. Rhode Island, which had been ignored, offered to raise sixty men. The fleet under Admiral Sir Hovenden Walker, consisting of fifteen ships of war and some forty transports, carried seven regiments of the line, five of whom were among the best of Marlborough's troops; in all there were 5,000 men, including artillery and marines. Osgood, *Eighteenth Century*, i. 441.

more than a fortnight. Fears were aroused that Massachusetts was fully expected to reject this impossible programme, thus excusing England from pursuing an expedition she did not really favour.[1]

On the English side evidence of suspicion of New Englanders is overt, having survived in personal accounts of the military commanders and their aides. The comment is highly subjective and has little justification in fact. Its tone was encouraged by the receptive climate prevailing in English society and government, in which there was already a background of distrust of New England motivation and values. It gained support from certain independent but important quarters. On more than one occasion, and once in the presence of a delegation from New France, Samuel Vetch spitefully reviled the New England people as liars.[2] They were already in ill-repute among the English as haters of monarchy, illegal traders, and narrow-minded bigots who believed in witches. Accordingly, military leaders of mediocre quality but of developed self-esteem could be assured that their petulant complaints and suspicions would be sympathetically considered, and their arrogance uncritically regarded, by the Tories in old England.[3] The virtuous acts of New Englanders went unnoticed because the commentators perceived only what, by conviction, they believed to be present: a self-regarding religious faith which encouraged and under-wrote narrow materialistic objectives. Such a view rested

[1] Thomas Hutchinson was persuaded that these fears were groundless. But it is indicative of the deterioration in the Anglo-Massachusetts relationship that they should have arisen at all. They were of course to be anticipated as a consequence of British failure in the recent past to show adequate consideration for colonial interests. Sewall, who gives less attention to the Canada expedition than to the enterprises of the two preceding years, makes no mention of such sentiment.

[2] The threat of Vetch to support these accusations in print caused serious concern to members of the Massachusetts Council. See 1 Feb. 1711, Sewall, Diary, ii. 298–9.

[3] Among the leading figures was Admiral Sir Hovenden Walker, himself a Tory selected by St. John, and of whom it has fairly been said that nothing in his previous career would seem to justify his appointment to command the naval forces of such an important expedition; he was not regarded as a very expert seaman. Brigadier-General Jack Hill was the commander-in-chief. Hill, brother of Abigail Hill, now Lady Masham, who with the support of Harley had achieved an ascendancy over the queen in supersession to the Duchess of Marlborough, gained his appointment for political reasons. His military record was wholly undistinguished. The quartermaster-general was Colonel King. All three men produced private journals which have survived.

upon a fundamental premiss derived from the experiences of the seventeenth century, that New Englanders were inferior to Englishmen who had remained at home.

But whatever their faults New Englanders were demonstrably something more than mere provincials. Equally undeniable is the vigour with which not only the Tory governor but also the Assembly responded to the problems posed in supporting and equipping the large army which arrived at Boston. Hutchinson contends that this was a consequence, in part, of the resolve to counter unreasonable demands and insincere intentions by creating a momentum from which it would be impossible for the English ministry and its military leaders to withdraw. Bills of credit to the amount of £40,000 were issued by the General Court, and loans made available for two years to merchants and others associated with the enterprise. The price of provisions was fixed and when some stores were closed or goods concealed, on the grounds that this practice was an offence against normal commercial procedure, the administration issued orders to impress whatever was needed.[1]

Individual malpractice such as this was taken by some of the military as a basis for generalization about the population as a whole. Occasional concealment of deserters was regarded as confirmation of malice directed against England. The constructive efforts of the provincial administration were discounted or ignored, as were the exemplary actions of some principal members of the public who resolved to eat only salt provisions while the fleet lay at anchor. It is true the government failed to undertake the impressment of men to replace deserters, but Massachusetts legislation against assisting them became a model for all other colonies.[2] In short the people, though lacking wild enthusiasm for

---

[1] Hutchinson, *History of Massachusetts*, ii. 142–3. There were difficulties over the rate of exchange though Waller observes that criticism of New Englanders was extended to 'North American merchants' as a whole when it was discovered that the English suffered even greater disadvantage in New York than in Massachusetts: *Samuel Vetch*, p. 212. See also Graham, 'Walker Expedition', pp. 82, 109, 112, 319, and 341; *C.S.P.C.*, 1711–2, no. 46, enclosure i; Sewall, *Diary* ii. 313, 317. Provincial officers and royal officers were conjointly empowered to search for provisions and liquors and to force entry, if necessary. Parkman, *Half Century of Conflict*, i. 161.

[2] Nicholson personally put up a reward of £100 sterling for the recovery of deserters and offered £5 to encourage the town marshal to impress seamen as replacement for those who absconded. Waller, *Samuel Vetch*, p. 214.

the enterprise, generally submitted to their property being taken from them, while the administration showed a readiness to override individual rights, upholding its policy by severe punishment and summary judicial procedure.[1] Moreover it underwrote these supporting measures by exceeding the quota of men to which it was committed. Nine hundred effectives, including 100 Indians, had been voted by the General Court in May.[2] Further than this no community could be normally expected to proceed and only the purblind could have misconstrued its intentions.

Admiral Walker showed a better appreciation of the positive qualities of his Indian allies than he did of his New England associates, confessing himself impressed by the thought and understanding, the sincerity and grave bearing, of those leaders invited to review the British fleet. The colonials received scarcely the equal of this in respect and attention comparable to their numbers and contribution, but such courtesies as were paid were not unfruitful. Both Walker and Hill attended the annual commencement celebrations at Cambridge on 4 July 'to put the people in a humour to comply with the necessary demands of our troops', wrote the general. In spite of the false reports of smallpox in the camp sufficient quantities of all sorts of provisions were brought in after this event.[3] Moreover the discipline of the troops and their

---

[1] Parkman made a clear distinction between the fervent action of the Assembly, which he described as 'worthy of a military dictatorship', and the coolness of the populace as a whole. Ibid., i. 161.

[2] Cf. New York, which in meeting its quota had included 150 Long Island Indians and 100 Palatines, leaving only 350 to be taken from the permanent white population. A further 100 Palatines were eventually added and £10,000 appropriated for the support of the force. Like Massachusetts, Connecticut exceeded its quota—by 60 men—but New Jersey was short of it, and Pennsylvania in August sent £2,000 but no men whatsoever. Ibid. i. 161; Osgood, *Eighteenth Century*, i. 443; *New York Col. Docs.* v. 253; *Pennsylvania Col. Records*, ii. 534–8.

[3] Colonel Richard King, the quartermaster-general, was in some respects more outspoken in his criticism of the colonists than either Walker or Hill. When the Massachusetts troops embarked on 24 July the transports were not ready to receive them. On considering in crude terms the ample resources which Massachusetts had at its disposal, he adjudged failure to provide beds and other necessaries, including sailors to man the ships, as evidence that the colonists designed to keep the expedition at Boston until the approach of cold weather should force its abandonment. He accused the New Englanders of indolence and indifference. See Graham, 'Walker Expedition', p. 325.

dazzling splendour, seen by the colonists in the review of 10 July, stirred the emotions of the dour New Englanders and revealed to them some of the more colourful features of metropolitan ceremonial.

Serious difficulties were encountered in providing pilots sufficiently skilled to navigate the St. Lawrence. Shipmasters who had some familiarity with the river were diffident or unwilling to serve on men-of-war, a factor which undermined Walker's belief in the wisdom of the enterprise. In face of public reluctance the government resorted to impressment at Marblehead and other ports. Vetch, who had been appointed commander of the colonial contingent, persuaded Captain John Bonner to accompany him. Cyprian Southack, himself a skilfull and experienced mariner, respected Bonner as the best pilot in New England. But Bonner doubted his own competence to take charge of the flagship or any large vessel, having navigated the St. Lawrence only once and that in a sloop. Walker on the other hand relied more on Captain Paradis, a French prisoner of war, though Vetch shook his confidence in this man before the fleet came to the Canada River.[1] The gloomy admiral, already unsure that he was adequately equipped to face the navigational hazards of the St. Lawrence, had led his fleet from Boston harbour on 30 July, finally provisioned a few days earlier by ships from New York. That same day Nicholson left for New York to command the land expedition which Hunter, the newly commissioned governor there, had organized.

The sea voyage was uneventful until 21 August, the day after the fleet left Gaspé, when the weather turned foggy and the wind began to freshen from the east-south-east. At this time Walker was in the broad mouth of the St. Lawrence but out of sight of land and out of soundings. By 22 August, in a navigational sense, he was lost. His pilots advised that his position was near the northerly shore but several hours later, after a warning from Captain Paddon of the flagship *Edgar* that they were approaching land to the south, he turned back on a northerly course. Within a short while, late in the evening, eight transports and a provision ship foundered on the

---

[1] Graham, 'Walker Expedition', pp. 28, 110, 132, 133, and 143. After ten days at sea Vetch came gloomily to the conclusion that he himself was the best pilot the fleet produced. He confessed to faith in no other. Waller, *Samuel Vetch*, p. 222.

rocks of the north shore. Only Walker's presence of mind and seamanship prevented the flagship from sharing their fate. No colonials were lost but between 800 and 900 British regulars perished, and many sailors were drowned.[1]

Two days were spent saving men and salvaging stores and then on 25 August Admiral Walker called a council of war. Both he and General Hill had lost heart. Neither wished to continue with the attempt on Quebec. They found support from all the naval captains who declared that the ignorance of the pilots made it impracticable to go up the St. Lawrence any further. None of the six pilots called in was able to contradict this view and Vetch, though he offered to guide the fleet for the remainder of the way to Quebec to the best of his ability, was less forceful than he might have been in opposing the counsel of retreat. Later, having pondered the consequences of such action for Britain and the colonies, he wrote to Walker in the strongest possible language urging him to reconsider his decision to retire. He requested a further consultation with the captains to no avail. The fleet retraced its course to the Gulf of Gaspé and then steered for Spanish River in the island of Cape Breton. Here a second council of war was called where it was deliberated whether to make Placentia an alternative objective for the force. The conclusion reached was that autumnal storms and the problem of supply made such an attempt too serious a risk. In the meantime the frigate *Sapphire* had been sent to Boston to warn Nicholson's land force of how the expedition had been obliged to turn back. The fleet and the transports now divided, the former returning to England and the latter to Boston.[2]

One of the immediate consequences of the collapse of the Walker expedition was a worsening of the image Englishmen held of the New Englander. How this came about is readily understandable. The naval principals in this expedition, having failed to employ their immense resources for the reduction of Quebec, could otherwise expect possible court martial or, at least, popular censure. Under these circumstances diversion of criticism to elements of the English nation traditionally suspect was the simplest and most

[1] Waller, *Samuel Vetch*, pp. 224–5.
[2] Graham, 'Walker Expedition', pp. 36–8; Parkman, *Half Century of Conflict*, pp. 169–70.

predictable line of action for them to take.[1] Thus a notion of the
true causes of failure was created, a conspiracy in which New
Englanders were assigned a central and diabolical role. That their
assumed motivation and behaviour were opposed to reason and
demonstrable interest would not appear to have inhibited a general
credence in this account, in quarters already convinced that the
'Saints' were a people perverse, by nature and, in their basic
intent, malicious to the mother country. It was implied that New
England had made repeated applications for help, which had been
answered despite serious pressures in Flanders, Spain, and Portugal, but that once England's resources had been committed then
New Englanders did everything in their power to defeat the success
of the venture.

In particular support of this view, it was asserted that as soon
as the fleet arrived the people debauched men from the service
and concealed them in their houses. But the direct interest involved was represented as that of the Boston merchants who, it was
alleged, carried on a clandestine trade with the French and were
resolved not to have their commerce broken up. To serve these
ends the supply of adequate provisions was delayed until the date
was past for a successful venture against Quebec, and so ill-
assured that, when in the Canada River, the expedition was prevented from proceeding to its objective for fear of starvation.
Destruction of the force, however, was virtually assured by providing ignorant and unskilled pilots.

Jeremiah Dummer, the colonial agent of Massachusetts in
England, published a refutation of these wild and unfounded
charges based upon a careful examination of provincial history.[2]
He opened his apologia with the observation that men will lie but
that interest will not, and continued with instruction in the

---

[1] 'All the blame of the Canada miscarriage is laid on your backs', Sir William
Ashurst to Revd. Increase Mather, 31 Jan. 1711/12, London, J. W. Ford
(ed.), *Correspondence between the Governors and Treasurers of the New England
Company in London and the Commissioners of the United Colonies in America . . .
1657–1712* (London, 1896), p. 95.
[2] *A Letter to a Noble Lord Concerning the Late Expedition to Canada* (Boston,
Mass., 1712). It is noteworthy that in 1720 Sir Hovendon Walker in his published *Journal* reiterated the story of La Ronde Denys implying that New
Englanders were influenced by the negotiation 'against the duty of allegiance
and the apparent interest of the province'. J. Dummer, 8 Apr., London, *Mass.
Hist. Soc. Coll.*, 3rd ser. i. 143.

character of that interest. Apart from demonstrating that the preparations for the expedition were scrupulously undertaken and that the objectives were of outstanding importance for both Crown and nation, his most difficult task was to counter the accusation, revived with even greater force in the Seven Years War, that Boston merchants traded with the enemy. This was given substance by the trial and conviction several years earlier of six of the port's merchants similarly charged. Not only was the governor indirectly involved in this scandal but one of the principals was Samuel Vetch himself. Dummer, in a rather weak defence, reduced their number to three, neither of whom were of English extraction or natives of the place. The New England element was ignored. The strongest part of his case rested upon the sustained integrity of the Assembly and its forthright methods of dealing with disloyal traders. Would its representatives, he argued, forfeit their reputation with the queen and betray their native land in order to gratify a few smugglers? Boston merchants in general he defended as having more honour, conscience, and love of country, than to engage generally in so criminal a commerce.

It is difficult to assess how effective were these words. Cotton Mather, who praised the elegance and sufficiency of Dummer's vindication, thought that even before Colonel Nicholson arrived with considerable supporting material, much of the clamour against New England had died down.[1] Walker's reputation for poor seamanship was not helpful to his case nor were the inconsistencies in the matter of pilots and provisions.[2] The decision to turn back, not a New England one, could in logic be seen to rest on an assessment of the importance of the lost transports. The capacity of the pilots and the questioned adequacy of the provisioning arrangements were unchanged by the disaster at Isle aux Oeufs. These things facilitated the influence of Dummer and Nicholson but alone could not suffice to destroy an unreasoning

---

[1] Mather, *Diary, 1709–1724, Mass. Hist. Soc. Coll.*, 7th ser. (Boston, Mass., 1912), ii. 173. Col. Nicholson, probably because of his unquestionable Toryism, escaped blame and was thus enabled to give Dummer very effective backing. See Sir William Ashurst to Governor of the Company, Governor Nicholson, 15 Jan. 1711/12, Ford, *Correspondence*, p. 94.

[2] In 1708 six English men-of-war had a running fight with the French on the Flemish coast. Walker's conduct on this occasion was much criticized. He was desired to cruise off Dunkirk but pretended he wanted pilots to carry him to the Dutch coast. W. Thomas to [Edward Harley] 27 Mar. 1708, *Portland*, iv. 482.

sentiment predisposed to regard the colonists as barbarous in their culture, machiavellian in their politics and disloyal in their objectives. The legend of colonial ingratitude for English sacrifice had been given a new and dramatic foundation. In fact there had been sacrifice for a common end on both sides of the Atlantic but since 1709 that of New England had been proportionately greater.

The task of rehabilitating the New England image might have been eased had Massachusetts been able to contribute to a renewal of the Canada expedition the following year. But to promise a major enterprise for the fourth year running, after so much treasure had been expended for a negative return, was beyond the politics of Joseph Dudley. The Bay province and New Hampshire alike were financially exhausted not through the expedition alone but also from the continuing strain of defending an extensive northern frontier. Resources were significantly running down as Massachusetts manpower quitted the province to avoid the burdens of taxation and the risks of military service, or signed on at sea never to return. With sickened hearts and some dissentient voices the General Court urged England to try once more to destroy the seat of French power in North America but pleaded an inability to provide a New England quota of men, at least one equal to 1711 when a fifth of all arms-bearing males had been directly in Her Majesty's service.[1] In the forefront of men's calculations throughout the northern colonies was the retribution which might be anticipated from French and Indian released from defending Quebec and the St. Lawrence valley.

As a counter-move to French power a conference of New England governors, attended by Nicholson and Vetch, met to consider united effort. The outcome was disappointing but fortunately the capacity of the enemy had been exaggerated.[2] Although in France at least one voice had called for the complete destruction of Boston and Rhode Island, in fact the resources of New France alone were too limited to attempt very much and the Eastern

[1] T. Lechmere to Wait Winthrop, 18 Sept. 1711, Dudley to John Winthrop, 27 Sept., *Mass. Hist. Soc. Coll.*, 6th ser., v. 246, 247; Address of the Governor, Council and Assembly of Massachusetts Bay to the Queen, 17 Oct. 1711, *C.S.P.C.*, 1711–12, nos. 123; Address of the Gov. and Council of New Hampshire to the Crown, 30 Oct. 1711, *C.S.P.C.*, 1711–12, no. 147. The New Hampshire address claimed that one-third of all the young men 'go abroad' yearly. Sewall felt himself unable to support the address from Massachusetts.

[2] Waller, *Samuel Vetch*, 234.

Indians had almost shot their bolt.[1] Yet no frontiersman felt secure. Jonathan Bridger, H.M. Surveyor of Woods, operating in the Piscataqua region and protected by at least six horsemen still feared for his life. In Massachusetts as in New Hampshire the threat of major assault as well as of scattered slayings persisted. The endangered frontier was surveyed in the autumn by Lieutenant-Governor Tailer of Massachusetts and Colonel Redknap. During the winter months of 1711–12 two parties of fifty men apiece ranged from their hideouts in the woods, while a larger seaborne force, conveyed in sloops gave support along the coast. Saint-Castin's settlement near Penobscot bore the brunt of the assault, which destroyed six or eight houses, two sloops and a considerable quantity of provisions. This ruined the enemy's plans for a small expedition. Although the New Englanders had slain very few Indians and Dudley's policies had seemed costly and unfruitful, in fact co-operation with a harsh environment to wear their numbers down had been more successful than was realized. Since the beginning of the war cold, hunger, and sickness had reduced those west of the Penobscot from 450 to 200.[2]

In the spring and summer of 1712 there was the last alarming flurry of isolated slayings on the eastern frontier at Exeter, Spruce Creek, and Dover. Wells suffered worst with four slain in two attacks. But though there were many parties of the enemy at large their number were few and a strengthening of the frontier guard under Captain Davis effectively secured the province against any further damage. The following summer, on 11 July 1713, three

---

[1] The voice was probably that of La Ronde Denys after the failure of his mission in 1711 to secure New England's neutrality. See Parkman, *Half Century of Conflict*, pp. 155–6. A later fear was that the French and Indians were forming for a descent against Annapolis, but Hutchinson believed that the Walker expedition had, if nothing else, already saved Annapolis from falling into the hands of the French, by inducing a concentration of strength for the defence of Quebec. Thomas Lechmere to Wait Winthrop, 5 Nov. 1711, *Mass. Hist. Soc. Coll.* 6th ser. v. 250–1; 17 Sept. 1711, Sewall, *Diary* ii. 322; Hutchinson, *History of Massachusetts*, ii. 148. Boston did not entirely escape unharmed. The shock to New England, when news was received of the failure of the Walker expedition, was deepened when on 2 Oct. much of the centre of the town was devastated by fire. What the French failed to do was accomplished by the carelessness of a poor Scottish woman, Mary Morse. Increase Mather in a subsequent sermon attributed the destruction to sabbath-breaking by Boston tradesmen. Sewall, *Diary*, ii. 323; Thomas Lechmere to Wait Winthrop, 8 Oct. 1710, *Mass. Hist. Soc. Coll.* v. 249.

[2] *C.S.P.C..* 1711–12. nos. 147, 229, 292, 375; Penhallow, *Wars of New England*, pp. 58, 60, and 71–3.

delegates from the St. John's Indians and three delegates from the Kennebec, including the other settlements from Pennacook, met with the English at Portsmouth, New Hampshire, to acknowledge that as subjects of Great Britain they had been in open rebellion against the queen. They confessed to having broken articles agreed to with Sir William Phips and the Earl of Bellomont, and reiterated their allegiance to the throne of England.[1] This, however, was consequent to the settlement of affairs in Europe.

Peace negotiations in Europe had followed a prolonged and tortuous course. French overtures concerning the Spanish inheritance of Charles II, first to the United Provinces, then to England, followed the shattering defeat of Ramillies in 1706. But the allies had not as yet concerted the preliminaries of their demands, save to agree upon the entire renunciation by the Duke of Anjou (Philip V); and France did not attempt to renew her offer in the following year. But until 1709 when the preliminaries of the peace began in earnest the impression was kept alive by Petkum, a well-meaning go-between, the Duke of Holstein's envoy at The Hague, that France was willing to negotiate.[2] In May of that year the Duke of Marlborough and young Lord Townshend met the principal French plenipotentiary, the Marquis de Torcy, at the Dutch capital. Britain, the States General, and the Austrian emperor presented an ultimatum of forty articles which included acknowledgement of Queen Anne's title and the Protestant Succession, the cession of Newfoundland, and additionally the exclusion of French trade from the Spanish Indies. France was to bind herself to secure the surrender of the Spanish monarchy to the Allies' candidate Charles III within two months after 1 June 17 In the event of a refusal on the part of Philip V to abdicate, French troops were to assist the allies in enforcing the evacuation of Spain.

The harshness of the demands took the French court by surprise but negotiations continued until 1710 before breaking down over the difficult question of the evacuation of Spain. Meanwhile in England the power of the Whigs was crumbling. Sunderland's fall was followed by the dismissal of Lord Treasurer Godolphin on 7 August. Harley became Chancellor of the Exchequer and the Treasury was put into commission. After the dissolution of the

---

[1] Ibid., pp. 74, 77, and 78.
[2] Leadam, *History of England*, ix. 147.

House of Commons a Tory Parliament met in November, and by
the end of the year scarcely a Whig was left in any office of importance. The disasters with which the Spanish campaign of
this year had ended convinced the ministry that possession of
Spain by the Austrian claimant could no longer be insisted upon as
a condition of peace, a concession communicated to France at the
very end of the year.[1] Moreover, Harley had long been opposed to
a war which in his view destroyed trade and exhausted the strength
of the kingdom. Under these circumstances France was encouraged
to re-open formal negotiations and Matthew Prior, in July, took
new terms to Paris.

British proposals now included retention of the captured
Gibraltar and Port Mahon in Minorca, and the *Asiento*, or contract
to provide negro slaves for the Spanish colonies in America, to be
transferred from France to England. The trade of Hudson's Bay
and the position in America were to remain *in statu quo*. The
demand for the surrender of Newfoundland remained unaltered.
Marlborough advised the queen against the preliminaries and the
Whigs, by promising to pass an occasional conformity bill, gained
to their side the support of Daniel Finch, the Tory Earl of Nottingham. In an amendment to the queen's address to Parliament
the Opposition motioned that there could be no safe and honourable peace if Spain and the West Indies were allowed to any branch
of the house of Bourbon. Successful in the Lords, the censure
motion was defeated in the Commons and Harley and St. John
moved cautiously to avenge themselves upon Marlborough, the
author of their discomfiture. At the end of December 1711, he was
dismissed from all his offices, an act coinciding with the creation
of twelve new Tory peers to ensure the ministry a confident position in the House of Lords. At the opening of the next parliamentary session in January Anne was enabled to announce the arrival
of the plenipotentiaries for peace at Utrecht: the conference was
formally opened on 18 January.

In the settlement Louis XIV acknowledged the right and title
of the queen and pledged himself to accept the succession of the
house of Hanover, to exclude the Pretender from France and to
abstain from giving him any assistance. He further accepted the
renunciation by Philip V of his claims to the succession of France.

---

[1] Leadam, *History of England*, ix. 186.

Most of the demands relating to the American continent were gained without significant modification. Possession of Acadia, conquered by the New Englanders, proved a valuable bargaining counter in English hands.[1] Louis had been deeply concerned to regain it, and for its return had offered St. Christophers and the islands of St. Martin and St. Bartholomew. When this exchange was refused he raised his bid promising to give up the fortification of Placentia untouched, to leave undisturbed the cannon in the forts of Hudson Bay, and to debar Frenchmen from the Newfoundland fisheries. This latter was a marked concession since Torcy in 1711 had resisted the claim to the whole of Newfoundland as 'the nursery of our seamen'. Louis, however, looked to Acadia as a substitute, and for this reason refused to consider that its bounds included the island of Cape Breton. Only in the final extremity, that is if rupture threatened the negotiations, was he prepared to cede both Acadia and Cape Breton since by this double cession he believed Canada would be rendered useless, the fisheries destroyed for France, and the French marine rendered useless.[2]

The Board of Trade, consulted by St. John in April 1712, and influenced by Nicholson, advised against conceding Cape Breton island to the French and urged that a careful description of the boundaries should be included in any peace treaty. When Louis realized that Nova Scotia would not be re-ceded he strengthened his demands for Newfoundland and fishery rights. In fact, save for the cession of Cape Breton, no definition of Canadian or Nova Scotian boundaries had taken place and the British by their negligence had not only paved the way for a resurgence of French strength in the fortification of Louisburg but also risked the territorial separation of Maine and Nova Scotia through French claims to the region south of the Cape of Gaspé.[3]

Reaction to the peace was generally one of unqualified relief even among those colonies which had suffered relatively little. The Maryland government claimed that most of its inhabitants were miserably impoverished and many quite ruined. Virginians, who had suffered heavy losses in the tobacco trade, thought that nothing

---

[1] H.M.C., *Portland MSS.*, v (*Harley Papers*, iii), 34–41, cited in Waller, *Samuel Vetch*, 243.
[2] Parkman, *Half Century of Conflict*, pp. 178–9; *C.S.P.C.*, 1711–12, nos. 365, 374, and 385.
[3] Waller, *Samuel Vetch*, 243, 254.

but peace could give hope to repair what had been suffered during so long and burdensome a war. Only Jamaica, disappointed in its hopes of regaining the *Asiento* trade, criticized the provisions of Utrecht and refused to send a congratulatory address, but Governor Hunter for New York sounded a warning note about increased French activity upon the Mississippi which was alarming New Yorkers.[1]

New Englanders who had feared to lose the whole of Acadia were not displeased. Dudley expressed the delight of all British subjects in North America at the securing of Newfoundland, Nova Scotia, and the Bay of Fundy. Connecticut too gave formal notice of its pleasure. Samuel Sewall, as a private individual, was less effusive. He was irritated that no mention of the achievements of Massachusetts in the Indian wars had been made in the address to the queen of 16 July. Earlier, upon the General Court passing an Order for Thanksgiving, when the Secretary 'writ "Peace" and the Governor added "Happy" ', he had objected because it was not then clear how much territory France had been able to retain.[2] Mather was less critical; he was thankful for the final accommodating spirit shown by France and, in approving the gains in North America, he wryly observed: 'As we have nothing left now to fight *for*; so we have as little to fight *with*.'[3]

The financial position of Massachusetts indeed remained parlous: at the end of the wars as at their start in 1689. In the *Duodecennium* Mather expressed the exhaustion and near despair which characterized the sentiments of the province; the loss of relatives, the many deaths, the fire which a few years earlier had so desolated Boston. But over all hung the fiscal problem.[4] Official Massachusetts acknowledged this. Earlier, statements of the effects of the war on the colonial economies had been forwarded to London by the governor to encourage support for the Canada expedition but in 1712 the General Court more precisely informed the queen how heavily the province was immersed in debt.[5]

---

[1] *C.S.P.C.*, 1712–14, nos. 145, enclosure ii; 453, enclosure i; 295.

[2] Sewall, *Diary*, i. 365; ii. 33, n. 1.

[3] To Samuel Penhallow, 17 Apr. 1712, Mather, *Diary*, ii. 171.

[4] *Mass. Hist. Soc. Coll.*, 1st ser. v. 52; Mather, *Duodecennium*, pp. 7, 14, 16; Waller, *Samuel Vetch*, p. 272, n. 20.

[5] *C.S.P.C.*, 1708–9, no. 60, pp. 47–9; Address of Governor, Council, and Assembly, 14 June 1712, ibid., 1712–14, no. 448.

How able was it to bear this burden? Poll tax and estate assessment figures provide some indication.[1] As is to be expected the various regions of Massachusetts reveal a contrasting pattern of decline and growth. Even within the various regions important distinctions are to be drawn. In south-eastern Massachusetts, to begin with, the increased assessment of a number of townships suggests a sudden accession of wealth, for the seaports the possible consequence of captures at sea. For sheltered inland locations it may indicate the arrival of adult males bringing with them substantial goods. In Barnstaple county the assessment of Harwich, which rose an unremarkable 5% in 1706, increased by a further 15% in 1708. Rochester rose more spectacularly: 10% in 1708 and a further 12% in 1712. Sandwich, Yarmouth, and Barnstaple town all showed a modest increase of 5%-6% in 1708, whilst inland in Plymouth County Marshfield experienced a slight rise in 1707–10, and Middleburgh 7% in 1706, and a further 11% in 1710. In parts of Bristol County there was similar growth. Tiverton and Swansea both sustained slight increases, the former 5% in 1708 which was held until the end of the war. Taunton similarly rose by about 3·5% in 1712 but the increase was not maintained. Freetown's assessment was augmented significantly in 1708: by 16%. Dartmouth experienced some remarkable irregularities during the War of the Spanish Succession; a fall of 20% in 1707 was offset the following year by a rise of 30%, but partially reversed the following months by a drop of 17%. Bristol and Little Compton showed little change. But in this more protected part of the south-east only Rehoboth and Taunton suffered a diminution of assessment, by 13% and 11% respectively in 1712. Elsewhere in the region variations were often much more marked.

Nantucket, for which taxation had risen between 1707 and 1710, showed a slight fall in 1712, and Scituate, hitherto constant, a minimal fall in that year. Plymouth, which experienced a spectacular decline in 1695, followed by a rapid recovery, had its long period of stability brought to an end in 1708 when its assessment fell by one-third. For most towns, however, the years 1708–12 were the critical ones. Bridgewater was adjusted downwards 6%

[1] See Goodell, *Acts and Resolves*, i. 106–7, 165–9, 177–80, 185–8, 197–9, 228–30, 239–45, 257–63, 277–81, 301–5, 337–42, 358–64, 389–91, 413–16, 438–86, 494–7, 520–4, 533–4, 548–50, 566–9, 589–93, 607–11, 624–8, 658–62, 691–4, and 711–15.

in 1712. But Eastham, in Barnstaple, fell 24% in 1710, Duxbury 36% in 1713, and Edgarstown and Tisbury, which both fell 14% in 1708, were reduced a further 50% in 1710. Chilmark's assessment was also reduced 50% in 1710. Clearly those townships which suffered the most serious loss of wealth, whether human or material, were those on the exposed southern and eastern coast of Cape Cod, Edgarstown, and to a lesser degree Nantucket.

Further north Suffolk, though with a seaboard—mainly Boston Bay, was probably the best-protected county. Middlesex was to the north of her, Hampshire to the west, Plymouth and Bristol to the south-east, and Rhode Island to the south. Throughout the War of the Spanish Succession five Suffolk communities carried unvarying tax assessments: Roxbury, Dorchester, Weymouth, Wrentham, and Medfield. For a sixth, Hull, the variation was extremely small. Five other communities by the end of the war were more highly assessed than they had been in 1704: Braintree, Hingham, Dedham, Mendon, and Oxford. Mendon, after a temporary abatement in 1710, held a rate in 1712 and 1713 a third higher than it had been in 1707. Oxford similarly rose after 1707. Dedham after some fluctuations between 1705 and 1709 was subsequently rated 11% higher than it had been in 1704. Other increases were smaller: Hingham 4%, Braintree less than 3%. But in all no less than seven communities had increased assessment in 1708.

Apart from Boston, Milton was the only Suffolk community which suffered adverse fluctuation. Having risen in 1708 4·5% above the figure for the previous year, it thereafter in 1710 fell 7% to a figure a little below that imposed for the earlier years of the war. But the difference is negligible. Assessment for Boston, the provincial capital, fell in 1706 but rose to its wartime peak in 1708. Thereafter it declined until in 1712 and 1713 it was almost £300 or 7% lower than it had been soon after the opening of the War of the Spanish Succession. Bearing in mind the city's population-growth between 1700 and 1710, there was conceivably a decline in real wealth particularly after 1708. But it is not possible to generalize very freely from the above analysis. What seems most likely is that the areas of Suffolk which were relatively well protected, absorbed migrants from areas more exposed, within and outside the county, causing the poll tax to rise. In Boston, before 1710, such increase in population was offset by a loss of property, presumably a consequence of the activity of French privateers.

In Essex, the most north-easterly county, some eight townships, of which three—Salem, Beverley, and Lynn—were ports, show stable assessment figures.[1] These ports were on the south-east coast, on the edge of Boston Bay. Generally speaking south of a line from Newbury to Andover the county was either prosperous or not suffering markedly from the effects of war. Bradford's taxes increased over 14% in 1707 and sustained this rise through to 1713. Wenham rose nearly 8% in 1708 and Gloucester 4·7%, and both towns held to this new figure until the end of the war. Six and one-quarter per cent was added to the figure for Marblehead in 1712. But in the northern part of the county Amesbury's assessment was lowered in 1705 from £120 to £110, and Haverhill's from £200 to £160 (20%) in 1707, which though restored in 1708 was held for only one year before returning to the 1707 figure. Salisbury's rate was reduced by 5% in 1705 and a further 2·5% in 1707.

In Middlesex County most of the communities either retained throughout the war the levy imposed at its beginning or had it raised. In a number of instances the year when the latter occurred was 1708. As far north as Billerica property was secure and the risk to life regarded as tolerable. The northernmost towns, predictably, were most affected by hostilities. Dunstable, close to the New Hampshire border, had its assessment lowered to one-third of the 1706 rate and even after 1710, by which time some partial recovery from Indian attack had taken place, continued for the remainder of the war to pay less than half the assessment of a decade earlier. Sherborn's assessment decreased after 1708 by almost one-fifth and that for Groton, in the north-west of the county, a few miles south of the New Hampshire border, was diminished by one-third in 1705 and fell a further fifth of the new figure in 1708. For the remaining years of conflict Groton bore a levy almost half that of 1703. Dracut had its taxes cut drastically in 1708 but recovered before the war closed. But the community worst hit was Lancaster (now in Worcester County), fifteen miles west of Concord. In June 1703 the General Court resolved that

---

[1] The other communities were Rowley, Newbury, Boxford, Topsfield, and Manchester.

the inhabitants had been driven out by the enemy and the place wholly deserted: the agreement with the minister was declared null and void. But though taxes for the following year were cut and in 1705 reduced again, this time by almost half, no moratorium was allowed as was granted to places severely hit in the counties of York and Hampshire.

In exposed Hampshire, the westernmost county, the rates for several communities went unrevised throughout the War of the Spanish Succession. Springfield, Northampton, Hadley, and Hatfield seem to have maintained a surprising stability in respect of property and numbers. But the assessment for Westfield was reduced 11% in 1705 and a further 20% in 1708 and at the end of the war had not recovered. By 1708 Suffield and Enfield had both fallen 22%. Deerfield, after the disastrous attack of 1704, was freed from all levies until 1712 when its assessment was restored to the 1703 figure. But in York county the impact of war is even more dramatically shown by the assessment figures. In 1708, at a time of reviving commercial activity, none of the three townships was paying a penny of rates to the provincial treasury. That for York had been reduced from £40 in 1703 to half this sum in the following year: thereafter all payment was excused until 1710. For the remainder of the war the rate was fixed at £20. Wells had its taxes reduced by one third in 1704 and subsequently ceased payment, save for a levy of £5 in 1710. Kittery's assessment rose from £80 to £100 in 1704 but then fell to half in the following year, and when it was restored in 1710 after the moratorium the figure was only £40.

How clearly did the people of Massachusetts distinguish between protected and exposed localities? The state provided its own definition of where the frontier was and accordingly identified townships to which special legislation applied, as has been observed. However, harsh as were the penalties for contravening the law, the majority of individuals did not stay put unless they adjudged their lives and their living reasonably secure. There is also some evidence of the difficulty in obtaining schoolmasters or ministers within these areas and perhaps at some distance outside them, as has been seen. In this respect society, or individual members of it, expressed an independent notion of where the frontier was. But the attitudes are more widely demonstrated by the demographic stability which may be assumed for townships within a defined boundary. This is not to rule out altogether loss from migration from specific towns inside this area. Clearly this took place to a sufficient degree in some places to offset natural growth. But it is probable that there was no sizeable net loss to the area as a whole. Moreover since so many towns bore an unchanging assessment, or were obliged to pay an increased rate, the loss for individual communities could not have been very great, save where in exceptional circumstances it may have been obscured by sizeable acquisitions of rateable property.

It may be observed that the boundary within which property and life was tolerably secure, or believed to be so, ran southwards from Newbury, passing thence westwards between Dracut and Dunstable in the north and Billerica and Chelmsford in the south. It continued south-westwards to divide Deerfield and Hatfield, then swung southwards close to the west bank of the Connecticut River to include the major valley towns but to exclude Westfield and Suffield. On the seacoast, however, it may be located less decisively. In 1706, alluding to Indian depredations, Governor Dudley commented that 'Boston and the seaports knew little of these troubles.' But the seaboard of Maine was dangerous because of the French and Indian attack, and the southern shore of Cape Cod, Dukes County, and Nantucket were particularly vulnerable to privateers. As a 'frontier to the sea' every port risked attack. Moreover sea-going property in the form of ships and commodities moved wherever profits were attractive. Thus community fortunes varied according to complex circumstances. Those of Salem, for example, were contrasted in two wars and an important part of Boston's wealth in particular was exposed to factors of insecurity external to New England. Yet there is some distinction, although not always a very clear one, between personal property exposed to risk and commercial ventures in which risk is calculated. For the ports of Massachusetts Bay community wealth was not seriously impaired by individual losses during the early years of the war.[1] But by 1708 and for some time thereafter the situation was critical if not grave. This period apart, a protective boundary enclosed the ports of central Massachusetts and on this coast, as in its hinterland, anxieties were less immediate and less intense. Soon after the termination of hostilities Cotton Mather would write of Boston with pride: 'We see the Metropolis of it [New England], and of the

[1] Above, ch. vi, pp. 222–30.

whole of English America, increase and flourish.'[1] Despite the
burden of taxes the damages of war to this substantial inner core
of towns, and their capital, was not irreparable.

How did the British view the economic situation of Massachusetts? Robert Quary's gloomy report on the diminution of Boston's
trade, the propaganda of Vetch and Dudley, and the development
of naval stores in the region, had made it possible for the Customs
Commissioners, the Board of Trade, and the queen's ministers to
piece together a picture of sufficient accuracy to justify support for
the Canada venture.[2] The generalized assessment of New England's value remained in essence economic: there was no significant
sentimental element. Money expended on this abortive enterprise,
the cost of the naval support was estimated at £121,600, was added
to other costs incurred directly on her behalf. The charge for
providing guard-ships for the whole New England region, for
example, during the four years 1708–11 was figured as £132,220.
This was £20,000 less than for Virginia but significantly below the
cost of a single year for Jamaica.[3]

On the debit side, in the mother country's reckoning, was also
to be found the amount of illegal trade which persisted when the
war ended. If Quary in 1708 had found fewer illegalities in Boston,
the record of Newport and the coast of Connecticut remained black.
Scandals such as that of John Stackmaple, collector of Connecticut,
and a 'Pillar of their Church', who encouraged illegal trade for his
own profit, besmirched the whole region in English eyes.[4] By 1714
Massachusetts herself was charged by Barbados with importing
rum, sugar, and molasses from Surinam, and trading with the
French West Indies. Such practices were seen as underwriting
the commercial revival and post-war boom, which also related to
the Newfoundland trade.[5] Thus the English had little reason to be

---

[1] Mather, *Duodecennium*, p. 24; S. E. Morison, *Maritime History of Massachusetts* (Boston, Mass., 1941), p. 14, and above, ch. iv, pp. 150–2, 157.

[2] See esp. *C.S.P.C.*, 1708–9, no. 60, pp. 47–9.

[3] The calculations are those of the Board of Trade estimated at £4 per man
per month. Protection was scanty during 1708 and 1709 but during the two
following years the number of men on station pretty well doubled. CO 390/5 ff.
45, 46,

[4] Barrow, *Trade and Empire*, p. 81.

[5] Steele, *Politics of Colonial Policy*, p. 157; Board of Trade to Queen, 9 Feb.
1714, *C.S.P.C.* 1712–14, no. 577; *Journal of Commissioners for Trade and
Plantations*, ii. 474–5, 504–5.

impressed by the picture of economic suffering which at worst was patchy and offset by growth. And for Newfoundland traditional violations of the acts of trade, though resented by the English government, raised less anger than the enticing away of English seamen in defiance of the act of 1699, when trained men were badly required for the navy. This practice in time of war was regarded as little short of treason.[1]

Notions of the physical suffering of the New Englanders were not current in English society. The trials of Deerfield are excluded from significant English annals: the heroism of the Dunstans failed to equal even the saga of Mary Rowlandson.[2] In a generation of harrowing war New England did not contribute to English folklore: she produced no heroes whose deeds crossed the Atlantic. The impact of New England was lessening. The *Duodecennium*, the second major tale of woes to be printed in Boston, was not noticed, even critically, in England. It is quite evident that the New English were never in the forefront of English vision, even in and after 1711. When they were viewed at all the images did not flatter. An important exception to this is Daniel Defoe's *Review of the State of the British Nation* which first appeared in February 1704, eventually thrice weekly, and continued in modified form until June 1713.

Defoe, undoubtedly one of the best-informed men on colonial affairs in England, gave New England considerable publicity. He related the savage losses at sea and at least mentioned the general effect of the incursions on land. His comments about the

---

[1] R. G. Lounsbury, *The British Fishery at Newfoundland, 1634–1763* (New Haven, Conn., 1934), p. 223. On the credit side the importance of New Englanders in provisioning Newfoundland in wartime was stressed on several occasions. John Jackson, later minister at Newfoundland, warned the House of Commons in 1706 that without these provisions the planters would starve. Commodore Aldred and Commodore Crow gave similar advice to the Board of Trade. *C.S.P.C.*, 1706–8, no. 74; ibid., no. 511; ibid., 1711–12, no. 149, enclosure i.

[2] Few writers gave any notice to New England at all. John Evelyn, who made occasional references to political events in New England before 1689, subsequently lost interest in her affairs. Swift, apart from an accurate prediction of the fate of the Walker expedition and, later, a brief comment on the career in New England of William Wood of Wood's Ha'ppence, ignores in his writings the English of this part of the world. The *Spectator* contains mention of one New Englander, Thomas Sapper, who died in London. And both the *Tatler* and *Spectator* record the visit of the Iroquois 'kings' to England in 1710. Narcissus Luttrell mentions the 'mast fleet' from New England being convoyed off Land's End in Nov. 1706.

French threat to encircle British holdings in North America were accompanied by an instructive map. Unlike Jonathan Swift, he gave great stress to the importance of trade and the value of economic ties as a cement of empire. He scoffed at the idea—'a chimera of some statesmen'—that to make colonies great would set them up as independent powers, separate from England. He also examined, and dismissed, the possibility of any colony seeking the protection of a foreign power, particularly the Netherlands, France, or Spain. But he chose New England as the core of his discourse because, as he later acknowledged, '*N. England* is the colony which our State Heroes who were frightened at Vapours thought most formidable: *first*, because they were too honest to be suffered to grow great and *secondly* because they were damn'd Phanaticks, who at that Time of Day, they thought it necessary to suppress and discourage.' He concluded: 'It is morally impossible that any of our colonies on the Continent of *America* but especially *New-England* should ever desire to be independent of *England*.'[1]

In the main, however, prejudices stimulated by political schism in old England and the tensions in New England kept the two peoples apart. Fear of Presbyterians and Independents being republicans in disguise lived on from the Commonwealth and Protectorate period. The concept of national unity, which after the coming of William of Orange had found support on both sides of the Atlantic, had in the mother country given place to clear party divisions. The years 1701–2 were the great watershed in post-Revolutionary politics.[2] New Englanders were slow to perceive and to react to these changes at home. Contemporary hostility to Dudley is related to the local scene and shows that for the extreme traditionalists, at least, suspicion of Tories and fear of enhancement of the prerogative was a continuum. This fear had survived the 1690s, during which time the Mathers and other leaders had sought to advance the singularity of purpose between the numeri-

---

[1] Arthur W. Secord (ed.), *Defoe's Review* (New York, 1938) nos. 30, 31, 44, 89, 97, vol. i, pp. 133, 135, 136, 138A, 181, 401, and 402; no. 135; vol. iv, pp. 539, 548, 551–2, and 555. Defoe's concern was pre-eminently in the promotion of naval stores. 'Embark *N. England* but in this Timber Trade', he wrote, 'and people her with 2 or 300,000 Families-Depending on that Trade; you have really got her with Child; and she must marry you, or she is undone.' Ibid., vol. iv, p. 548.

[2] G. Holmes, *British Politics in the Age of Anne* (London and New York, 1967), p. 47.

cally preponderant part of the English nation in old England and the theologically significant element of that nation in New England. But after the early years of Queen Anne's reign the adversities of the renewed struggle with France and her Indian allies lessened it and imposed a provincial unity between executive and legislature which through the instrumentality of the Canada projects became a popular consensus transcending provincial divisions.

For the purpose of bringing the military conflict to a successful conclusion Whig New England joined not with the Whigs of old England, who, though they recognized the War of the Spanish Succession as a 'war of religion', were nevertheless committed to a continental strategy in which the welfare of the colonies did not importantly figure, but with the Tories who placed greater value upon a maritime and a colonial strategy. Co-operation between such unnatural allies was no less easy than it had been between the moderate or mercantile element of Massachusetts and the representatives of James II under the Dominion of New England.[1] And though the failure of the Walker expedition in 1711 brought political consequences far less dramatic than did the revolt against General Governor Andros, like that experience it had been preceded by a Tory triumph, the election of 1710, and was followed by revelations of Jacobite schemes which raised fears that England would be saddled with a papist monarchy.

Though Queen Anne herself was not directly involved in the aftermath of the debacle of 1711, it had in fact reiterated the lessons of the 1680s that those who exalted the monarchy or who trusted the Stuarts were not themselves to be trusted. But were Englishmen of any political persuasion above suspicion? With whom could New Englanders effectively co-operate?[2] If following the Glorious Revolution they had looked for allies among the Whigs, through whose good offices Cotton Mather had aspired to a special relationship, after the death of William that alliance had faltered

---

[1] But see Alison G. Olson, 'William Penn, Parliament and Proprietary Government', *W&MQ*, 3rd ser. xviii (1961), 176, 177, 188, and *passim*.

[2] The view of the anonymous French writer who claimed there was great antipathy between the English of Europe and those of America was supported by Governor Bellomont's comment that the New Englanders seemed to hate those that are English-born as if they were foreigners. But such provincial sentiments were scarcely unique to Massachusetts or to the early part of the eighteenth century. See Parkman, *Half Century*, i, ch. viii; Bodleian Library Rawlinson MSS. A 272 f. 62–3, cited in Barrow, *Trade and Empire*, p. 71.

and collapsed. Interests diverged, but even where they did not there were now fewer men of influence concerned for the needs of the province. There had been no move to shield it from the calumnies which followed the wreck of the Walker expedition. Even the very integrity of the Whig leaders as guardians of religious toleration was called into question. From 1702 to 1705 they had successfully countered the attempt to challenge through Parliament the practice of occasional conformity and to prevent those who attended Nonconformist places of worship from holding municipal office. Though unable to remove all disabilities for the Protestants they nevertheless pursued the principle of complete freedom of worship and education, and full political rights. But as has been observed, in December 1711 the Whigs agreed to the passing of a new occasional conformity bill. From that point until the summer of 1713 it is true, they, like the Hanoverian Tories, became virtuous largely by contrast with their opponents. Yet as a party they had signally failed to succour and support the persisting and most valued elements of the New England tradition. Like their predecessors of the Glorious Revolution they had a Protestant contender waiting in the wings, but he was not a figure for whom New Englanders could have any special feeling nor through whom they could expect to establish any unique relationship.

Queen Anne herself never gained the spontaneous affection which was freely given to William, but she did benefit from comparison with the Old Pretender. In the worst Protestant nightmares the alternative was Louis XIV and the Universal Monarchy. At the end, French power remained on the St. Lawrence and the Mississippi. 'Should you become a French province how forelorn, how rueful would be your condition',[1] wrote Cotton Mather: an unnecessary reminder. But whoever was bogeyman, the form it took would mix absolutism with Catholic bigotry. However Anne, who was without heirs, could not live forever. And as peace dawned the problem of a successor loomed nearer. To what extent could trust to make the right choice be lodged in the wisdom of that part of the nation residing in England? Devotion to the nation, in part because of its lack of precision as a concept and because of its mystique, could be imparted

---

[1] Mather, *Duodecennium*, p. 20.

with fewer reservations than loyalty to the throne, faith in parties, or faith in the conscience of particular Englishmen. Kings might come and go but the identity of New England was preserved in the body and experiences of the nation.

But the nation was changing. After 1707 by the Act of Union something of the mystique of the English had been conceded to the necessity of creating a united British people. Moreover, it remained amenable to subjective definition. Cotton Mather gravely alluded to 'ferments' within it which were boiled up to such an astonishing and prodigious heighth as fills all people with consternation.[1] Sir William Ashurst spoke bitterly of how he had lived to see the greatest merit condemned and the greatest benefits the nation had ever received exposed to ridicule and contempt.[2] To some on both sides, Tories and Whigs, it seemed as if there was a dual heritage, two incipient nations within the body of one state. Matthew Prior voiced his disappointment at the Canadian disaster by ascribing it to 'the avarice or treachery of the godley at New England'. 'The same party', he opined, 'are doing all the mischief they can in Old England, they are really such a race of men that the Palatins are more our countrymen than they.'[3]

Yet the New Englanders, not wholly at one with dissenters even, were emotionally, if not ideologically, further separated from the Jacobite wing of the Tories than were their Whig counterparts in England. They themselves denied the importance of a differentiating radicalism. Their informed defenders tried to disprove it. Writers such as Neal and Penhallow, Dummer and Oldmixon, thoughtful officials such as Bellomont and Bannister retailed the services done for the nation by New England. For those with eyes to see these were not insignificant. Important achievements such as the acquisition of Nova Scotia, the value of which was carefully assessed as a national gain by Prior the diplomatist, were not universally acknowledged. Even in bare economic terms a sensitive calculation rated them as a beneficial component of empire. Their value as a market helped to offset their role as competitors in the carrying trade of the colonies. As the Whig historian John Oldmixon observed, New England imported 'Stuffs, Silks, Linen,

---

[1] Mather, *Diary*, ii. 172.
[2] To Nicholson, 15 Jan. 1711/12, Ford, *Correspondence*, p. 94.
[3] *Hammer Correspondence*, p. 131.

Birmingham-ware, 'Tools for the Mechanicks'. In assisting the Leeward Islands with provisions, 'they were rather a service to the Publick Interest than a prejudice; for without help from them, the sugar plantations could not maintain three thousand mouths, whites and blacks. Provisions could not be sent thence from England with that ease, speed and certainty, as from this Colony.[1] This was certainly true of wartime. But the quality of New England shipbuilding and the white pine masts she grew for the English Navy, along with the expectations for naval stores, were indications of a yet more valuable service which would increase in importance as Baltic supplies became less accessible.[2]

Like Cotton Mather, most dissenters who examined New England, particularly Daniel Neal, Samuel Penhallow, and the Earl of Bellomont, minimized the differences of religion which separated them from their fellow-countrymen on the European side of the Atlantic. Daniel Neal, a London dissenter, educated at Thomas Rowe's academy and at Utrecht and Leiden, developed an attachment for New England second only to that for his own countrymen which, profound though it was, never destroyed his objectivity and honesty as an historian. In his popular history, modelled on Mather's *Magnalia*, he did not endeavour to hide the more distasteful aspects of the behaviour of the early planters. Yet he stressed the abiding affection for England and the love of the English constitution. Penhallow, a Cornishman who went to New England at the age of twenty-one, denied that New Englanders were enemies of the Church of England. He believed his New England countrymen differed from the Anglicans 'only in the ceremonies, which none of them [the Anglicans] will allow to be essential. Many of those that are of the church, dissent more from one another than we do—many of them are dissenters from their own articles of faith. Is not our own doctrine the same? The Sabbath as strictly solemnised and our mode of worship as agreeable to the primitive constitution, as any other church in the world'[3]

John Oldmixon thrust aside the differences in economic activity and discounted the influence of geography. 'I have no notion', he commented, 'of any more difference between *Old-England* and

---

[1] John Oldmixon, *History of the British Empire* (London, 1708), i. 96–7.
[2] Thomas Bannister to Council of Trade, 7 July 1715, *C.S.P.C.*, 1714–15, no. 508.
[3] Penhallow, *Wars of New England*, p. 73.

New than between *Lincolnshire* and *Somersetshire*; neither can I see, why the English in *America* should not be suffered to cultivate the Ground, and improve it as they think fit, anymore than that feeding and grazing should be prohibited in *Somersetshire* for the Advantage of *Lincolnshire*. The people of *New-England* deal as with *Old-England* as either of those Counties in proportion to their Numbers.'[1] Oldmixon was not blinded by love, though he imaginatively saw Massachusetts as a land of sheep-covered hills, like Devonshire in the old country.

But if blood was thicker than water, the skin of kin was, in contrast, strikingly thin. In the minds even of some dissenters, New Englanders were a form of degenerate Englishmen. Oldmixon was highly critical of their scholarly equipment and believed they had misused education. He had borrowed heavily from Cotton Mather's writing yet he held the style in contempt. Mather's history, he thought, resembled 'School Boys' Exercises Forty years ago'.[2] It sufficed to give one 'a Surfeit of Letters', if all the schools in the world were like Harvard College. It was not the design of their university which was at fault, so he believed, but rather the execution of it—the form of cant which was in fashion. Grudgingly he admitted that some of the ministers who had published sermons and other discourses were good scholars but he did not distinguish between their writing and Mather's. It was the convolutions of Mather's crabbed writing, not sermons in the plain style, which to him characterized New England. Either he did not perceive or did not acknowledge the existence of the latter. 'But', he observed, in a passage which seemed to fly in the face of what he had earlier written, ''tis in stile as in Painting, ev'ry Nation has a Manner, by which 'tis known, and which will be more or less Polite according to the Genius of the People.'[3]

Thus Oldmixon defined these New English as a nation living in a land like Devonshire and holding an economic relationship with England like that of Somerset. He did not, however, raise doubts about their loyalty to the Crown, nor even about the natural nobility of men who had made a fortune from the wilderness. For all his inaccuracies and deficiencies as a historian he saw some

---

[1] Oldmixon, *British Empire*, i. 96.
[2] Ibid., i. 109.
[3] Ibid., i. 112–13.

important things more clearly than many of his countrymen. But how influential were he and his fellow-writers in countering ignorance, prejudice, and indifference? At best it was the half-blind leading the blind. How many Englishmen knew even the elementary geography of the New World? The historian Narcissus Luttrell, and Abbé Gaultier, confidential agent of Louis XIV in London, jointly confused Canada with the West Indies. They were not alone in their error.[1] The Reverend Mr. Barnard relates how a young lady of society was similarly bewildered, having imagined all New Englanders were black. Believing they were not naturally versed in the English tongue, she complimented him on his facility in learning the language so rapidly.[2] Barnard, though he had many friends and admirers and several offers of an incumbency, felt the cultural distances which separated him from the dissenters of old England. Only among those merchants who traded with New England did he feel really at home.

While the number of English friends seemed to be thinning out hostile elements within the nation were gathering afresh. During 1713, powerfully supported by Governor Nicholson and some of the Anglican colonists, consideration was given to the creation of a colonial bishopric. New England ministers were questioned in the most guarded terms for their reactions to a move which denied any intention of interfering with their churches. The need for more accurate information to prevent the Anglican hierarchy being misinformed or misguided was given as the short-term justification. The long-term aspiration, still believed to muster major support among Independents as well as Anglicans, was the union of all Protestants, or at least all English in America.[3] This project had the support of the Society for Propagation of the Gospel and before Anne's death, which put a stop to proceedings, a parliamentary bill was drafted for carrying it out. But advice was passed to New England that there was a 'civil nature in this affair' and such a concurrency of civil and ecclesiastical business that it was

---

[1] See W. T. Morgan, 'The South Sea Company and the Canadian Expedition in the Reign of Queen Anne', *Hispanic American Review* viii (1928), 143ff.; Narcissus Luttrell, *Brief Historical Relation of State Affairs, 1678–1714* (Oxford, 1857), vi. 572, 687. This point is made guardedly for it may not have been an uncommon usage to describe the North American mainland as the West Indies *Terra Firma*. See *Defoe's Review*, i. 135.

[2] *Mass. Hist. Soc. Coll.*, 3rd ser. v. 200.

[3] Cross, *Anglican Episcopate*, pp. 98–9.

impossible to foretell the outcome.[1] At this juncture the charter of 1691, which had been viewed as the framework of a new relationship, offered no secure shelter from further change. Justified fears were raised of a renewal of the judicial procedure of *quo warranto* which in 1684 had resulted in the vacation of the charter of 1629.[2] Since the time of Sacheverell's sermon the sky had been darkening. Now for some months men faced the future with alarm.[3]

There was to be no repetition of the disturbances of 1689. Neither Massachusetts nor her neighbours produced a political reaction before the English crisis was solved by the Protestant succession and the failure of the Jacobites. Dudley avoided the fate of Andros without being obliged to make any precipitate move. Perhaps conditioned by war and its experiences, New Englanders had become reconciled to the major decisions which shaped their destiny being taken in England. In 1713 there was a docility which points to exhaustion of the spirit if not of physical resources. A generation of conflict had broadened and diluted the New England psyche so that it was more nearly co-terminous with the wider range of economic enterprise in which its citizens indulged, but it had brought no glories equal to the achievements of the colony's founders. Nor had it provided security against the enemies of the province. Against this background the well-known warning of Governor Hunter of New York to the English government may be considered.

Hunter advised reflection on Harrington's thoughts in *Oceana*: as Nationall or Independant Empire is to be exercised by them that have ye proper ballance of Dominion in the Nation, soe Provincial or Dependant Empire is not to be exercised by them that have the ballance of dominion in the province, because that would bring the Government from provinciall and dependant to Nationall and Independant.[4]

But Massachusetts had matured in the seventeenth century and had moved some distance towards independence and national stature. After her humiliating experiences of the 1680s she had sought, perhaps pretentiously, a more sophisticated relationship

---

[1] Ibid., p. 101.

[2] *A Letter from One in Boston to his Friend in the Country* (Boston, Mass., 1714), p. 12.

[3] E. Pemberton to John Winthrop, 5 Oct. 1712, *Mass. Hist. Soc. Coll.*, v. 261.

[4] *C.S.P.C.*, 1711–12, no. 96, pp. 103–4.

with the parent state the characteristic of which was interdependence. This relationship had neither been formalized nor acknowledged by informal courtesies, save in the uncertain months following the revolution of 1688. That there was no real partnership was evident by 1711, if not earlier. But the lessons of exposure to the frontiers of New France were also plainly written. Neither Massachusetts nor the region which embraced the neighbouring provinces could have believed in all sanity that they possessed the resources to stand alone.

Bibliography

MANUSCRIPT MATERIAL

1. BOSTON, MASSACHUSETTS

Massachusetts Archives, State House.

Volume:
ii	Colonial, 1638–1720.
iii	,, 1629–1720.
vi	Court Records, 1689–98.
vii	Commercial, 1685–1714.
xx	Foreign Relations, 1658–1751.
xxxv	Miscellaneous Inter-Charter.
xxxvi	,, ,,
xxxvii	,, ,,
xxxviia	,, ,,
xlvii	Laws.
xlviii	,,
lxi	Maritime, 1671–94.
lxii	,, 1694–1706.
lxiii	,, 1706–40.
lxx	Military, 1680–1703.
lxxi	,, 1704–11.
lxxii	,, 1712–42.
cvi	Political, 1638–1700.

2. RICHMOND, VIRGINIA

(a) Virginia State Library.
Henrico County Records: Deeds, Wills, etc. 1688–97 (transcript).
Stafford County Records: Orders, 1664–8; 1689–93. (, , , ,).

(b) Virginia Historical Society Library.
William Byrd Letter Book. MSS5: 2B 9965/1.
Wormeley Estate Papers, 1701–16. MS.22711.
Robert Bristow Letter Book, 1705–50. MS.22953.

3. COLONIAL WILLIAMSBURG, VIRGINIA

The Blathwayt Papers (Microfilm).

Vol. i Includes letters from Edward Randolph during his period
of imprisonment under the Provisional government of

Massachusetts. Provides valuable comment on the early
months of the war with France.

ii 14 letters from Isaac Addington, Provincial Secretary of
Massachusetts, to William Blathwayt. Informed opinion on
the conduct of military affairs and the state of the province
at war, 1692–8.

v Includes 7 letters from Increase Mather and a draft letter
from William Blathwayt on the raising of men for the conquest
of Nova Scotia and Canada; and 5 letters from William
Stoughton on the wartime hardships suffered by the province.

4. LONDON, ENGLAND

Public Record Office.

Save for statistical information and documents known to be inade-
quately abstracted, the CO series were mainly examined through the
printed calendars. Most of the sources given here are for purposes of
reference.

(a) Plantation Office and Board of Trade.

CO 1/68	General Series. Addenda, 1690–7.
5/751	Original Correspondence, 1689–1713.
5/785–91	Sessional Papers. Massachusetts and New Hampshire, 1686–1713.
5/848	Shipping Returns. New England.
5/905–13	Entry Books of Letters, Grants, Instructions, etc., 1688–1713.
5/898	Original Correspondence. Letters from Governors, 1703–32.
5/9	Canadian Expedition, 1710–13.
5/1045	Original Correspondence. New York. 1700–1.
195/3	Newfoundland Entry Book, 1701–5.
390/5	Board of Trade, Exports and Imports, Shipping, etc., 1688–1792.
391/9–16	Journal of Board of Trade, 1696–1704. After 1704 the volumes are printed.

(b) Admiralty Papers.

ADM 1/1435	Captains' Letters
1/2033	,, ,, , 1698–1702.
1/2638	,, ,, , 1700–1.
1/4093	Letters from Secretaries of State, 1709–10.
1/4085	Contains letter to Edward Randolph, 29 June 1697, warning of French designs on New England.
2/1048	Letters relating to Admiralty and Vice-Admiralty Courts, 1699–1702.
49/123	Contains details of Royal Navy ships built in New England between 1689–1713.

British Museum.
Add. MSS. 9105   Correspondence of John Churchill, first Duke
    *   of Marlborough.
    9109   ,,

PRINTED SOURCES

I. PRINTED DOCUMENTS

Acts and Resolves Public and Private of the Province of the Massachusetts Bay. Ed. by E. Ames and A. C. Goodell. 21 vols. Boston, Mass., 1868–1922. Vols. i, vi, viii, ix.

Acts of the Privy Council of England, Colonial Series. Ed. by W. L. Grant and J. Munro. 6 vols. London, 1908–12. Vol. ii (1680–1720).

'American Colonial Documents to 1776'. Ed. Merrill Jensen. London, 1955. *English Historical Documents.* Vol. ix.

The Andros Tracts. Ed. by W. H. Whitmore. 3 vols. The Prince Society, Boston, Mass., 1868–74.

Archives of Maryland. Ed. by W. H. Browne, *et al.* 65 vols. Baltimore, Md., 1883. Vols. viii, xiii.

Archives of the State of New Jersey, 1631–1800. Ed. by W. A Whitehead, *et al.* 30 vols. Newark, N. J., etc., 1880–1906. 1st ser., vols. ii, iii.

Boston News-Letter (weekly publication, beginning 24 April 1704).

'Byng Papers', Ed. by Brian Tunstall. *Publications of the Navy Records Society.* 2 vols. London, 1930–3. Vol. ii.

Calendar of State Papers, Colonial Series. America and the West Indies. Ed. by J. W. Fortescue and Cecil Headlam. 16 vols., for 1689–1715. London, 1901–28.

Calendar of Treasury Books. Ed. by William A. Shaw. 32 vols. London, 1904–62. Vol. xix.

Calendar of Treasury Papers. Ed. by Joseph Redington. 6 vols. London, 1868–89. Vol. xciii.

Collections of the Massachusetts Historical Society:
'The Hutchinson Papers', 3rd ser. (Boston, Mass., 1846), vol i.
'Sewall Papers', 5th ser. (Boston, Mass., 1878–82), vols. v-viii.
'Sewall Letter Book', 6th ser. (Boston, Mass., 1886), vol. i.
'Winthrop Papers', 6th ser. (Boston, Mass., 1889), vol. iii.
'Belcher Papers', 6th ser. (Boston, Mass., 1893), vol. vi.
'Diary of Cotton Mather', 6th ser. (Boston, Mass., 1911–12), vols. vii, viii.

Colonial Records of Pennsylvania, 1683–1790. 16 vols. Philadelphia, Pa., 1852–3. vol. ii.

Connecticut Historical Society Collections. Hartford, Conn., 1860. vol. i.

Correspondence between the Governors and Treasurers of the New England Company in London and the Commissioners of the United Colonies in America.... *1657–1712.* Ed. by J. W. Ford. London, 1896.

Correspondence between William Penn and James Logan and others, 1700–1750. Ed. by E. Armstrong. 2 vols. Philadelphia, Pa., 1886. Vol. ii.

Correspondence of Sir Thomas Hanmer, Bart. Ed. by Sir Henry Bunbury. London, 1838.

Defoe's Review. Ed. by Arthur Wellesley Secord. 22 vols. New York, 1938.

Dictionary of American Biography. Ed. by Allen Johnson. 22 vols. London and New York, 1928. Vols. ii, xiv, xviii.

The Documentary History of the State of New York. Ed. by E. B. O'Callaghan. 4 vols. Albany, N.Y., 1849.

Documents and Records Relating to the Province of New Hampshire 1623–1800. Ed. by Nathaniel Bouton, *et al.* 39 vols. Concord, N. H. 1867–1941. Vols. ii, iii.

Documents Relative to the Colonial History of the State of New York. Ed. by E. B. O'Callaghan and Berthold Fernow. 15 vols. Albany, N. Y., 1856–87. Vols. iii, ix.

Edward Randolph ... Including his Letters and Official Papers, 1676–1703. Ed. by R. N. Toppan and A. T. S. Goodrick. 7 vols. The Prince Society, Boston, Mass., 1898–1909.

Essex Institute Historical Collections. Salem, Mass., 1906. Vol. xlii.

Executive Journals of the Council of Virginia. Ed. by H. R. McIlwaine. Richmond, Va., 1925.

The Glorious Revolution in America. Ed. by Michael G. Hall, *et al.* Chapel Hill, N. C., 1964.

Higginson, T. W. *Letters and Journals.* Boston, Mass., 1921.

H.M.C., *House of Lords Manuscripts,* New Series. London, 1908. Vol. iv.

H.M.C., *Portland mss.,* vol. v. (*Harley Papers,* iii.) London 1899.

Journal of the Commissioners for Trade and Plantations. 14 vols. London, 1920–38. Vols. i, ii.

Journal of the Jasper Danckaerts, 1679–80. Ed. by B. B. James and J. F. Jameson. New York, 1959.

Journals of the House of Burgesses of Virginia, 1659/60–93. Ed. by H. R. McIlwaine. Richmond, Va., 1914.

Journals of the House of Commons. Vol. xv.

Massachusetts Historical Society Proceedings, 1863–4, 1878, 1901.

Narratives of the Indian Wars, 1675–99. Ed. by C. H. Lincoln. New York, 1913.

Narratives of the Insurrections. 1675–90. Ed. C. M. Andrews. New York, 1915.

New York Historical Society Collections. 1868.

The Private Correspondence of Sarah, Duchess of Marlborough 2 vols. 2nd edn., London, 1838.

Records of the Colony of Rhode Island and Providence Plantations in New England, 1636–1792. Ed. by J. R. Bartlett. 10 vols. Providence, R. T., 1856–65. Vol. ii.

Report of the Record Commissioners of the City of Boston. Ed. by W. H. Whitmore, *et al.* 39 vols. Boston, Mass., 1876–1909. Vols. i, vii, viii, ix, xi, xxiv.

The Statutes of the Realm. 9 vols. London, 1810. Vols. vi, vii, viii, ix.

Virginia Calendar of State Papers, 1652–1781. Ed. by W. Palmer. Richmond, Va., 1875.

'The Walker Expedition to Quebec, 1711', Ed. by G. S. Graham. *Publications of the Navy Records Society,* xciv. London, 1953.

2. CONTEMPORARY SERMONS, PAMPHLETS, HISTORIES, etc.

The rich and extensive resources of the John Carter Brown Library, Providence, R.I., include a high proportion of the printed works listed below. Most of the Massachusetts Election and Artillery Sermons and the Boston Almanacs, as well as much of the vast output of Cotton Mather are to be found here. Election Sermons printed in 1693, 1696, 1698, 1699, 1702, 1704, 1705, and 1712 are in the Boston Public Library. The sermons for 1695 and 1709 are held by the Massachusetts Historical Society in Boston. Those Election Sermons listed below are indicated by the letters 'E.S.' after the title.

A. B. (identity unknown) 'An Account of the Late Revolutions in New-England', Boston, 1689, *Andros Tracts*, ii, 231–70.

ANONYMOUS 'The Deplorable State of New-England By Reason of a Covetous and Treacherous Governour and Pusillanimous Counsellors', London, 1708, *Mass, Hist. Soc. Coll.,* 5th ser. (1879), vi. 96–131.

——'The Humble Address of the Publicans of New-England, containing the Second Petition of the Boston Episcopalians', London, 1691, *Andros Tracts*, ii. 231–70.

——'A Modest Enquiry Into the Grounds and Occasions of a Late Pamphlet, Intituled, A Memorial of the Present Deplorable State of New-England', London, 1707, *Mass. Hist. Soc. Coll.* 5th ser. (1879), vi. 65–95.

——'A New and Further Narrative of the State of New-England; being a Continued Account of the Bloudy Indian War', London, 1676 *Narratives of the Indian Wars*, pp. 77–99.

——'The Present State of New-England . . . Faithfully Composed by a Merchant of Boston and Communicated to his Friend in London' London, 1675, *Narratives of the Indian Wars*, pp. 24–50.

BELCHER, Revd. Joseph. *The Singular Happiness of Such Heads or Rulers as are able to chuse out their People's Way and will also endeavour their People's Comfort.* E.S. Boston, Mass., 1701.

BARNARD, Revd. John. 'Autobiography', Marblehead, Mass., 1766, *Mass. Hist. Soc. Coll.*, 3rd ser. (1836), v. 177–243.

BULKELEY, Revd. Gershom. 'The People's Right to Election', Philadelphia, Pa., 1689, *Conn. Hist. Soc. Coll.* (1860), i. 57–8.

'BULLIVANT'S JOURNAL', *Massachusetts Historical Society Proceedings.* 1878.

BURCHETT, J. *A Complete History of the Most Remarkable Transactions at Sea.* London, 1720.

BYFIELD, NATHANIEL. 'An Account of the Late Revolution in New-England', London, 1689, *Andros Tracts*, i. 3–10.

C. D. 'New-England's Faction Discovered; or, A Brief and True Account of their Persecution of the Church of England', London, 1690. *Narratives of the Insurrections.* pp. 251–67.

CHARLEVOIX, Pierre Francois-Xavier DE. *Histoire de description générale de la Nouvelle-France.* 6 vols. Paris, 1744.

CHEEVER, Revd. Samuel. *God's Sovereign Government Among the Nations.* E.S. Boston, Mass., 1712.

CHILD, Sir Josiah. *A New Discourse of Trade.* London, 1694.

CHURCH, Benjamin. *History of the Eastern Expeditions of 1689, 1690, 1692, 1696, and 1704 Against the Indians and French.* Ed. by Henry M. Dexter. Boston, Mass., 1867.

COLMAN, Revd. Benjamin. *The Piety and Duty of Rulers: To Comfort and Encourage the Ministry of Christ.* Boston, Mass., 1708.

DUDLEY, Col. Joseph. 'An Account of the State of Religion in the English Plantations in North America', *Prot. Episc. Hist. Soc. Colls.* (New York, 1851), vol. i.

DUMMER, Jeremiah. *A Letter to a Noble Lord Concerning the Late Expedition to Canada.* Boston, Mass., 1712.

——*A Letter from One in Boston to His Friend in the Country.* Boston, Mass., 1714.

EASTERBROOK, Revd. Joseph. *Abraham the Passenger; his Privilege and Duty described.* E.S. Boston, Mass., 1705.

HENNEPIN, Fr. Louis. *Nouvelle découverte d'un trés-grand pays, situé dans l'Amérique.* Utrecht. 1697.

HUBBARD, William. *A Narrative of the Troubles with the Indians.* Boston, Mass., 1677.

HUMPHREYS, David. *An Historical Account of the Incorporated Society for the Propagation of the Gospel in Foreign Parts.* London, 1730.

HUTCHINSON, Thomas. *History of the Colony and Province of Massachusetts Bay.* Ed. by L. S. Mayo. 3 vols. Cambridge, Mass., 1936.

LAWSON, John. *A New Voyage to Carolina, containing an Exact Description and Natural History of that Country.* London, 1709.

LE CLERQ. *Premier établissement de la foi dans la Nouvelle France.* Paris, 1691.

LITTLETON, Edward. *The Groans of the Plantations. Or a true account of the Grievous and Extreme Sufferings by the Heavy Impositions upon Sugar and other Hardships Relating more particularly to the Island of Barbados.* London, 1689.

LUTTRELL, Narcissus. *A Brief Historical Relation of State Affairs, 1678–1714.* Oxford, 1857.

MAKEMIE, Francis. *Truths in a True Light, or a Pastoral Letter to the Reformed Protestants in Barbados.* Edinburgh, 1699.

MATHER, Revd. Cotton. *Blessed Unions. An Union with the Son of God by Faith, And, an Union In the Church of God by Love, Importunately Pressed.* Boston, Mass., 1692.

——*A Brief Relation of the State of New-England.* London, 1689.

——'Decennium Luctuosum. An History of Remarkable Occurences in the Long War, which New England hath had with the Indian Salvages, From the year 1688', Boston, Mass., 1699. *Narratives of the Indian Wars,* pp. 169–297.

——*Duodecennium Luctuosum. The History of a Long War with Indian Salvages and their Directors and Abettors from the Year 1702 To the Year 1714.* Boston, Mass., 1714.

——*Early Piety, Exemplified in the Life and Death of Mr. Nathaniel Mather.* London, 1689.

——*Ecclesiastes. The Life of the Reverend & Excellent Jonathan Mitchel.* Massachusetts, 1697.

——*Magnalia Christi Americana.* 2 vols. Hartford, Conn., 1853.

——*Pietas in Patriam: The Life of His Excellency Sir William Phips.* London, 1697.

——*A Pillar of Gratitude. Or, A brief Recapitulation, of the Matchless Favours, with which the God of Heaven hath obliged the Hearty Praises of His New-England Israel.* E.S. Boston, Mass., 1700.

——*The Present State of New-England. Considered in a Discourse on the Necessities and Advantages of a Public Spirit In every Man; Especially at such a time as this.* Boston, Mass., 1690.

——*The Serviceable Man.* Boston, Mass., 1690.

——*A Short History of New England. A Recapitulation of Wonderful Passages which have Occurr'd First in the Protections, and then in the Afflictions of New England.* Boston, Mass., 1694.

——*Soldiers Counselled and Comforted. A Discourse Delivered unto some part of the Forces Engaged in the Just War of New-England against the Northern and Eastern Indians.* Boston, Mass., Sept. 1689.

——*The Way to Prosperity.* Boston, Mass., 1689.

——*The Wonderful Works of God—a Thanksgiving Sermon.* Boston, Mass., 1689.

MATHER, Revd. Increase. 'A Brief Account concerning Several of the Agents of New-England', London, 1691, *Narratives of the Insurrections,* pp. 269–96.

——*A Brief History of the Warr with the Indians in New England.* London, 1676.

——*The Great Blessing of Primitive Counsellours.* Boston, Mass., 1693.

——*A Relation of the Troubles which have hapned in New-England By reason of the Indians there. From the Year 1614 to the Year 1675.* London, 1677.

——'The Revolution in New England Justified, And the People there Vindicated', Boston, 1691, *Andros Tracts,* i. 63–132.

——*The Surest Way to the Greatest Honour.* E.S. Boston, Mass., 1699.

NORTON, Revd. John. *An Essay Tending to Promote Reformation.* E.S. Boston, Mass., 1708.

NOYES, Revd. Nicholas. *New England's Duty and Interest, To be an Habitation of Justice and a Mountain of Holiness Containing Doctrine, Caution, and Comfort.* E.S. Boston, Mass., 1698.

OLDMIXON, John. *History of the British Empire.* 2. Vols. London, 1708.

PEMBERTON, Revd. Ebenezer. *The Divine Original and Dignity of Government Asserted; and an Advantageous Prospect of the Rulers Mortality recommended.* E.S. Boston, Mass., 1710.

——*Sermon Preached in the Audience of the General Assembly.* Boston, Mass., 1705.

PENHALLOW, Samuel. *The History of the Wars of New England with the Eastern Indians.* Cincinnati, Ohio, 1859.

ROGERS, Revd. John. *A Sermon Preached at the Election.* E.S. Boston, Mass., 1706.

ROWLANDSON, Mary. *The Sovereignty and Goodness of God . . . being a Narrative of the Captivity and Restauration of Mrs. Mary Rowlandson . . . Written by Her Own Hand for Her private Use, and now made Publick at the earnest Desire of some Friends.* Cambridge, Mass., 1682.

SCOTTOW, Joshua. *A Narrative of the Planting of Massachusetts Colony Anno 1628.* Boston, Mass., 1694.

SMITH, William. *The History of the Province of New York from the first discovery to 1732.* London, 1776.

STODDARD, Revd. Solomon. *An Appeal to the Learned.* Boston, Mass., 1709.

——*Doctrine of Instituted Churches Explained and Proved from the Word of God.* London, 1700.

——*The Inexcusableness of Neglecting the Worship of God, under a Pretence of being in an Unconverted Condition.* Boston, Mass., 1708.

——*The Way for a People to Live Long in the Land that God hath given them.* E.S. Boston, Mass., 1703.

THOMAS, Gabriel. *An Historical and Geographical Account of the Province and Country of Pensilvania and West New-Jersey in America.* London, 1698.

TURRELL, Ebenezer. *The Life and Character of the Reverend Benjamin Colman.* Boston, Mass., 1749.

URING, Captain. 'Notices of New England (1709)', *New Hampshire Hist. Soc. Colls.* (1832), vol. iii.

WADSWORTH, Revd. Benjamin. *Mutual Love and Peace among Christians.* Boston, Mass., 1701.

WARD, Edward. *A Trip to New-England*. London, 1699.

WILLARD, Revd. Samuel. *Character of a Good Ruler, as it was Recommended in a Sermon*. E.S. Boston, Mass., 1694.

——*The Man of War. A Sermon preached to the Artillery Coy*. Boston, Mass., 1699

WISE, Revd. John. *The Churches Quarrel Espoused*. New York. 1713.

3. LATER WORKS

ADAMS, James Truslow. *Revolutionary New England, 1691–1776*. Atlantic Monthly Press, Boston, Mass., 1923.

ADAMS, Nathaniel. *Annals of Portsmouth*. Privately printed for Adams, Exeter, N.H., 1825.

ADAMS, W. Paul. 'Republicanism in Political Rhetoric Before 1776', *Political Science Quarterly*, vol. lxxxv, no. 3 (1970).

ANDREWS, Charles, M. *Colonial Self-Government, 1652–1689*. Harper and Bros., New York, 1904.

——*Fathers of New England*. Yale University Press, New Haven, Conn., 1919.

BAILYN, Bernard. *The New England Merchants in the Seventeenth Century*. Harvard University Press, Cambridge, Mass., 1955.

——*Education in the Forming of American Society: Needs and Opportunities for Study*. University of North Carolina Press, Chapel Hill, N.C., 1960.

BAILYN, Bernard and Lotte. *Massachusetts Shipping, 1697–1714. A Statistical Study*, Belknap Press of Harvard University Press, Cambridge, Mass., 1959.

BALDWIN, Alice. *The New England Clergy and the American Revolution*. Duke University Press, Durham, N.C., 1928.

BANKS, C. E. *History of York, Maine*. The Calkins Press, Boston, Mass., 1931.

BARNES, Viola F. *The Dominion of New England*. Yale University Press, New Haven, Conn., 1960.

BARROW, Thomas C. *Trade and Empire. The British Customs Service in Colonial America, 1660–1775*. Harvard University Press, Cambridge, Mass., 1966.

BAUER, John E. 'English Protestant Attempts at Reunion, 1689–1710', *Hist. Mag. Prot. Episc. Church*, vol. xviii. (1949).

BELKNAP, Jeremy. *The History of New Hampshire*. J. Belknap, Philadelphia, Pa., and Boston, Mass., 1784.

BELL, C. H. *History of the Town of Exeter, N.H.* J. E. Farwell & Co., Exeter, N.H., 1888.

BENNETT, G. V. *White Kennett, 1660–1728. Bishop of Peterborough.* S.P.C.K. for Church Historical Society, London, 1957.

BOND, R. P. *Queen Anne's American Kings.* Clarendon Press, Oxford, 1952.

BONNAULT, Claude DE. *Histoire du Canada français, 1534–1763.* Presses Universitaires de France, Paris, 1950.

BOORSTIN, Daniel. *The Americans: The Colonial Experience.* Random House, New York, 1964.

BOURNE, E. E. *History of Wells and Kennebunk.* B. Thurston & Co., Portland, Me., 1875.

BOWDEN, James. *A History of the Society of Friends in America.* W. & F. G. Cash, London, 1850, 1854.

BREWSTER, Charles W. *Rambles about Portsmouth.* C. W. Brewster, Portsmouth, N.H., 1859.

BRIDENBAUGH, Carl. *Cities in the Wilderness: The First Century of Urban Life in America, 1625–1742.* Capricorn Books, New York, 1964.

——*Mitre and Sceptre. Transatlantic Faiths, Ideas, Personalities and Politics 1689–1775.* Oxford University Press, New York, 1962.

BRODHEAD, J. R. *History of the State of New York.* 2 vols. Harper & Bros., New York, 1871.

BROWN, Robert E. *Middle Class Democracy and the Revolution in Massachusetts, 1691–1780.* Cornell University Press, Ithaca, N.Y., 1955.

BRUCE, P. A. *Institutional History of Virginia in the Seventeenth Century.* G. P. Putnam's sons, New York, 1910.

BUFFINGTON, A. H. 'Dudley and the Treaty of Neutrality', *Mass. Col. Soc. Publ.* vol. xxvi. (1925).

BURT, H. M. *The First Century of Springfield.* 2. vols. C. W. Bryan Co., Springfield, Mass., 1899.

CHALMERS, George. *Political Annals of the Present United Colonies, from their Settlement to the Peace of 1763.* 2 vols. J. Bowen. London, 1780.

CHANNING, Edward. *History of the United States.* 6 vols. Macmillan & Co., New York, 1926–7.

CHASE, G. W. *History of Haverhill.* G. W. Chase, Haverhill, Mass. 1861.

CLARK, Dora M. *The Rise of the British Treasury*. Yale University Press, New Haven, Conn., 1960.

COHEN, Sheldon S. 'The Diary of Jeremiah Dummer', *W & MQ*, 3rd. ser, vol. xxiv. (1967).

COWIE, Leonard W. *Henry Newman. An American in London, 1708–1743*. S.P.C.K. for Church Historical Society, London, 1956.

CRANE, Verner. *The Southern Frontier, 1670–1723*. University of Michigan Press, Ann Arbor, Mich., repr., 1956.

CRAVEN, Wesley F. *The Colonies in Transition, 1660–1713*. Harper & Row, New York, 1968.

CREIGHTON, Donald. *The Dominion of the North*. Houghton Mifflin Co., Boston, Mass., 1944.

CROSS, A. L. *The Anglican Episcopate and the American Colonies*. Harvard University Press, London, 1902. Harvard Historical Studies, vol. ix.

CROUSE, Nellis M. *Lemoyne d'Iberville. Soldier of New France*. Cornell University Press, Ithaca, N.Y., 1954.

CUNDALL, Frank. *The Governors of Jamaica in the Seventeenth Century*. The West India Committee, London, 1936.

CURTI, Merle E. *Social Ideas of American Educators*. C. Scribner & Sons, New York, 1935.

DICKERSON, Oliver M. *American Colonial Government*. Arthur H. Clark Co., Cleveland, Ohio, 1912.

DIXON, W. Hepworth. *History of William Penn: Founder of Pennsylvania*. New Amsterdam Book Co., New York, 1902.

DOW, G. F. and EDMONDS, J. H. *The Pirates of the New England Coast, 1630–1730*. Marine Research Society, Salem, Mass., 1923.

DRAKE, S. A. *Border Wars of New England*. C. Scribner's Sons, New York, 1897.

DRAKE, S. G. *Antiquities of Boston*. 2 vols. L. Stevens, Boston, Mass., 1857.

DUNN, Richard S. *Puritans and Yankees. The Winthrop Dynasty of New England, 1630–1717*. Princeton University Press, Princeton, N.J., 1962.

EASTMAN, Mack. *Church and State in Early Canada*. T. A. Constable, Edinburgh, 1915.

ECCLES, C. J. *Canada under Louis XIV, 1663–1701*. Oxford University Press, New York and London, 1964.

——'Frontenac's Military Policies, 1689–98: A Reassessment', *Canadian Historical Review*, xxxvii (1956), 201–24.

EDWARDS, Newton and RICHEY, Herman G. *The School in American Social Order*. Houghton Mifflin Co., Boston, Mass., 1947.

EGERTON, Hugh E. *A Short History of British Colonial Policy 1609–1909*. Methuen & Co., London, 1920.

EHRMAN, John. *The Navy in the War of William III*. Cambridge University, Cambridge, 1953.

EVERY, George. *The High Church Party*. S.P.C.K. for Church Historical Society, London, 1956.

FELT, Joseph B. *Annals of Salem*. J. Munroe & Co., Salem, Mass., 1827.

FLICK, A. C. *History of the State of New York*. New York State Historical Association, New York, 1933.

FOLSHOM, G. *History of Saco and Biddeford*. A. C. Putnam, Saco, Me., 1830.

FUESS, Charles M. *Andover. Symbol of New England*. Andover Historical Society, Portland, Me., 1959.

GIRAUD, Marcel. *Histoire de la Louisiane*. 3 vols. Presses Universitaires de France, Paris, 1953.

GOSSELIN, Abbé de. 'Education in Canada under the French Régime', in *Canada and its Provinces*. Edited by A Short and A. C. Doughty. Publishers' Association of Canada, Toronto, 1914.

——'Mgr. de Saint-Vallier et Son Temps', *Revue catholique de Normandie*. Paris, 1899.

GOULD, William. *Portland in the Past*. W. Gould, Portland, Me., 1886.

GRAHAM, Gerald S. *Empire of the North Atlantic*. University of Toronto Press, Toronto, 1951.

GREEN, Samuel A. *Groton during the Indian Wars*. S. A. Green. Groton, Mass., 1883.

GREENE, Evarts B. 'The Anglican Church in the American Colonies in the Early Eighteenth Century', *American Historical Review*, vol. xx (1914–15).

GROULX, Abbé L. *L'Enseignment français au Canada*. 2 vols. Librairie Granger Frères Ltd., Montreal, 1933.

GUTTRIDGE, George H. *The Colonial Policy of William III in America and the West Indies*. Cambridge University Press, Cambridge, 1922

HAFFENDEN, Philip. 'France and England in North America, 1689–1713', *New Cambridge Modern History*, ed. J. S. Bromley. Cambridge University Press, Cambridge, 1970. Vol. vi.

——'The Crown and the Colonial Charters, 1675–88', *W&MQ*, 3rd ser., vol. xv (1958).

HALL, Michael G. *Edward Randolph and the American Colonies, 1676–1703*. University of North Carolina Press, Chapel Hill, N.C., 1960.

HAMILTON, Lady Elizabeth. *The Backstairs dragon: a life of Robert Harley, Earl of Oxford*. Hamilton, London, 1969.

HAMMANG, Francis H. *The Marquis de Vaudreuil. New France at the beginning of the Eighteenth Century*. Université de Louvain, Bruge, Belgium, 1938. Pt. I.

HANOTAUX, Gabriel et MARTINEAU, Alfred. *Histoire des colonies françaises et l'expansion de la France dans le monde*. Société de l'histoire nationale, Paris, 1929. Vol. i. *L'Amérique*.

HEMPHILL, John. 'Virginia and the English Commercial System, 1689–1713.' Unpublished Ph.D. thesis. University of Princeton, 1964.

HILDRETH, Richard. *The History of the United States of America*, 6 vols. Harper & Bros., New York, 1877. Vol. ii.

HOLMES, Geoffrey. *British Politics in the Age of Anne*. Macmillan, London, St. Martin's Press, New York, 1967.

JACOBSEN, Gertrude. *William Blathwayt: a Late Seventeenth Century English Administrator*. Yale University Press, New Haven, Conn., 1932.

JAMESON, J. F. *Privateering and Piracy in the Colonial Period*. Macmillan Co., New York, 1923.

JARAY, Gabriel L. *L'Empire français d'Amerique, 1534–1803*. A. Colin, Paris, 1938.

JONES, Rufus M. *The Quakers in the American Colonies*. Macmillan Co., London, 1923.

JORDAN, Winthrop. D. *White over Black*. University of North Carolina Press, Chapel Hill, N.C. 1968.

JUDAH, Charles B. *The North American Fisheries and British Policy to 1713*. University of Illinois Press, Urbana, Ill., 1935.

JUDD, Sylvester. *History of Hadley*. Metcalf & Co., Springfield, Mass., 1905.

KEITH, C. P. *Chronicles of Pennsylvania, 1688–1748*. 2 vols. Patterson & White Co., Philadelphia, Pa., 1917. Vol. i.

KELLAWAY, William. *The New England Company, 1649–1776*. Longmans, London, 1961.

KELLOGG, Louise P. 'The American Colonial Charter', *American Historical Association Report for 1903*. 2 vols. Washington, D.C., 1904, 187–234.

KIMBALL, Everett. *The Public Life of Joseph Dudley*. Longmans, Green & Co., London, 1911.

KIRBY, Ethyn W. *George Keith, 1638–1714*. American Historical Association, New York, 1942.

KITTREDGE, George L. *Witchcraft in Old and New England*. Harvard University Press, Cambridge, Mass., 1929.

LANCTOT, Gustave. *A History of Canada*. 2 vols. Clarke Irwin, Toronto, 1964.

LEACH, D. E. *The Northern Colonial Frontier, 1607–1736*. Holt, Rinehart, & Winston, New York, 1966.

LEADAM, I. S. *The Political History of England 1702–60*. 12 vols. Longmans, Green & Co., London, 1909. vol. ix.

LEDER, Lawrence H. *Robert Livingston, 1654–1728 and the Politics of Colonial New York*. University of North Carolina Press, Chapel Hill, N.C., 1961.

LOCKWOOD, Revd. J. H. *Westfield and its Historic Influence, 1699–1919*. 2 vols. Lockwood, Springfield, Mass., 1922.

LORIN, Henri. *Le Comte de Frontenac*. A. Colin, Paris, 1895.

LOUNSBURY, Alice. *Sir William Phips*. C. Scribner's Sons, New York, 1941.

LOUNSBURY, R. G. *The British Fishery at Newfoundland, 1634–1763*. Yale University Press, New Haven, Conn., 1934.

——'Yankee Trade at Newfoundland', *New England Quarterly*, vol. iii (1930).

LOVEJOY, E. S. 'Equality and Empire: The New York Charter of Liberties, 1683', *W&MQ*, 3rd ser., vol. xxi (1964).

MACNUTT, W. S. *The Atlantic Provinces: The Emergence of Colonial Society, 1712–1857*. McClelland & Stewart, London, 1965.

MAHON, J. K. 'Anglo-American Methods of Indian Warfare, 1676–1794', *Miss. Valley Hist. Rev.*, vol. xlv (Sept. 1958).

MALONE, Joseph J. *Pine Trees and Politics, 1691–1775*. University of Wisconsin Press, London, 1964.

MAY, Ralph. *Early Portsmouth History*. Goodspeed & Co., Boston, Mass., 1926.

MILLER, Perry. *The New England Mind from Colony to Province.* Harvard University Press, Cambridge, Mass., 1953.

MORGAN, Edmund. 'The Puritan Ethic and the American Revolution', *W&MQ*, 3rd ser., vol. xxiv (1967).

MORGAN, W. T. 'Some Attempts at Imperial Co-Operation during the Reign of Queen Anne', *Royal Hist. Soc. Trans.* 4th ser., vol. x (1927).

——'The South Sea Company and the Canadian Expedition in the Reign of Queen Anne', *Hispanic American Review*, vol. viii (1928).

MORISON, Samuel E. *Harvard College in the Seventeenth Century.* Harvard University Press, Cambridge, Mass., 1936.

——*Intellectual Life of Colonial New England.* New York University Press, New York, 1956.

——*The Maritime History of Massachusetts.* Houghton Mifflin Co., Boston, Mass., 1941.

MURDOCH, Beamish. *History of Nova Scotia.* 2 vols. B. Murdoch, Halifax, N.S., 1865.

NEAL, Daniel. *The History of New England.* 2 vols. J. Clark *et al.* London, 1720.

NETTELS, Curtis P. *Money Supply of the American Colonies.* University of Wisconsin Press, Madison, Wis., 1934.

——*The Roots of American Civilization.* Appleton-Century-Crofts, New York, 1963.

OGG, David. *England in the Reigns of James II and William III.* Clarendon Press, Oxford, 1955.

OLSON, Alison G. 'William Penn, Parliament and Proprietary Government', *W&MQ*, 3rd ser., vol. xviii (1961).

OSGOOD, Herbert L. *The American Colonies in the Seventeenth Century.* 4 vols. Peter Smith, Gloucester, Mass., 1957.

——*The American Colonies in the Eighteenth Century.* 4 vols. Peter Smith, Gloucester, Mass., 1958.

OWEN, J. H. *War at Sea under Queen Anne.* Cambridge University Press, Cambridge, 1938.

PALFREY, John G. *A Compendious History of New England.* 4 vols. H. C. Shepard, Boston, Mass., and New York, 1873.

PASCOE, Charles F. *Two Hundred Years of the S. P. G.* Society's Office, London, 1901.

PARKMAN, Francis. *The Old Régime in Canada*. Macmillan Co., London, 1909.

——*Half Century of Conflict*. Little Brown & Co., Boston, Mass., 1892.

PARRINGTON, Vernon L. *Main Currents in American Thought*. 2 vols. Harcourt, Brace & Co., New York, 1954, paperback.

PECKHAM, H. H. 'Speculations on the Colonial Wars', *W&MQ*, 3rd ser., vol. xvii (1960).

——*The Colonial Wars, 1689–1762*. University of Chicago Press, Chicago, Ill., 1964.

PERLEY, Sidney. *History of Salem*. 2 vols. S. Perley, Salem, Mass., 1928.

PHILLIPS, James D. *Salem in the Eighteenth Century*. Houghton Mifflin Co., Boston, Mass., 1937.

PHILLIPS, Paul C. *The Fur Trade*. 2 vols. University of Oklahoma Press, Norman, Okla., 1961.

PLUMB, J. H. *The Growth of Political Stability in England, 1675–1725*. Macmillan, London, 1967.

POLE, J. R. *The Seventeenth Century. The Sources of Legislative Power*. University of Virginia Press, Charlottesville, Va., 1969.

POMFRET, John E. *The Province of East New Jersey, 1609–1702*. Princeton University Press, Princeton, N.J., 1962.

——*The Province of West New Jersey, 1609–1702. A History of the Origins of an American Colony*. Princeton University Press, Princeton, N.J., 1956.

PROWSE, D. W. *History of Newfoundland*. Macmillan Co., London, 1895.

REED, Susan M. *Church and State in Massachusetts, 1691–1740*. University of Illinois, Urbana, Ill., 1914.

ROBBINS, Caroline. *The Eighteenth Century Commonwealthman*. Harvard University Press, Cambridge, Mass., 1959.

ROSE, J. Holland, *et al. The Cambridge History of the British Empire*. Vol. i. *The Old Empire from the beginnings to 1783*. Cambridge University Press. London. 1929.

ROY, Antoine. *Les Lettres, les sciences et les arts au Canada*. Paris, 1930.

RUSSELL, Elmer B. *The Review of American Colonial Legislation by the King in Council*. Columbia University Press, New York, 1915.

SACHSE, William L. 'Harvard Men in England, 1642–1714', *Col. Soc. of Mass. Trans.*, vol. xxxv (1944).

——*The Colonial American in Britain.* University of Wisconsin Press, Madison, Wis., 1956.

SCUDI, Abbie T. *The Sacheverell Affair.* Columbia University Press, New York, 1939.

SCALES, John, ed. *Historical Memoranda of Ancient Dover, New Hampshire.* Dover, N.H., 1900.

SHEA, J. Dawson. *A History of the Catholic Church within the United States.* 4 vols. J. G. Shea, New York, 1886–92.

SHELDON, George. *History of Deerfield.* 2 vols. E. A. Hall & Co., Deerfield, Mass., 1895–6.

SHRIPTON, C. K. 'Immigration to New England, 1680–1740', *Journal of Political Economics*, vol. xliv (1936).

SIMMONS, Richard C. 'Massachusetts: Godliness, Property and the Franchise in Puritan Massachusetts', *Journal of American History*, vol. iv (1968).

SMALL, Walter H. *Early New England Schools.* Ginn & Co., Boston, Mass., 1914.

SMITH, Peter H. 'Politics and Sainthood: Biography by Cotton Mather', *W&MQ*, vol. xx (1963).

SPENCER, Charles W. 'The Cornbury Legend', *New York State Hist. Proc.* vol. xiii (1914).

SPRAGUE, W. B. *Annals of the American Pulpit.* 9 vols. R. Carter & Bros., New York, 1857–69. Vol. i.

STACKPOLE, Everett S. *Old Kittery and Her Families.* Press of Lewiston Journal Co., Lewiston, Me., 1903.

STEELE, I. K. *Politics of Colonial Policy. The Board of Trade in Colonial Administration, 1696–1720.* Clarendon Press, Oxford, 1968.

STEINER, Bernard C. 'The Protestant Revolution in Maryland', American Historical Association, *Annual Report for 1897*, Washington, D.C., 1898.

SWIFT, Lindsay. 'The Massachusetts Election Sermons', *Mass. Col. Soc. Publ.*, vol. i (1895).

TRUMBULL, J. R. *History of Northampton.* 2 vols. Press of Gazette Printing Co., Northampton, Mass., 1898.

TREVELYAN, George M. *England under Queen Anne. The Peace and the Protestant Succession.* 3 vols. Longmans Co., London, 1946. Vol. iii.

TYLER, L. G. 'Education in Colonial Virginia', *W&MQ*, vol. vi (1897).

UPHAM, Charles W. *Salem Witchcraft*. Wiggin & Lunt, Boston, Mass., 1867.

VAN ALSTYNE, Richard. *Empire and Independence. The International History of the American Revolution*. Wiley, New York, 1965.

WALKER, Williston. *The Creeds and Platforms of Congregationalism*. C. Scribner's Sons, repr. Boston, Mass., 1960.

WALLACE, David D. *History of South Carolina*. 4 vols. American Hist. Soc., New York, 1934.

WALLER, George M. *Samuel Vetch: Colonial Enterpriser*. University of North Carolina Press, Chapel Hill, N.C., 1960.

WASHBURN, Emory. *Sketches of the Judicial History of Massachusetts from 1630–1775*. C. C. Little & J. Brown, Boston, Mass., 1890.

WEEDEN, W. B. *Economic and Social History of New England, 1620–1789*, 2 vols. Houghton Mifflin Co., Boston, Mass., and New York, 1890.

WENDELL, Barrett. *Cotton Mather, The Puritan Priest*. Dodd, Mead, & Co., New York, 1891.

WERTEMBAKER, Thomas J. *Virginia under the Stuarts*. Princeton University Press, New York, 1959.

WHITSON, Agnes. *The Constitutional Development of Jamaica, 1660–1729*. University of Manchester, 1929.

WILLIAMSON, W. D. *History of the State of Maine*, 2 vols. Hallowell Glazier & Masters, Hallowell, 1832.

WILLIS, William. *History of Portland*, 2 vols. Day, Fraser & Co., Portland, Me., 1833.

WICKERSHAM, James P. *History of Education in Pennsylvania*. Inquirer, Lancaster, Pa., 1886.

WINSOR, Justin. *The Struggle in America between England and France, 1697–1763*. Sampson Low & Marston, London, 1895.

WRIGHT, Louis B. *The Cultural Life of the American Colonies, 1607–1763*. Harper & Bros., New York, 1957.

Index

Acadia, 72, 85 n. 3, 238, 248, 273, 274
See also Nova Scotia
Accault, Michel, 197
Adiwando, Indian chief, 212
Allen, Arthur, 6
Allen, William, 136
Allerton, Isaac, 6 n. 3
Amesbury (Mass.), 87, 217, 277
Anderson, William, 6
Andover (Mass.), 218, 277
Andros, Sir Edmund, governor of Dominion of New England, xii, 8, 11, 14, 17, 23, 33, 34, 38, 52, 78, 79, 120, 132, 150, 165, 168, 174, 175, 241, 253
Anglican Church, 121
and colonies, 167
and episcopal supervision, 170, 288–9
and Henry Compton, bishop of London, 168, 188
and potential resources, 168
and S.P.G., 168, 170, 172, 194, 288
and trial of Dr. Sacheverell, 171, 281
Annapolis, 270 n. 1
See also Port Royal
Anne, queen of England, 45, 46, 172, 238, 249, 284
compared to William III, 45
devotion to Protestant religion, 183
supports New England, 43, 45
and titles, 271, 272
threatens withdrawal of bounty from Massachusetts, 186, 186 n. 2
and Walker expedition, 283
Antigua, 27
See also Leeward Islands
Arbella, sermon on, xiii
Argoud, sieur de, 197, 198
Armistead, John, 6 n. 3
Ashurst, Sir Henry, provincial agent, 173, 175, 182, 194, 215, 267, 268 n. 1
opposes northern union by Act of Parliament, 117 n. 1
Ayers, Obadiah, 140

Bacon, Nathaniel, president of the Virginia Council, 25
Bahamas, recovery considered, 253
Bannister, Thomas, 126, 285
Barbados, 280
James Kendall appointed governor in, 34
non-jurors in, 28
offers help to Leewards, 28
William III proclaimed in, 28
Barnard, Revd. John, 246 n. 1, 288
Barnstaple (Mass.), 275
Basse, Jeremiah, 172, 194
Bayard, Nicholas, 32
Beaubassin (N.S.), 107, 216
Beaubassin, sieur de, 212
Bedford, first Duke of, see Russell, William
Beeman, Mrs., 139
Belcher, Andrew, Commissary-General, 235, 257
Bellomont, second Earl of, see Coote, Richard
Benbow, vice-Admiral John, 234
Bentinck, William, first Earl of Portland, 173
Berwick (Me.), 213, 214, 247
Beverley (Mass.), 277
Biddeford (Me.), 133
Billerica (Mass.), 101, 218, 277, 279
Bishop, James, deputy governor of Connecticut, 22
Black Point (Me.), 213
Blair, James, 149
Blakiston, Nehemiah, collector of customs, 26
Blathwayt, William, 173, 188, 189, 191, 192, 195, 196, 233
Blenac, Count de, 28
Board of Trade, 166, 183, 192, 193, 195, 220, 221, 232
and attack on Port Royal, 234
and charges against Governor Dudley, 240
and Canada project, 249, 280

Board of Trade and fishery protection,
    230
and Utrecht peace settlement, 273
Bolingbroke, Viscount, *see* St. John,
    Henry
Bonaventure, M. de, 247
Bonavista (Newfoundland), 113, 236
Bond, William, 179
Bonner, Capt. John, 265
Boston (Mass.), 157 n. 4, 160, 163,
    219, 230, 231, 237, 238, 240, 246,
    256, 263, 281
    alarmed, 212
    boats registered at, 151
    and Castle Island, 220, 221, 257
    and Council for the Safety of the
        People, 14
    and crime, 146
    and decline in trade, 228
    and departure of Phips expedition
        for Canada, 90
    and departure of Walker expedi-
        tion, 265
    and dominance as entrepôt, 154
    and dominance of General Assem-
        bly, 179
    and fear of attack, 78 n. 6
    and fever in, 251
    and fire of, 270 n.
    and fortifications, 78, 78 n. 1, 220
    and French threat to, 210, 226, 269
    and grammar school at, 131
    and herring boats in, 150
    and illegal trading, 155 n. 3
    and impressment by Royal Navy,
        231
    and north church of, 174
    and Port Royal
        forces gathered for attack on, 247,
            257
        reception of unsuccessful troops
            from, 247
        reception of victorious troops,
            258
    printing press in, 147
    prosperity of, 280
    protected from Indian depreda-
        tions, 279
    and refugees, 82
    and revolution in, 9–15, 70
    and trade with mainland colonies,
        154
    and vessels using port, 152

Boston News-Letter, 111, 147, 166,
    202, 227, 229 n. 2, 236 n. 2, 241
Boucherville (New France), 142
Bowman, Henry, 25
Boyle, Henry, sec. of state, 249, 257
Bradford (Mass.), 277
Bradstreet, Simon, governor of Mass-
    achusetts, 83, 89, 123
Braintree (Mass.), 151, 169, 275
Brattle Street Church, 125, 126
Brattle, Thomas, 122, 125, 126, 127,
    220
Brattle, William, 122, 125–9
Bray, Dr. Thomas, 147, 169, 172
Bridger, Jonathan, H.M. Surveyor
    General of Woods in America,
    270 (Forts)
Bridgewater (Mass.), 275
Bridgewater, third Earl of, *see* Eger-
    ton, John
Bristol (Mass.), 275
Bristol co. (Mass.), 164, 167, 275
Brooke, Chidley, 109
Brookfield (Mass.), 101, 102, 218, 259,
    270
Brouillan, M. de, 113, 207, 237 n. 3
Bruyas, Fr. James, S.J., 201
Bull, Henry, governor of Plymouth
    colony, 23
Bulkeley, Gershom, 4 n. 2, 22
Buzzard's Bay (Mass.), 164
Byfield, Nathaniel, 14 n. 2, 180, 181
Byrd, II, William, 147, 149

Cadaracqui, fort at, 205
Callières, Louis Hector, chevalier de,
    governor of Montreal, 197, 199,
    204, 213
Calvert, Charles, third Lord Balti-
    more, 3, 5, 7, 19
Cambridge (Mass.), 131, 151, 170,
    264
Canada, 228, 242, 253, 273
    and projects for conquest of, xiii,
        77, 89, 108, 113 (*see also* Walker
        expedition)
    expedition, diverted to Port Royal,
        252
    and Marlborough, 256
    and Phips expedition, 90, 107
        English losses, 92
        consequences of, 92–3, 149
    See also New France

Cape Ann, 169
Cape Breton Isle, 266, 273
Cape Cod, 276, vulnerability of, 279
Cape Nègre (Newfoundland), 113
Cape Newaggin (N.S.), 209
Cape Race (Newfoundland), 114
Cape Sable (N.S.), 209
  maritime losses off, 226
  fishery protection of, 230
Carbonear (Newfoundland), 113, 236
Carolina, 3
  insurrection in, 29
  traders of, 237
Casco Bay (Falmouth), 85, 86, 133,
  156, 207, 208, 211, 212, 215, 225,
  247
Chamberlayne, Willoughby, 5, 28
Champigny, Jean Bochart de, in-
  tendant of New France, 74, 199
Charles co. (Md.), 20
Charles II of England, x, 3
Charles II of Spain, 199, 271
Charles III of Spain, 271
Charleston (Mass.), 146, 131, 151, 152
Charleston (S.C.), 146
Chelmsford (Mass.), 218, 259, 270, 279
Chesapeake colonies, 251 (see also
  Maryland; Virginia)
Cheseldyne, Kenelm, speaker of Md.
  Assembly, 20
Chignecto Bay (N.S.), 107
Child, Sir Josiah, ix, 54
Chilmark (Mass.), 276
Chilton, Edward, 149
Chingford (Mass.), 180
Chubb, Captain,
  surrenders Pemaquid, 106
Church, Col. Benjamin, 85, 100, 107,
  200, 215
Churchill, Dr., chief pastor of Jam-
  aica, 4
Churchill, John, first Duke of Marl-
  borough, 252, 256, 271, 272
Churchill, Sarah, Duchess of Marl-
  borough, 262 n. 3
Clarke, Capt. Timothy, 220, 221
Clarke, Walter, governor of Rhode
  Island, 23
Cochecho (Dover, N. H.), 81 n. 2
Codrington, Christopher, appointed
  governor of Leeward Islands, 33
Coinage, royal proclamation of rates,
  158

Colbert, Jean-Baptiste, marquis de
  Seignelay, 74, 75, 197
Colchester (Mass.), 153
Colman, Revd. Benjamin, 122, 125,
  128, 167, 170
Collins, James, 25
Conception Bay (Newfoundland), 115,
  116
Concord (Hampshire co., Mass.), 219
Concord (Middlesex co., Mass.), 277
Connecticut, 3, 87, 88, 90, 107, 115–
  117, 130, 153, 193, 194, 196, 213
  n. 4, 214–15, 229, 249
  and defence of Connecticut valley,
    103, 215
  and farm produce, 154
  illegal trade of, 280
  and legislation against heretics, 165
  militia control passes to New York,
    104
  ordered to co-operate with New
    York, 108
  provincial government resumed, 22
  quota for Canada project, 261 n. 3,
    264 n. 2
  refuses help against Port Royal,
    256
  support requested by Massachu-
    setts for national war, 100
  supports Canada project, 250
  and transports for Port Royal, 256
  and Utrecht peace settlement, 274
  See also individual towns
Connecticut valley, 126, 127, 132, 138,
  140, 209, 212, 219, 225, 279
Converse, Capt., 100, 104
Coode, John, militia captain in Maryland, 20, 21
Cooke, Elisha, Senior, 123
  alliance with Bellomont, 175
  attitude towards 1691 charter, 51,
    184
  leads Country Party, 120
  promotes Wait Winthrop for gover-
    nor of Massachusetts, 182
Coote, Richard, second Earl of Bellomont, governor of New York and
  New England, 68, 69 n. 1, 114,
  118, 150, 157, 174, 175, 182, 204,
  205, 271, 285, 286
Cornbury, Viscount, see Edward
  Hyde, Viscount Cornbury and
  third Earl of Clarendon

Costibelle, M. de, governor at Placentia, 260
Courtemanche, sieur de, 237
Cowassic, Indian strongpoint, 214, 215
Coxe, Dr. Daniel, 198
Culpeper, Lord Thomas, governor of Virginia, 7
Cutts, Lord John, Baron of Gowran, 173

Darnall, Henry, Maryland councillor, 20, 21
Dartmouth (Mass.), 275
Dartmouth, second Baron and first Earl of, see Legge, William
Davenant, Charles, English propagandist, 198
Davis, Capt., 270
Dedham (Mass.), 276
Deerfield (Mass.), 101, 102, 137, 139, 140, 214, 215, 218, 225, 241, 278-80
Delanoy, Peter, 117 n. 1
Denonville, René de Brisay, marquis de, governor of New France, 76, 200
Denys, La Ronde, 260, 267 n. 2
Deshayes, Jean, hydrographer royal, 148
Detroit, fort at, 200, 209
Digges, Col., Maryland councillor, 20
Dongan, Thomas, governor of New York, 8, 76, 87, 248
Dorchester (Mass.), 153, 276
Dover (N. H.), 136, 211, 217, 247, 270
Dracut (Mass.), 219, 277, 279
Dudley, Joseph, governor of Massachusetts, 9, 36, 45, 46, 69 n. 1, 123, 128, 151, 156, 157, 160 n. 1, 166, 172, 173, 173 n. 1, 174, 177, 178, 180, 183-6, 188, 192-5, 206, 208-11, 213-15, 217, 219, 221, 224, 226, 228, 231, 233, 235, 237, 238-40, 243, 245-9, 270, 274, 280, 289
Dudley, Samuel, 64
Dudley, William, 237, 240 n. 4
Dummer, Jeremiah, provincial agent for Massachusetts, 229 n. 3, 254, 259, 267, 268
Dunstable (Mass.), 218, 225, 239
Durham (N.H.), 85
Du Ru, Paul, S.J., 201

Duxbury (Mass.), 276

Eastham (Mass.), 276
Easthampton (N.Y.), 16
Edgarstown (Mass.), 276
Edward I, king of England, 186 n. 2
Effingham, Lord Howard of, 6, 26
Egerton, Charles, 6
Egerton, John, third Earl of Bridgewater, president of the Board of Trade, 190
Eliot, John,
    archetypal New Englander, 56
    importance in spreading gospel to Indians, 55
Ellwood, Thomas, 165
Enfield (Mass.), 278
English colonial policy, 189
    and attack on colonial charters, 193-5
    and Canada project, 251
    and creation of Board of Trade, 189
    and Customs Commissioners, 190
    and defence, 107
    and imperial centralization, 2, 189, 195
    and mercantile objectives, 31
    and Navigation Act of 1696, 190
    and Newfoundland, 236
    and proprietary power, 193
    and requisitions, 107
    and support for Port Royal project, 255-7
    and suspicion of New Englanders, 262
    and the Treasury, 191, 192
Essex co. (Mass.), 101, 130, 212-14
Exeter (N. H.), 87, 217, 247, 270

Falmouth (Mass.), 164
Fermouse (Newfoundland), 113
Ferryland (Newfoundland), 113, 236
Field, John, 165
Finch, Daniel, second Earl of Nottingham, 208, 233 n. 3
Flanders, 267
Fletcher, Benjamin, governor of New York, 109, 111
Forest, Fr. de, 5
Forillon (Newfoundland), 113
Forts
    Albany (Hudson's Bay), 112
    Anne, 78, 80

Bon Secours (Lake Pepin), 197
Casco, 212, 244
Frontenac, 142
Hill (Boston), 78 n. 6
James (New York), 17
Loyal, 78, 80, 86, 212 n. 4
Newcastle (William and Mary, N.H), 224, 232
Pemaquid, 78, 94, 183, 183 n. 2, 206, 209, 219, 220, 225, 232
    captured, 85, 106
    cost of building, 220 n. 1
    French decline to attack, 105
    guns recovered from, 86
    peace conference with Indians at, 105
    rebuilding begins, 100, 104
    rebuilding reconsidered, 183, 187
    trading post at, 156
Pojebscot, abandoned, 80, 100
Saco, 78, 225
Sagadahoc, 80
Teconnet (Winslow), 104
William Henry, 114
York (Hudson's Bay), 112
Fortune (Newfoundland), 113
Foster, John, 187 n. 2
Foxcroft, Justice Francis, 12, 180 n. 1
Framingham (Mass.), 219
France, 272, 274, 282, 283
Franklin, Benjamin, ix
Freeman, Nathaniel, 134
Freetown (Mass.), 275
French Empire, see New France
Frontenac, Louis de Buade, comte de, governor of New France, xiii, 74, 94, 112, 200, 204
    expansionist aims of, 197
    frontier policy of, 84
    plans conquest of New York, 77
    recall of, 76
Fundy, Bay of (N.S.), 88, 107, 247
    naval patrol in, 99

Gannock, William, 26
Gaultier, Abbé Francois de, 288
Gayhead (Mass.), 229 n. 4
Gedney, Col. Bartholomew, 107
George, Capt., R.N., 12, 96
Gibraltar, 272
Glorious Revolution of 1688, x, 1, 202
Gloucester (Mass.), 151, 230, 277

Godolphin, Sidney, first Earl of, lord treasurer, 189, 190, 192, 256, 271
Gookin, Charles, governor of Pennsylvania, 251
Grand Pré (Minas, N.S.), 216
Graydon, vice-Admiral John, 235
Grayfoot, Bridget, 136
Groton (Mass.), 105, 217–19
Guadeloupe, 27
Guilford (Conn.), 153

Hadley (Mass.), 138, 218, 225, 278
Hampshire co. (Mass.), 84, 101, 102, 138–9, 219 n. 1
Hampton (N.H.), 164
Hanover (Mass.), 151, 153
Harley, Robert, first Earl of Oxford and Mortimer, 250, 259, 271, 272
Harrison, Buer, 26
Harrison, Edmund, 116, 117
Harvard College, 127, 128, 178, 287
    and graduates, 131
    and proposals for new charter, 128, 130
Harwich (Mass.), 132, 275
Hastings, Dr., 138
Hastings, Thomas, 138
Hatfield (Mass.), 102, 138, 214 n. 3, 218, 225, 278, 279
Haverhill (Mass.), 136–8, 140, 164, 167, 211, 212, 214, 217, 218, 277
Hawthorn, Col. John, 107
Heathcote, Caleb, 152
Heather, William, 26
Hedges, Sir Charles, 194
Hennepin, Fr. Louis, 148, 197
Henry III of England, 186 n. 2
Hertel, M. Francois, 86
Higginson, John, 122, 127
Hill, Abigail, Lady Masham, 262 n. 3
Hill, Brigadier-General Jack, 262 n. 3, 264, 266
Hilton, Col., 200, 259
Hinckley, Thomas, governor of Plymouth colony, 23
H.M.S. Arundel, 97, 208
    Chester, 229, 253, 256
    Conception Prize, 97, 99
    Deptford, 227, 244, 245
    Dragon, 256
    Edgar, 265
    Falkland, 99
    Falmouth, 256

H.M.S. *Feversham*, 256
 Gosport, 208, 226, 228
 Jersey, 208
 Litchfield, 227
 Lowestoft, 227, 256
 Mary, 79, 94
 Nonesuch, 95, 97
 Orford, 97, 99
 Oxford, 227
 Rochfort, 256
 Rose, 12, 14
 Sapphire, 266
 Speedwell, 79, 94
 Strombula, 227
 Swift, 231
Hopewood, Indian chief, 86
Holmes, Capt. William, 113
Howe, John, 166
Hubbard, William, 69
Hudson's Bay, 107, 112, 200
Hull (Mass.), 208, 276
Huntington (N.Y.), 16
Hutchinson, Elisha, 220, 246
Hutchinson, Thomas, historian, 85,
 175 n. 2, 247, 262, 263, 270 n. 1
Hunter, Robert, governor of New
 York, 289
Hyde, Edward, Viscount Cornbury
 and third Earl of Clarendon, 152,
 170, 194, 195, 221, 248, 250

Iberville, Pierre Le Moyne Sieur de,
 assaults Pemaquid, 106
 and Louisiana, 197–9, 201, 209
 tactical innovations of, 112, 113
Indians:
 Eastern Indians—
  Abenaki (Tarrentines), 89, 100,
   205, 206, 211, 213, 237, 238,
   270, 271
  Canibas (probably Penobscots),
   81
  Etechemins, 200
  Kennebecs, 200
  Norridgewocks, 105, 210
  Pennacooks, 8, 211, 225
  Penobscots, 200, 206, 212
  Sokokis, 81
 Cape Sable Indians (Micmacs),
  211
 Arkansas, 201
 Malicites, 81
 Micmacs, 81

Fox, 76
Iroquois, Confederacy of the Five
 Nations (Cayugas, Mohawks,
 Oneidas, Onondagas, Senecas),
 75, 76, 206
 and fur trade, 75
 christianised community at Sault
  St. Louis, 201
 defection of, 232, 237
 excluded from Peace of Ryswick,
  204
 and Jesuits, 201, 206
 Mohawks—
  almost extinct, 204
  army of, 105
  criticise Boston government, 78
 Oneidas, 201
 Onondagas, 205
 Senecas, 25
 proposal to send leaders to Lon-
  don, 254
 reach Michilimackinac, 76
 renew friendship with English,
  205
 shield New York settlements, 109
 Miamis, 76
 Missouri, 201
 Nanticoke, 26
 Osages, 201
 Ottawas, 76
 Oumas, 201
 Tonicas, 201
Isle Dauphine, Louisiana, 202
Isle aux Œufs, 268
Isle of Shoals (N.H), 209

Jacobites, 24, 24 n. 1, 53 n. 3, 171,
 174, 182, 283, 285, 289
Jamaica, 192, 233, 234
 martial law in, 29
 and Utrecht peace settlement, 274
Jamaica (Mass.), 164
Jamaica (N.Y.), 16
James II of England, xi, 2, 5, 8, 10,
 12, 16, 17, 20, 22, 35, 40, 66, 118,
 185, 283
Jephson, William, sec. to William III,
 13 n. 1
 and circular letter to colonies, 35
Jesuits, 5, 201, 205, 206
Johnson, Nathaniel, governor of Leeward Islands, 27, 169
Joliet, Louis, French explorer, 75

Jordan, Capt. Robert, 6
Joseph, William, President of Maryland Council, 21
Jowles, Henry, 20

Keith, George, 170
Kennebunk (Me.), 133, 212
Kennet, White, Dean of Peterborough, 170
Kidd, Capt. William, 157
King, Col. Richard, 262, 264 n. 3
Kittery (Me.), 133, 217, 239 n. 3, 278

La Chauchetière, Fr. de, 144
Lachine (New France), 142
La Hogue, naval battle, 110
Lahontan, Louis Armand, baron de, 143
Lake Atibibi, 76
Lake Champlain, 90
Lake Nipigon, 76
Lambert, George, 26
Lancaster (Mass.), 101, 139, 217, 218, 277
La Prairie de-la-Magdeleine (New France), 142
La Rochelle, France, 258
La Ronde Denys, M. de, 260
Larrimore, Capt. Thomas, 233, 235
La Salle, Robert Cavalier, sieur de, French explorer, 197
Laval, Francois Xavier de Montmorency, b. of Quebec, 74, 142
Lawson, John, 148
Leake, Capt. John, governor at St. John's, 235
Le Blonde de la Tour, Jacques, 144
Le Clerq, Fr. Chrétien, 148
Leeds, Duke of, see Osborne, Thomas
Leeward Islands:
    fears of French invasion, 28
    Irish Catholics in, x, 27, 207
    New England compassion for, 235, 286
    and Utrecht peace settlement, 273
Legge, Samuel, 180
Legge, William, second Baron and first Earl of Dartmouth, 256
Leiden, 286
Leisler, Jacob, 3, 17, 18, 31, 34
    more to reverse attainder against, 173
    refuses to acknowledge royal governor, 33

Leverett, John, president of Harvard, 122, 125, 128, 129, 188, 246
L'Hermitage (Newfoundland), 113
Little Compton (Mass.), 169, 275
Littleton, Edward, 68 n. 2
Livingston, Robert, 205
Lords of Trade, 97, 99, 111
    and centralization, 35
    consider re-unifying northern colonies, 117-18
    inquire about colonial defences, 80
    and Massachusetts charter (1691), 36
    and ordnance for Massachusetts, 80
Louis XIV of France, 3, 30, 43, 45, 63, 72, 77, 182, 197, 199, 200, 202, 238, 273, 284
Louisiana, 128, 209
    and Canadian settlers, 198
    and climate, 198
    and Jesuits, 202
    and Louis XIV, 199
    and trade goods for New France, 199
Lynn (Mass.), 164, 165, 277

Machias Bay (Me.), 216
Madockawando, Indian chief, 105
Maine, 36, 132, 134, 140, 216, 217, 273
    barbarism in, 218
    and French raiding parties, 243
    and frontier defence, 100
    and new settlement in, 187
    and shipbuilding in, 151
    and suffering in Spanish Succession War, 209
    and vulnerable seaboard, 279
    See also Acadia; individual towns
Makemie, Francis, 122
Manchester (Mass.), 230
Marblehead (Mass.), 169, 180, 208, 223, 265, 277
March, Col. John, 244, 246
Marlborough (Mass.), 212, 216, 218, 219, 247, 259, 270
Marquette, Fr., S.J., 75
Marshfield (Mass.), 275
Martha's Vineyard (Mass.), 229 n. 4
Martin, Capt., 225
Martinique, 5, 7, 28
Mary II, queen of England, 15, 17, 19, 22, 41, 62

Maryland, 3, 5, 7, 192
  and clash between proprietors and
    lower house, 19
  and Protestant Association, 20
  and Protestant fear of conspiracy,
    7, 20
  and revolution in, 19–21, 24, 30
  and support for New York, 108, 111
Mason, George, 26, 26 n. 4
Massachusetts, 132, 175, 191, 194,
    195, 196, 213, 224, 243, 249
  accepts monarchy, 40
  adultery in, 147
  and bad kings, 40
  and Boston regiment, 80
  and British at Harvard commence-
    ment, 264
  and British imperial power, 260
  and burden of taxation, 159
  and charter of 1629, 9
  and charter of 1691, 52, 164
  and chartered liberties, 39
  and clashes with Col. Romer, 221
  and coasting trade, 229
  and compassion for St. Christo-
    phers, 235
  and convention of 1689, 15
  and criticism of merchants, 263 n. 1
  and decline in trade, 228
  and defeat of French landing party,
    164
  and defence problems, 102
  and desertion from British forces,
    263, 267
  and draft Proposals of ministers,
    124, 166
  and drunkenness in, 146
  and ecclesiastical legislation, 162–3,
    167
  and Education Act of 1647, 130
  and election sermons in, 164, 255
  and election of 1706, 239
  and emigration, 269
  and English nation, 238
  and failure of Port Royal expedition,
    245
  and financial exhaustion, 105, 269,
    274
  and fisheries and fur trade, 66
  and fortifications, 186, 220
  and French privateers, 227, 229,
    229 n. 4, 248
  and French proposals for truce, 237

  and gains from provisioning British
    forces, 157
  and General Court, 92, 137, 156, 163,
    174–6, 178, 218, 230, 238, 239,
    243, 250, 257, 258, 263, 264, 274
  appoints special committee for
    frontier defence, 83
  and Bills of Credit, 263
  compared to other provincial
    assemblies, 187
  urges further English attempt
    against Canada, 269
  and provincial debt, 274
  and gunpowder supply, 225 n. 3
  hegemony of, 66
  import bill lowered, 153
  and illegal trade, 280, 281
  and Israel, xii
  and King Philip's War, xii, 1, 10,
    84 n. 3
  and legislation, 179
  and Levellism, avoidance of, 49
  and maritime wealth, 150
  and militia, 79, 80 n. 3, 211
  and Murmuring, 50
  and naval protection, 227, 230
  and need to assist rulers, 50
  notified of renewal of war, 208
  and obedience, 50
  and opposition to the Mathers
    leadership, 124
  and opposition to mercantile legis-
    lation, 68
  ordered to support New York, 111,
    111 n. 2
  and ordnance, 232–3
  and paper money, 158–9
  and partnership with old England,
    232, 289
  and population in, 39 n. 1
  and prisoners of French, 239
  and privateering, 227, 248
  and protected localities, 278
  and provisioning Newfoundland,
    281 n. 1
  and purposeful past, 38
  and Quakers, 163
  and reasons for renewed assault on
    Port Royal, 246
  and rebuke by Board of Trade, 166
  and religious toleration, 10
  and renewal of Indian attacks
    (1706), 239

and Revolution, avoidance of, 49
requests neighbours to share defence costs, 88
and role of governor after 1691, 177
and salary of governor, 185–7
and shipbuilding, 151
and stores of war, 93, 208
supported by Connecticut and Plymouth, 85
and trade with the enemy, 239
and veto of councillors by governor, 184
and vulnerability, 278, 279
See also individual towns of; New England
Mather, Cotton, 203
and Canada project, 251, 268
and charter privileges, 52, 55
and Decennium Luctuosum, 61, 114, 119 n. 1, 149
describes countrymen as English, 87 n. 1
and Duodecennium, 274, 280, 281
and importance of New England, 283
and 'leprosy of sin', 147
library of, 147
and Magnalia Christi Americana, 70, 149, 166
and Peace of Ryswick, 118
and pessimistic view of New England, 61
and Phips expedition to Canada, 94
and Political Fables, 178
preaches on Heads of Agreement, 166
and Protestant succession, 41
and reaction to fall of Pemaquid, 106
and religious achievements of the English nation, 59
and reputation of New Englanders, 56
and selfishness of New Englanders, 58
Mather, Increase, 4 n. 1, 4 n. 2, 11, 122, 123, 125, 128, 163, 176, 188, 203, 267 n. 1, 283
assumes partnership with old England, 37, 176
and charter of 1691, 51
co-operates with English dissenters, 166

fails to restore charter of 1629, 36
and George Keith, 170
and King Philip's War, 69
and organization of New England Churches, 123
and praise for King William and Queen Mary, 42
and protection for Harvard, 40
and sabbath-breaking in Boston, 270 n. 1
and William Stoughton, 181
Mather, Samuel, 13
Matthews, Capt., R. N., 239
Mead, Matthew, 166
Medfield (Mass.), 276
Mendon (Mass.), 276
Michilimackinac, fort at, 209
Mico, John, 126
Middleburgh (Mass.), 275
Middlesex co. (Mass.), 101, 130, 212, 213, 277
Milford (Conn.), 226
Milet, Fr. Peter S.J., 201
Milton (Mass.), 276
Minorca, 272
Mistick (? Mystick River, Mass.), 140
Mobile, 201, 202
Molesworth, Hender, governor of Jamaica, 29
Monck, George, Duke of Albemarle, 4, 29
Monegin (Monhegan) Island, 209
Montgomery, Sir Thomas, 5, 28
Montreal, 72, 90, 197, 205, 249
Moody, Joshua, 135
Moody, Revd. Samuel, 134
Morse, Mary, 270 n. 1
Mount Desart, 88, 211, 216
Moxus, Abenaki chief, 105, 206, 211

Nantasket (Mass.), 88, 257
Nantucket (Mass.), 275, 276
Neal, Daniel, historian, 285, 286
Nelson, John, leads Massachusetts insurrection, 11, 14 n. 1, 88
Netherlands, and New England, 282
Nevis, 27, 28; and see Leeward Islands
Newbury (Mass.), 140, 164, 169, 277, 279
New England, 10, 209
and Ancient Israel, xii, 57
and Anglican Church, 7, 288–9

New England and Anglo-Scottish
    Union, 285
and Armageddon, 65 n. 2
arrogance of, 69
assurance of, 70
and British defence expenditure,
    280
and Canada project, 71
    arrival of Nicholson in Boston,
        261
    British fleet diverted to Portugal,
        252
    cost of preparations for, 253
    distrust of English leaders by
        New Englanders, 261
    enthusiasm for, 250
    influences reputation of New
        Englanders in England, 262,
        266–7
    revived, 254, 259, 261
and captives of New France, 237
    n. 4
and Christian attitude to war, 64,
    65
and collapse of theocracy, 61
and concern of Board of Trade for,
    232
and confluence with Anglo-Scottish
    interests, 250
and courage of inhabitants, 54, n. 1
and covenant with God, 56
and decline of spiritual awareness,
    121
and disallowed legislation, 131
and disobedience, 69
and Divine Law, 47
Dominion of, 3, 7, 23, 77, 87, 114,
    120, 189, 191, 283
and drain on manpower, 231
and the Dunstans, Thomas and
    Hannah, 281
and educational system,
    compulsory elements, 130
    purposes of, 129
and economic relationship with
    England, 68
and English destiny, 242
and English interest in Newfound-
    land, 113
and the English nation, 59–60, 62,
    68, 71, 202–3,
and English reading public, 69, 70
and English rights, 68

and English writers,
    Defoe, Daniel, 281–2
    Evelyn, John, 281 n. 2
    Luttrell, Narcissus, 281 n. 2, 288
    Oldmixon, John, 285–6
    Swift, Jonathan, 281 n. 2
    Wood, William, 281 n. 2
and European protestantism, 59
and European victories of Britain,
    241, 242
and French privateers, 95, 226 n. 4,
    227
and fear of dissolution, 61
and fear of Indian rising, 12
and the French menace, 66
and French warships, 95
and Frontenac, 63
and Harrington's Oceana, 289
and illegal trade in, 280
and importance of family life, 57
and imports, 153
and instruction of youth, 58
and Louis XIV, 63
and loyalty to the Crown, 287
and mercantile elements in, 120
and migration from, 231n, 4
and militia, 79
and naval patrols, 96
and naval stores, 68, 153, 249
and need for internal unity, 58
and neutrality of New York, 232
and New England Company, 194
and Newfoundland, 236
and notion of pre-eminence, 53
and notion of separateness, 55
and Occasional Conformity Bill,
    171, 284
and Peace of Ryswick, 204
and piracy, attitude towards, 157
and price of provisions, 152
and privateering, 210, 230, 231
and proprietary charters, 194
and Protestant interest, 59, 241
and Quaker persecution, 70
and rejection of James II, 66
and religion's loss of dynamic force,
    132
and resemblance to old England,
    59, 287
and respect for cultural foundations,
    61
and rumour of war with France, 207
and re-unification, 115

and Sagadahoc fort, 80
and sentimental attachment to old England, 67
and success on the eastern frontier, 243
and trade,
  cost of protection, 161
  in furs, 156
  with Newfoundland, 153, 155
  with southern Europe, 153
  in specie, 155
  with West Indies, 155
and Turkish power, 63, 67
and Universal Monarchy, 70, 202, 241, 260, 281
and utility of garrison houses, 82, 83
and Utrecht peace settlement, 274
and vulnerability of sea-coast, 226
and Walker expedition, 159, 167
and West Indian expedition, 226 n. 3
and Whigs and Tories, 283–5
and woollen manufacturing, 68, 153
See also Connecticut; Maine; Massachusetts; New Hampshire; Rhode Island; individual towns
Newfoundland:
  and attack on St. John's, 235–6
  Banks of, 234
  and check to British, 236
  cession of French possessions demanded, 271
  and fishery, 118
  and importance to New Englanders, 112–15, 281
  and Jamaica expedition, 234, 235
  and Utrecht, 272–4
  and post-war boom, 280
New France:
  and abandonment of western posts, 197
  and brandy trade, 73
  and defence of Ohio valley, 197, 200
  and education, 142–4
  and exploration of Mississippi, 75
  and fur trade, 73, 75, 196
  and *habitants*, 73, 112
  and intendants, 142
  and missions, 200, 201, 202
  and Mississippi, 197, 198
  and precarious hold in Maine, 200
  and regained prestige among Indians, 77
  and role of Church, 74, 196

and successes in Hudson's Bay, 76
and system of government, 72, 73
and Sulpicians, 201
New Hampshire:
  and attacks on Dover, 84, 106
  and attacks on Oyster River, 85, 105, 217, 247
  and attack on Portsmouth, 106
  and attack on Salmon Falls, 86
  and emigration of young men, 269 n. 1
  and financial exhaustion, 269
  and loan of men and stores by Massachusetts, 79 n. 2
  and lumber, 153, 154
  and manpower resources and militia, 79 n. 2, 103
  and military control by Massachusetts, 79 n. 2
  and naval stores in, 153
  and political fears of proprietors, 103, 116
  and population, 39 n. 1, 159
  and Quakers, 164, 165 n. 1
  and transports for Port Royal project, 256
  See also individual towns
New Jersey, 3, 117, 168
  support for New York, 111
  opposition to Canada project, 251
  proprietors yield political power, 195
  quotas for Canada project, 251 n. 3, 264 n. 4
New Jersey, East, 23, 24, 227
New Jersey, West, 23
Newmarch, Revd. John, 133
Newmarket (N.H.), 87
Newport (R.I.), 157
New York, 3, 5, 8, 22, 24, 175, 191, 193, 195, 205, 207, 209, 221, 227, 232, 238, 256, 260
  and Albany front, 107, 109, 111, 114, 118
  and Albany traders, 240
  and Committee of Safety, 18
  and fears of conquest, 76
  and fear of Irish papists, 16
  and inter-colonial conference, 87
  and Jesuit school, 17
  and neutrality, 237–8, 240
  and news of William of Orange's landing, 15

New York and privateers off Sandy Hook, 227
and quotas for Canada project, 261 n. 3, 264 n. 2
and raid on Schenectady, 32, 77, 86, 205
and plot against liberties, 8
and revolution in, 15–19
and royal government in, 31
and union with New England, 115–18
and Utrecht peace settlement, 273
and Virginia tobacco fleet, 227
New York city:
administrative machinery of, 16
crime in, 146
Nicholson, Sir Francis, lieutenant-governor of New York, 8, 15–18, 33, 193, 207 n. 3, 228, 249, 251, 254, 256, 257, 258, 261, 266, 268, 269, 273, 288
Norridgewock (Me.), 215, 217
Northampton (Mass.), 214, 218, 225, 278
Northfield (Mass.), 101, 102
Nottingham, second Earl of, see Finch, Daniel
Nova Scotia, 88, 107, 176, 209, 216, 239, 247, 248, 253, 259, 273, 285
and arrival of Brouillan, 207
and capture of St. John, 157
and French warships off coast, 94
and patrol in Bay of Fundy, 99
and New England council in, 89
and oath of loyalty to King William, 89
See also Port Royal
Noyes, Nicholas, 122, 127

Oakes, Thomas, 184, 185
O'Brien, William, Earl of Inchiquin, governor of Jamaica, 33
Oldmixon, John, historian, 149, 285
and Cotton Mather, 287
and New England's economic value, 286
Osborne, Thomas, first Earl of Danby and Duke of Leeds, 230

Paddon, Capt. R. N., 265
Panama, bishop of, 5
Paquasset (Me.), 211

Paradis, Capt., French prisoner of war, 265
Parkman, Francis, historian, 218
Pemasquoddy (Eastport, Me.), 216
Pemberton, Revd. Ebenezer, 122, 128, 255
Penhallow, Samuel, 135
Penhallow, Samuel, historian, 285, 286
Penn, William, 24, 165, 194, 195
Pennacook (Me.), 271
Pennsylvania, 1, 7, 168, 193
and charter, 172, 194
and educational plans, 141
and Jacobitism, 24 n. 1
and James II, 24
and military control by New York, 33
and New York's request for aid, 111
and Quaker opposition to Canada project, 251
and quotas for Canada project, 251 n. 3, 264 n. 4
Penobscot, 88, 270
Pequawket (Fryeburg, Me.), 81
Petkum, Hermann, 271
Petre, Fr., 5
Phelps, Isaac, 139
Philip, duke of Anjou (Philip V of Spain), 199, 156
Phillipse, Frederick, 32
Phips, Constantine, Massachusetts agent, 173, 175, 188
Phippis, Thomas, 135
Phips, William, governor of Massachusetts, 88, 104, 108, 109, 172, 173, 174, 177, 179, 187 n. 2, 271
and Assembly of 1694, 180
and Canada (1690) expedition, 90
and criticism of, 93–4
and dismissal of Speaker of the House, 181
and expedition against Port Royal (1690), 88, 156
and Indian hostages, 206
and New England militia, 102
and quarrels with naval captains, 98
and refusal to support Albany front, 109
Pickering, Capt., 230
Pigeon, Major, 254
Pike, Henry, 25
Pike, Major Robert, 100

Piracy, legislation against, 69 n. 1, 158
Piscataqua (N.H.), 188, 230
Placentia (Newfoundland), 113, 235, 236
Plymouth (Mass), 36, 37, 87, 88, 208
   and population, 39 n. 1
Pointe-aux Tremble (New France), 142
Pointe Levis (New France), 142
Pointe-Verte (Newfoundland), 113
Pontchartrain, Jerome Phélypeaux de, 238, 260
   resists abandonment of Louisiana, 199
Pontchartrain, Louis Phélypeaux de, and Louisiana, 198
   orders abandonment of western posts, 197
Port Biloxi, 201
Portland, Earl of, see Bentinck, William
Port Mahon, 272
Portneuf, 86, 101
Port Royal (N.S.), 115, 143, 156, 215, 217, 226, 228, 236 n. 1., 242, 244, 245, 252, 253, 255, 259
   assault rejected by naval captains, 253
   expedition against, 88, 89
   capture urged, 228, 235
   English fleet before, 257
   failure of expedition, 245
   and French privateers, 226 n. 3
   and fur trade, 156
   projected revived, 255
   surrender of, 258
Portsmouth (N.H.), 135, 216, 271
Portugal, 267
Prior, Matthew, negotiates peace terms, 272, 285
Province Galley, 97, 99
Province Snow, 216
Provincial sloops, 79, 99, 209, 229, 231 n. 4, 244, 256
Purpooduck (Me.), 86, 212
Pye, Edward, Maryland councillor, 20

Quary, Robert, 189, 193, 195, 228, 246 n. 1, 249, 281
   and Boston's trade, 280
Quebec, 72, 90, 91, 112, 142, 200, 205, 211, 226, 237, 248, 266, 267, 269
   French fleet arrives at, 94
   and Newfoundland refugees, 112

provisions captured, 210
   strengthened, 205
Queens (N.Y.), 16
Quochecho (see Cochecho)

Râle, Fr., S.J., 200
Randolph, Edward, 3, 9, 14, 30, 36, 69, 150, 172, 178, 189, 190, 191, 192, 193, 220 n. 2
Raymond, a Virginian priest, 6
Redknap, Col. John, royal engineer, 225, 244, 245, 270
Rehoboth (Mass.), 153
Rémonville, sieur de, of Louisiana, 197
Rhode Island, 23, 107, 115–17, 130, 193–6, 213 n. 4, 226, 228, 229, 244
   and Block Island,
   frigates patrol, 226
   plundered by privateers, 95
   ships seized by French, 96, 99
   and foreign coin in, 154
   and French privateers, 229
   ordered to co-operate with New York, 108, 111
   and population, 39 n. 1
   and quotas for Canada project, 261 n. 3
   replaces Boston as privateer base, 231
   and threat to charter, 172
   and transports for Port Royal project, 256
   and zeal for Canada project, 250
Richards, John, 139
Richmond's Island (Me.), 209
Rivers:
   Androscoggin, 74, 84, 100
   Arkansas, 198
   Canada (see St. Lawrence), 267
   Chaudière, 200, 201
   Damariscotta, 78, 104
   Hudson, 209
   Kennebec, 78, 84, 104, 200, 206, 210, 217, 271
   Lampereel, 87
   Merrimac, 80
   Mississippi, 284
   Missouri, 198
   Nashua, 217
   Penobscot, 104, 109, 206, 210, 215, 270

Rivers (*contd*):
  Piscataway, 224
  Richelieu, 72
  Saco, 224
  St. Croix, 206, 215
  St. John (Me.), 200
  St. Lawrence, 266, 269, 284
  Sheepscot, 104
  Wabash, 201
  Wisconsin, 75
Rochefort, 258
Rochester (Mass.), 275
Rognouse (Newfoundland), 113
Romer, Capt. Wolfgang, royal engineer, 220, 221, 224, 225
Rowlandson, Mary, 69, 69 n. 1, 281
Rowse, William, 230, 240
Roxbury (Mass.), 131, 276
Ruddick, Henry, 6
Rulers:
  Character of a Good Ruler, 48
  dangers of incapacity, 50
  Gods vicegerents, 47
  and promotion of religion, 48
  and royal birthdays, 45
  and royal governors, 44
  and stewardship, 48
  transgressions of, 48
Russell, William, first Duke of Bedford, 230
Ryswick, Peace of, 118, 204, 208

Saco (Me.), 87, 105, 156, 207, 211, 212
Saffin, John, 184
St. Bartholomew (W.I.), 273
Saint-Castin, Baron de, 85, 88, 101, 106, 216
Ste. Famille (New France), 142
Ste. Foy (New France), 142
St. Joachim, 142
St. John, Henry, Viscount Bolingbroke, 192, 259, 272, 273
St. John (N.S.), 115
St. John's (Newfoundland), 235
St. Martin (W.I.), 273
St. Mary's co. (Md.), 20
St. Mary's (Newfoundland), 235
St. Ovide, sieur de, 236
Salem (Mass.), 88, 167, 178, 277, 279
  losses at sea, 95
  naval protection of, 95
  panics, 84 n. 1
  quakers in, 164

ships registered at, 151, 154
witchcraft trials, 175 n. 1
Salisbury (Mass.), 140, 164, 218, 277
Salmon Falls (N.H.), 86
Sandwich (Mass.), 275
Scarborough, Charles, high sheriff of Accomack co. (Va.), 25
Schenectady (N.Y.), 32, 100, 205
Schuyler, Col. Peter, 201, 254
Scituate (Mass.), 151, 164, 275
Scottow, Joshua, fears dissolution of New England, 61
Seagar, Henry, 219 n. 3
Seamen,
  desertion from royal navy, 97
  employment ashore, 98
  impressment of, 98, 98 n. 1
Seignelay, Jean-Baptiste Colbert, marquis of, 197
Sewall Samuel, 45, 63, 67, 111, 146, 164, 175, 235, 240 n. 4, 248, 255, 258, 262, 274
Shannon Viscount, *see* Boyle, Henry
Sherborn (Mass.), 219, 277
Shrewsbury, Duke of, *see* Talbot, Charles
Sillery (New France), 200
Simsbury (Conn.), 259, 270
Sloughter, Henry, governor of New York, 31, 91
Small, Henry, ship's carpenter, H.M.S. *Rose*, 14
Smith, John, 6
Smith, William, historian, 17–19
Sothell, Seth, governor of Carolina, 3
Southack, Cyprian, 256, 265
Southampton (N.Y.), 16
Spain, 199, 267, 272
  and *Asiento*, 274
  and Indies trade, 156, 271
Spencer, Charles, third Earl of Sunderland, 228, 249, 250, 252–4, 256, 271
Spencer, Nicholas, president of Virginia Council, 25–7, 30
Springfield (Mass.), 138, 214 n. 3
Spruce Creek (Me.), 2
Spurwink (Cape Elizabeth, Me.), 86, 212
Stackmaple, John, customs collector, 280
Stafford co. (Va.), 6, 7
Stamford (Conn.), 153

Stede, Edwyn, deputy-governor of Barbados, 28

Stoddard, Solomon, Revd. 54, 122, 123, 126, 128, 146
  advocates national church, 127
  and Hampshire Association, 127
  and Saybrook *Platform*, 124
  and *Stoddardeanism*, 126

Stoll, Joost, New York envoy to England, 18 n. 1

Stoughton, William, lieutenant-governor of Massachusetts, 114, 115, 172, 174, 180–2, 220 n. 2

Stow (Mass.), 219

Stukely, Capt. R. N., 245

Subercase, Auger de, governor of Acadia, 235, 245

Suffolk (Mass.), 101, 278, 279

Suffolk co. (Mass.), 101, 276

Suffolk (N.Y.), 16, 19

Sunderland, third Earl of, *see* Spencer, Charles

Swansea (Mass.), 169

Sydney, Henry, Earl of Romney, 173

Tailer, William, Lieutenant, Governor of Massachusetts, 270

Talbot, Charles, Duke of Shrewsbury, 230

Taunton (Mass.), 275

Taylor, Edward, Massachusetts poet, 148

Tew, Thomas, pirate, 157

Tisbury (Mass.), 276

Tiverton (Mass.), 275

Torcy, Jean Baptiste Colbert, marquis de, French foreign secretary, 271

Townshend, Charles, second Viscount, 271

Townshend, Col. Penn, 246

Treat, Robert, governor of Connecticut, 22

Trepassey (Newfoundland), 235

Trinity (Newfoundland), 113

Trois Rivières (New France), 72, 142, 143

Tyng, Lieut-col., Jonathan, 211, 225

United Brethren, and New England, 120, 122, 124

Ussher, John, lieutenant-governor of New Hampshire, 103, 213 n. 1

Utrecht, peace settlement of, 286
  and Acadia, 273
  and *Asiento*, 273
  and Gibraltar, 272
  and negotiations for, 271
  and Newfoundland, 272
  and Port Mahon, 272

Van Cortland, Stephen, 32

Vaudreuil, Philippe Rigaud, chevalier de, governor general at Quebec, 213, 237 n. 4, 238, 241

Vaughan, George, agent for New Hampshire, 249

Vetch, Samuel, 64, 228, 237, 241, 248–52, 259, 262, 266, 268, 269, 280

Virginia, 3, 5, 107, 192, 193, 207, 227, 232
  Anglican church in, 167
  armed bands in, 25
  avoids revolution, 25–7, 30
  and British contributions to defence, 280
  and breakdown of government in Rappahannock co., 25
  and Canada project, 249
  economic depression in, 84 n. 2
  education in, 141
  and fear of Catholics, 5
  and governorship of Andros, 33
  and request to aid New York, 108, 111
  and support for James II, 25
  and Utrecht, 273–4
  and William III, 25

Wainwright, Francis, 247

Waldron, Major, 85 n. 1

Walker, Admiral Sir Hovenden, 262 n. 3, 264, 265, 267 n. 2, 268

Walker expedition (1711), 68
  collapse of, 266, 271, 273
  council of war, 266
  transports wrecked, 265–6

Walley, Major John, 90

Walton, Col. Shadrach, 233, 235, 259, 270

Ward, Ned, poet, 54, 196 n. 1

Watanuman, Indian chief, 211, 212

Waterbury (Conn), 259, 270

Watson, Sir Francis, president of Jamaica Council, 29
Waugh, John, minister of Stafford co. (Va.), 25
Wells (Me.), 78, 87, 100, 133, 133 n. 2, 135, 211, 216, 218, 225, 237 n. 4, 239, 247, 248, 270
Wenham (Mass.), 277
Westchester (N.Y.), 16
Westfield (Mass.), 102, 138, 218
West Indies, 227, 233, 235, 272
  See also individual islands
Wethersfield (Conn.), 22, 23
Weymouth (Mass.), 276
Wharton, Edward, 70
Wharton, Richard, 123
Wheler, Sir Francis,
  commands force for West Indies, 108
  pillages St. Pierre (Newfoundland), 113
  reaches New England, 108
Willard, Revd. Samuel, President of Harvard, 170
William III, xi, 1, 4, 11, 13, 15, 17, 19, 22, 24, 30, 40, 62, 89, 163, 173, 176, 191
  attempted assassination of, 45
  and colonial defence, 30, 31
  importance to New Englanders, 42
  views on centralisation, 30
Williams, Commodore, leads raid on Placentia, 113
Williams, John, 139 n. 2
Winthrop, Fitz-John, governor of Connecticut, 215
Winslow, John, 12
Winter Harbour (Me.), 212, 247, 248, 259, 270
Winter Island (Salem), 223
Winthrop, Wait, 180, 182
Woodstock (Mass.), 218
Wrentham (Mass.), 276

Yale college, 129
York (Me.), 81 n. 2, 82, 133 n. 2, 134, 136, 213, 217, 218, 225, 247
  attacks on, 82, 100
  requests a chaplain, 135